MANAGING
YOUR OWN
FINANCES

Thomas W. McRae

INTERNATIONAL THOMSON BUSINESS PRESS
I ⓣ P ® An International Thomson Publishing Company

London • Bonn • Boston • Johannesburg • Madrid • Melbourne • Mexico City • New York • Paris
Singapore • Tokyo • Toronto • Albany, NY • Belmont, CA • Cincinnati, OH • Detroit, MI

Managing Your Own Finances
Copyright © 1997 Thomas W. McRae

First published by International Thomson Business Press

I⒯P® A division of International Thomson Publishing Inc.
The ITP logo is a trademark under licence

British Library Cataloguing-in-Publication Data
A catalogue record for this book is available from the British Library

Library of Congress Cataloging-in-Publication Data
A catalog record for this book is available from the Library of Congress

First edition 1997

Typeset by D.E. Michael, Laindon, Essex
Printed in the UK by T.J. International Ltd, Cornwall

ISBN 1-861-52049-2

International Thomson Business Press
Berkshire House
168–173 High Holborn
London WC1V 7AA
UK

International Thomson Business
Press
20 Park Plaza
13th Floor
Boston MA 02116
USA

http://www.itbp.com

To Aidan Thomas

Contents

Preface

The decline of the welfare state means that individuals are increasingly expected to assume responsibility for their own long-term financial security. They must protect their own future by designing a set of financial plans to safeguard themselves and their families against the vicissitudes of life.

The main objective of *Managing Your Own Finances* is to assist individuals who would like to plan their own finances rather than leaving this task to a financial adviser. Certain aspects of personal finance, such as setting up a trust or buying a complex financial product like a pension, require specialized knowledge, but a good deal of personal financial planning requires no more than a basic knowledge of the key facts together with some common sense.

Readers who decide to use the services of a financial adviser will find that *Managing Your Own Finances* provides useful background information that should improve the quality of the communication between the reader and the adviser. Many complaints about the quality of financial advice arise from the ignorance of the client as much as from the incompetence of the financial adviser. The best financial plans are produced when a knowledgeable client works with a competent adviser.

In July 1994 the magazine *Moneywise* commissioned a Gallup poll to ask a representative sample of 1046 adults in Great Britain what they thought about the honesty and competence of personal financial advisers (PFAs). The results were not good. Fifty per cent considered that clients of PFAs were frequently sold the wrong investments and only 28% were quite confident or very confident that a PFA would be completely honest. Twenty per cent claimed that they had been given poor investment advice by PFAs in the past. This suggests that gaining a little knowledge of personal finance before using the services of a personal adviser may be no bad thing.

Managing Your Own Finances provides the background knowledge that readers need in order to invest sensibly: the information they need to select the appropriate insurance policies, to build a pension, to buy a house or flat, to raise short-term credit at minimum cost and to minimize their tax bill. It also explains how to maintain a set of personal book-keeping records by hand or on a computer and how to protect oneself against poor financial advice. Topics covered include the following:

- How can the wealth portfolio of the family be arranged in such a way that it will provide a reasonable return while keeping its value against the hazards of inflation and economic slump? What are the characteristics of the many types of investment available to the investor? What are the advantages and disadvantages of investing in 'real' assets like antique clocks and Lalique glass?

- What are the various different types of annuity on offer from the insurance companies and which type of annuity is best suited to which type of investor? (An annuity is a form of investment much favoured by the older investor.)

- Just how much money is needed to provide an 'adequate' pension? What are the various types of State, company and personal pension products on offer, and what are their relative benefits and limitations? (Nothing is more important in personal finance than arranging a safe and adequate pension.)

- What needs to be considered when financing a home using a mortgage or a loan? (This is usually the most important single financial transaction undertaken by an individual or family.) What are the various forms of mortgage currently on offer and what are the advantages and disadvantages of each? Is property a sound investment and how do the costs of buying a house compare with the cost of renting one?

- Many of life's hazards can be covered quite cheaply by taking out insurance. A form of insurance audit is presented together with a discussion of the more important insurance products currently on offer. We consider which of these are worth buying and which should be avoided.

- What techniques are available for reducing one's total insurance bill and how can individuals who have purchased insurance complain if the service is unsatisfactory?

- Tax is a key issue in personal finance. The basics of income tax, capital gains tax and inheritance tax are explained and some elementary advice is provided on reducing tax bills.

- It is difficult for anyone to manage their own finances without some form of regular financial record keeping. This is true even if an adviser handle one's financial affairs. Several relatively simple personal book-keeping systems are sold on the market. Some use pen and ink and others use a microcomputer. How do these work and what are the advantages of using a computer-based system?

- The apparatus for protecting the personal investor is up and running in the UK but it still needs a deal of fine tuning if it is to work satisfactorily. What are the regulations at present and what are the complaints procedures to be followed by investors who feel that they have lost out from bad or fraudulent advice from his or her personal financial adviser?

- What are the key sources of information on personal finance currently available in the UK? Information on personal finance can be gleaned from the daily and weekly newspapers (good sources of information on personal finance), from books and specialist monthly magazines, from computer data bases, from CD ROM discs and even from the internet (although this last source, in the writer's experience, is still a long way from being really useful to the individual enquirer, it has enormous potential).

- There is also a 'test your knowledge' section at the end of most of the chapters. Brief solutions are provided.

- Finally, a simple financial planning strategy has been provided together with a list of useful addresses, some suggestions for further reading and a glossary of financial terms.

I have tried to avoid the use of technical financial language and have kept examples simple.

The new self-assessment regime for personal tax will force around nine million tax payers to keep personal financial records as from April 1997. This presents an excellent opportunity for readers to use these records as a basis for designing a complete financial plan for the future.

TWM
March 1997

Acknowledgements

The data in Exhibit 2.10 are adapted from BZW figures with permission of BZW Securities Limited.

Exhibit 6.14 is based on material from the BCIS *Guide to House Rebuilding Costs 1996* and is reproduced with permission of the Building Cost Information Services Ltd.

Abbreviations

APR	Average percentage rate
AVC	Additional voluntary contributions
CBPFP	Computer-based personal financial planning program
CBPP	Computer-based planning program
CGT	Capital gains tax
CII	Chartered Insurance Institute *or* critical illness insurance
DB	Data base
EPS	Earnings per share
FIMBRA	Financial Intermediaries, Managers and Brokers Regulatory Association
FSAVC	Free-standing additional voluntary contributions
IBRC	Insurance Brokers' Registration Council
ICAEW	Institute of Chartered Accountants in England and Wales
ICAS	Institute of Chartered Accountants of Scotland
ICS	Investor's Compensation Scheme
IMRO	Investment Managers Regulatory Organization
IRR	Internal rate of return
LAUTRO	Life Assurance and Unit Trust Regulatory Organization
LTCI	Long-term care insurance
MIG	Mortgage Indemnity Guarantee
MPS	Money-purchase scheme
NPV	Net present value
PE	Price earnings ratio
PFA	Personal financial adviser
PHI	Permanent health insurance (income replacement)
PIA	Personal Investment Authority
PMI	Private medical insurance
RO	Regulatory organization
RPI	Retail price index
SFA	Securities and futures authority
SIB	Securities and Investment Board
SRO	Self-regulating organization

Why manage your own finances?

1

THE PERSONAL FINANCE CRISIS

The long-term personal finances of individuals and families in almost all modern industrialized countries are in a state of crisis. The odd thing is how few individuals and families are aware of this.

The root of the problem lies in the fact that citizens in most countries are nowadays refusing to accept any increase in taxes, particularly income taxes, so governments are no longer able to afford the cost of providing State welfare systems that care for their citizens 'from the cradle to the grave'.

A key factor contributing to the problem is the ageing of the population. In the UK the ratio of retired persons to working persons will increase from 1:5 in 1995 to 1:3 in the year 2025. Who will pay to provide adequate pensions for the retired then? Only the retired themselves, we must presume.

In recent years, the cost of pensions, health care, insurance, education, housing and so forth has been rising inexorably year-by-year in most advanced industrial countries. If these facilities are being paid for by the State the proportion of the nation's annual income taken in taxes must inevitably rise. If the voters are not prepared to pay higher taxes then these voters have no option but to pay for these services, or at least some of them, themselves.

This inexorable logic has escaped the notice of most voters. Facilities such as a decent pension on retirement, proper health care, an adequate insurance shield to protect against the unexpected hazards of life, the secure investment of one's savings and wealth, the financing of accommodation for the family, even the education of one's children can no longer be taken for granted.

Self help is the order of the day. Whether most voters will actually relish having to arrange to finance all of these services for themselves, rather than allowing the State to provide them from taxation, is a mute point. What is not in doubt is that this is the way things are moving. These services will be arranged through personal pensions, life and health insurance, personal savings and investment, mortgage finance, and other financial services.

Such a dramatic shift in the provision of personal welfare will place a considerable burden on the individual citizen. The scant evidence available suggests that few people are able to handle their personal financial affairs adequately. Few appear to keep financial records on a regular basis and even fewer make a regular check on the value of their net worth and the proper diversification of their assets. How many individuals have estimated their long-term annual cash flow up to the age of 80, an essential step in long-term financial planning? All the evidence suggests that few employees really understand their pension rights or how to estimate the value of their pension on retirement, especially if they have worked for several firms throughout their lives and are not certain as to their eventual retirement date. Most families seem to be underinsured; for example they are not providing adequately for dependants, especially for spouses, and the tax benefits available from certain kinds of investment are often ignored, particularly with regard to pension-fund investment.

THE COST OF ADVICE

If an individual lacks sufficient knowledge to organize his or her own financial affairs, the obvious solution is to seek advice from a personal financial adviser. There are many highly competent financial advisers offering useful advice on personal financial matters but there are also many inadequate advisers who are little more than salesmen living off of the commission generated by the products they sell.

In 1994 a poll by the Gallup organization, which had been commissioned by the magazine *Moneywise*, found that 20% of clients of financial advisers thought that they had been given poor advice and only 28% stated that they were confident that the advice they would be given was honest. Some 50% of the respondents considered that the clients of financial advisers were frequently sold the wrong investment product.

There is the also the issue of cost. A fee-based personal financial adviser must charge between £80 to £120 an hour to cover his costs and make an adequate living. Even if this fee takes the form of a commission, it still has to be paid. A full personal financial analysis and plan will take from six to 10 hours to prepare, so the total fee will be in the region of £500 to £1200.

A LITTLE KNOWLEDGE IS A USEFUL THING

If clients have some knowledge of personal finance they can discuss their cases more intelligently with their advisers and work out a solution that is more likely to meet their needs. A basic knowledge of personal finance also allows clients to test the competence of their advisers. Some financial advisers are rather better at putting on an impressive front, driving a BMW, or wearing a mohair coat than they are at giving relevant financial advice.

THE 'DO-IT-YOURSELF' APPROACH

Individuals who are willing to take the time and trouble can avoid the consultation fee altogether by designing their own financial plan. Preparing one's own personal financial plan is not as difficult as might be imagined. Many factors assist do-it-yourself financial planners. If the basic format of the planning process is understood, it is not difficult to fit the components of a plan together.

PROTECTION AND REGULATION

The 1986 Financial Services Act was introduced following some spectacular financial scandals in the early 1980s. This Act set up a battery of self-regulating agencies to protect the investor against fraudulent and incompetent financial advice. The Securities and Investment Board (SIB) is the overall regulator of the market and a variety of minor regulators with strange acronyms like PIA, IMRO and SFA operate under the SIB's auspices, regulating their respective sectors of the financial market. The regulator that protects the private investor is called the Personal Investment Authority (PIA). An *investor's compensation scheme* (ICS) was established in tandem with these developments to compensate investors who lose money through fraud or bad advice. The ISC is funded in the form of an annual levy by the SIB on the financial advisers themselves.

These attempts at self-regulation by the market operators have met with only limited success, but at least some form of protection is available to the investor. The protection that is available is explained in some detail in Chapter 11.

SOME KEY QUESTIONS TO ASK ABOUT PERSONAL FINANCES

1. How much will my pension be worth if I retire at 60?

2. What happens if I fall seriously ill long before I retire?

3. What happens to my dependants if I die suddenly?

4. How safe is my pension?

5. Is my wealth properly protected against high inflation and the danger of economic slump?

6. Is my wealth diversified among a sufficient number of different kinds of assets?

7. If I am over 65 should I buy an annuity?

8. Are my assets fully insured at reasonable cost?

9. Will the endowment policy attached to my mortgage be able to pay off my mortgage at the end of the agreed repayment period?

10. Should my mortgage be switched to another company or be repaid early?

11. Am I spending enough to maintain my home in prime condition?

12. Do I know how to complain if I receive misleading advice from a financial adviser?

13. Am I paying too much for credit?

14. Am I paying too much personal tax?

15. Have I written a will? Have I arranged my estate to minimize inheritance tax?

16. Do I keep proper records of my financial affairs?

If the answer to any of these questions is 'no' you should start planning your financial future before it is too late.

Managing your personal wealth

2

INVESTING IN FINANCIAL ASSETS

Let us first dispose of a common fallacy. Investment is not about 'picking winners'. Efficient personal investment is not about choosing those shares that will be the next to jump in value on the stock exchange. Some investment columns in newspapers and many investment newsletters are devoted to such an approach but an investment strategy based on this strategy will more likely than not lose you a lot of money. Why this is so will be explained later in the chapter. Your overall investment strategy may have a place for 'picking winners' but this will be the very last step in the long process of building an investment portfolio. Research on investment over the last 30 years has concluded that it is simply not possible to 'pick winners' on a consistent basis if the stock exchange trading the stock making up your portfolio is efficient.

When you invest your personal wealth you should aim to achieve two objectives. First, aim to obtain a reasonable income from the investment. Second, try to move the value inherent in your investment securely through time. The first of these objectives is obvious to every investor; the second is much less so. For most people during most of their lives the second objective, that of moving value securely through time, should be more important than the first objective of maximizing the income from the investment.

Unfortunately the evidence suggests that many investors, perhaps even the majority, are prepared to sacrifice security for a higher income. Many investors do not even realize that this trade-off between income and risk is taking place. Yet the trade-off between income and risk should lie at the heart of your investment strategy.

WHAT DO WE MEAN BY MOVING VALUE SECURELY THROUGH TIME?

Let us suppose that a doting aunt, on her deathbed, leaves you £100 000 in her will. You are 35 years of age and married with two children. You have an income from employment of £30 000 a year. You already own investments of £150 000 plus a house worth £150 000 with a mortgage of £100 000. You have no real need for this money at this time. However you are hoping to set up an independent business some 20 years from now when you expect to retire from your present employment. How should you invest the £100 000 in the meantime to ensure that it will generate an 'adequate' income while at the same time also ensuring that, after adjusting for inflation, it will still be worth at least £100 000 or more 20 years from now? Maintaining the value of this money through time is a good deal more difficult than ensuring an adequate annual return from the investment.

First we will explain *how to measure the income from an investment*, then we will explain *how to protect the capital value inherent in an investment* from being reduced by the many vicissitudes that threaten the financial markets of the world at all times.

CLARIFYING INVESTMENT OBJECTIVES

The correct investment strategy depends on your investment objectives. It is important to differentiate between long-term objectives (a pension), medium-term objectives (school fees) and short-term objectives (an expensive holiday next year). The types of financial strategy you choose should be strongly influenced by the length of time before you need the money. There is a premium on lack of liquidity. If you do not need the money for some years then higher returns are available to you.

Another important factor is risk. How much risk are you prepared to take with your wealth? High-risk investments provide a higher return than low-risk investments. Are you prepared to trade safety off against a higher potential return?

TYPES OF INVESTMENT

You have an immense choice as to where to invest your wealth. A complete inventory of investments open to you would run to several million possibilities. Fortunately the choice can be reduced somewhat by breaking the investment possibilities down into a few basic types. Exhibit 2.1 sets out a simple classification of the investment opportunities available to the average personal investor. Each of the basic investment types shown in this figure can be exploded into a wide range of further possibilities but the fundamental choice is between financial assets and real assets.

FINANCIAL ASSETS VERSUS REAL ASSETS

Financial assets consist of investments such as ordinary shares in quoted companies, tracker funds, unit and investment trusts, index-linked gilts,

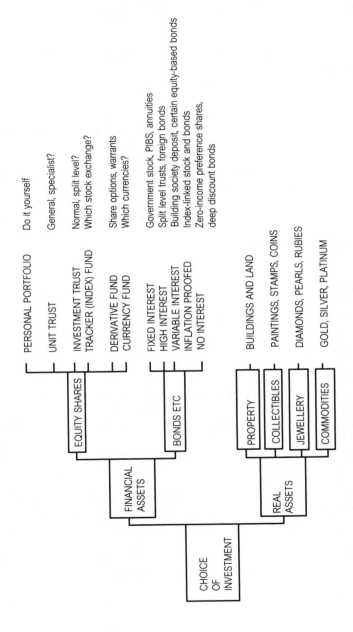

			PERSONAL PORTFOLIO	Do it yourself
			UNIT TRUST	General, specialist?
		EQUITY SHARES	INVESTMENT TRUST	Normal, split level?
			TRACKER (INDEX) FUND	Which stock exchange?
			DERIVATIVE FUND	Share options, warrants
	FINANCIAL ASSETS		CURRENCY FUND	Which currencies?
			FIXED INTEREST	Government stock, PIBS, annuities
			HIGH INTEREST	Split level trusts, foreign bonds
		BONDS ETC	VARIABLE INTEREST	Building society deposit, certain equity-based bonds
CHOICE OF INVESTMENT			INFLATION PROOFED	Index-linked stock and bonds
			NO INTEREST	Zero-income preference shares, deep discount bonds
		PROPERTY	BUILDINGS AND LAND	
	REAL ASSETS	COLLECTIBLES	PAINTINGS, STAMPS, COINS	
		JEWELLERY	DIAMONDS, PEARLS, RUBIES	
		COMMODITIES	GOLD, SILVER, PLATINUM	

EXHIBIT 2.1: A wide choice of investments are available to the discriminating investor

As an investor you can choose between financial assets and real assets. The range of financial and real assets on offer are very wide, the choice is particularly wide among real assets. However, financial assets are easier to protect and maintain and equity shares have consistently provided the highest real return among the assets available for inclusion in a wealth portfolio. Both equity shares and real assets have been shown to provide a good hedge against inflation.

building society deposits, annuities, fixed and variable interest bonds plus a wide range of exotics such as traded endowment policies, options and warrants. *Real* assets consist of physical objects such as expressionist paintings, Lalique glassware, gold coins, Chinese ceramics . . . and houses.

We will concentrate on investment in financial assets in this chapter and investment in real assets in the following chapter.

WHY ARE FINANCIAL ASSETS SUCH A POPULAR FORM OF INVESTMENT?

Financial assets, such as ordinary shares, gilts, and building society deposits, are legal contracts between the investor and the issuer of the asset. They give the investor certain rights. The more common rights conferred on an investor are:

- the right to an income from the investment, such as a dividend from a share or the interest on a bond;

- the right to a capital sum if the investment is wound up or liquidated;

- the right to a vote if the investment confers ownership rights on the investor;

- the right to be consulted if the rights mentioned above are to be altered;

- various other rights such as the right to buy a share in the future at a given fixed price.

Financial assets are popular because most of them are *liquid* in the sense that they can be sold quickly at relatively low cost. Liquidity confers a major benefit on the investor. Not all financial assets are liquid, however. Annuities, for example, and some insurance and pension investments, are very illiquid.

The cost of selling and protecting a financial asset is low compared to the equivalent costs associated with most real assets. Financial assets are usually divisible: the whole asset need not be liquidated at one time. They can be transported easily from one place to another. The current value of many financial assets can be monitored on a regular basis since the current market value of the asset is quoted daily in the financial pages of the press.

Financial assets often provide an efficient mechanism for storing value and this encourages the citizens of a country to save and to participate in the increasing wealth of the country at relatively low cost and risk. This is not true of the financial assets available for investment in many developing countries.

INVESTING IN REAL ASSETS

Few people invest in real assets primarily for financial return. Most collectors buy real assets such as stamps or antique clocks or Japanese *netsuke* for reasons other than investment. The buyer admires the beauty of the object, or is a collector of such objects, or wishes to avoid the attentions of the local tax inspector. There are investors, however, who choose to invest in real assets rather than financial assets because they genuinely believe that these assets will provide them with a higher income or greater security than they could achieve by investing in a financial asset. Alas, such people are almost certainly mistaken. Research has shown that *in the long run* financial assets, if carefully chosen, almost invariably provide the investor with a higher real income and greater security of value than real assets. There are, however, exceptions to this rule.

Note that most real assets provide no cash income until the asset is sold and they incur a value added tax (VAT) charge if they are bought from a dealer.

THE MOST COMMON INVESTMENT PRODUCTS

The most common investment products bought by private individuals are ordinary shares and government 'gilts' and bonds.

Ordinary shares, as the name suggests, give you a part share in the ownership of a limited company. If the company has issued one million shares and you own 10 000 of them, you own 1% of the company. If the company makes a profit, and if the directors of the company decide to declare a dividend, then you will receive 1% of the dividend paid out of profits. The directors need not declare a dividend even if the company is very profitable. However if they do not declare a dividend out of profits, the market value of your shares will rise because profits will be reinvested, so you can sell a few shares if you are short of cash. You may also get one vote per share which you can use at meetings of the company, although a vote does not seem to be worth much in real terms. Some companies issue shares both with and without a vote. The difference in price between these two types of share is very small. If the company goes into liquidation you will receive 1% of the net proceeds of the assets sold.

A portfolio of ordinary shares, even randomly selected, has proved to be the best bulwark against inflation in recent years. For this reason ordinary shares make up the foundation of most wealth portfolios.

There are so many different kinds of bonds on the market that the non-financial specialist is likely to become very confused as to the meaning of this financial product. A *simple bond* is a fixed-interest investment. It is called a *gilt-edged security* or *gilt* if it is issued by the Government. If it is issued by a company it is called a *commercial bond.*

Gilts usually offer you a fixed-interest payment twice a year and your money back, in nominal terms, at the end of the investment period. You pay income tax on the income from gilts but not capital gains tax. So far as income is concerned, gilts provide the safest income there is. Unfortunately, ordinary gilts do not guarantee that you will get your capital back *in real terms*. Inflation might eat into the real value of gilts. If £100 000 of gilts are invested for 10 years the investor will only receive back £100 000 at the end of the 10-year period. If inflation has averaged 5% per year over the 10 years you will only receive back

$$\frac{\pounds100\ 000}{(1+0.05)^5} = \pounds78\ 353$$

in real terms. If the rate of interest is high enough to compensate for this loss you might get your money back in the interest payments, but normally you do not.

The government has issued *index-linked gilts* to solve this problem. A wide range of investment periods are offered since the index-linked gilts mature in various years between 1998 and 2030. Both the interest paid and the capital value are linked to the retail price index *eight months back,* so you are protected from the ravages of inflation if you invest in index-linked gilts.

Since index-linked gilts are the safest investments you can buy, they provide a lower return than more risky government stock but at around 3% it is still a real return after inflation.

Gilts and bonds offer a much higher cash return than ordinary shares. Currently ordinary shares yield about 4% per annum gross of tax; most bonds yield from 8% to 10% per annum gross of tax. Ordinary shares are likely to provide a much higher capital gain (increase in capital value) than bonds and gilts however. We discuss how to measure the return on a financial investment later in this chapter.

A few Government gilts, such as War Stock, are not dated. This means that they may never be repaid.

The market value of gilts and bonds depends on the current market rate of interest. If the market rate (the rate paid by top-class borrowers) moves above the fixed interest rate on the bond the market value of the bond falls, if the market rate falls below the fixed interest rate on the bond, the market value of the bond rises. The maturity date of the bond is important here, if the maturity date of the bond is near (say a few months away) the market value of the bond is much less sensitive to the market interest rate. The further away the maturity date of the bond is, the more sensitive the market value of the bond is to movements in the market interest rate. If fluctuations in the market value of your bonds worry you only buy bonds with repayment dates close to the present. Gilts and bonds with relatively high fixed interest rates are less sensitive to the market interest rate than gilts and bonds with low fixed interest rates.

In addition to simple fixed interest bonds there are a plethora of other financial products called 'bonds'. Some of the more interesting of these 'bonds' are:

- permanent interest-bearing shares;

- distribution bonds;

- guaranteed income bonds;

- guaranteed equity bonds;

- zero coupon bonds;

- premium bonds.

PERMANENT INTEREST-BEARING SHARES (PIBS)

Permanent interest-bearing shares are issued by building societies. They are called shares but they are really irredeemable bonds. The interest is almost certain to be paid but it need not be. These shares pay a higher rate of interest than gilts, perhaps 1.5% to 2% higher, but they are almost as safe as irredeemable gilts. Since they are irredeemable, the market value of PIBS is highly sensitive to movements in the market rate of interest. Income tax is paid on the interest, but not capital gains tax.

DISTRIBUTION BONDS

Distribution bonds are issued by insurance companies. They are in theory single premium whole of life assurance policies. However the life cover is very small. The investor can take out 5% of the value of the bond each year without having to pay any income or capital gains tax.

These financial products are really a type of equity investment. The funds raised by the bond are invested by the insurance company in a mix of safe equities, fixed-interest securities and property. The manager of the distribution bond aims to increase the income of the bond-holder over time. The investor is sometimes allowed to switch between different kinds of funds that have different mixes of equity and fixed interest securities. The minimum investment can be as high as £10 000. A typical initial charge is currently 5% with an annual management fee of 1%. Your financial adviser gets around 5.25% commission. Beware of exit charges. Early surrender can be very expensive. Distribution bonds are a useful investment if you want a safe regular income plus the possibility of capital growth, but the stock market can fall as well as rise.

GUARANTEED INCOME BONDS

These are fixed interest bonds issued by insurance companies. They are issued for a fixed number of years after which a major portion of your capital will be returned to you – but not necessarily all of your capital. Neither the income nor the capital is really guaranteed. The returns offered can be very high, say 10% or 11%, but the lack of guarantee on the principal amount invested means that some of this 'income' might turn out to be simply a return of some of your own capital. If the income is accumulated and paid out at the end of the period the bond is called a *growth bond*.

The interest on guaranteed income bonds is paid net of basic rate income tax and there are no additional charges. Higher rate taxpayers must pay additional tax, currently at 16%. Early surrender of the bond is likely to be an expensive exercise.

GUARANTEED EQUITY BONDS

The money invested in these bonds is reinvested in stock index options and fixed interest securities by an insurance company or bank. You will receive a high fixed guaranteed return for a given number of years, usually five or six. The income can be paid monthly, annually or at the end of the period in a lump sum. The income is guaranteed but the return of your capital is not. The value of your capital at the end of the period depends on the performance of the stock exchange over the period during which you hold the bond since the capital value is tied to a stock exchange index such as the FT-SE 100 index. Again, your annual income may include the return of a portion of your own capital! Early surrender is expensive and is not advised.

If the stock market rises you can do well with a guaranteed equity bond but not as well as if you had invested in a tracker fund. Guaranteed equity bonds provide a high secure income but the underlying capital is at risk. These income bonds will suit investors who want a steady income and are prepared to take a small risk of losing a fraction of their capital (say 20% to 30%). The tax position is a little complicated, so you must check this out before you buy these products.

Growth bonds, which are similar in structure, are designed to allow investors to take advantage of a rise in the stock market without putting their capital at risk. If you invest £100 000 in a growth bond you are guaranteed to receive this back at the end of the period and you may get back a great deal more if the stock market is substantially higher when the bond is repaid.

ZERO COUPON BONDS

These bonds, which are issued by companies, do not pay interest to the holder regularly but instead are issued at a substantial discount on their face value. The return is the difference between the issue price and the maturity value. There is no regular income, only a capital gain on maturity. You might buy a £100 bond for £60 to be repaid as £100 in, say, five years' time. If you want a fixed amount of money after a given number of years these bonds might appeal to you but they are a minority taste.

The market value of zero bonds is very sensitive to the market rate of interest so, if you are a gambler and you think current interest rates are high, you might find zero bonds preferable to the national lottery.

PREMIUM BONDS

Premium bonds are a gamble that offers you much better odds than the national lottery. The bonds are issued by the government in units of one pound each. The minimum investment is £100. No income tax or capital gains tax is paid on the winnings from premium bonds. This might appeal to higher-rate taxpayers. The average return over a long period of investment should be close to 4% per annum or 6% grossed up for income tax. The monthly prizes vary from £50 to £1 000 000. Unfortunately there is only one £1 000 000 prize each month.

What are your chances of winning? You had one chance in 17 500 of winning *some* prize for one bond in each draw in 1995. If you held £200 worth of bonds you had about a one-in-seven chance of winning a £50 prize during one year (if you bought four lottery tickets a week, that is if you spent £204 a year, your chance of winning a £10 lottery prize was around one chance in 14). Premium bonds are not really viable as a serious investment but if you fancy a small flutter you might win £1 000 000. Your chances of winning this, for each bond you buy, are one in five billion. You can also get your money back by cashing in the bond. You cannot do this with lottery tickets.

HOW DO YOU MEASURE THE INCOME FROM YOUR INVESTMENT?

The income from an investment is made up of two parts. First there is the dividend or interest, which is paid out regularly on the investment. Secondly, there is the change in the market value of the investment from when it is purchased until it is sold.

Note that income is not the same as cash. The interest on a 12% government bond provides you with an income and a regular inflow of cash; the increase in the value of a share in ICI provides you with an income, the increase in the value of the share, but no cash until the share is sold.

Let us work through an example to illustrate how to measure the income from an investment for a given year. Suppose you purchase 8000 ordinary shares of a company called Software UK PLC. Software pays you a £2000 dividend in cash during the year. Let us ignore tax effects for the moment to keep the example simple. At the beginning of the year the shares of Software UK PLC are quoted at £5 a share on the London Stock

Exchange,[1] thus the shares have a market value of

$$8000 \times £5 = £40\ 000.$$

At the end of the year these same shares are quoted at £7 a share on the same stock exchange. What is your income for the year from the 8000 ordinary shares in Software UK PLC?

The dividends alone have generated an income of

$$\frac{£2000}{£40\ 000} = 5\%$$

but the total return on the shares is much higher than this. The capital gain over the year is £7 – £5 = £2 a share, or 8000 x £2 = £16 000. Thus the total return for the year is £2000 + £16 000 = £18 000. Your true return on the shares in Software PLC for the year is £18 000/£40 000 = 45%!

Notice one very important point. The £2000 dividend is received in cash. The £16 000 of capital gain is only a 'paper' profit. It has not been realized. It can only be realized by selling the shares on the last day of the period in question.

The capital gain of £16 000 could be lost in the next period if the value of the shares in Software PLC were to fall back to £5 per share. There are also trading costs to consider.

Financial analysts measure the return on a share by adding the dividend received to the capital gain or loss during the period. This form of measure can be misleading unless the shares are sold and the capital gain converted into cash. If the shares are not sold the capital gain is only a *probability*, not a certainty.

Many of the advertisements offering financial assets for sale fail to emphasize the ephemeral nature of capital gains in their presentation of the return from an investment over several years past. The quoted return would only be the true realized return for the period if the investments were cashed-in at the end of the period under consideration. It is not difficult to manufacture a very high 'return' by carefully choosing a period that starts at the bottom of a stock exchange boom and ends at the top.

To make a proper measure of the return on an investment for a given period you must add the annual return in the form of dividends or interest to the change in the value of the investment over the period to arrive at the percentage return on the opening investment. Exhibit 2.2 provides two examples of measuring the return on an investment over a given period.

Tax, the buying and selling costs of the investment, and the current rate of inflation can complicate the calculations somewhat, but the basic principle remains that the income from an investment is measured by adjusting the periodic dividend or interest for any change in the market value of the investment over the given period.

In the case of some assets that are stable in price over long periods of time the income from dividends or interest makes up the major portion

Calculating the precise yield on an investment can be quite complicated. However the approximate yield is often all that is required.

The following formula will allow you to calculate the approximate yield on an investment given the current and expected future price and the expected annual average dividend or interest. The yield should be calculated net of tax.

Average annual dividend = *D*
Current share price = *C*
Future share price = *F*
Approximate yield = *Y*

$$Y = \frac{(D + (F - C))}{((F + C) \div 2)}$$

For example:

D = 6 pence per period
C = 110 pence
F = 150 pence

The approximate yield is:

$$\frac{(6 + (150 - 110))}{((150 + 110) \div 2)} = 35.4\%$$

Suppose that £1000 of war stock paying 2.5% per annum is bought for £320 at the beginning of the year. At the end of the year the war stock can now be sold for £380. What is the yield on the war stock?

$$\frac{(25 + (380 - 320))}{((380 + 320) \div 2)} = 24.3\%$$

EXHIBIT 2.2: Calculating the approximate yield

of the return, but this is unusual. The main factor determining the return on most investments is the change in the value of the market price of the investment between the beginning and end of the period in question. This is obviously so in the case of assets that have no annual cash return, such as gold coins or antiques. Such assets are more risky to hold since all of the return is accumulated and condensed into the final sale of the asset. There is no bird in the hand.

NOTHING IS FOR NOTHING – RISK VERSUS RETURN

How much of a return should you be aiming at from your investments? The answer might seem to be obvious – 'I want as high a return as possible!' This is not only the wrong answer, it is a very dangerous answer. Day after day we read about unfortunate investors who have lost their worldly wealth by pursuing this particular investment objective. The mistake they have made is to ignore the *risk factor*.

In an efficient market, investments that produce a higher-than-average return must inevitably have a higher-than-average risk attached to that return. In recent years financial analysts who measure such things as investment risk have found that there is a very close relation between return and risk. The return on an investment portfolio can only be increased if the investor is prepared to carry a higher-than-average risk. On the other hand, a lower degree of risk can be achieved if the investor is prepared to accept a lower return on his or her investment.

Option funds can provide a very high return to the investor but they are a very risky type of investment. Investing in inflation-indexed gilt-edged stocks will never make you a millionaire but they will provide you with a very safe return for life.

Exhibit 2.3(a) illustrates this point. Let is suppose that the return on an investment with average risk (we will call this a risk factor of 1) is 22% per annum. A more risky investment, carrying a risk factor of 1.4, will provide you with a return of 27% per annum. A less risky investment, carrying a risk factor of only 0.8, 20% less risky than the average investment, will provide you with a return of only 20% per annum.

Exhibit 2.3(b) illustrates the risk and return characteristics of a range of investments, varying in their risk levels.

A higher return on an investment can only be bought at the cost of a higher risk being attached to the return on that investment. As an investor you must decide on the particular risk-return mix that suits you. A young electrical engineer with glowing future prospects might choose a high return, high risk mix. A retired architect might choose a low return, low risk mix. Retired people cannot afford to take risks with their future income. The return on the investment and the associated risk factor can be, and has been, measured for most UK equity shares.

Is accepting a lower return the only way to reduce the risk on an investment? Fortunately the answer to this question is 'no'. The risk in a portfolio of investments can be reduced without reducing the future income from the investments. The classic way to reduce the risk on the return from your funds is to *diversify* the total pool of funds over many investments.

If we restrict your choice of investments to investing in ordinary shares then a pool of around 30 randomly selected ordinary shares can reduce the total risk attached to your total portfolio of shares by 70% to 80%.

Exhibit 2.4 illustrates the degree of reduction in risk achieved by investing a fund of a given size into up to 30 different shares chosen at random from all of the shares listed on the London Stock Exchange. Note that beyond about 20 shares very little reduction in total risk is achieved by adding an additional share. Since buying and selling shares costs money, *you can overdiversify your portfolio of shares.* Many unit trusts overdiversify their portfolio of shares, which may account for the relatively modest returns achieved by many unit trusts in recent years.[2]

Financial analysts have identified two kinds of risk associated with all assets. The first of these risks is called *specific* risk. The second is called *market risk.* You can reduce *specific* risk by diversifying your wealth over a sufficient number of different assets.

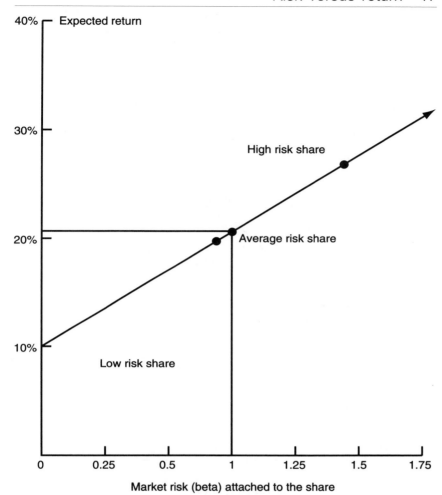

Market risk (beta) attached to the share

Let us assume that a riskless investment such as a government security provides a return in excess of 10%. An equity share of average market risk is said to have a risk factor (beta) of 1. Such a share is shown to provide a return of about 22%. A share with a beta of 0.5 provides a return of about 16%. A share whose return varies more than the market return, having a beta (market risk) of, let us say, 1.5 must provide a return of at least 28%. Otherwise the owner of the share will sell it and buy another that provides a better return.

Note that the risk we are discussing here is 'market risk'. 'Specific risk' has already been eliminated by diversifying the portfolio of shares in the wealth portfolio.

EXHIBIT 2.3(a): The risk versus the return on an investment

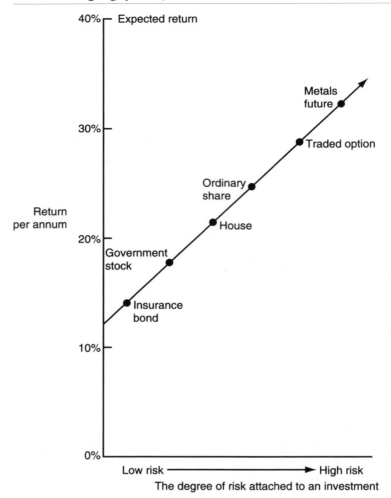

EXHIBIT 2.3(b): Risk versus return on some types of investment

In an efficient market the return flowing from an investment can only be increased by increasing the risk attached to the return from that investment.

In the above diagram the cash flowing from a government security enjoys a low risk and so provides a low rate of return. Company shares provide a higher return and so are more risky. Options and other derivatives can provide a very high return but for this very reason are very risky investments.

EXHIBIT 2.3(b): Risk versus return on some types of investment

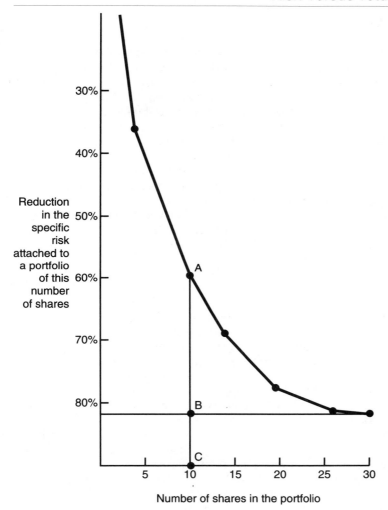

The specific risk attached to an individual share can be reduced by investing in a portfolio of shares. When the return from one of the shares falls because of the specific risk attached to that share the return on one or other of the other shares in the portfolio is quite likely to rise, thus compensating for the fall in the return on the other share.

A portfolio of 20 shares selected at random removes about 80% of the specific risk attached to the portfolio. Diversification does not reduce the market risk attached to a share.

EXHIBIT 2.4: Reducing the risk on a portfolio by diversification

WHAT IS SPECIFIC RISK?

If we limit our discussion of risk to ordinary shares for the moment then 'specific' risk means the risk attached to the return from an individual share. If we hold shares in Zeneca PLC and a substitute drug comes onto the market to compete with Zeneca's main product then the value of Zeneca's shares will fall sharply as soon as this fact is known to the market. However if we also hold shares in Prudential Insurance, Tarmac, British Aerospace and General Electric then the impact of a drug substitute on our future investment income is much reduced. It is unlikely that the introduction of a new drug will have any impact on the future profits of companies in the insurance, building, aeroplane manufacture or electrical industries.

As we noted above, the specific risk attached to the returns on an individual share can be almost completely eliminated by diversifying your portfolio of wealth over 20 or more shares.

WHAT IS MARKET RISK?

Market risk examines the relation between a change in the return on a specific share quoted on a stock exchange and the change in the return on all of the shares quoted on that stock exchange.

Suppose, for example, that you own a block of shares in British Aerospace (BAe). Suppose the return on all of the shares quoted on the stock exchange falls by 10% over a given year and the return on the block of BAe shares falls by 15%. What would this fact tell us about the 'market' risk attached to BAe shares?

The figures would tell us that BAe shares were 50% more sensitive to market movements than the average share quoted on that stock exchange. Financial analysts talk about the *beta* of a share. The beta tells us the sensitivity of the returns on a share to movements in the return on the whole market. The above figures would tell us that BAe shares would have a beta greater than one. The shares would be very sensitive to movements in the whole market.

Shares with a high beta attached will compensate the owner of the shares by awarding the owner a higher return than shares with a low beta attached. High risk, high return. Low risk, low return.

A REVIEW OF THE ARGUMENT

We have sailed into rather deep waters in the last few paragraphs so let us try to clarify matters by going over the same course again. These matters are important and do-it-yourself investors need to have a basic grasp of the two different types of risk, specific risk and market risk, before they can build up an effective investment portfolio.

The objective of personal investment is to obtain an income from the investment and yet to secure the value of that investment against the hazards that can deplete its value over time.

Your primary objective as an investor is to control the risk factor attached to your total investment portfolio. We now know that the return obtained from any investment is closely related to the risk attached to that investment. The return is measured as the dividend or interest paid per period plus (or minus) the change in the market value of the investment over the period.

The risk attached to one particular share is composed of two parts: *specific* risk caused by variations in the return applying to that one particular company whose share you hold, and the *market* risk arising from the fact that the return on this share is more-or-less sensitive to changes in the overall market compared to the average share.

One part of this risk, the specific risk, can be eliminated by diversifying your total wealth portfolio over several shares (20 to 30 shares chosen at random should suffice). Unfortunately market risk cannot be eliminated in this way. However shares that are sensitive to market risk reward investors by giving them a higher potential return.

ADJUSTING YOUR SHARE PORTFOLIO FOR RISK: THE BETA

'Market' risk cannot be eliminated by diversifying your portfolio, but it can be controlled. An investor can set up a portfolio with a high market risk attached (one with a higher-than-average expected return) or a portfolio with a low market risk attached (one with a lower-than-average expected return). The investor can do this because the degree of market risk is measured by the beta of the share. In most advanced industrial countries, like the UK, organizations exist that measure the betas of company shares on a regular basis. For example, the betas of UK companies are measured every few months by the London Business School Risk Measurement Service. Exhibit 2.5 provides an introduction to the calculation of the beta.

Someone who is approaching retirement and who wishes to construct a low-risk, low-return portfolio of shares can select their portfolio from among the many shares offering betas of less than one. On the other hand, a young upwardly mobile executive might think of including higher risk shares with a higher potential return. The executive has less to lose and may finish up a rich man.

An alternative strategy, which is easier to follow in practice, is to set up a portfolio of average risk – a portfolio with an average beta of one – and invest a fraction of your wealth portfolio in fixed interest stocks (very safe) to reduce the overall risk attached to your portfolio to below average, or, if you want to construct a high-risk, high-return portfolio, you can borrow money to buy additional stocks with an average beta of one. This will increase both the risk and the return attached to your portfolio since your portfolio of investments is now 'levered' by the funds you have borrowed. This strategy is not difficult to effect if you are

The total risk attached to the future earnings from a share can be segregated into two types of risk. First there is the *specific* risk. This type of risk includes all of those risky factors that apply exclusively to the individual company. A lawsuit or factory fire are examples of specific risk. The second type of risk is called *market* risk. This includes all those risky factors that will affect all of the shares quoted on a given stock exchange. A rise in the market rate of interest is an example of a market risk.

Specific risk can be almost eliminated from a share portfolio by simply diversifying the total wealth invested over 20 or 30 shares chosen at random from all of the shares quoted on the Stock Exchange. Market risk cannot be eliminated by diversification but it can be measured. Not every share quoted on a given stock exchange is affected equally by market risk. If the average return on all of the shares quoted rises by, say, 15%, the return on some shares will rise by more than 15%, others by less than 15%.

A statistical device called the *beta* measures the impact that a given rise or fall in the market return has on the return of any individual share. For example, if a share has a beta of 1.7 then the return on this share is likely to suffer around 70% more market risk than the average share. A share with a beta of 0.90 is around 10% less risky than the average share. The 'risk' we are considering here is market risk, not the specific risk discussed earlier. The betas of most of the shares quoted on the London Stock Exchange are calculated regularly by the London Business School Risk Service. The beta measures the covariance* between the market return and the return on any individual share over many periods in the past. The beta of a share is relatively stable over time. The beta concept is only useful if the stock market processes information efficiently. Once the beta of a share is known the management of a quoted company can find out the rate of return on capital that the market expects from the share in the next accounting period. The required equation, somewhat simplified, is:

$$R = G + B \times (A - G)$$

where:

R =   the return required by the market from this share in the next period
G =   the return on a very safe, riskless investment
B =   the beta of the share
A =   the current return on a share of average market risk

For example, if the share of Teleware PLC has a beta of 1.7 and the return on a share of average risk is 22% and a riskless government stock returns 10% per annum then the required return for Teleware PLC in the coming year is:

$R = 10\% + 1.7 \times (22 - 10) = 30.4\%$

If Surewater Plc has a beta of 0.7 the required return is:

$R = 10\% + 0.7 \times (22 - 10) = 18.4\%$

* The covariance is a sort of amalgam of the variance on the return on the given share and the correlation between the returns on the share and the returns on all the shares quoted on this market.

EXHIBIT 2.5: The calculation of the beta (market risk) on a share

---

investing a substantial part of your portfolio in a general unit trust, an investment trust or a 'tracker' or 'index' fund. These so-called 'collective' investments are likely to have a beta close to one since they are widely dispersed among many types of stock. Thus all you have to do is to borrow funds and invest them in collective investments. Another alternative is to invest in a highly levered investment trust.

COLLECTIVE INVESTMENTS: UNIT TRUSTS, INVESTMENT TRUSTS AND TRACKER (INDEX) FUNDS

So far we have considered an investor who wishes to construct a do-it-yourself share portfolio. Investment trusts were born when advisers discovered that most investors prefer to leave the construction and management of an investment portfolio to experts. Unit trusts followed and, much later, tracker or index funds appeared (see Exhibit 2.6).

These so-called *collective investments* encourage the investor to hand over a lump sum to the investment manager who buys a well-diversified selection of shares and other financial assets on behalf of the investor. The manager of the fund charges the investor an initial investment fee of, say, 5% plus an annual management fee of 1% to 1.5%.

General collective investments (as distinct from the specialized sort) remove specific risk from the investment equation.

So far as collective investments are concerned, if the shares bought are not limited to a specialized sector, such as hi-tech companies, then the 'market risk' or beta of the portfolio is likely to be close to one. In other words the market risk of the portfolio will be close to the average market risk of all the shares quoted on the Stock Exchange and the specific risk will be close to zero. Units in a unit trust are thus a safe, if somewhat unexciting, investment and are likely to provide a safe, if somewhat unexciting, return. A collective investment will tend to attract the average return for all the shares quoted on that particular exchange.

OTHER IMPORTANT ATTRIBUTES OF INVESTMENTS

So far we have concentrated on two aspects of investment: the income from the investment and the risk attached to this income in the future. These are the two most important characteristics of investment so far as most investors are concerned. There are, however, several other attributes of investment products that can be crucial to the investment decision in certain situations. These other attributes are:

- the nature of the periodic cash flow from the investment;

- the pattern of growth in the capital value of the investment;

- the security;

- liquidity of the investment;

- the buying and selling costs associated with the investment;

- maintenance and protection costs associated with the investment;

- the degree of divisibility inherent in the investment;

- the transportability and international marketability of the investment;

and, last but by no means least

- the impact of tax on the return from the investment.

We will now examine each of these issues in turn.

THE NATURE OF THE PERIODIC CASH FLOW

The specific characteristics of the cash flow from an investment are important to an investor. The investor may wish to consider issues such as:

- Is there a regular cash flow or is the cash flow irregular?

- How often is the cash paid out to the investor monthly or annually?

- Can the investor vary the timing and amount of the periodic cash flow?

- For how long will the cash continue to flow before the investment matures?

Some high-rate taxpayers will be happy to receive no cash (and so pay no tax on their investment) until the investment is sold after they retire (when they will be paying tax at a lower marginal rate). Certain zero-interest bonds and roll-up funds in offshore finance havens like the Isle of Man cater for such investors. Other investors, particularly retired investors, will need a regular flow of cash each month. Thus the regularity and periodicity of the cash flow from an investment will often determine its suitability for a particular investor.

CAPITAL GROWTH

Many investments are held because the investor believes these investments will enjoy a substantial capital growth in the future even if the current cash flow from the investment is meagre. Younger investors are more likely to be interested in the prospects for capital growth in their investments than in the current cash flow. Certain investments, for example shares in 'emerging country' funds, shares in companies which have high price : earnings ratios, growth bonds, zero income bonds, the capital portion of split level trusts and some real assets such as antique silver or old English furniture hold out the prospect of capital growth over time while providing a low cash flow, or no cash flow at all, at present.

Investments that provide high capital growth allied to a meagre cash flow can present tax benefits to an investor. For example, those investors who have set up discretionary trusts to reduce personal taxes on the family income are likely to seek out investments combining high capital

	Index funds over five years (to July 1995)	Charges Initial %	Charges Annual %
SOME UK INDEX FUNDS			
Gartmore UK Index	166	0.00	0.50
HSBC UK Index	154	0.00	0.50
Morgan Grenfell UK Index	152	3.00	0.75
Norwich UK Index Tracking	155	3.00	0.20
Virgin UK index tracking (set up 1995)	not relevant	0.00	1.00
Average performance of UK trust funds	146		
FT All-Share Index	168		
SOME US INDEX FUNDS			
HSBC American index	149	0.00	1.00
Morgan Grenfell US Index	152	3.00	0.75
Average performance of US trust funds	147		
Standard & Poor's US index	155		
SOME EUROPEAN INDEX FUNDS			
HSBC Eurotrack 100		0.00	1.00
Legal & General Euro Index	134	0.00	0.75
Average performance of European trust funds	131		
SOME EMERGING MARKET FUNDS			
HSBC Tiger Index	198	0.00	1.00
Morgan Grenfell Japan Tracker		3.00	0.75
Average performance of Japanese trust funds	99		
Nikkei Dow Index	88		
SOME INTERNATIONAL INDEX FUNDS			
Norwich international tracking	145	4.00	0.90
Morgan Stanley World Index		3.00	0.75

Tracker funds attempt to mimic the composition of an all-share index. Thus tracker funds remove almost all specific risk from the shares in the tracker portfolio and have an average market risk. That is, the tracker fund has a beta of 1. The annual management charges for tracker or index funds are lower than for other managed investments at around 0.5% to 0.7% compared to 1% to 1.5% for other funds. Tracker or index funds are available that mimic the UK, USA, European, emerging markets and world indices.

EXHIBIT 2.6: A listing of some tracker (index) funds

growth with low cash income. The income tax due can be postponed at least until the investment is sold.

HOW SAFE IS THE CAPITAL INVESTED IN AN ASSET?

There is no guarantee that shares will maintain the capital value invested in them or provide a particular level of income (in the form of dividends). The income from fixed-interest government stock or gilts is very safe but the capital value of the stock may not be safe if the market rate of interest rises above the rate on the investment.[3]

This stricture also applies to most commercial bonds issued by large companies. In times of low inflation, building society variable rate deposits provide excellent security for the capital value invested but the income from such an investment may be relatively poor and subject to wide variation as market rates of interest and expectations about the future rate of inflation change. The average yield on building society deposits from mid 1975 to mid 1994 was 7.8% gross of tax and inflation.

Some income and insurance bonds provide guarantees regarding the security of both capital value and future income but they may suffer from some other shortcomings such as inflexibility, lack of liquidity or low returns.

The building societies introduced permanent interest-bearing shares (PIBS) in 1991. Despite their name, these are really bonds that will not be repaid. They pay higher rates than gilts but are more risky. The interest need not be paid.

Good security is an important attribute of any investment but it must usually be paid for in the shape of low returns. Nothing is for nothing in the world of investment.

LIQUIDITY

A *liquid asset* is one that can be quickly converted into cash. Certain investments like building society and bank deposits provide high liquidity at the cost of a relatively modest return. However most ordinary shares that are quoted on major stock markets and collective investments such as unit and investment trust holdings can also be converted into cash quickly and easily but at a higher conversion cost. These investments tend to provide a higher return than fixed-term deposits.

Most real assets such as houses, works of art, antiques and collectibles are rather illiquid and converting them into cash can be a time-consuming and costly business. Gold coins can be converted to cash fairly quickly but the buy-sell spread is around 3% and there may be VAT to pay plus an assay fee.

Certain financial investments such as annuities and endowment insurance policies are very illiquid and converting such investments into cash before their terminal date, even if it is possible, can prove to be a prohibitively expensive business.

The key to liquidity lies in the existence of an *efficient* market which trades in the asset. The existence of such a market, like a stock exchange, or a gold-coin market, or a market for nearly-paid-up 'with-profits' endowment policies, improves liquidity immeasurably. Before choosing to invest in a specific asset you should first verify that an efficient market exists where you can convert the asset back into cash quickly should the need arise. Exhibit 2.7 provides a listing of some of the markets and dealers who trade or sell financial products.

BUYING AND SELLING COSTS

The difference between the cost of buying an asset and selling the same asset can be a key factor in your choice of investment. For example the difference between the buying and selling cost of a diamond can be 30% or more of the buying cost while the cost of selling a Government stock may set you back less than 1% of the market value of the stock.

The spread between the buying and selling costs of real assets is usually much higher than the spread between the buying and selling cost of financial assets. In some cases the cost of selling an asset is proportionate to the value of the asset, in other cases it is only weakly related to the value of the asset. In some cases both the buyer and the seller of the asset have to pay a commission to the dealer or auctioneer. Some real assets, like antiques and pictures, have a buyer's premium of as much as 15% added to the purchase price.

The width of the buy-sell spread is a useful indication of the efficiency of the market trading the asset. The wider the spread, the less efficient is the market trading the asset.

Exhibit 2.8 provides a rough estimate of the buy-sell spread for several popular financial assets.

PROTECTION AND MAINTENANCE COSTS

The cost of protecting some of your assets against loss or damage can commit you to considerable expense. Fortunately this stricture only applies to real assets. The cost of protecting and maintaining financial assets is usually low or even negligible since they are registered with some authenticating authority. This is one of their more useful attributes. Financial assets that are not registered, such as bearer stocks, need more careful protection. We will discuss the costs associated with protecting and maintaining real assets in the next chapter.

Object traded	Market or issuer
Commercial bonds	Stockbroker, Stock Exchange
Company shares	Stockbroker, Stock Exchange
Futures contracts	LIFFE Futures Exchange, London
Government gilts	Post Office, Stock Exchange
Guaranteed equity bonds	Insurance companies, banks and building societies
Guaranteed income bonds	Insurance companies
Investment bonds	Insurance companies
Investment trust shares	Stock Exchange
National lottery tickets	Lottery shops
PEPs	Many financial institutions
PIBS	Building societies
Premium bonds	Post Offices
Specialized bonds	Many financial institutions
TESSAs	Many financial institutions
Traded endowment policy	Securitized Endowment Cont. Plc.
Traded option contracts	LIFFE
Unit trust units	Unit trust managers
Zero coupon bonds	Many large companies

A wide range of markets that trade a wide range of financial assets are available in the UK. Many markets, such as the Stock Exchange, do not exist at a physical location but trade using the telephone and computer screens. Specialist dealers exist who are willing to buy or sell almost any conceivable financial asset. Such dealers will advertise in the trade press of the given asset in which they trade. The above list represents only a random selection from among the many markets and dealers who buy and sell financial assets in the UK.

EXHIBIT 2.7: Some markets and dealers that trade in financial assets

---

DIVISIBILITY

This important attribute is often overlooked when buying an asset. A painting, a jewel, a house, or even a life assurance policy is a single indivisible unit. It is difficult, if not impossible, to sell off part of such an asset, although a loan can be raised against it. Other assets such as 1000 ordinary shares in a quoted company, £10 000 of gilts, 100 bottles of claret, a collection of vintage postage stamps, or 100 krugerrands can be sold off in parts. Divisibility can provide substantial advantages for an investor by allowing the investor to release income and capital gains gradually over time, thus providing a steady income while at the same time reducing the liability to capital gains and inheritance tax.

SIZE, TRANSPORTABILITY AND INTERNATIONAL MARKETABILITY

A house or a plot of land cannot be transported from one country to another, while 'blue chip' share certificates, gilt edged stock, a collection of Japanese *netsuke*, a valuable collection of postage stamps, or a quality jewel can be transported quite easily across a national frontier.

The international marketability and transportability of an investment may well be important to you if you are living in a country with an unstable political climate. A revolution or a change in government, or even an impending change in the laws on tax or exchange control, may require you to switch countries quickly with your assets intact.

	Percentage of buying price
Building society deposit	0%
Premium bonds	0%
Government gilt-edged stock (from Post Office)	0.7%
Currency	2% to 5%
Ordinary shares: spread	2% to 10%
brokerage charges	0.3% to 10% (depends on value of deal)
Unit trust units: spread	2% to 5%
initial charge	0% to 6%
exit charge	0% to 5% (exit charge unusual)
Investment trust shares: spread	1% to 3%
brokerage charges	0.3% to 10% (depends on value of deal)
Commercial debentures: spread	1% to 2%
brokerage charges	0.1% to 3%
Derivative funds: options, futures: spread	3% to 8%
brokerage charges	1% to 10%
Commodities	4% to 7%
Enterprise investment scheme	4% to 8%
Life assurance policy (viatical)	30% to 40% (discount on face value)
National lottery (balance goes to costs, government and charities)	50%

The list provides an illustration of the wide variation in the buy-sell spreads and other charges applied to some financial assets. The figures emphasize the fact that over-trading of assets is an expensive exercise.

The spread is expressed as a percentage of the buyer's buying price. The dealer's selling price.

The size of the spread is strongly influenced by the efficiency of the market trading the stock. The spreads on most financial assets are much lower than the spreads on real assets.

EXHIBIT 2.8: The buy-sell spreads and costs for some financial assets

---

'Value per unit of weight' is a useful measure of international transportability. Financial assets in the form of certificates score well here but some valuable real assets also transport well. Gold, for example, is an international currency with a value of around US$350–US$400 an ounce. Rare postage stamps, jewels and coins possess an excellent value to weight ratio.

One important question is whether the financial asset is tradable outside its country of origin. Some financial assets are less tradable than others but bearer shares and bonds are designed to be traded internationally.[4]

TAX IMPLICATIONS OF THE INVESTMENT

Last, but by no means least, we must consider the tax implications of holding certain investments. In the UK, for example, there is no income tax payable on the income from certain assets (see Chapter 9 for a list of such assets). No capital gains tax is due on capital gains from many government stocks. In many foreign countries the income from certain government securities are entirely tax free. In the UK, certain government schemes such as personal equity plans and tax-exempt

EXHIBIT 2.9: Annual rate of inflation in the UK from 1914 to 1996

Year	Percent. of index based on 1961	Times 1996 index	Annual inflation (%)	10-year average (%)	20-year average (%)
1914	21.3	53.00			
1915	26.3	42.92	23.5		
1916	31.1	36.30	18.3		
1917	37.6	30.02	20.9		
1918	43.4	26.01	15.4		
1919	45.9	24.59	5.8		
1920	53.2	21.22	15.9		
1921	48.2	23.42	−9.4		
1922	39.1	28.87	−18.9		
1923	37.2	30.34	−4.9		
1924	37.4	30.18	0.5	6.7	
1925	37.6	30.02	0.5	4.4	
1926	36.7	30.76	−2.4	2.4	
1927	35.8	31.53	−2.5	0.0	
1928	35.4	31.89	−1.1	−1.6	
1929	35.0	32.25	−1.1	−2.3	
1930	33.7	33.50	−3.7	−4.3	
1931	31.5	35.84	−6.5	−4.0	
1932	30.7	36.77	−2.5	−2.4	
1933	29.9	37.75	−2.6	−2.1	
1934	30.1	37.50	0.7	−2.1	2.3
1935	30.5	37.01	1.3	−2.0	1.2
1936	31.4	35.95	3.0	−1.5	0.4
1937	32.9	34.31	4.8	−0.8	−0.4
1938	33.3	33.90	1.2	−0.6	−1.1
1939	36.3	31.10	9.0	0.5	−0.9
1940	40.1	28.15	10.5	1.9	−1.2
1941	43.6	25.89	8.7	3.4	−0.3
1942	45.2	24.97	3.7	4.0	0.8
1943	48.4	23.32	7.1	5.0	1.4
1944	51.1	22.09	5.6	5.5	1.7
1945	53.5	21.10	4.7	5.8	1.9
1946	56.4	20.01	5.4	6.1	2.3
1947	60.2	18.75	6.7	6.3	2.7
1948	64.9	17.39	7.8	6.9	3.2
1949	66.4	17.00	2.3	6.2	3.4
1950	68.3	16.53	2.9	5.5	3.7
1951	74.5	15.15	9.1	5.5	4.5
1952	79.0	14.29	6.0	5.8	4.9
1953	80.3	14.06	1.6	5.2	5.1
1954	81.8	13.80	1.9	4.8	5.2
1955	84.4	13.36	3.3	4.7	5.3
1956	88.3	12.78	4.5	4.6	5.3
1957	91.1	12.39	3.2	4.3	5.3
1958	93.6	12.06	2.7	3.8	5.3
1959	94.2	11.98	0.6	3.6	4.9
1960	95.1	11.87	1.0	3.4	4.4
1961	100.0	11.29	5.2	3.0	4.3
1962	101.6	11.11	1.6	2.6	4.2
1963	103.6	10.90	2.0	2.6	3.9
1964	107.0	10.55	3.3	2.7	3.8
1965	112.1	10.07	4.8	2.9	3.8
1966	116.5	9.69	3.9	2.8	3.7
1967	119.4	9.45	2.5	2.8	3.5
1968	125.0	9.03	4.7	2.9	3.3
1969	131.8	8.56	5.4	3.4	3.5
1970	140.2	8.05	6.4	4.0	3.7
1971	153.4	7.36	9.4	4.4	3.7
1972	164.3	6.87	7.1	4.9	3.8
1973	179.4	6.29	9.2	5.7	4.1
1974	211.7	5.33	18.0	7.1	4.9
1975	265.5	4.25	25.4	9.2	6.0
1976	305.0	3.70	14.9	10.3	6.6
1977	344.5	3.28	12.9	11.3	7.0
1978	373.2	3.02	8.3	11.7	7.3
1979	437.8	2.58	17.3	12.9	8.2
1980	504.2	2.24	15.2	13.8	8.9

Year	Percent. of index based on 1961	Times 1996 index	Annual inflation (%)	10-year average	20-year average
1981	565.2	2.00	12.1	14.0	9.2
1982	599.3	1.88	6.0	13.9	9.4
1983	629.8	1.79	5.1	13.5	9.6
1984	669.2	1.69	6.3	12.4	9.7
1985	696.1	1.62	4.0	10.2	9.7
1986	721.3	1.57	3.6	9.1	9.7
1987	751.8	1.50	4.2	8.2	9.8
1988	800.3	1.41	6.5	8.0	9.9
1989	860.9	1.31	7.6	7.1	10.0
1990	940.9	1.20	9.3	6.5	10.1
1991	983.3	1.15	4.5	5.7	9.9
1992	1014.8	1.11	3.2	5.4	9.7
1993	1034.0	1.09	1.9	5.1	9.3
1994	1064.0	1.06	2.9	4.8	8.6
1995	1098.1	1.03	3.2	4.7	7.4
1996	1128.8	1.00	2.8	4.6	6.8

1914–45: Ministry of Labour Cost of Living Index; 1946–62: Consumer Expenditure Deflator; 1963–96: Government's Retail Price Index

The rate of inflation in retail prices in the UK averages out at about 5% per year over the period 1914 to 1996. However, the rate has been falling since 1991 and expert opinion predicts that the average rate of price inflation may fall to around 3% over the next 20 years. It might be wise to budget on a relatively conservative rate of 4% over the next 20 years.

savings schemes are very tax efficient. The tax treatment of the income on certain types of investments which are held in a trust fund for the benefit of a third party can be crucial in efficient inheritance-tax planning. Such exemptions can provide a substantial benefit to the high marginal rate taxpayer.

Tax-efficient investment planning is an important and complex subject in its own right. Chapter 9 will discuss tax-efficient investment planning in more detail.

COPING WITH INFLATION

One of the primary risks you face as an investor is that the future rate of inflation, the fall in the real value of money compared to other goods, will destroy the real value of your wealth over time.

Exhibit 2.9 shows the annual rate of inflation in the UK from 1914 to 1996. The average rate over this period was close to 5%, but over certain 10-year periods the average rate rose to 10% and above. As shown in the table, annual inflation rates as high as 25% are not unknown in the UK.

So long as the return on your investment after tax exceeds the rate of inflation, you can live with inflation. The danger is that while the annual interest or dividend on the investment appears to exceed the rate of inflation, the capital base generating this income is being gradually eroded. The money value of the capital base may seem to be unchanged but after it is adjusted for the falling value of money you may find that it has been reducing in value.

The secret of coping with inflation is to invest in assets the value of which has been proven to be capable of floating on the rate of inflation. If the rate of inflation rises then the return on these assets will rise as fast as, or even faster than, the inflation rate. (In this section we are referring to normal inflation such as one encounters in the UK, not hyperinflation such as one meets in certain South American countries where you pay for a meal when you order it since the costs on the menu may be altered upwards during the meal.)

Real assets such as gold, antiques, or rare postage stamps tend to float up with inflation. However, as we shall see in the next chapter these same real assets suffer from certain disadvantages that tend to offset their use as a counter to inflation.

Research has shown that over the years the best bulwark against inflation in most of the countries of the world has proved to be ordinary shares quoted and traded on a recognized stock exchange. BZW Merchant Bank published a regular measure of the real return on various types of financial assets in the UK. Part of this study is shown in Exhibit 2.10. Exhibit 2.10 compares the real return on ordinary shares and UK fixed-interest government stock, net of inflation and gross of tax, over various periods in the past. Over all periods in the recent past, ordinary shares have provided the investor with a real return, after allowing for inflation, of between 6% per annum and 9% per annum. By contrast the performance of fixed interest stocks has been poor at matching inflation. In some periods in the recent past fixed-interest stocks have provided the unfortunate investor with a zero or even negative real return.[5]

An alternative way of coping with inflation is to invest in inflation-indexed government stock. The return on these stocks is adjusted regularly to allow for the degree of inflation (eight months back). Thus if the stock promises a 3% annual return and the inflation rate for the period is 5% per annum, the government stock will pay out 8% per annum. These inflation-proofed stocks provide an excellent bulwark against inflation. The real return is low but very safe. Again we see the strong link between return and risk. A large amount of capital needs to be invested in such a stock to provide a substantial return. Over the period from 1921 to 1995 in the UK ordinary shares have provided the investor with a degree of protection against inflation equal to inflation-proofed government stocks but have also, in recent years, provided the investor with at least double the return provided on these inflation proofed stocks. Inflation-proofed annuities are another way of coping with inflation. We will discuss these annuities in a later chapter.

A wide range of investments can now be index-linked if the investor so desires. For example there is an index-linked building society account, there are index-linked national savings certificates, and index-linked managed funds run by some insurance companies.

Unit trusts, investment trusts, distributor funds, some annuity funds, and many bonds place a high proportion of their assets in ordinary shares. These assets thus have an inbuilt protection against inflation.

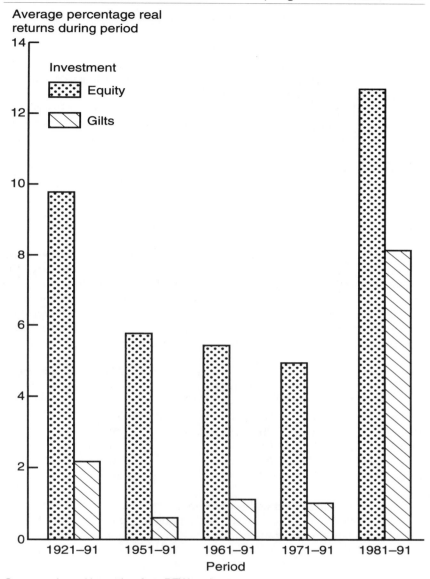

Average percentage real
returns during period

Source: adapted by author from BZW estimates

On average the return on equity (ordinary) shares have consistently beaten the return on fixed-interest government securities over the last 70 years in the UK.

EXHIBIT 2.10: The long-term returns on equity shares and gilt-edged (government) securities; estimates 1921–91

BUILDING YOUR WEALTH PORTFOLIO

How do you decide on the particular assets to include in your wealth portfolio? In order to build a suitable wealth portfolio you must match your needs to the characteristics of the different kinds of assets that can be placed into the portfolio.

You need to consider your objectives in building the portfolio, and other relevant characteristics that will influence the type of investment chosen such as your age, state of health, attitude to risk, lifestyle, the needs of dependent relatives, future employment prospects, future need for funds, and one or two special factors that affect specific investors such as domicile (these are too numerous to set down here in detail).

AGE

Your age is a very important factor in designing your wealth portfolio where long-term investment is concerned. The younger you are, the greater the risk you can take with your wealth portfolio as there are still many years ahead to save additional funds if something should go wrong with your portfolio. The older you are, the higher the proportion of your funds you should place in safe investments such as fixed interest stocks and inflation-indexed bonds. A suitable mixture might be:

Age	Ordinary shares (percentage)	Fixed-interest stocks (percentage)
20–35	90	10
36–50	70	30
51–65	50	50
66–75	30	70
Over 75	20	80

A stable and reliable income becomes more important to you as you get older. A 75-year-old widow is not likely to be interested in gambling on capital gains on zero-income bonds.

A *distributor bond* (see below) is a useful investment vehicle that provides a stable income together with the advantages of equity investment. However, note that some of the 'income' from a distributor bond might be a disguised return of capital. There is no harm in this so long as you are aware that this is the case. As one grows older it often becomes inevitable that one uses up some capital as income.

STATE OF HEALTH

The impact of your state of health on your investment strategy is very similar to the impact of your age. If you suffer from poor health you will be unwilling to take excessive risk with your wealth. A higher proportion of your total wealth portfolio should be invested in 'safe' securities providing a lower but safer return.

If you suffer from very poor health and so have an *impaired life* (an expectation of life much lower than normal) you might consider applying for an *impaired annuity* which will offer you a much higher income than would be offered to a healthy investor of the same age. Chapter 4 will discuss this option in more detail. You might also be interested in the viatical settlement market, which buys life-assurance policies before death.

ATTITUDE TO RISK

Investors do not all have the same attitude to taking risks. Some investors prefer the high-risk, high-return approach to investment (choosing investment vehicles such as warrant funds); others prefer the low-risk, low-return option (investing in government inflation-indexed gilts, for example). You must decide for yourself what degree of risk you wish to take and build an appropriate portfolio from the investments discussed in this chapter.

The degree of risk can be reflected in the proportion of your total wealth portfolio that you invest in equities, the higher the percentage invested in equities, the greater is the return and the greater is the attendant risk.

Some investors may choose to invest a good proportion of their portfolio in 'high beta' shares which might be expected to produce a high return (via capital gains) in the future. If an even higher risk-return mix is required an investor can consider investing in a *geared* asset. Most geared assets are selected from a class of financial assets called *derivatives*.

Examples of geared assets are *warrant* and *option* funds. These assets allow a small investment to achieve truly massive returns if the underlying investment on which the derivative is based moves up in price. On the downside such investments can also result in the loss of the entire investment if the underlying asset moves down in price (as Nick Leeson discovered).

Geared assets, such as warrants and options, are only really suited to the professional investor who knows what he or she is doing. They do, however, offer very high returns in a very short time span for the daring investor. Certain fund managers offer investment in funds consisting exclusively of geared assets. The amateur investor can invest in these managed funds and so enjoy the advantage of professional management plus some diversification of risk plus the possibility of very high returns compared to alternative investments. *These funds are still risky and incur very high management charges.*[6]

Many professional portfolios, such as pension fund portfolios, contain a small proportion of geared assets.

LIFESTYLE

Your lifestyle may influence the assets you choose to place into your wealth portfolio. If you move around the world a great deal, not settling in one country for long, you may choose to invest in an international investment fund based on a tax haven which charges zero or low personal tax on your income. Bermuda, the Cayman Islands, the Isle of Man, Jersey and Nassau are among the dozens of tax havens offering investment services to the itinerant private investor. Every tax haven has an information office that will be delighted to send you full details free of charge. Pay particular attention to the compensation terms offered if the fund you are investing in goes bust. These terms vary a great deal from haven to haven. Offshore compensation terms in some countries are almost as good as in the UK, the Isle of Man being one example.

Certain types of investment such as the 'bearer' shares we mentioned above are not registered and so income arising from them is not easily accessible to tax authorities. Such shares might appeal to some investors.

Investors domiciled but not resident in the UK, working abroad, might choose a rather different mix of investments from those they would choose if they were working in the UK. For example some UK government stocks are paid gross of tax to non-resident investors. Many investment funds held and managed abroad are paid gross of tax to UK citizens or any other citizens working or living abroad.

If you are nearing retirement and if you wish to enjoy an expensive lifestyle after retirement you may prefer to invest in a portfolio with higher income potential and higher risk than we suggested above. This is a potentially hazardous option, gambling with your future quality of life.

DEPENDENT RELATIVES

You need to consider those for whom you are responsible when designing your investment portfolio. If you are nearing retirement it is probable that your spouse is the only dependent relative you have. If the age of the investor and spouse is about the same a portfolio suited to the needs of the investor is likely to suit the needs of the spouse just as well but if there is a substantial age gap between the two this is not the case. A younger portfolio might be more suitable.

The needs of a dependant, say a handicapped child, should be covered by term or some other form of insurance or via an annuity. We will discuss this problem in some detail in Chapter 7. Tax-efficient investments placed in a suitable form of trust are the conventional way of looking after the interests of younger dependent relatives after you are gone.

An elderly investor will find that an annuity can provide a very good return on the money invested especially after taking income tax into account. A simple annuity terminates on the death of the investor unless some form of guaranteed or joint annuity is taken out. Such guarantees usually only cover a period of five years after inception or, in the case of a joint annuity, they cut the income generated from the annuity by a substantial margin. The point we are making is that the interests of dependants should be considered if you intend to place a substantial fraction of your wealth into an annuity.

FUTURE EMPLOYMENT PROSPECTS

If you are in a secure, highly paid job you can obviously afford to take a much greater risk with your wealth portfolio than if your future is insecure. The investor in an insecure job needs to maintain a much more liquid wealth portfolio and invest in assets that do not fluctuate too wildly in value. In other words, such an investor should invest in fixed interest securities plus an index fund with a low risk attached.

The investor with an insecure future needs liquidity because he or she may need rapid access to funds to finance a period of unemployment or a new lifestyle. Liquidity has a price and any investment which suffers from low liquidity, such as an insurance bond, will offer a premium above the market return to compensate for the low liquidity inherent in this kind of asset. The premium can be substantial, running to 2% to 3% per annum.

The investor in a secure job is able to lock away financial assets for long periods into the future. This self-denial of liquidity can provide the fortunate investor with a much higher average return over this period. The organization holding the investor's funds knows that the investor cannot withdraw them over this period and is willing to pay a premium rate to the investor for this privilege.

THE FUTURE NEED FOR FUNDS

Few of us save in a vacuum. We normally save with some objective in view. The normal objectives include building up retirement income or saving to cover for some unexpected misfortune like ill-health or loss of job.

Sometimes we save to build up a fund for a specific purpose such as setting up an independent business or saving to provide private school fees or to buy a home. The nature of this investment objective will effect the composition of the investment fund set up to meet the objective. For example if we know that private school fees currently costing £6000 a year for five years will begin to be paid in 10-years' time then we can select a tax-efficient investment, such as a split-level trust or a discounted bond, which comes to fruition in 10-years' time. The proceeds can then be invested in another, more liquid, fund which can be cashed-in gradually over the five-year period during which the fees are due to be paid. Savings made to buy a home can be invested with an institution which will provide the mortgage finance in later years.

Various tax allowances are provided by the government to encourage business investment. An investor considering setting up an independent business would be foolish to ignore these benefits and this might effect the composition of his investment fund. The rules are complex and you would need to take advice from a business tax adviser on such matters.

OTHER FACTORS

A legion of other factors might have some influence on the composition of your wealth portfolio. Most of these factors, such as attitude to environmentalism, political attitude, affiliation to a particular company, the equity shares held by another member of the family, and your likely future domicile or residence are of limited interest to the general investor but can have a decisive influence on the investment plans of specific investors.

COMPOSING YOUR OWN PORTFOLIO OF SHARES

Let us assume that you have now considered your key characteristics, such as your age and health, and have studied the characteristics of the various individual investments that are available to you. You are now in a position to design a portfolio of shares suited to your particular needs.

First you must decide whether you wish to put together a do-it-yourself portfolio of shares or whether you will hand this job over to the manager of a *collective* investment fund such as a unit trust or investment trust or tracker fund.

Let us suppose you decide to do it yourself. This is the cheaper but more risky option. Which company shares will you buy? The odd thing about this question is the answer: 'it does not matter very much'. Research by financial analysts have shown that shares on the stock exchange in London and New York are efficiently priced. In other words if a share in Glaxo PLC is quoted at 333 pence today on the London exchange, that is a fair price to pay. Where shares are concerned you cannot outguess the market. You cannot 'pick winners' on a consistent basis. Remember that tracker funds, which mirror the index, have beaten around 80% of managed funds in recent years if we measure performance by return minus management costs. Tracker funds charge very low management costs.

Research over the last 20 years has demonstrated that all publicly available information that investors can use to pick 'winners' is almost immediately incorporated into the value of the share once it is published. By the time you, or any analyst not watching the screens continuously, obtain the information it is 'old hat'. The share price has already adjusted to this information. One study showed that, on average, new information is incorporated into the share price within eight minutes of it being announced.

The fact that you cannot 'pick winners' in an efficient share market is of great benefit to the amateur investor. Any random selection of 20 to 30 shares will remove most of the specific risk attached to these individual shares in the portfolio. The market will always outguess you, and professional investors as well it seems, when it comes to picking particular 'winners'.

In the long run you can only make money on the stock exchange from 'picking winners' if you have 'insider knowledge' of the company concerned. This activity is called 'insider trading' and it is illegal in most countries and can land you in jail.

Should you just select 30 shares at random from the *Financial Times* list? No. You may be able to improve on that option by selecting two shares each from each of the 15 industrial groups quoted in the *Financial Times* and some other newspapers. Which two shares should you select from each industrial group? It is safer to choose large companies. The market value of the equity shares in each of the companies quoted is calculated and shown each week in some newspapers such as the *Guardian*. This approach will provide you with a safer portfolio at the cost of a slightly lower average return.

We conclude that you can design a perfectly adequate portfolio of shares for yourself by choosing around 30 shares, for example two shares in large companies from within each of 15 industrial groups, quoted in any of the leading newspapers.

Why go to all this trouble when a 'collective' investment such as a unit trust or investment trust or a tracker fund will make the selection for you? Unit trusts and investment trusts charge investors a management fee of around 1% to 3% of the value of the shares held in the trust each year. If the yield on the collective investment is around 4% to 6% a year this is a substantial reduction in the return on your investment. Why not save yourself this cost and do it for yourself?

The professional investor may be able to gain a slightly higher return but we doubt if the incremental return will be above 1.5% a year on average. In other words if you can achieve 5% per annum the managers of the collective investment must achieve at least 6.5% per annum to be competitive.

The managers of collective investments will also charge a 'signing on' fee of 1% to 5% of the value of your investment when you enter the scheme. Spread over a long period this charge is much less important than the annual management fee.

Building and running your own portfolio can also be fun. You can avoid owning shares in companies you do not like and take a punt at companies you believe to be 'winners' even although you are unlikely to make much money out of this activity in the long run.

Much depends on the opportunity cost of your own time. If this is very high or you just can't be bothered, then take the easy route and invest in a collective investment that will be managed for you.

Note that the cost of buying and selling shares is rather high. The spread between the buy and sell price can be from 2% to 6% of the selling price. Stockbrokers charge very high fees per deal for selling small quantities of shares. Selling 500 shares might cost you 10% of the value of the shares. Selling 5000 shares in the same company might cost you only 1% of the value of the shares. It is not economic to trade much below £5000 worth of shares on each trade. This means that churning your initial portfolio is not sensible: it will kill the return on your investment. You must set up your own portfolio but trade infrequently.

THE EASY WAY: SELECT A COLLECTIVE INVESTMENT

Unit trusts, investment trusts, tracker funds, insurance funds and some types of equity-based bonds are called *collective investments.* You hand your money over to the manager of the fund and the manager invests this money in the collective fund. The fund itself will be managed by a team of professional analysts who watch the market day-by-day. They sell some shares or stocks and buy others. In other words they update the collective fund in line with market developments.

This saves you a lot of trouble but, as argued above, it also costs you an annual management fee which can be quite expensive at 1% to 3% of the value of the fund each year. Some 'exotic' funds such as warrant funds charge upwards of 5% per year as a management fee. There will also usually be an initial fee that currently runs at around 3% to 5% of the amount invested, although some funds do not charge an initial fee.

Exhibit 2.11 illustrates several portfolios of managed funds designed to meet the needs of three investors with differing requirements.

Not all collective investments have the same objective. Some funds are general funds that invest in a wide range of securities from every sector of the market. Other collective funds invest in specialized sectors. For example one can invest in a small companies fund, an emerging country fund, a venture capital fund or an ethical fund. Since these funds are more specialized they are likely to be more risky and so will have to offer a higher return to attract investors. Specialized collective funds offer the investor the option of investing in a chosen sector while avoiding exclusive investment in a single company in that sector. For example an emerging country fund could invest in companies in Brazil, Malaysia, India and South Africa. All of these markets are likely to offer high growth rates in the future but from time to time each of these markets will individually plummet in value . . . not, we hope, all at the same time. Research has shown that the returns show only a low correlation in time. Diversification offers security of return.

UNIT TRUSTS

Unit trusts invest the funds entrusted to them in a wide range of shares. Unit trusts are *open-ended:* they can buy and sell shares within the trust fund. The trustee is usually a bank.

The fees consist of an initial charge of 1% to 5% and a management charge of 1% to 2%. This is quite expensive considering that the yield on UK shares is currently running at below 4% per annum gross of tax. The buy-sell spread can be up to 5% of the selling price. There may even be an 'exit' charge of 5% to 1%, diminishing depending on the number of years you hold the units. You can ask the fund manager to reinvest your annual income in the same fund if you wish. Unit trust funds can be general or specialized. There are different types of specialization: large companies, venture companies, 'hi-tech' companies, or geographic specializations such as portfolios of shares from the UK, USA, Europe, the Far East, or South America. Obviously the specialized companies are more risky than the general trusts and should provide a higher average return on your units. The magazine *Money Observer* provides extensive information on the type and performance of unit trusts available to investors in the UK. The return on general unit trusts has been somewhat less than spectacular in recent years.

INVESTMENT TRUSTS

Investment trusts, unlike unit trusts, are allowed to raise debt and invest this debt in further shares for the fund. In other words investment trusts can *gear* their portfolios with debt. What is the advantage of such a procedure? If the return on the shares so invested exceeds the cost of the debt then the investors in the fund will benefit by the difference. If the cost of the debt exceeds the return from the additional shares the investors will lose out. Historically the return on shares has exceeded the cost of debt so, on average, investors have benefited from the gearing of investment trusts.

Investment trusts have provided a higher return than unit trusts in recent years. In fact since around 1990 investment trusts have been all the rage in the personal investment market.

Most investment trust shares trade at a discount to the value of the shares in the trust. The discount on the market value of the shares and so forth held in the trust is currently around 5% but the discount was as high as 35% in 1976.

In a few cases the value of the trust shares actually exceed the value of the shares held in the underlying fund. This is therefore a risky investment.

Shares in investment trusts are quoted on the Stock Exchange and can be bought there like any other share, unlike units in a unit trust which can only be bought from and sold to the managers of the trust. Investment trust shares were not marketed as strongly as unit trust units until recently when it was decided to pay investment advisers a commission for selling them. Most investment trusts have provided a rather better return than the average for general unit trusts in recent years. However the current surge in their popularity may have reduced this comparative advantage over unit trusts somewhat since 1994.

EXHIBIT 2.11: Financial asset portfolios of three investors at different ages with different responsibilities

The composition of your wealth portfolio depends on your objectives. How much cash do you need on a regular basis? Will you need to keep your funds liquid or can you invest for the long term? How much risk are you willing to take with your investments? Will you be staying in the UK or moving abroad when you retire? What arrangements are you making with regard to inheritance tax?

A. A 35-year-old (married) designer of computer software

Investment product	Value	Return	Risk	Subject to tax?
Building society deposit	£11 000	low	low	yes
TESSA account with bank	£9 000	medium	low	no
With profits bond	£20 000	high	medium	yes
Equity shares with growth potential (in PEP)	£30 000	high	medium	no
Zero dividend preference shares (for future school fees)	£20 000	high	low	no (use CGT allowance)
Highly geared technology investment trust	£10 000	very high	very high	yes
	£100 000			

B. A doctor who is married but will retire in five years time

Investment product	Value	Return	Risk	Subject to tax?
Building society deposit	£11 000	low	low	yes
TESSA account with bank	£9 000	medium	low	no
Guaranteed income bond	£20 000	high	medium	yes (for higher tax rates)
Equity shares in six large stable companies (held in a PEP)	£30 000	medium	medium	no
High income shares from split trust	£20 000	high	medium (capital at risk)	yes
Medium geared safe investment trust	£10 000	medium	medium	yes
	£100 000			

C. A 72-year-old widow

Investment product	Value	Return	Risk	Subject to tax?
Building society deposit	£2 000	low	low	yes
TESSA account with a building society	£9 000	medium	low	no
PIBS building society share	£10 000	high	low	yes
Guaranteed income bond	£10 000	high	medium for capital	yes
Equity shares in four large, stable companies (held in a PEP)	£20 000	medium	medium	no
Level term life annuity at 13% per annum	£40 000	high	zero	at very low rate
Medium geared safe investment trust (held in a PEP)	£9 000	medium	medium	no
	£100 000			

The annual management charges on investment trusts are lower than on unit trusts, at 0.5% to 1%. Since investment trust shares are bought and sold on the stock market there is the buy-sell spread of 2% to 3% to contend with plus stamp duty at 0.5%.

SPLIT-LEVEL INVESTMENT TRUSTS

One exotic form of investment trust is the split-level investment trust. In this case the income derived from the shares in the trust is separated from the capital in the trust. One group of investors buys the rights to the income the other buys the rights to the capital.

The investors in the capital portion of the trust buy *zero dividend preference shares*. When the trust is wound up at the end of its fixed term of life these shareholders will receive a fixed sum of money that was agreed when they bought the shares. They will receive no dividend from the shares.

Zero dividend preference shares are an example of what is called a deep discounted financial product. The terminal value will almost certainly be achieved by the fund but if it is not the shareholders will not receive the full capital due. A shareholder might pay £70 for a zero which will be repaid in seven years' time at £100. Most zeros have a life of around five to seven years.

Since no dividends are paid there is no income tax to pay and the capital gains may not be taxed if you use your capital gains tax allowance efficiently.

Zeros are useful for high marginal-rate taxpayers who face a large bill in the future. Parents saving for school fees are a good example: a block of zeros can be released year-by-year to pay the annual fees.

The income portion of the split-level investment trust goes to the holders of the *income shares*. These shares receive all of the income and a small portion of any capital gain. The holders of income shares may not receive all of their capital back: they may only get back, say, 90%. This protects the interests of the zero shareholders who, you will recall, may not receive the promised terminal sum if the trust does not perform as expected.

Lawyers use split-level investment trusts to alleviate problems with inheritance tax planning. You can retain the income from the income shares in the trust during your lifetime and give the zeros to your children some years before your death (see Chapter 9).

PERSONAL EQUITY PLANS

Personal equity plans, or PEPs, are free of both income tax and capital gains tax. You can currently invest up to £6000 a year in a PEP plus another £3000 in a single company PEP. You cannot place your existing shares in a PEP: you must sell them and reinvest. If you invest in shares, the company you invest in must be registered in the European Community. You can invest in ordinary shares, preference shares, and company bonds so long as the bonds have five years to run. If you invest in a unit or investment trust the trust must have invested at least 50% of its portfolio of financial assets in the UK or EC. This makes it a *qualifying trust*. You can invest up to £1500 of your PEP allowance in a non-qualifying trust. There are numerous other restrictions on PEP investment.

You can set up the PEP via a self-select route run by a company which allows you to run your own portfolio. Most investors invest through a managed PEP or through a unit or investment trust PEP.

Personal equity plans are clearly a profitable option for the higher-rate taxpayer: particularly those who use up their capital gains allowance each year. The benefits to the basic-rate taxpayer are more problematic. Most basic-rate taxpayers do not use up their capital gains allowance each year so the avoidance of CGT is of no value to them. If you are going to invest in a unit trust it makes sense to invest £6000 or £9000 in a PEP. The benefit, however, is rather less than you might think it is.

Note that if you do not use your PEP allowance in one year it is lost for ever.

OPEN-ENDED INVESTMENT COMPANIES (OEIC)

This European innovation is about to enter the UK market. The OEIC (pronounced 'oik') is likely to become a substitute for unit trusts over the next few years. The UK unit trust managers will convert their unit trusts to OEICs since this form of investment combines some of the benefits inherent in unit trusts and investment trusts. However OEICs will not be allowed to invest in other funds, derivatives[7] or cash.

An OEIC is open ended, like a unit trust, but it has share capital like an investment trust.

The share units in an OEIC will be offered at a single price rather than at a buy-sell spread. This would be an advantage to the buyer but for the fact that there will be a sales charge and possibly a redemption charge to pay when you buy or sell your units.

We doubt whether the net benefit to the investor will be worth the change from unit trusts to OEICs but we must wait and see.

TRACKER OR INDEX FUNDS

A third popular form of collective investment, mentioned previously, is the *tracker* or *index* fund.

Tracker funds have been introduced into the UK financial markets relatively recently. This novel financial product incorporates many of the advantages of unit and investment trusts but at a much lower management cost to the investor.

Tracker funds build up a composite fund which mimics a well-known share index such as the Financial Times All-Share Index or the Japanese Nikkei 225 index. These indices are used by analysts to measure the changing value of all the shares quoted on a given stock exchange. If a tracker fund mimics an index correctly it will move in tandem with it. Most tracker funds have been successful in achieving this objective. Shares need only be bought and sold to keep the composition of the tracker fund in line with the index. Thus annual management charges are very low, being typically 0.5% of the value of the fund as against an average of 1.5% for most unit trusts and 1% for investment trusts.

If tracker funds provide benefits similar to unit and investment trusts, why not invest in a tracker fund rather than in another type of collective investment? As we have seen, studies of the performance of tracker funds have shown that their return beat 80% of the actively managed collective funds over the five year period 1991–95. There is no guarantee that this sequence will continue but why pay 1.5% a year in management fees when you can achieve the same objective at a cost of only 0.5%?

It is perhaps significant that when Richard Branson started out in the personal finance industry he chose a tracker fund as his first financial product.

A tracker fund diversifies away specific risk, has a beta (market risk) factor close to one, and enjoys low management charges. An additional benefit is that the value of the investment can be easily monitored since it mimics a given share index which is published daily.

Under current conditions in the UK, tracker or index funds appear to offer the best bet for the amateur investor. Both the risk and the costs of running the fund are low while the returns obtained are above the average for safe collective funds. A listing of some tracker or index funds available in the UK is provided in Exhibit 2.6 above.

INSURANCE FUNDS

The insurance industry provides a form of collective investment in the form of *endowment funds*. We will say more about endowment funds in Chapter 7 on insurance.

All the forms of collective investment mentioned above, the investments such as unit and investment trusts, are provided under the insurance fund umbrella. Exhibit 2.12 shows the return on 10-year and 25-year endowment policies in recent years. The average yield is good but the size of the variance in yield between different funds is rather alarming.

HOW TO OBTAIN A GOOD UNIT OR INVESTMENT TRUST

Each month personal finance magazines such as *Money Management* and *Money Observer* publish lists of unit and investment trusts showing their relative performance over the last six months to five or even 10 years. It might be thought that finding a good unit or investment trust entails no more than picking one of the larger trusts at the top of the list. Unfortunately there is no evidence supporting this proposition. Financial research by very reputable researchers has found that a good performance in the past gives no guarantee for the future.[8]

In fact some research indicates that poor past performers do better in the future than good past performers. There is a tendency to move towards the mean performance. The efficient market theory would support this finding.

It *has* been found that new unit trusts tend to do better than old ones. Moreover, small trusts perform better than large ones. Trusts specializing in the shares of small businesses do better than trusts holding the shares of large businesses but the higher return in these cases might well be attributed to taking on a greater risk.

Pick a trust from the top half of the draw by all means but do not believe that by following this strategy you are guaranteeing yourself a superior performance in the future. Since the quality of fund management is not so important why not invest in a 'tracker' or 'index' fund instead? These funds incur much lower management charges and the evidence suggests that they will provide you with just as good a return as actively managed funds.

	10-YEAR POLICIES		25-YEAR POLICIES	
	Redemption value	Annual yield	Redemption value	Annual yield
	£	%	£	%
Best	8427	14.8	45 999	14.4
Average	7444	12.2	39 466	13.3
Worst	5786	6.8	29 443	11.5

Source: *Money Marketing*, April 1994

Note:

Inflation averaged 5.1% per year over the period 1984–93.

Inflation averaged 9% per year over the period 1969–93.

The table shows the redemption value and the annual yield gross of inflation for 10-year and 25-year endowment policies managed by various UK insurance companies over the periods 1984–93 and 1969–93.

Note the very wide variation in yield and terminal value. The highest terminal value is 56% above the lowest value. The highest yield is more than twice the yield of the lowest yield.

The problem with such policies lies in choosing the 'winners' 10- or 25-years in advance. One must question the ability of anyone, even a competent personal financial adviser, to achieve this objective.

EXHIBIT 2.12: The rate of return on endowment policies over 10 and 25 years

ADJUSTING YOUR PORTFOLIO FOR RISK

Let us now return to the issue of building your own portfolio. We assume that you have built a portfolio of shares suited to your particular needs. You have matched your particular characteristics and requirements to the attributes of the many financial products on the market. You have built or bought a diversified portfolio that has removed the specific risk attached to any individual share. If you have bought a tracker fund or a general unit trust you will face an average market risk. Suppose you now want to take on a higher market risk with a higher potential return or conversely a lower market risk with a lower potential return. How do you effect such a change in the market risk inherent in your portfolio of shares?

There are several approaches to handling this problem, some of them very complex, but we will take the easy path here. Let us assume that you decide to control the degree of risk attached to the return on your wealth portfolio by varying the proportion of the total fund that is invested in fixed-interest securities. A tracker fund is fairly safe but if the stock market should plunge you could be in financial trouble, at least for a time. If you wish to design a safer portfolio that provides a rather lower income you might invest a fraction of your total portfolio in fixed-interest stocks such a gilts or PIBS or their equivalent. A 50-year-old man retiring in 10 years time might decide to invest 30% of his portfolio in fixed interest stocks. A 70-year-old widow might choose to place 80% of her portfolio in fixed interest stocks. An annuity is another possibility but we will discuss the complexities of investing in an annuity in a later chapter.

Suppose you want to increase risk and so go for a higher return on your funds. As we stated earlier in the chapter if you wish to build a risky but potentially very profitable portfolio you have several options. You could take out a bank or other loan and invest the proceeds in equity shares. This strategy *levers* your portfolio upwards. If the return on the additional shares bought with your loan is higher than the cost of the debt taken on to buy these shares the returns on your portfolio can be increased quite dramatically, but note that the overall risk is also increased. If the return on the new shares proves to be less than the cost of the loan you will be in trouble! We do not recommend such a strategy for the amateur investor – at least not without professional guidance.

EXOTIC INVESTMENTS

An alternative strategy for increasing the risk and return on your portfolio is to place certain high-risk, high-return financial products into your portfolio. We have discussed *warrant* funds, which are highly geared products. Some of these funds have produced very high returns in recent years. Unfortunately they impose spectacularly high management charges on the investor. Some option funds are also available in this category. Speculative currency funds, such as the well-known fund run by George Soros, have made spectacular gains but also spectacular losses. Usually only very large amounts of money are accepted into such funds. Exotic investment products of this nature are not for widows and orphans, or for those with a heart-condition, but a small fraction of a personal fund invested in such exotica can be fun and just might be very profitable but don't blame me if you lose the lot!

THE COST OF BUYING FINANCIAL PRODUCTS

Financial products such as shares, unit trust units, investment trust shares and equity bonds can be expensive to buy. First there is the cost of the share itself but on top of this there will be a charge by the broker who buys the share for you on the Stock Exchange. In addition there is the spread between the buying and selling price of the share which might be 3% to 5% of the cost of the share. In some cases there is also stamp duty at 0.5%. If you are not careful, the cost of buying and selling a financial product can add up to 10% of the market value of the product. Fortunately there are ways to reduce these costs:

- To reduce the charge by the broker the best approach is to ask for an *execution-only* deal. A full broker service deal would allow you to ask advice from the broker. If you don't want this advice don't pay for it. Execution-only deals are much cheaper than full service deals.

- You should not make deals that are worth less than about £5000. A £5000 deal will cost about 1% or £50. A £500 deal would cost about 6% of the value of the deal which would be hopelessly uneconomic. Incidentally a £50 000 deal would cost about 0.3%.

The *Investor's Chronicle* regularly publishes lists of brokers and charges. Buying unit trusts from a trust company can be expensive at 5% of the value of the units bought. There are dealers called *discount brokers* who will sell you unit trust units much more cheaply. They advertise in the financial press. Why pay 5% if you can buy the same product at 3%? Some unit trust managers now make a much lower initial charge.

WHEN TO BUY

Shares move within a cyclical trend. If you study the price history of any share you will find times when it was 'cheap' and other times when it was 'dear'. How can you time your purchase so that you only buy when the share is cheap?

The answer is: you can't! Even the most expert financial analysts get their timing wrong so you have no chance of *consistently* beating the market. The solution is to follow a strategy that is called *pound cost averaging*. You buy shares continuously when they are both cheap and dear, thus over time you buy at the moving average price of the share. You will not make a fortune but on the other hand you will not lose your shirt. Although some may tell you otherwise it is just not possible to consistently buy at the bottom of the cycle.

MINIMUM PORTFOLIO SIZE

If you need around 20 shares to properly diversify your portfolio, and the minimum deal is £5000, then the minimum portfolio size must be 20 × £5000 which is equal to £100 000. A do-it-yourself portfolio below this size is really too small to be economic. If you are investing less than £100 000 go for a collective investment.

SAVING AND INVESTMENT

Research on personal finance has found that most personal investment comes from *lump sums* received from inheritance, the sale of an asset, or from the terminal value of a pension or insurance fund.

If you want to build up a substantial investment fund from saving you need to set up a savings plan. All financial institutions will be only too happy to organize such a fund for you. Even a small amount set aside each month can build to a substantial sum through the power of compound interest. The power of compound interest is truly marvellous to behold. For example £100 a month saved each month over 10 years will build a fund of £16 500 at a compound rate of interest of 6%; over 20 years the figure is £46 200. This 6% rate is not too optimistic if the fund is invested in a PEP. The PEP will be mostly invested in equities which have achieved a higher rate than this over the last 30 years. You will pay no income or capital gains tax on the fund in the PEP.

If £100 per month is deducted from your regular income you will simply adjust expenditure down to the lower level. If you don't set up a savings scheme your expenditure may rise to meet the income available.

SOME CONCLUDING THOUGHTS

You have reviewed your investment needs, chosen suitable investments from among the many financial products available, decided whether to build the wealth portfolio yourself or leave it to a professional manager and controlled the risk attached to the portfolio by splitting the total fund between equities and fixed interest or other safe securities. The less risk you were willing to take with your wealth the higher the proportion you will have invested in fixed interest securities and the lower income (income not cash) you will receive per pound invested. This assumes a period of relatively low inflation. If you expect a future inflation rate of above 5% a year to return you should invest a higher proportion in equities. Inflation is the traditional scourge of the fixed-income classes.

You must take care to buy financial products at minimum cost. The costs of purchase, management and sale can easily wipe out the return on any financial investment if you do not seek out cheaper methods of purchase and annual management charges.

This chapter was concerned exclusively with investing in financial assets, particularly in equity shares. Equity shares have provided investors with a good return over the last 50 years or so and have also provided strong protection against inflation. The next chapter will consider the question of investing in real assets such as houses, antiques, gold coins or rare postage stamps. Real assets have also provided the investor with a good bulwark against inflation over the past 50 years but real assets suffer from some deficiencies which we shall discuss in the next chapter.

SUMMARY

1. When you make an investment you are seeking income and you are also seeking to maintain the value of the investment through time.

2. The immense range of possible investments open to an investor can be clarified somewhat if we divide investments between financial assets, which are legal contracts, and real assets, which are mainly physical assets. Financial assets can be further classified into equity shares and fixed-interest investments.

3. Financial assets, rather than real assets, provide the best haven for saving since they are more easily protected, provide a regular income, are often quite liquid, are usually divisible and transportable and can be bought and sold quite easily at low cost.

4. The income from an investment consists of two parts: the annual dividend or interest payment, and the difference between the market value of the investment at the beginning and end of a period. The latter normally provides a larger part of the income than the former.

5. The return on an investment and the risk attached to it are as closely bound together as Siamese twins. In an efficient financial market higher returns can only be achieved by taking on additional risk.

6. The risk attached to an investment can be segregated into two types: *specific* risk and *market* risk. Specific risk can be almost eliminated from a portfolio of shares by diversifying the portfolio over 20 to 30 shares.

7. Market risk measures the sensitivity of the return on a share to movements in the overall market. Shares that are highly sensitive to market movements are called *high beta* shares.

8. The beta of a share allows an investor to design an average risk, average return portfolio, a high risk, high return portfolio, or a low risk, low return portfolio.

9. If investors do not wish to take the trouble of constructing their own portfolios of shares, they can invest in a collective investment like a unit trust, investment trust or tracker fund. The manager of these funds will charge an initial fee of 1% to 5% plus an annual fee of 0.5% to 3% for handling the fund for the investor.

10. Tracker funds mimic the Stock Exchange index. They provide a wide diversification of shares in large companies and a beta close to one. The management fee is very low, usually only 0.5% per annum. In recent years they have equalled the performance of general unit and investment trusts at a lower cost.

11. In addition to risk and return some other aspects of investments are important. Factors such as cash flow, capital growth, security,

liquidity, buying and selling costs, protection costs, divisibility, transportability and tax implications.

12. An investment portfolio must be able to cope with inflation. Ordinary shares have proved to be a strong bulwark against inflation for almost the whole of this century. Inflation-indexed government bonds and inflation-indexed annuities are alternative ways to handle inflation. These latter, however, provide a rather low return compared to equity shares.

13. The secret behind building a sound investment portfolio is to match the characteristics and needs of the investor to the wide range of financial products available on the market. The key characteristics of the investor are age, state of health, attitude to risk, lifestyle, needs of dependent relatives, future employment prospects and the future need for funds.

14. When it comes to choosing particular investments to place in your wealth portfolio you can forget about picking winners. This cannot be done on an efficient stock exchange like London or New York. What you should do is decide on the risk-return mix you favour and use the proportion of fixed interest stocks in the portfolio to achieve this objective. If you want a high risk, high return portfolio, borrow money and invest it in a range of ordinary shares.

15. The same objective can be achieved by investing in a suitable collective investment like a unit trust but this is expensive. The typical trust charges 1.5% per year in management fees. If the total return is only 5% per year, this is a lot. Tracker funds are cheaper. Investment trusts can gear up their earnings, unlike unit trusts.

16. If the reader requires a more interesting investment, he or she might consider the *exotic* investments now offered on the market. Warrant and option funds are *geared* investments that offer a kind of double or quits game to the brave investor. Speculative currency funds are even riskier but potentially very profitable. Whilst a small gamble with exotics can be fun, we suggest that not too much should be wagered.

TEST YOUR KNOWLEDGE

1. What are the two main objectives of personal investment?

2. Personal wealth can be invested in either financial assets or real assets. What is the difference between a financial asset and a real asset? Give two examples of each type of asset. Why are financial

assets considered to be superior as an investment medium compared to most real assets?

3. If you buy an ordinary (equity) share in a quoted company you buy certain *rights* attached to the share. Describe four rights that are attached to most ordinary shares.

4. The income from a financial investment usually consists of two parts. What are these two parts? Calculate the rate of return on the following shares for the year to 31 August 1997 given the assumed opening value, closing value and dividend for the year.

Company	Opening pence	Closing pence	Dividend pence
Zelda	245	270	12
Tarant	160	148	8
CIK	375	399	18

5. 'So far as investment is concerned return and risk are Siamese twins.' Explain.

6. What is a *collective investment*? Give three examples of collective investments. What advantages would you hope to derive from investing in a collective investment rather than selecting a range of shares for yourself?

7. What is a *tracker* or *index* fund? What does it track? Suggest three important benefits provided to an investor by a tracker fund.

8. Let us suppose you want to invest your assets in such a way that if a political crisis were to occur in your country the assets could be quickly transferred to another country and sold in that country. Suggest three suitable assets.

9. If you expect the rate of inflation to rise above 5% in the near future and remain high for some years to come which assets should you invest in to protect your wealth against the ravages of inflation?

10. How does the age of an investor effect the composition of his or her wealth portfolio?

11. If an investor is in poor health, how will this effect the composition of his or her wealth portfolio?

12. The Isle of Man and Jersey and the Cayman Islands are called 'tax havens'. What is a tax haven? What type of benefits are offered to a private investor by a tax haven?

13. Suppose you know that you will incur school fees for your child in 10 years' time. The fees will be incurred for a five year period. The current cost of these school fees is £6000 per annum. What sort of an investment fund should you set up now to ensure that you will be able to pay these school fees when the time comes?

14. Suppose that, rather than choosing 30 shares from the London stock market at random, you wish to improve diversification and reduce risk even further (at the cost of a slightly lower return). What simple strategy can you employ?

15. Why is the strategy of 'picking winners' dangerous? You can only 'pick winners' among shares in an efficient stock market under very special conditions. What are these conditions?

NOTES

1. This is the selling price on the Stock Exchange. The buying price will be somewhat higher. The difference is called the 'spread' on the buy-sell price. This spread can be anything from 1% to 6% of the buying price. Trading shares is an expensive business! It is the width of the buy-sell spread that makes running your own portfolio so expensive.

2. High management charges are a second reason!

3. The market value of a fixed-rate investment is sensitive to the changing market rate of interest. As the market rate rises, so the market (capital) value of the fixed-rate investment will fall. The longer the maturity of the stock is, the more sensitive the market value will be to changes in the market rate of interest. Fixed-interest stocks that have no maturity date, such as war stock and some consols, are exceedingly sensitive to changes in the market rate of interest.

4. Most financial assets are registered by the issuing company. If you lose the share it can be replaced by writing to the issuer and requesting a replacement. Bearer bonds are assumed to be owned by the person holding the bond. These bonds are often not registered – at least not in the normal way.

5. This trend may be changing. Some analysts believe that fixed interest stocks may provide higher returns than equities over the 1990s.

6. Some warrant and currency funds charge 5% a year in management charges.

7 Except as a hedging device to protect the fund.

8 A well-known recent study by B.G. Malkeil (using US data) concluded that no fund outperformed other funds consistently over more than a few years. These performing funds could not be selected in advance. In other words there are no consistently outstanding fund managers. Malkiel B.G. (1995) Returns from investing in equity mutual funds 1971 to 1991. *Journal of Finance,* 50, pp. 549–72.

Investing in real assets 3

WHAT DO WE MEAN BY A REAL ASSET?

A real asset is a physical asset like an antique clock, a Victorian doll, a postage stamp, a royal navy brass bell, a painting or your home. Real assets can be contrasted with financial assets such as ordinary shares, government stock certificates, annuities, or a postal deposit in a building society. A financial asset is, in essence, a piece of paper, a legal contract between you, the owner of the financial asset, and the institution which sells you the financial asset. This contract gives you certain rights, which we outlined in the last chapter.

Few people buy financial assets for reasons other than to gain a profit from the deal. You buy a financial asset in the expectation of gaining a future income from it.

By contrast, few individual investors buy real assets for the sole, or even the primary, purpose of making a profit (although if a profit is forthcoming they are not displeased). They buy real assets because they enjoy the possession of such objects: they enjoy looking at beautiful objects or they like to build up a collection, or they want to show off their wealth to their friends.

One exception to the above rule involves those real assets that are bought specifically as a store of value and have no other purpose. Gold coins are an example of this, but there are others.

Another possible exception to the rule involves investment in raw materials such as wool, copper and soya beans. Few private individuals choose to invest in such assets and if they do they will almost certainly do so by buying *futures* or *options* on the given product in the *derivatives* market. Futures and options are financial assets, not real assets.

Investing in real assets can be fun but the evidence suggests that, on average, over the long term, the return on real assets is lower than the return on a diversified portfolio of financial assets which includes a substantial portion of equity shares. Real investments have, however, provided a much better return than fixed-interest investments over long periods of time during this century, at least in the UK. Most real investments have also provided the owner with a fairly good hedge against inflation over the last 30 years or so.

Year	UK FT All-Share Index	Old Master's Index	Impressionist Art Index	English Silver Index	Ceramics Chinese Index	Ceramics Continental Index	English Furniture Index	UK Inflation Index (RPI)
1981	100	100	100	100	100	100	100	100
1982	130	106	114	122	106	95	103	105
1983	160	129	148	162	115	108	135	111
1984	192	172	181	201	143	129	181	116
1985	225	201	214	257	146	131	195	123
1986	276	185	362	285	157	140	288	127
1987	430	229	362	285	157	140	288	132
1988	340	265	598	317	195	178	379	141
1989	421	465	975	369	274	243	444	156
1990	360	478	610	374	286	250	448	166
1991	450	478	500	357	286	310	447	174
1992	432	532	498	358	264	337	438	180

Note the variance in the value of some of these real assets over time. The period from 1981 to 1989 was a boom period for real assets. Note that all of these assets beat the inflation index over the period by a substantial margin. These figures ignore the selling and buying costs which might range from 2% to 20% of the price at which the asset is brought from the auctioneer. The FT All-Share index is adjusted for reinvestment of dividends received.

Sources: adapted from indices produced by Sotheby's, Art Market Research, Salomans and the Stock Exchange

EXHIBIT 3.1: An index of the changing market value of some real assets over time

Under normal circumstances real investments do not provide a cash income until the investment is sold.[1] This is a major problem if you want a steady income from your wealth portfolio.

SOME CHARACTERISTICS OF REAL ASSETS

The reader will recall that, in the previous chapter, we listed certain characteristics of assets that are important when we are assessing their worth as investments. These attributes were cash flow, capital growth, security, liquidity, the buying and selling costs, the protection and maintenance costs, divisibility, size, transportability, international marketability, and tax aspects of the investment. Let us now examine how real assets measure up under each of these headings.

CASH FLOW AND INCOME

Most real assets provide you with no cash flow until the asset is sold. You may be able to raise cash from a real asset if you are prepared to put the asset forward as collateral for a loan, but under normal circumstances the only cash forthcoming from a real asset will be the cash realized from the eventual sale of the asset. A profit will only be forthcoming if the inflation-adjusted selling price, less the inflation-adjusted cost of sale, exceeds the original cost of the asset. Real assets are non-starters as income or cash generators when compared with financial assets.

GROWTH IN MARKET VALUE

Real assets have better potential for capital growth than many financial assets – the increase in their sales value over their purchase value is greater over time.

As Exhibit 3.1 shows, the growth in the value of many real assets, assets such as Impressionist paintings, Old Masters and English furniture, have matched the performance of a diversified portfolio of ordinary shares. The share index figure is calculated by assuming that the dividends declared are reinvested in the index.

On the whole, in recent years, the rise in the value of real assets has compensated their owners for inflation, which is more than can be said for fixed-interest stocks throughout most of the twentieth century. One problem, however, is that the variance in the value of real assets tends to be higher than the variance in the value of ordinary shares. The market value of real assets tends to fluctuate by a substantial margin. In other words most real assets provide you with a substantial growth in capital value but these assets are much riskier investments than ordinary shares.

SECURITY OF CAPITAL VALUE

How safe is the capital invested in a real asset? The safety of the cash flow is not too important here because few real assets produce any cash flow. Some financial assets guarantee the nominal value of the capital invested in the asset – building society deposits and some guaranteed bonds for example. Very few real assets provide the owner with a guarantee to maintain the value of the capital invested in the asset.[2]

Since there is seldom any cash to be derived from a real asset until it is sold, and since the entire capital value is at risk, the risk of loss is very great and this risk increases in direct proportion to the length of the period during which the asset is held.

Real assets are risky investments but, as shown in Exhibit 3.1, they may provide the owner with a return high enough to compensate for this risk. You need to decide whether the pleasure you derive from owning a particular asset compensates for the potential loss if its value suddenly drops. In the case of assets such as works of art, it should be remembered that value often depends on fashion and fashion is notoriously fickle.

LIQUIDITY

Liquidity means the speed at which you can convert your assets into cash. Most financial assets can be converted into cash with great speed. There are efficient markets available, such as the Stock Exchange, which will provide you with a price for your asset and will buy the asset from you at that price at almost any time.

The liquidity situation is quite different when you hold real assets. There are markets for real assets, such as auction houses, but they do not operate continuously and the price at which you can sell the real asset is not certain. You may, at best, if you are lucky, be given a 'guide price'. Another problem with real assets concerns the time it takes to sell them. It will take you at least three months to sell your home and it *could* take several years. You may have a problem finding a buyer for a valuable but exotic asset such as a rare antique clock or an arcane stamp collection. You could, of course, sell your asset to a dealer but this will cut the price you will receive by a substantial margin. Dealers will offer you a price 30% to 50% below the current market price in the catalogue.

Liquidity is the Achilles' heel of real assets. You will normally have to be patient and wait for a good price.

BUYING AND SELLING COSTS

The efficiency of a market can be measured by the *spread* between the price at which you can sell an asset and the price at which you can buy the same asset. Some of the markets that buy and sell financial assets such as gilt-edged stock, shares and currencies are remarkably efficient, especially for large value sales. In the case of financial assets the spread between the buying and selling price of the asset is often as low as 1% of the selling price and rarely exceeds 5% of the selling price.

The situation is rather different when it comes to selling real assets such as Victorian paintings, ships' bells or old Japanese prints. At an auction the auctioneer may charge you from 5% to 15% of the sale price as his commission and the buyer may also be charged a fee of up to 15%. Dealers' margins on real assets are notoriously high. If you buy an asset, such as a diamond or a print from a dealer, walk out of the shop, and then walk back in and try to resell it to the same dealer you may be offered one-third or even one-half less than you have just paid for it.

There is also the problem of value added tax (VAT). If you buy a real asset from a dealer you will be required to pay VAT on the purchase. If you are a final consumer of the good in question you will not be able to recover this cost. Value added tax is currently charged at 17.5% on the sale value of the item sold.

Exhibit 3.2 presents an estimate of the spread between the buying and selling price on some real assets. Notice the dramatic contrast between the width of the spread on buying and selling real assets such as paintings and antiques compared to the spread on buying and selling financial assets such as ordinary shares and government stock. (See Exhibit 2.8 in Chapter 2 above.)

The spread between the buying and selling price of real assets is high – seldom less than 15% of the dealer's selling price. Gold coins are a noteworthy exception with a spread of a mere 2% to 3%. Note that the buy-sell spread is reduced as the quality of the asset increases.

PROTECTION AND MAINTENANCE COSTS

A valuable asset needs to be protected and kept in prime condition. This presents no problem with financial assets that are mostly legal contracts. Most financial assets are registered in the name of a particular person by the issuer, so if you lose a share certificate, for example, you can get it replaced at a minimal cost from the original issuer. As we noted in Chapter 2 bearer bonds are a rare exception to this rule.[3]

The cost of protecting a real asset and maintaining it in prime condition can be very high. Protection can mean anything from insuring the asset to employing security guards.

Real assets like jewellery can be insured, but the cost of insurance is high and the insurance contract will almost certainly place restrictions on the number of days on which the jewellery can be worn during a given period. The insurance contract may stipulate where the real asset must be stored when it is not on display. Insurance companies will usually accept valuations of real assets based on a standard catalogue price. A Lloyd's broker will find insurance on an unusual or very expensive asset.

The cost of maintaining an asset in prime condition can also be high. For example you may have to spend several thousand pounds a year to

	% OF BUYING PRICE
Gold coins	3
Land	4
House (£200 000)	7
Antiques (good quality)	20
Antique jewellery	30
Antique cars (pre-1920)	30
Netsuke	30
Collectors' coins	30
Antique silver ornaments	30
Stamps (collectors' items)	30
Other antiques	30
New jewellery	40
Diamond (small)	40
Modern furniture	50
Victorian painting (not by a master)	50
Modern painting (out of fashion)	90

The spreads noted above are only approximations but they give some indication of the cost of trading an asset through a dealer. The spread is expressed as a percentage of your buying price and is much affected by the quality of the asset. Top-quality assets enjoy much lower buy-sell spreads.

EXHIBIT 3.2: The buy-sell spreads of some assets

maintain a house in prime condition, particularly an older house. If you fail to do this the house will fall in value over time and this fall in value is just as much of a cost to you as the cost of maintenance. By contrast, in most parts of the UK, the cost of insuring a house is low compared to its market value. (See Chapter 6 for a fuller discussion of these points.) With a few exceptions, the cost of protecting and maintaining real assets is much higher than the equivalent cost for financial assets.

When real assets are being valued forward, for example when you are calculating their value at your retirement date when you are thinking of cashing them in, these additional costs, which might accumulate over many years, ought to be taken into account in your calculations.

DIVISIBILITY

A few financial assets, such as life insurance policies and annuities, cannot be sold off a part at a time, but these are unusual. Most financial assets are divisible in this way. If you own 10 000 shares in Tarmac PLC you can sell off 1000 shares, or 3000 shares, or any other fraction of the 10 000 shares at any time.

Some real assets offer a similar facility. For example you can sell off a few krugerrands or a few bottles of a vintage wine or a few items from a collection of postage stamps and leave most of the collection intact. However most real assets are not divisible. For example you cannot break up a glass bowl or an antique car or a valuable expressionist painting and sell off the parts one at a time without affecting the value!

Divisibility is important. Once you retire you may wish to liquidate your assets over a given time period. Selling off your house in parts will present you with something of a problem. Home income schemes were devised to solve just this problem.[4] You can raise a loan on the security of an indivisible real asset but this is an expensive option, and you cannot be certain that the eventual sale value of the asset will repay the loan.

It may also be necessary to sell off your assets in parts in order to take full advantage of your annual capital gains tax allowance. See Chapter 9 for a fuller explanation of this point.

The advantage of being able to divide up an asset and sell it off in parts is often overlooked.

SIZE, TRANSPORTABILITY AND INTERNATIONAL MARKETABILITY

Most financial assets are small in bulk (they are mostly documents such as share certificates), can be easily transported across international boundaries and have a reasonable international marketability depending upon local exchange-control regulations.

Real assets vary greatly in this respect. Some real assets (postage stamps, *netsuki*, jewels) are ideally suited to transferring value across an international frontier. They are small and can find buyers in almost any country in the world. The key factor here is the value-to-weight ratio. How much value can be carried in one ounce of the good in question? Rare postage stamps, *netsuki* and jewels come out well on this score. Gold and rare coins also provide you with a good value-to-weight ratio.

However most real assets come out badly on this count. Land cannot be transported from one place to another and so must be sold first and then converted into some other asset for transportation. Houses are little better. Many real assets such as antique cars and clocks are bulky and so are both difficult and expensive to move from one country to another.

If you live in a politically stable country with no exchange-control regulations then this characteristic is not of much significance to you. If you live in a politically unstable country you need to take great care where you place your wealth. Invest in real assets by all means, they may be far superior to local financial assets as repositories of value, but do not invest in immovable real assets. Many expatriates in African countries have learned this lesson the hard way over the last 30 years.

If a crisis forces you to leave with the clothes you stand up in, then rare postage stamps and high quality jewels are useful assets to have tucked away.

TAX ASPECTS OF REAL ASSETS

Real assets are treated for the most part in the same fashion as financial assets so far as UK tax is concerned. However there are one or two differences in tax treatment.

You pay capital gains tax on profits from the sale of both financial and real assets, but any profit made on the sale of a first home is not subject to capital gains tax. Your heirs will pay inheritance tax on both your financial and real assets. If you put your funds into a tax-protected investment plan, like a PEP or a TESSA, you pay no tax on either income or the profit on sale. Profits on the sale of certain government stock are tax free. These kind of plans are available only to investors in financial assets, although financial assets may represent underlying real assets. See Chapter 9 for a fuller discussion of these matters.

Apart from these points, so far as tax is concerned, there is not much difference between investing in financial and real assets except that it might be easier to hide the profits on the sale of a real asset from the eyes of the tax authorities. I am sure no reader of this book would consider such a thing.

FINANCIAL VERSUS REAL ASSETS AS INVESTMENTS

We conclude that so far as financial return is concerned there is no real competition between financial and real assets. If the usual risk/return criteria is used as the criteria of choice financial assets win hands down. On seven of the nine criteria listed above financial assets provide the superior service. As for the others, capital growth and international marketability, there is little difference between the two types of investment. Financial assets, particularly equity shares, are the better investment option on almost all counts.

If we return to Exhibit 3.1, which shows the growth in the value of real assets in money terms over the period from 1981 to 1992 we find that all of the real assets studied beat the inflation index over the period and a few even beat the FT All-Share index (assuming that dividends are reinvested). Note, however, that none of these real assets provides the owner of the asset with a cash income over the period of ownership.

We repeat what we said at the start of this chapter. Few real assets are bought *primarily* as an investment. Real assets such as French jewellery or miniature paintings or lacquered Chinese clocks provide enjoyment over and above any cash income that may be forthcoming from the investments when they are sold. The long-term investment return on 'collectibles' is no more than a minor consideration for most collectors.

Most of the remainder of this chapter will be concerned with advice on investing in real assets that are bought for reasons other than maximizing future investment return.

HOW CAN YOU ENSURE THAT A REAL ASSET BOUGHT FOR SOME OTHER PURPOSE IS ALSO A GOOD INVESTMENT?

Even if the rate of return on your investment is not the primary reason for you buying a Tuscan vase, you will still want to ensure that you have made a good investment. What are the key factors involved in ensuring that when you buy a real asset it is *also* a good investment ?

There are two key factors to consider if you decide to invest in a real asset: quality and authenticity.

Quality is all important when investing in real assets. Only the very best is worth buying if the future value of the asset is an important factor in your choice.

Such items as first editions of books, first night theatre programmes, Japanese prints or Chinese porcelain lose a very large part of their value if they suffer from even the slightest blemish. Only items of the highest quality, in prime condition, can be guaranteed to transfer value safely down the generations. For example, Seaby classifies rare coins into seven different quality classes: fleur-de-coin, uncirculated, extremely fine, very fine, fine, fair and poor.

If you can choose between items in a given class, for example between diamonds of varying weight (in carats), always choose the most expensive you can afford to buy. If you have a given sum to invest, it is better to buy one item of high quality rather than three or four items of lower quality. Rare items have tended to rise in real value through time as the population of well-heeled collectors worldwide rises in number.

The second factor to consider when you are investing in real assets is *authenticity*. For most real assets there is usually some institution or individual who is an expert on the topic, whether the assets are Japanese *netsuki*, Italian violins, medieval English furniture or Roman vases, and who, for a fee, will authenticate the item you are about to buy as genuine. The *certificate of authenticity* will authenticate the approximate age of the item, the maker of the item, the place of manufacture or whatever other attribute gives the item lasting value. Many real assets are of little value without such a certificate. Make sure you are given one when you purchase a real asset or inform the seller that you will only complete the purchase after you have received a certificate of authenticity from an accredited source.

The clandestine industry that manufactures 'fakes' has blossomed in recent years and such is the quality of some of these fakes, particularly from the Far East, that even the experts are sometimes deceived. A certificate of authenticity can provide you with a reasonable degree of assurance that the piece under scrutiny is authentic.

HOW DO YOU BUY AND SELL REAL ASSETS?

There are so many different kinds of real assets that can be bought and sold that no single market like the Stock Exchange exists to organize the buying and selling of *all* real assets. Almost any asset you care to name can be bought or sold in a market somewhere. The markets for selling certain real assets are well defined, such as the auction houses that sell paintings and antiques. Some markets are held on specific sites at fixed intervals such as the Ilkley market for dolls or the London market for antique cars. Some real assets are bought and sold through the listings pages of specialist magazines (books, micro-computers, railway memorabilia). Most real assets are handled by a dealer somewhere.

The problem lies in finding the specific market or dealer for your particular interest. Specialist magazines are the best source of information. Many of these are stored in your local central library.

The London and Provincial Antiques Dealers Association (LAPADA) can assist you in finding experts to authenticate antiques and can also assist in finding any particular antique. It provides a listing of dealers in around 250 specialist types of asset. Most real assets that are collectible are traded by well-known dealers. For example, in the case of rare coins, Seaby and Spinks provide standard catalogues with selling prices, but not buying prices, attached.

Many types of real assets have associations of collectors who will be only too happy to supply you with information about finding, storing, selling or insuring a particular collectible. Exhibit 3.3 presents a listing of markets and dealers who trade in a selection of real assets.

INSURING YOUR REAL ASSETS

If you own valuable antiques, paintings or other assets, a normal insurance policy is unlikely to be your best bet.[5] Specialist insurers provide flexible policies that can reduce the cost of insuring such items by one-half to one-third. The cost can be as low as 30 pence per £100 compared to £1 to £2 per £100 under a standard general contents policy.

If your antique is damaged, the insurance company will pay for the damage to be repaired but will it pay for the subsequent fall in the retail value? Specialist high value insurers will do so if the policy covers this possibility. If one part of a set goes missing will the insurance policy compensate for the loss in value of the whole set? Will you be allowed to buy back a stolen item when recovered if the insurance company has paid out on your claim? These are all matters to be checked out if you own valuable real assets.

You should photograph your valuable antiques, paintings or collectibles. A company called Artist will record your valuables digitally in a secure computer database. This image can be fed to a police computer if the article is stolen.

BUYING, SELLING AND THE INTERNET

One of the major problems associated with investing in real assets is the high costs involved in selling and buying them. By contrast the cost of buying and selling most financial assets is very low. Usually the cost of selling a financial asset is less than 3% of the selling or buying price. It can be as low as 1%. This is not so with real assets. The costs associated with selling and buying real assets can be formidable.

Object traded	Dealers
Antiquities	Robin Symes
Antique cars	Brooks
Furniture	Patridge Fine Art
Coins	Spink & Son; Seaby
Jewellery	S.J. Phillips Ltd
Diamonds (high quality)	CSO Valuations (De Beers)
Gold coins	City market
Houses	Regional estate agents
Land for houses	Regional estate agents
Postage stamps	Stanley Gibbons; dealers
Specialist antiques	Sothebys; Phillips
Wines	John Armit
Artworks: oriental	Spink & Sons
old masters	Richard Green
Chinese	Eskenazi Ltd
contemporary	Anthony D'Offay Ltd
British	Simon Dickonson
Impressionist	Thomas Gibson

A wide range of markets are available for trading real assets in the UK. Many markets do not exist at a physical location but trade through telephones and computer screens, Specialist dealers exist who are willing to buy or sell almost any conceivable asset. Such dealers will advertise in the trade press of their given asset. The above list represents no more than a random selection from among the many dealers who operate in the UK markets.

EXHIBIT 3.3: Some dealers who trade real assets in the UK

If you buy or sell through a dealer you must pay for the *dealer's turn*. This is the spread, discussed above, between the price at which the dealer buys and sells you the same asset. Auctioning goods in a recognized auction house of standing is clearly an expensive business.

All of this means that if you can sell direct to the buyer you can make an extra 30% to 50% on the sale, but how do potential buyers and sellers make contact with one another? Apart from specialist magazines it has been suggested that the ubiquitous Internet might solve this problem once a sufficiently high proportion of the population learn how to communicate through this medium. There are already auction houses running on the Internet such as Auctionweb (http://www.ebay.com/aw/) which offers a wide variety of collectibles to bidders, and Rampages (http://rampages.onramp.net/) offering costume jewellery but these auctions are operating within the USA. Outside the USA I have found that the number of participants in such auctions are few in number. One major problem with the Internet auction is authenticity. How do you ensure the authenticity of the seller and the product? Most of us will want to see more than a coloured photograph before we buy.

The situation may change over the next few years as more people join the Internet. Certainly the dealer's spread is likely to come under pressure if computer auctions catch on.

SUMMARY

1. A real asset is a physical asset. A financial asset is a legal contract.

2. Buying real assets is fun but you should not expect the return on your real asset portfolio to match the return on your portfolio of financial assets.

3. Few real assets provide the owner with a cash income. The income on a real asset comes from the growth in the capital value of the asset. This can only be realized on sale unless the asset is used as security for a loan, which is a risky option.

4. Most real assets are less secure and less liquid than financial assets, suffer from higher buying and selling costs, cost more to protect, and are bulkier and less easy to transport. However most real assets have proved to be a sound bulwark against inflation over the years and can sometimes provide a convenient means of transporting value across international frontiers.

5. If you decide to invest in a real asset of some value you should ensure that it is of the highest quality in that class of asset. In addition a certificate of authenticity should be obtained to ensure that the article is genuine.

6. Both buying and selling real assets can be something of a problem, but this is particularly so in the case of selling. Finding a willing buyer for an exotic asset is not the easiest of tasks. Markets and auctions exist for many real assets but by no means for all. Specialist magazines are the best source of information. Finding a current market value for some real assets can also present you with a tricky problem.

7. Even if you can find a buyer for your asset, the value offered may be well below your expectations. Dealer catalogues provide you with their selling prices not their buying prices. The difference between these two figures can be anything from 10% to 50% of the selling price. Dealers take a very wide 'spread' when buying from you. Auctions can charge up to 20% commission on sale and then an

additional 15% commission to the buyer. The buying and selling of real assets can be an expensive business. This is not true of most financial assets which have a ready market and low dealing costs.

8 Some recent developments on the computer front may assist you in buying and selling real assets. The Internet already runs auctions in various products and if the 'authenticity' problem can be overcome this seems like a promising avenue of development, allowing the amateur collector to buy and sell at a reasonable cost.

TEST YOUR KNOWLEDGE

1. Name a real asset that will provide you with a regular cash income.

2. Do real assets such as good quality paintings provide the owner with a defence against inflation?

3. What is meant by the liquidity of an asset? Are real assets more liquid or less liquid than financial assets? How liquid are the following real assets?

   (a) A rare postage stamp.

   (b) 100 krugerrands.

   (c) A house.

   (d) A 1928 Lagonda car in good condition.

   (e) A collection of first-night programmes of Noel Coward plays from the 1920s.

4. What is meant by the *dealer's spread* when trading assets? Why is this factor so important to an amateur collector? What does the width of the spread tell us about the efficiency of the market selling the asset?

5. What kind of conditions do insurance contracts usually place on the handling of a real asset?

6. Can you think of three kinds of real assets where the total value is divisible into individual units that can be sold separately? Why is divisibility important?

7. 'Some real assets are ideally suited to transferring value across an international frontier.' Give three examples.

8. What tax advantages do financial assets enjoy over real assets?

9. What are the two key factors you need to check out before investing in a real asset, assuming that you want to ensure that the asset retains its value over time?

10. If you buy a valuable real asset, such as a Roman vase or a Chinese burial urn, how can you verify its authenticity?

11. If you wish to buy a specific type of asset, say an eighteenth-century French clock, how do you go about finding a market, auction or dealer who handles such an item?

12. Why is the spread between the buying and selling price so much greater in the case of real assets than it is for financial assets?

13. Electronic auctions through the Internet are already up and running. What factors will you need to check up on before you conclude a contract to buy a real asset such as an antique through an auction on the Internet?

NOTES

1. Renting a house to a tenant is an obvious exception to this rule.

2. Certain real assets that are also raw materials have access to the derivatives market. An example is the *futures* or *options* market in gold and silver. Dealers may use these derivatives markets to provide value guarantees to investors on resale for short periods (at a price).

3. Bearer bonds are not registered in the name of a particular person by the issuer. Ownership is implied by possession. If you lose a bearer bond the finder can cash it.

4. See Chapter 6 for a discussion of the advantages and disadvantages of home income schemes.

5. Such as Harringtons, Artscope International and Hiscox.

Investing in an annuity 4

The annuity is such an important investment medium for the personal investor that this entire chapter will be dedicated to the subject. There is a wide range of annuities on offer to meet the particular needs of different investors. In this chapter we will discuss annuities purchased as an investment to provide a future income, usually to supplement an existing pension income. Such annuities should be differentiated from salary-based pension-fund annuities, which are purchased out of what are called 'money purchase' pension schemes. 'Money purchase' pension schemes must be converted into an annuity on the retirement of the employee. Annuities bought with funds from 'money purchase' schemes enjoy various tax privileges that are not available to simple purchased annuities. We will discuss annuities bought out of 'money purchase schemes' in Chapter 5.

WHAT IS AN ANNUITY?

An annuity is a contract between an insurance company and the person or persons buying the annuity whereby the insurance company guarantees to pay the annuitant a fixed sum of money each period until some event occurs. The most likely event that will terminate the annuity is the death of the annuitant but an annuity can also be paid for a fixed period of time. If you are a 70-year-old male you can buy a lifetime annuity from an insurance company for £100 000. This annuity guarantees that the insurance company will pay you a fixed sum, let us say £12 000 a year, each year until you die. The payments are likely to be made to you monthly, that is £1000 per month. Such a simple annuity is rare nowadays; it is more likely that you will also buy some kind of insurance guarantee along with the annuity. The insurance policy will guarantee that if you die soon after the annuity is taken out then the annuity payments, or a lump sum in lieu, will fall into your estate for the benefit of your heirs.

Guarantees are important to your heirs but not to you. You will be dead if they are needed. The key point is that if you take out a £100 000 annuity, which is not guaranteed, on the 5 September 1997 and you die on 6 September 1997, your heirs will lose the entire £100 000 from your estate! No capital is returned from an annuity – only the annual income. If, however, you take out a five-year guarantee on the annuity, which might cost you 5% of the annual income from the annuity, then if you die on any date up to, say, 4 September 2002, your heirs will inherit the balance of the annuity income up to the year 2002. Most annuities include some kind of guarantee on future income. The longer the period insured the higher the premium. A 10-year guarantee will cost around 8% of the annual income from the annuity.

HOW MUCH INCOME DO YOU GET FROM AN ANNUITY?

In the previous example we quoted an income of £12 000 a year on an annuity of £100 000. This is a very high rate of return – much higher than you can expect from a portfolio of equity shares or government bonds. How can an annuity pay such a high annual income?

An annuity includes a partial return of your capital in the annual payment. The £12 000 includes a return around £8000 of your capital on top of the £4000 of annual income. If you, at the age of 70 today, live the normal expected number of years for a man of 70, you will live to an age of 80. You have, *on average*, 10 years to live. Thus $\frac{£100\ 000}{10}$ = £10 000 a year of capital could be returned to you in addition to the return on the average investment of £50 000 ($\frac{£100\ 000}{2}$) over the period. In fact rather less than £10 000 of capital is returned each year since the insurance company must make a profit on the deal. The fact that a high proportion of your annual 'income' is actually a return of capital and is not income has important tax implications as we shall see later in this chapter.

The return on a whole-of-life annuity is very sensitive to your age. Once you reach the age of 70 an annuity is a good investment; between 65 and 70 it is quite good. Unless you have an 'impaired' life, an annuity is not a good investment below the age of 65 for either men or women.

We conclude that, so long as you are old enough, by investing in an annuity you will receive a much higher guaranteed annual return than you would receive from most other forms of investment, but you must remember that this regular income includes a substantial portion of the return of your own initial capital. When the insurance company receives the £100 000 from you when you buy the annuity the company knows that it will never need to return the initial capital to you as a lump sum but it does, in effect, return it to you in the form of the regular payments on the annuity (if you live long enough).

WHAT HAPPENS TO YOUR MONEY?

When you buy an annuity from an insurance company the insurance company invests your money in medium-term fixed-interest stock, such as a 10-year-to maturity government stock. The stock probably has a maturity of about the same period as your life expectancy. If you are expected to live, on average, for another 10-years then the insurance company will buy £100 000 of fixed-interest stock with a life of 10 years before repayment.[1]

The returns offered by insurance companies on annuities at any one time vary a great deal both between periods and between insurance companies. For example, in early 1990 a 65-year-old man in the UK could have bought a simple whole-of-life annuity which would have paid him 15.5% income, gross of tax, on the capital sum for life. His death might have been 30 or even 40 years away! By early 1994 the highest rate offered on annuities to men of 65 was a mere 10.2% on the capital sum. A fall in income from £15 500 a year to £10 200 a year over only four years, or a fall in annual income of 34%. How can this be?

The explanation lies with the return received by the insurance company on its investments. The return on annuities is tied to the return on medium-term gilt edged securities issued by the government. The insurance company invests its annuity funds in such assets. If the return on these government investments should fall, the return offered by the insurance company on its annuities will also fall. Exhibit 4.1 illustrates the close correlation between the return offered on medium-term government-issued gilt-edged securities and the returns offered by insurance companies on 'whole of life' annuities.

This does not mean that if you retire when the return on gilt-edged securities is low you are stuck with a low income for the rest of your life. There are solutions to this problem that we will discuss later in the chapter.

The return on gilt-edged securities is much affected by market expectations about the future rate of inflation. Since 1992 the financial markets have come to expect lower rates of inflation in the medium term future so the return on gilts has fallen accordingly since there is no need to compensate for high future inflation rates by offering high interest rates.

WHAT DETERMINES THE RATE OF RETURN OFFERED ON AN ANNUITY?

We noted above that expectations about future rates of inflation can have a big impact on the returns offered on annuities in general but many other factors affect the return on annuities offered to individuals. The most important of these factors are your age, your sex and your state of health.

ANNUITY RETURNS AND AGE

As we noted above, the return offered on annuities varies a great deal depending on the age of the annuitant. If you are 75 years of age you are

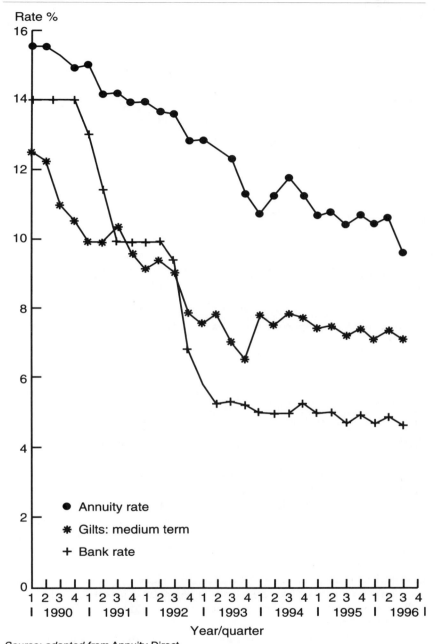

Source: adapted from Annuity Direct

**EXHIBIT 4.1:   The average returns offered on annuities for a 65-
year-old man (level, not guaranteed) compared to
the returns offered on gilts and the bank rate,
1990–96**

74 Investing in an annuity

Annuities: level rates as at January 1994

1. Based on £100 000 purchased annuity.

2. No guarantee or escalation.

3. Paid monthly in advance.

Age	Male	Index	Female	Index	Female/male %	Joint
	£		£			
50	8 450	100	7 400	100	88	
55	8 700	103	7 650	103	88	
60	9 600	114	8 400	114	88	
70	12 300	146	10 800	146	88	
M60, F57						7 500
M65, F63						8 100

The table illustrates the returns offered on level-term purchased annuities without guarantees in January 1994. The rates offered vary a great deal over time. They are linked to the current rate of return on medium-term government stock.

The variation in income offered is substantial. For example the income offered on level-term annuities fell by about 25% between 1990 and 1993. There is also a wide variation between the income offered on annuities by different insurance companies. You would be wise to shop around when buying an annuity.

The table illustrates how the income obtainable on an annuity increases rapidly over the age of 65. Note that the income offered increased by 46% between the ages of 50 and 70. Since women live longer than men they tend to be offered around 12% less income at any given age,

Note the substantial drop in income offered for joint annuities. A 60-year-old man could obtain £9600 per year. If this annuity is extended to both man and wife the income obtainable drops to £7500 per year – a drop of 20% for each future year until the death of both parties.

EXHIBIT 4.2 Some typical annuity rates available at various ages for men and women

offered a much higher return than if you are 60 years of age. In fact the returns offered on annuities sold to 60-year-olds of either sex are so low that they are not a good investment at this age. Annuities are for 65-year-olds and upwards who are in good health. Exhibit 4.2 shows the rates of return offered by one insurance company on a specific date to annuitants of either sex between the ages of 50 and 70 years of age. Women are offered less than men at any particular age since they live longer and a joint annuity on two lives offers much less than a single annuity.

The return becomes even better as you get older. For example a 95-year-old male might well be offered £25 000 a year on a £100 000 annuity, with very little income tax to pay. Difficult to beat, you might think. Unfortunately it is unlikely that many readers will ever be able to take advantage of this particular investment opportunity.

The reason why the rate of return on annuities increases with age is that the older you are the closer you are to departure. Since the regular annuity payments include a portion of return of capital, this portion will rise as you approach your life-expectancy date as given by life-expectancy tables. However you must always remember that life expectancy in any particular category is an average. You might well beat the average and receive a good annuity income for many years beyond your expected date of departure.

ARE ANNUITIES SIMPLY CHIPS IN A LIFETIME GAMBLING CASINO?

An annuity is a gamble between you and a life insurance company. If you live longer than the mortality tables say you should, you win. If you live for a shorter time, you lose. However this loss need not concern you too much since you would be dead. It might be of concern to your heirs.

The above statement implies that, if you are thinking of taking out an annuity, your state of health is important. You do not need to attend for a medical to take out an annuity. The insurance companies are happy to balance their annuity books using the latest mortality tables. Thus if you are 75 years of age and have recently climbed Ben Nevis in three hours, we suggest that you rush hot foot to your insurance company or annuity broker and take out an annuity.

The insurance company expects you to die in five to six years time but you know that you are going to live for 20 or more years yet and, thanks to your high income annuity, live on a very good income for the remainder of your life.

ANNUITIES AND SEX

Sex, they say, affects everything: it certainly affects annuities, although perhaps a more accurate word would be gender. Insurance companies do not look into your sex life before offering you an annuity, although perhaps they should. They do, however, enquire whether you are male or female.

The income offered to a female at any age is about 88% of the amount offered to a male of the same age, but before the 'wimmins' movement takes up arms in protest it must be said that this clear gender discrimination is based on the fact that women live, on average, for four more years than men. Since a 'whole of life' annuity pays out until death then the insurance company will, on average, pay out income on an annuity for four years more to a female annuitant than to a male. Thus the income offered to a female at any age above 60 is about 12% less than that offered to the male. The gap widens further as the age rises.

YOUR STATE OF HEALTH AND ANNUITIES

Your state of health is normally irrelevant when buying an annuity but it can be an important factor if you are relatively young and have a terminal disease. We shall return to this point later when we discuss 'impaired life' annuities.

THE BENEFITS DERIVED FROM AN ANNUITY

Annuities have been around for many hundreds of years. For this reason they are sometimes regarded as a rather 'old fashioned' form of investment compared to the modern equity based products. This attitude is misconceived. Annuities provide an excellent investment opportunity for older people who wish to ensure a steady high income for the rest of their days and are not too worried about leaving a substantial inheritance to their heirs.

The alternative is to invest in an equity based product which provides an uncertain return or another fixed-rate investment which provides a lower return than an annuity.

If you suffer from poor health an annuity is not a good idea unless you can buy an 'impaired' annuity. We will discuss 'impaired annuities' later in the chapter.

If you are a sprightly 70-year-old then an annuity will provide you with a high,[2] stable income for life.

TYPES OF ANNUITY

Insurance companies have designed a wide range of different types of annuity to meet the varying needs of annuitants.

The 'whole of life' flat rate annuity

This is the conventional annuity that has been around for hundreds of years. A 'whole life' flat rate annuity pays a fixed sum of money each month or year from inception until the death of the annuitant. The annual income paid is expressed as a percentage of the initial investment. The rates offered are published in several monthly journals.[3] The return offered, as we noted above, depends on the age and gender of the annuitant. The returns offered rise rapidly beyond the age of 70.

For example one insurance company might offer the following annual incomes on a 'whole of life' flat rate annuity bought by males or females of various ages for £100 000.

Age	Male (£)	Female (£)
55	11 700	10 980
60	12 620	11 550
65	13 760	12 380
70	15 350	13 620
75	17 560	15 480
80	20 670	18 310
90	25 110	22 100

GUARANTEED ANNUITIES

We noted above that, on a non-guaranteed annuity, nothing will be paid to the heirs of the deceased from an annuity on the death of the annuitant. A simple annuity is a gamble between the annuitant and the insurance company selling the annuity. For this reason most annuities sold today are sold in the form of *guaranteed annuities*. Guaranteed annuities will continue to pay out the annuity income into the estate of the deceased for some years after death of the annuitant if the annuitant should die soon after the annuity is taken out. The normal period of cover is for 5 or 10 years after death.

The cost of a guarantee is not high; it depends on your age. The cost of a five-year guarantee to a 65-year-old man with a life expectancy of 13 years is around 3% to 5% of the annual income from the annuity. The cost for 10-year cover is around 8% of the annual income from the annuity.

A long-term guaranteed annuity might be a useful substitute for a joint annuity. A joint annuity on the lives of both husband and wife is a rather expensive variety of annuity. A long period of guarantee attached to the annuity secured on the life of a husband would ensure that the higher income from the annuity on a man would be transferred to his wife for a given number of years after his death. This would be cheaper than a joint annuity.

JOINT ANNUITIES

If a simple annuity is taken out on the life of a husband, his wife loses the income from the annuity on her husband's death. The same would apply to the husband if the annuity were taken out on the life of the wife. Joint annuities are designed to solve this problem. The annuity income is paid out during the lifetime of *either* party. In other words the annuity income continues to be paid out until the last surviving partner dies.

A joint annuity provides useful financial protection for both parties but, unfortunately, this kind of annuity is very expensive since it is based on the life expectancy of *both* parties to the annuity. There is a higher probability of a long life for one or other of the two parties involved as compared to each individual probability. Suppose for example that a male aged 60 takes out a £100 000 annuity and receives an annual income of £9600; if his wife, aged 57, took out a similar annuity she would receive only £8100. But suppose the husband and wife take out a joint annuity of £100 000 when the husband is aged 60 and the wife 57? The joint annuity would pay out only £7500 a year. Note that this figure is not based on the average of £9600 and £8100.

The joint annuity pays out only 78% of the income that would be received by the husband alone, or 90% of the income that would be paid to the wife alone. We conclude that joint annuities provide admirable financial protection but are expensive. See Exhibit 4.2 for further details.

ANNUITIES CERTAIN

An *annuity certain* can be bought for a fixed period of years. Such an annuity can prove useful in guaranteeing that a specific amount of money will be available to make a series of payments in the future such as the payment of school fees. A grandparent could set up a deferred annuity certain to ensure that school fees will be available during some period in the future to guarantee a good education for her grandchild. The annuity can be placed in a trust for the benefit of the child.

A MANAGED ANNUITY

A *managed* annuity gives you a measure of control over the investment and income you receive from your annuity. For example it allows you to vary the level of income you want to receive from the annuity within certain limits. Some control can also be obtained over the investment of the annuity funds. For example the funds can be invested in equity shares, unit trusts, or a 'with-profits' life assurance policy, or some mixture of these. This diversified investment base allows you to manipulate the income you receive each year from the annuity.

This increased degree of control is bought at a greater degree of risk attached to the annuity income. The normal fixed income annuity guarantees the nominal value of the regular flow of income from the annuity. A managed annuity might not provide this guarantee.

THE PHASED ANNUITY

Until quite recently the income you received from a personal pension was something of a lottery. The income from the pension was based on an annuity. You could build up your pension fund from contributions made over 30 years but the income you actually received from your pension was dependent on the rate of return offered on annuities on the date of your retirement.

Income tax rules required that at least 75% of the terminal value of a pension fund had to be invested in an annuity. In the recent past, if the rates offered on annuities happened to be low on the date of your retirement, and the rates vary a great deal from month to month let alone from year to year, then you would receive a low income for the rest of your life.

Recent government legislation has relieved this problem somewhat and you need no longer convert 75% of your pension fund into an annuity on the date of your retirement. However one solution to the problem would have been to invest your pension fund in a *phased* personal pension plan. Your cumulating personal pension fund would be invested in a set of phased annuities that are more flexible than a single simple annuity. A phased pension fund is divided into segments. Each segment can be converted into a small annuity at a time chosen by the contributor to the plan. The conversions must all take place between the ages of 50 and 75. Thus all of your personal pension fund need not be converted into an annuity on the same date. If annuity rates are low on the date of your retirement, segments of the fund can be retained as investments and converted into an annuity later when annuity rates are running at a higher level. You are no longer dependent on the rate of return offered on annuities on a single date.

The income from the funds left in the pension fund, that is the funds not yet converted into an annuity, will be added to your pension fund thus building up a larger fund for future conversion into annuities. Such a strategy can improve the average return on your cumulated pension fund and so increase your future pension.

There is, however, one possible snag in this arrangement. The balance remaining in your retirement fund may vary in value over time depending on the composition of the fund and the state of the stock market at that time. It is at least theoretically possible that over the period when you are converting your pension fund into a pension through a series of annuities you could lose more by a fall in the stock market value of your personal pension fund than you gain from the averaging of your annuity income. It is a cruel world. However steps can be taken to hedge the value of your pension fund, at least in the short term, by buying index futures in the derivatives market.

Phased annuities are now of less importance than they were in the past since the UK government now permits you to delay the conversion of your pension fund into an annuity up to the age of 75.[4]

Phased annuities have other uses. For example if you have a substantial but declining income on the date of your retirement then a set of phased annuities can allow you to maintain a steady level of income after retirement. The annuities can be phased in such a way that the income from them compensates for the decline in your other income.

Phased annuities incur higher set up and other charges than most other forms of annuity.

ESCALATING ANNUITIES

An escalating annuity increases the income on your annuity by a fixed percentage period by period. For example you could buy a 4% escalating annuity rather than a flat-rate annuity. The 4% escalating annuity will increase your income from the annuity by 4% per year each year until you die. You can choose any rate of escalation you wish, within reason, but escalating annuities are a good deal more expensive to buy than flat rate annuities.

Exhibit 4.3 illustrates the annual income received from a series of escalating annuities that will increase your initial income from the annuity by 4% and 6% per annum respectively. The annual return from a flat rate annuity offering 10% per annum is also shown. All the annuities shown cost the same amount of money in year one.

Note that the initial income received from the 6% and 4% escalating annuities is well below the initial income received from the flat rate annuity. The annual income received from the escalating annuity gradually catches up with the flat rate annuity but it takes 9 to 11 years before this happens.

Let us translate these figures into actual ages. Suppose you retire at age 65 and take out an annuity escalating at 6% per annum. You have to reach the age of 74 before the income from your escalating annuity reaches what you would have earned if you had taken out a flat rate annuity at age 65.

We suspect that most retirees need more money at the age of 65 than they do at the age of 75. Thus, unless you are rich and can afford the security provided in the long term by an escalating annuity, or you believe that you will live to a ripe old age, or you are really worried about future inflation, then we think you should keep to the flat-rate annuity.

Escalating annuities can be used to compensate for inflation, the falling value of money, but if you are really worried about future inflation there are other solutions. You could take out an annuity the income from which is linked directly to the retail price index. These are called *index-linked annuities.* Alternatively you could invest in a *with profits* annuity that is invested in equity shares.

INFLATION-PROOFED ANNUITIES

Inflation-proofed annuities are offered by some insurance companies. There are several varieties. One has already been mentioned: the escalating annuity that is geared to the expected rate of inflation.

With an index-linked annuity the income from the annuity is revalued each year, using the retail price index (RPI), to allow for any fall in the value of money during the year. Some inflation-indexed annuities are *capped* in the sense that they only compensate for inflation up to some maximum annual figure, say 5%.

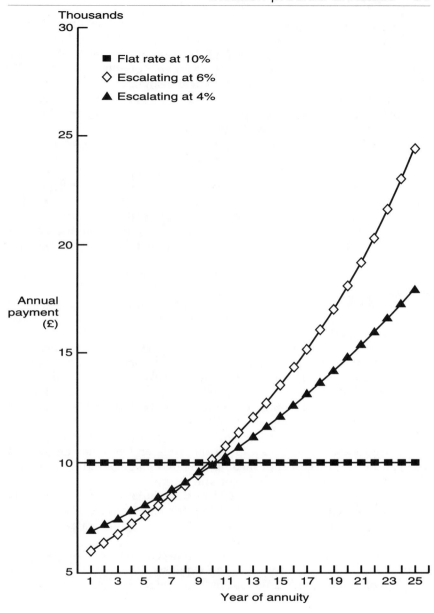

Thousands

- ■ Flat rate at 10%
- ◇ Escalating at 6%
- ▲ Escalating at 4%

Annual payment (£)

Year of annuity

An escalating annuity will provide an initial return well below that of a level term annuity but the return will catch up with the level term annuity around years nine to 11 and then bound ahead. If you live long enough the difference can become substantial. An escalating annuity compensates for inflation but you might well ask whether an excess return beyond the age of 75 or so is worth sacrificing the lower return over the first 10 years when you might be well able to enjoy it.

EXHIBIT 4.3: The return on an escalating annuity

In 1988 when the current UK rate of inflation was 6.5% a £100 000 flat-rate annuity would have provided an income of about £11 000 a year to a 65-year-old man. In this same year a £100 000 inflation-indexed annuity would have provided an income in the first year of only £7000. By 1993, when the rate of inflation had fallen to just below 2% a year, a £100 000 flat-rate annuity would have provided an income of £7500 a year to a 65-year-old man and an indexed-linked annuity would have provided an annual income in the first year of only £4800 a year.

Inflation-proofed annuities are, alas, very expensive. They may cost up to double the price of a flat-rate annuity that provides the same initial income. The flat-rate annuity is not, of course, inflation proofed. The cost of inflation proofing depends on market expectations about the future rate of inflation. If high inflation is expected then inflation-proofed annuities will cost very much more than those that are not inflation proofed. If low inflation is expected in the future then the cost of inflation-proofed annuities will be much closer to the cost of flat-rate annuities.

However if you are rich enough to afford an inflation-proofed annuity then I strongly recommend this investment. Such annuities will provide you with a very secure income for life. Your standard of living will never fall, or will only fall by a little, during your lifetime no matter what happens to inflation.

Note that inflation-proofed annuities may become affordable once you reach a good age, say 75. Recall how the income offered by an insurance company on an annuity rises sharply as you get older. This makes annuities cheaper for any given level of income as you get older. At 65 years of age an inflation-proofed annuity costing £100 000 may only offer an initial income of 6% per annum – not enough to live on. When you reach 75 years of age, however, the rate offered on an inflation-proofed annuity may have risen to 9% and you may decide that you can live on this level of income while no longer needing to worry about a falling standard of living in the future.

Insurance companies invest most of their inflation-indexed annuity funds in inflation-indexed bonds. Thus the rates of return offered on inflation-proofed annuities are much influenced by the rates of return earned on these inflation-proofed bonds.

We conclude that inflation-proofed annuities are an excellent form of investment if you can afford such an expensive luxury. They solve the problem of inflation reducing your real income for the remainder of your life.

THE EQUITY-BASED 'WITH PROFITS' ANNUITY

A less expensive protection against the ravages of inflation is to invest in an equity-based annuity such as a *with-profits* annuity. In this case the insurance company invests the annuity fund in a portfolio consisting mainly of equity shares. We noted in Chapter 2 that equity shares have historically provided an excellent cover against inflation. Thus a 'with-profits' annuity should provide good cover against inflation at a lower cost than either the inflation-proofed annuity or the escalating annuity. However, as we will note when we come to discuss 'with-profits' endowment policies in more detail in later chapters, the profit performance of *some* insurance funds based on equities and real assets has proved to be somewhat less than outstanding in recent years.

Another problem with the 'with-profits' annuity is that the precise amount of income you will receive each year is not fixed. The amount you receive on your 'with-profits' annuity depends on the dividends received on the investment portfolio held by the insurance company.

In the late 1990s it does not seem likely that a high rate of inflation will occur again in the UK for many years, especially if the countries taking part in the European Union set up a common currency. Under this scenario a flat-rate annuity would seem to offer the best choice among those available although the 'with-profits' and 'managed' annuities should also be considered.

ENHANCING YOUR PENSION

When a pension fund is converted into an annuity on retirement it is usually possible to take out 25% of the terminal fund in the form of cash. This fund can be spent or reinvested as you wish and so allows you to diversify your wealth portfolio into a wider range of alternative investments.

One possible alternative investment is another annuity: a *purchased* annuity. But why, you might well ask, take funds from one annuity and put the same funds into another annuity? Surely this tactic breaches the sacred diversification principle?

One possible reason is tax. The income received from a pension fund converted into an annuity on retirement is normally subject to tax at the marginal rate of the pensioner. If, however, 25% of this fund is converted into a purchased annuity then an alternative tax regime applies. A part of the regular income from the annuity is considered to be a return of capital and so a much lower average rate of tax is applied to the income from this kind of annuity.

TAX, PURCHASED ANNUITIES AND PENSION FUND ANNUITIES

The contributions to a pension fund are normally allowed against the highest rate of income tax assessed on the contributor. This reduces the cost of building up your pension fund. In addition the income from your pension fund investments, which are managed by an insurance company, are not subject to tax. This is a major concession by the Inland Revenue that might one day be withdrawn. Thus the terminal

UK Life expectancy tables, 1990

	Life expectancy				Most likely lifespan	
	Men		Women		Men	Women
Age	Years	Months	Years	Months	Age	Age
20	53	4	57	6	73	77
25	48	7	52	10	73	77
30	43	11	48	1	73	78
35	39	3	43	6	74	78
40	34	6	38	10	74	78
45	30	0	34	3	75	79
50	25	7	29	9	75	79
55	21	6	25	5	76	80
60	17	6	21	2	77	81
65	13	11	17	2	78	82
70	10	9	13	6	80	83
75	8	1	10	5	83	85
80	5	11	7	7	85	87
85	4	3	5	6	89	90
90	3	0	3	10	93	93
95	2	2	2	9	97	97
100	1	9	2	1	101	102

The life-expectancy table shows that a man retiring at 65 can expect to live for about 14 years and a woman retiring at 60 for about 21 years. However, in recent years both men and women are tending to retire at around the age of 60. This can present a financial problem to the male retiree since he will now live, on average, for 17.5 years. He may not have planned for this period of retirement.

The problem is that inflation at about 5% can reduce the real value of a pension by one half in 15 years. It is essential to make an allowance for inflation in pension planning.

EXHIBIT 4.4: How long can you expect to live?

value of your 'contributory' pension fund has received substantial tax subsidies from the government. For this reason the income from a pension is treated just like any other income and is subject to income tax at the highest marginal rate of the pensioner: usually either at the 25% rate or the 40% rate. However a part of the regular pension payment received by the pensioner out of the pension fund is actually a return of capital since, when the pensioner dies, his or her beneficiaries receive no capital sum from the annuity bought with the pension.

The income that is received from an annuity purchased out of taxed income, a *purchased annuity*, is treated in a different way for tax purposes. Recalling that there is no return of capital where an annuity is concerned, if you buy a £100 000 'whole-of-life' annuity on 5 September and die on 6 September your beneficiaries will lose the £100 000 unless you have bought a guarantee along with the annuity. The regular income that you receive from a purchased annuity thus includes the return of your own capital in addition to the income earned on the annuity fund.

The tax authorities admit this fact by not taxing the portion of the income from a purchased annuity that is deemed to be a return of capital. But how much of the regular income from a purchased annuity is made up of a return of capital?

The tax authorities use the latest life-expectancy tables to estimate this amount (see Exhibit 4.4). Let us suppose that a 71-year-old woman, a Mrs White, invests £100 000 in a flat-rate annuity that will pay her £1000 a month until she dies. How much of this £1000 per month is a return of capital and how much is income? A surprisingly small proportion is made up of income.

The tax authorities look up the latest life-expectancy tables and find that the average elderly lady aged at exactly 71 years has a life expectancy of 10 years or 120 months. The tax authorities divide the £100 000 by 120 to arrive at a figure of $\frac{£100\ 000}{120}$ = £833.33. Thus if Mrs White actually lives for the 120 months allotted to her, the time she is predicted to live by the life-expectancy tables, she will receive back £833.33 × 120 = £100 000 at the end of the 10-year period. The balance of £1000 − 833.33 = £166.67 is considered to be the investment income from the annuity and is taxed at Mrs White's marginal rate of tax as investment, not earned, income.

If Mrs White pays tax at a marginal rate of 20% she will have to pay only £166.67 × 0.20 = £33.34 income tax on her monthly income of £1000, an average rate of 3.33%. If Mrs White had earned this income from a 'contributory' pension annuity that had received tax benefits she would have had to pay income tax at her marginal earned income rate of 23%, that is £1000 × 0.23 = £230 each month assuming that her personal tax allowances are used up against other income.

Note that Mrs White will benefit from this tax concession until she dies – an event that might be some 30 years away!

A purchased annuity allows a retired person to use up capital in a tax-efficient manner, avoiding the inconvenience of selling off assets every year. A guaranteed annuity left to a beneficiary in a will is taxed as investment income on the trust or on the beneficiary.

ANNUITIES ON IMPAIRED LIVES

If you are suffering from ill health and you apply for a life-insurance policy you will find that you have to pay a much higher premium than you would have had to pay if you were healthy. The reason for this anomaly is that your life expectancy is shorter than average so the insurance company will probably collect fewer premiums from you before you die than it would collect from a more healthy person.

The reverse of this situation arises when you apply for an annuity. Your poor health means that the insurance company is likely to pay you out fewer annuity payments than it would have to do if you were a healthy individual, thus the cost of the annuity, at any given level of return, *should be* cheaper for the unhealthy annuitant.

An unhealthy individual is said to have an *impaired life* and *impaired life annuities* can be bought from some, but not all, insurance companies.

Each case is considered on its merits by the insurance company after a careful medical assessment of the health condition of the applicant has been made by a doctor working for the insurance company.

A 45-year-old man with an impaired life might receive an annuity income equal to that granted to a 65-year-old man if the 45-year-old man is expected to live for only another 12 years. The somewhat ghoulish practice of medical assessment is unavoidable.

The shorter your life expectancy, the higher the income granted you from the *impaired* annuity. Guaranteed annuities on impaired lives are either unobtainable or are very expensive. If you are diagnosed as having cancer, AIDS or some other serious illness that is likely to reduce your normal life span by a substantial amount you might consider applying for an impaired annuity.[5] However you might consider the prospect of following through a procedure which will try to precisely estimate your limited future lifespan to be unattractive.

An alternative to an impaired annuity is what is known as a *viatical settlement* whereby you sell your life-insurance policy to a company that specializes in the purchase of life-insurance policies from those with impaired lives. You might receive 70% of the value of the policy some five years before your predicted date of departure.

COPING WITH INFLATION

Exhibit 4.5 shows some data on the performance of a flat rate annuity, a 'with profits' annuity and an annuity from which the income escalates at 5% a year. The profits of companies that issue equity shares did particularly well over this period, so the 'with profits' annuity is well ahead in 1995 but the 5% escalator annuity will catch up in time.

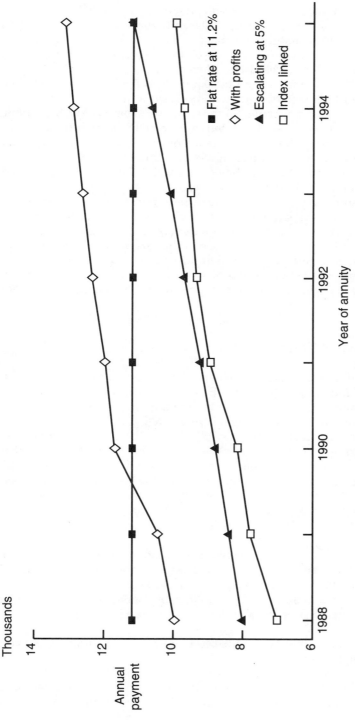

EXHIBIT 4.5: The relative returns on different kinds of annuity: flat rate, escalating and 'with profits'

The pattern of return over the life of an annuity differs depending upon whether the annuity is level term, escalating or based on a 'with profits' fund. The escalating and 'with profits'' type of annuity provide some protection against inflation; the level term annuity does not. The return on the 'with profits' annuity might be exaggerated since the return on equity shares was particularly good over this period.

We again ask the question: 'What is the best method of hedging your future annuity income against inflation?' The indexed-linked and escalating annuities reduce income for the first 10 years or so after retirement. If you retire at the age of 65 this means that you are poorer from the age of 65 to 75 but richer thereafter.

Both the flat-rate annuity and the equity-linked annuity are risky. The flat rate risks high inflation, the equity-based annuity risks occasional unpredictable dips in income. Despite this we suspect that the simple 'flat rate' annuity or an equity-based 'with profits' or 'unit-trust-linked' annuity will provide the package best suited to meeting the needs of most retirees. The next best package is probably an annuity based on a 5% per annum escalator. As shown in Exhibit 2.9, inflation averaged around 5% in the UK from 1914 to 1996.

Your attitude to risk is the key factor here. Some people will prefer to sacrifice a substantial part of their initial annuity income for the complete financial security provided by the inflation-indexed annuity; others will prefer to benefit from a higher income in the early years after retirement with their real income gradually diminishing as they progress towards old age. Whatever you choose, once you have made your choice you may have to live with it for the rest of your days. So think carefully about your choice.

ANNUITIES AND GILTS

As we noted above, annuity rates are closely tied to the rate of return offered on medium-dated gilts. Exhibit 4.1 shows the relationship between annuity rates, the return on medium-dated gilt-edged stock, and the bank rate over the period 1990 to 1995.

Note the close correlation over the period between the return on medium-term gilts and the rate of return on annuities. The return that will be offered to you on annuities in the future will be closely tied to the return offered on medium-term gilt stocks by the government of the day.

SUMMARY

1. An annuity is a contract between the annuitant and an insurance company whereby the annuitant pays a substantial amount of money to the insurance company and the insurance company agrees to pay the annuitant a regular sum of money until some event occurs. The event is usually the death of the annuitant.

2. No medical examination is needed to take out an annuity unless you are applying for an 'impaired' life annuity.

3. An annuity has no capital value. If you die, the value inherent in a whole-of-life annuity will be lost. Most purchased annuities are

now 'guaranteed' for a fixed number of years to compensate for this fact. This means that if you die within, say, five years of taking out the annuity then the balance of the income for the five-year period will be paid into your estate. This benefits your heirs but not yourself!

4. Since no capital is paid out by the provider of the whole-life annuity on your death, a part of the regular income from a purchased annuity is, in fact, a return of your own capital. The closer you are in age to your average life expectancy when you take out the annuity the greater is the proportion of capital in the regular income payments from the annuity. This fact has important tax implications.

5. Since part of the regular income from an annuity is a return of capital the return from an annuity is likely to be greater than the return from other comparable investments. These other investments, such as government stock or equity shares, provide a return of capital when you wish to cash it in.

6. An annuity is a gamble between you and the insurance company. If you live beyond your life expectancy you win; if you live less than your expected life-span the insurance company wins. The return offered on an annuity increases with age since your life expectancy decreases with age. Very high returns can be obtained from an annuity when you reach an age beyond 75.

7. The returns offered by insurance companies on annuities vary a great deal through time. Returns as high as 15% per annum and as low as 7% per annum were offered between 1989 and 1996. The return depends on the current returns offered by medium-term government stock. Expectations about future inflation have a big impact on the returns offered on government stock and on annuities.

8. The return you are offered on an annuity is also affected by your age, gender and state of health. The older you are, the higher is the annuity income offered to you. Women are offered a lower income than men at any given age because women live longer than men. Your state of health becomes important if you apply for an 'impaired life'. The worse your health condition, the higher the return you are offered. The reason is that the insurance company will have to pay out the annuity income for a shorter period.

9. If you are very healthy and over 70 years of age, an annuity is likely to be a good investment for you.

10. Many types of annuity are on offer from insurance companies. An annuity can be for the whole of your life or for a fixed period and can

be paid on a single lifespan or on a joint lifespan. An annuity can be 'flat rate' or the rate of return can be increased by a given percentage each period, or even tied to the rate of inflation. You can purchase an annuity that you can manage yourself or one that can be 'phased' over several years. It is up to you to select the annuity best suited to your future needs.

11. The real return on an annuity is much affected by future inflation. If you believe that inflation will rise substantially between taking out the annuity and your death you should take out an annuity that compensates for inflation to some extent. An equity-based annuity, or an escalating or inflation-proofed annuity can achieve this objective but at a cost.

12. The tax treatment of annuity income is quite complex. Annuities bought out of pension funds are normally taxed liked ordinary income. Income from purchased annuities (bought out of taxed income) are treated differently. The tax paid on purchased annuities is much less since part of the regular annuity income is treated as a return of capital.

TEST YOUR KNOWLEDGE

1. What is the difference between investing £100 000 in fixed-interest Government stock and investing £100 000 in a flat rate 'whole-of-life' annuity?

2. What effect do the following factors have on the return you can expect from a flat-rate 'whole-of-life' annuity: age, sex, estimated future inflation, health, current market return on medium-term gilts?

3. Let us suppose you take out a £100 000 annuity on 12 October 1998 and you die on the 7 February 1999. What proportion of the £100 000 will be inherited by your heirs?

4. What benefit do you gain by taking out a *guaranteed* annuity? What is guaranteed?

5. 'If you buy a "whole-of-life" annuity from an insurance company you are entering into a bet with the insurance company.' Explain this statement. How can you ensure that you win this bet?

6. Why does the rate of return offered on annuities vary such a great deal through time (for example 9% to 15.5% per annum in the UK between 1989 and 1996 for a 65-year-old male) and between insurance companies?

7. What is an *impaired* annuity? Who can qualify for an impaired annuity? What benefits can you hope to gain by taking out an 'impaired' rather than a 'normal' whole-of-life annuity?

8. What is an *annuity certain*? How can it be used?

9. What is a *phased annuity*? Suggest a situation where a phased annuity might prove useful? What problem might arise in relation to the part of the pension fund not yet converted into a phased annuity? What is *income drawdown* with regard to a pension?

10. Suppose you take out an *escalating* annuity on which the income is increased by 5% per year. How long, approximately, would it take for the income from this annuity to catch up with the income from a *flat rate* annuity taken out at the same time as the escalating annuity?

11. Inflation-proofed annuities seem like a good idea. What is the catch?

12. What is the difference between the tax paid on income derived from an annuity bought from a tax privileged pension fund and tax paid on the income derived from a *purchased* annuity bought out of taxed income? What is the reason for this difference in tax treatment?

13. Let us suppose that on 1 January 1998 you are a 67-year-old male. You buy an annuity for £50 000 out of taxed income and receive an annual income for life of £6000 per year, or £500 per month, from this annuity. Your expectation of life is 136 months. If you pay tax at 23% on your marginal income, what tax will you pay on the £6000 per annum income from the annuity? Assume that all tax allowances have been used up by other income. What tax would you pay if the £6000 were received from a normal salary-based pension?

14. Suggest three methods of hedging your annuity income against the impact of future inflation.

NOTES

1. This is a simplified version of what actually happens, but this explanation is useful in explaining the link between the returns offered on an annuity and the market rate of interest.

2. High, that is, relative to the return on other investments from the same amount of money.

3. See, for example, the annuity tables in Stone and Cox. The monthly magazine *Money Management* provides a sample of current annuity rates.

4. See April 1994 budget statement on personal pensions.

5. Some insurance brokers specialize in finding 'impaired' annuities for clients. The Insurance Brokers Association will supply the name of such brokers.

Managing your pension

5

Nothing in the world of personal finance can cause you more grief than an inadequate or ill-designed pension plan. The period during which you will be retired now accounts for about one quarter of your life. An inadequate income during this final period can cast a dark shadow over the end of an otherwise happy life.

The basic problem in pension planning is that an adequate pension cannot be funded in a short period unless you are seriously rich. An individual of moderate means requires a minimum period of 20 years to save up sufficient funds to generate an adequate pension and 30 years to build up a good pension. In other words an employee or self-employed person needs to start saving for a pension at 30 to enjoy a good pension at 60. Unfortunately few people give much thought to their future pension rights at 30; it is too remote a problem.

The age at which most people begin to worry about an adequate pension is around 45 or even as late as 55. Some basic financial calculation will reveal that it is very difficult to build up an adequate pension for retirement at 60 or even 65 years of age if you start building your pension fund at an age later than 35. Unless you enjoy a very high salary you cannot build an adequate pension fund after the age of 40 without making a substantial financial sacrifice in the short period remaining before you retire. We will present some figures later in this chapter to persuade you of the truth of these claims.

THE THREE FINANCIAL AGES

Exhibit 5.1 illustrates the lifetime cash flows of an individual who spends approximately 40 years of his or her life in paid employment. The lifetime cash flow of most professional people can be divided into three 'ages'. During the first age, from birth to about 23 years of age, we suffer from a negative cash flow. We consume more than we earn, if we earn anything at all. From our early twenties until around the age of 55 to 65 we take up employment and enjoy a positive cash flow. We consume less than we earn. Once we have retired we could revert to a negative cash flow once more. We can consume more than we earn. Pension planning

Thousand pounds

	Cash outflow
	Net cash flow
	Cash inflow

80

60

40

20

0   Lifetime
     cash
     flow

-20

-40

-60

1   11   21   31   41   51   61   71   81

Age

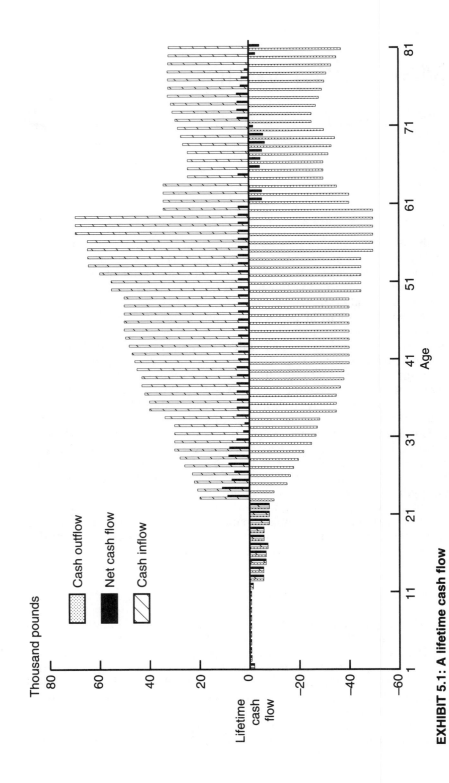

EXHIBIT 5.1: A lifetime cash flow

tries to avoid this last phase by building up a fund to plug the gap between expenditure and income once we have retired.

Note that the period of positive cash flow covers little more than one half of a lifetime. During the first 20-odd years of life others have had to accept the responsibility for eliminating our negative cash flow. These 'others' are most likely to be our parents but they might be other relatives or representatives of the State. However the responsibility for funding the last period in our life cycle, the period from around the age of 60 to 80-odd, is very much our own responsibility. Some of the surplus income earned during our middle 'earning' period must be invested in some way to produce an income during the later 'retired' period. We need to arrange a sufficient retirement income to ensure that the negative cash flow that occurs during the last quarter of our life can be reduced or eliminated.

This process of organizing a fund during our working lives to provide ourselves with an adequate cash flow in later life is called *pension planning*. Pension planning is a crucial component of personal financial planning. Every individual who wishes to build a personal financial shield to protect the interests of themselves and their family must acquire a thorough and systematic knowledge of pension planning.

THE PENSION NUTCRACKER

As our modern industrialized society moves forward towards the twenty-first century the provision of an adequate pension for the retired portion of the population is posing a serious problem to the governments of most industrialized countries. The problem stems from the fact that the proportion of the total population at work is decreasing while the proportion who are retired is increasing. Exhibit 5.2(a) illustrates this trend for several industrialized countries by providing future projections of the proportion of workers and retired persons in those countries for various dates in the future.

From Exhibit 5.2(b) we can see that the ratio of workers to pensioners in the UK is expected to decrease until well into the next century. In 1995 there were 3.4 workers for every retired person. By 2030 there will be 2.4 workers for every retired person.

Interestingly enough, as is also shown in Exhibit 5.2(a) the 'workers-to-retired' ratio is expected to be even worse in Germany, the USA and Japan over this period.

The British State pension fund is unfunded: no State pension fund exists. Thus if, in the future, the declining working population in the UK is required to pay for the pensions of the increasing number of the retired, the cost of pension provision will take an increasing and possibly unacceptably high proportion of the wages of the working population.

Matters are made even worse by the fact that workers are retiring at an earlier age than in the past and life expectancy is increasing. This means that the length of the period between retirement and death is

Percentage of population retired

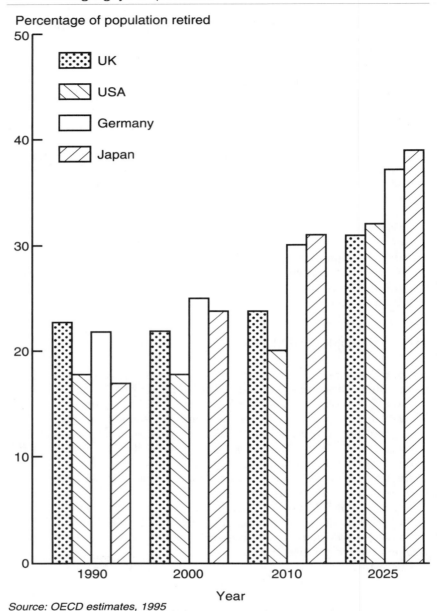

Year

Source: OECD estimates, 1995

All industrialized countries face the problem of an ageing population. Over the long term the situation in the UK is better than that in
the USA, Germany and Japan.

**EXHIBIT 5.2(a): Percentage of the population retired in various
countries, 1990–2025**

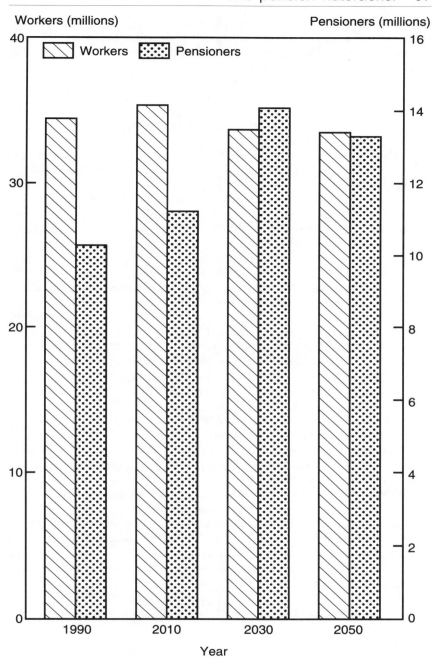

EXHIBIT 5.2(b): Workers and pensioners (Government estimates)

increasing while the number of years at work is decreasing. The average age of retirement for a worker in the UK is 57 years of age in 1997. The average length of life in the UK is increasing, although, fortunately, not by much.[1] Thus the average male needs to finance a period of 15 to 20 years after retirement whereas 20 years ago he only needed to finance a retirement period of 10 years, after 40 years of work. The situation is much worse for females. Women retire earlier, on average, than their male colleagues and die later. A typical female executive will need to finance a retirement period of 20 to 25 years during her shorter working life.[2] You can check your own average life expectancy by consulting the life expectancy tables for men and women in the UK provided in Exhibit 4.4 in Chapter 4.

A recent Gallup Poll sponsored by Norwich Union found that 56% of the employees interviewed who were contributing to pension funds feared that their pension would be insufficient to finance an adequate lifestyle when they retired.

What conclusions can we draw from these rather gloomy statistics? You must begin to save for a pension at an early age to ensure that you have sufficient funds to provide an adequate pension for yourself and possibly, your spouse for the last quarter of your life. Because of the pressure on governments, of whatever political hue, to cut taxation in the future, the value of the State pension is likely to decline in real terms. It is also possible that the supplementary benefits provided to retirees on a low income will diminish.[3] In 1997 the State pension for an individual in the UK had a value equal to only around 15% of average earnings. By the year 2025 this percentage will have fallen to 7% of average earnings if present trends continue.

Thus a key responsibility of every breadwinner must be to arrange an adequate and secure pension provision for himself or herself and family. A breadwinner who fails to make proper provision for an adequate pension after retirement can lead himself and his spouse into a state close to destitution in later life.

This statement is not excessively dramatic: retirees close to destitution are, unfortunately, only too common in the UK at the present moment. The reason for this lamentable state of affairs arises out of the inadequate pension provided by the State in the UK compared to most other rich European countries. When compared to the average industrial wage the UK pension provision is amongst the poorest in the industrialized world.

Your first priority in designing a personal financial plan must be to organize an adequate pension provision for yourself and spouse.

FIVE KEY QUESTIONS TO ASK YOURSELF WHEN PLANNING YOUR PENSION PROVISION

In order to work out a plan to provide yourself with an adequate pension when you retire you need to ask yourself five key questions.

1. *How much income will I need, net of tax, to maintain an adequate standard of living after retirement?*

The amount of money needed to provide an 'adequate standard of living' after retirement will vary a great deal between different retirees. You may be looking forward to retiring to a small country cottage deep in the country where you can devote your time to serious gardening or breeding cocker spaniels or entering local politics. None of these occupations call for a substantial income. On the other hand you may envisage your retirement as a long and much-deserved holiday from a lifetime of hard work. You may be looking forward to frequent sea voyages to exotic parts, regular visits to the top London shows and a very active social life. Such a lifestyle calls for a substantial income.

It is important to concentrate your mind on expectations that are realistic relative to your anticipated lifetime income. You may be prepared to sacrifice spending now to ensure a higher income after retirement. The important thing is to make a rational choice about your pension planning now and not be faced with a *fait accompli* later.

As we noted above, few people seem to realize how early one needs to start saving to provide an adequate retirement income. Twenty-five years is the absolute minimum period. Thirty years is preferable. Thirty-five years is ideal. The power of financial compounding over a long period like 35 years is, as we shall see later in the chapter, quite marvellous to behold.

The first step in calculating how much money you will need after retirement is to draw up an *after-retirement income and expenditure account* based on current expenditures adjusted for the various reductions and increases in income and costs caused by retirement.

An example of just such a post-retirement budget is provided in Exhibit 5.3 for Mr Bates. This shows that the total gross income of Mr Bates after retirement is expected to fall by about 39%. However net cash flow after tax, when regular deductions like pension contribution and NHI are ended, will fall by only 28%. Some expenditures will be reduced by retirement while others will rise. For example, in this case, the mortgage will be paid off and less money will be spent on such things as children and communication. However more will be spent on medical care, security, gas and electricity, and transportation. Mr Bates' total estimated expenditures after retirement will be around 76% of the figure before retirement.

Mr Bates has budgeted to save about half the amount of his income after retirement that he saved before he retired. This surplus could be spent on taking out a term or other insurance policy on his life to be placed in trust for his wife or children. If, on Mr Bates' death, the value of the occupational pension paid to his wife is only half of that paid to Mr Bates before his death, a common occurrence, then some such arrangement is advisable to protect the financial interests of Mrs Bates.

Not all costs will fall after retirement. Some costs will rise by a substantial margin. For example many executives have most of their car

EXHIBIT 5.3: A post-retirement budget

Name: Richard Bates

Retirement estimate

Income and expenditure account

	Final year's expenditure	Post retirement budget	Change in expenditure
Income	1997	1998	
	£	£	
Basic salary/pension	46 000	23 000	
Commission	8 000	0	
Dividends etc.	1 800	10 000	
Other income	540	1 200	
Total income	56 340	34 200	61%
Less Taxation	18 029	9 918	
Other deductions	4 500		
Net cash inflow	**33 811**	**24 282**	72%
Expenditure			
Mortgage (net of tax)	6 800	0	0%
Household			
Rates	1 400	1 400	
Gas	1 230	1 400	
Electricity	884	950	
Food/meals out	768	1 000	
Repairs	532	200	
House insurance	490	490	
Security	600	600	
Other	639	400	
Total household	6 543	6 440	98%
Transport	(Mr Bates has a company car)		
Fares	785	1 200	
Mrs Bates' car	1 400	2 000	
Car licence	140	140	
Petrol	396	500	
Insurance	442	442	
Repairs	275	300	
Total transport	3 438	4 582	133%

	Final year's expenditure	Post retirement budget	Change in expenditure
	1997	1998	
	£	£	
Communication			
Postage	88	85	
Telephone	784	300	
Computer	496	500	
Total communication	1 368	885	65%
Risk hedging	(company pays for family health care plan under PPP)		
Insurance	650	650	
Medical care plan	0	1560	
Children	1 400	0	0%
Personal			
Clothing	1 400	1 200	
Holidays	2 500	2 600	
Entertainment	853	1 200	
Subscriptions	800	200	
Sundry			
Cash expenses	2 800	2 400	
TOTAL EXPENDITURE	**28 522**	**21 717**	76%
NET SAVING	**5259**	**2 565**	49%

Mr Bates estimates his post-retirement budget based on an adjusted pre-retirement budget. He invests a lump sum on retirement to increase his investment income. His mortgage is paid off in his last working year but he no longer has a company car or health insurance. He has terminated all allowances to his children.

His gross income is only 61% of his pre-retirement income but his net income is 72% of his pre-retirement income. His mortgage is paid off in his last working year but he no longer has a company car or health insurance. He has terminated all allowances to his children.

His gross income is only 61% of his pre-retirement income but his net income is 72% of his pre-retirement income. The termination of mortgage payments has resulted in a substantial reduction in his expenditure thus his net of expenditure savings is still positive at £2565. Thus despite a 30% fall in his net cash inflow, his financial position is still sound without incurring an undue fall in his standard of living.

ownership costs and medical care costs met by the firm which employs them. These free 'perks' will cease on retirement.

The post-retirement budget should be designed to arrive at a realistic estimate of your net cash flow after retirement. However this does not really answer the question of how much money you need after you retire. You have simply calculated how much money you are *likely to have* if your pension turns out as expected and your expenses continue on much the same lines as at present.

The question 'How much post retirement income do I need?' can only be answered by you, but some rough estimates can be made for professional people. Using the 1997 value of the pound sterling as our yardstick we can state with some confidence that for a professional couple in the UK a post-retirement net cash flow (income less tax) of £1000 a month is absolute survival level. You can survive on this but it is not going to provide much of a life. A net cash flow of £1500 per month is 'comfortable'. Many couples will find this an adequate income, but you will not live fat on £1500 a month. A net cash flow after tax of £2000 per month is a desirable goal. A couple can live fairly well on such a figure without cutting into their capital base *so long as the mortgage is paid off*. Anything above £2000 per month of net cash flow represents the good life. Three holidays a year to exotic parts, two London shows a month and a wide choice of new cars and clothes to brighten the declining years.

It should be said that only around 2% of the working population of the UK can hope to aspire to the last of these three budget scenarios!

We conclude that the average professional couple should strive to set up a pension fund sufficient to provide at least £1500 per month net of tax after retirement and it would be wise to budget for £2000 per month if this is feasible. This is the estimated figure for 1997. Estimates beyond this year will need to be adjusted for future inflation.

At this stage in constructing your retirement plan you should have made an estimate of your most likely post-retirement income and expenditure. This will alert you to any impending income deficit on retirement. You might also decide to make an estimate of how much money you would *like to* have when you retire in contrast to how much money you will *actually* have when you retire.

Pension planning can help you turn the latter figure into the former . . . so long as you have enough years at your disposal before retirement.

2. At what age will I retire?

The second matter you need to decide when planning your pension scheme is the age at which you will retire. The average retirement age in the UK is falling year by year. In the 1950s most executives and professional people retired at age 65; by the 1980s 60 was a typical retirement age and by the year 2000 the typical retirement age for an executive in the UK may have fallen to 55, the current retirement age for most executives in the USA and Japan. The earlier your retirement age, the less time you have to accumulate adequate retirement funds.

It is best to be conservative when estimating the age of your retirement by designing a retirement scheme that assumes you will retire some five years earlier than you actually expect to retire, especially if the date of your retirement is still some way off.

If your company 'invites' you to retire before your official retirement date, some additional years of employment will probably be added to your pension value formula. If you have a choice in the matter, before accepting early retirement, you should compare the benefit added to your pension by these additional years with the pension you would receive by retiring on your official retirement date. The difference might surprise you. We will return to this important point later in the chapter. Early retirement can prove to be an expensive option.

3. How secure are my pension rights?

Government pensions are very secure. The legal security attaching to company 'occupational' pension schemes has been much improved in recent years but these schemes are still inadequate in some respects. New regulations are about to be introduced. In the past one company could be taken over by another company and a 'surplus' on the pension fund of the target company raided. This is no longer feasible.[4]

A greedy or fraudulent management is not the only hazard which might threaten the security of your pension rights. Inflation can destroy the worth of a fixed value pension as effectively as any fraudster. The antidote to inflation is to ensure that your pension fund is invested in inflation-proofed securities. Most government pensions are fully inflation-proofed but many company and personal pensions are not. In Chapter 2 we discovered that equity investment is the best shield against inflation although other strategies for coping with inflation are available. We will return to the inflation proofing of pension funds later in this chapter. We conclude by noting that you should check how well your pension fund is proofed against inflation.

If you are not contributing to an 'occupational' final salary-based pension fund but to a managed fund a further, less publicized, threat to the future value of your pension arises from the possibility of a poor investment strategy being pursued by the managers of your pension fund. Poor pension fund management can see your pension income expectations eclipsed if your pension depends on the terminal value of the fund. The range of the returns achieved by managed pension funds over time is very wide. MICROPAL has reported a variation of 40% between the terminal value of the best and worse managed pension fund over a 20-year period. You are allowed to switch between funds although this option may be costly.

Another hazard applies to married contributors to pension funds. Recent changes, both in common law and pension regulation, imply that a married contributor to a pension fund may have to share his or her pension rights with a divorced spouse. Money purchase schemes and personal pensions are more vulnerable to this legal hazard than are salary-based schemes.

If you have worked for several companies during your career you might be at risk of losing some past pension contributions. In order to assist with this problem the government has set up the Pension Registry and Tracings Service. This organization is able to trace frozen pensions back to 1975 and possibly even earlier.[5]

4. Are you employed or self-employed?

The majority of professional people are employed by large companies or large public organizations. The remainder are employed by smaller companies or are self-employed.

Pension planning is much influenced by your employment category. If you are employed by a large organization with a fully developed 'occupational' final-salary based pension scheme you are one of the 'lucky' third of the population who fall into this category. Your pension problem, if you have one, reduces to supplementing the income from your existing pension scheme with a tax-efficient additional voluntary contribution scheme in order to bring your post-retirement pension up to the level you estimate you will require on your retirement from work.

Employees working in large companies usually enjoy generous pension provision, especially if they hold a senior position in the company. In such cases the final value of your pension on retirement will be based on a fraction of your final salary.[6]

Such 'final salary based schemes' are the best type of pension scheme currently available on the market. If you have one hold on to it.

Unfortunately we do not all enjoy the benefits of a pension scheme based on final salary. If you are employed by a small company you are likely to be invited to participate in a pension scheme called a 'money purchase' plan. In such cases the eventual value of your pension depends on the terminal value of the pension fund set up under the plan and the annuity rates offered at that time or later. On your retirement, or later, this fund must be used to buy an annuity although under current tax legislation an amount equal to 25% of the fund can be taken out in the form of cash if you favour this option.

If you are self-employed many tax-efficient pension schemes are at your disposal. You can make pension provision by placing regular contributions or a lump sum into a personal pension plan managed by an insurance company or some other financial institution. As with the money purchase plan, the value of your personal pension on retirement will depend on the terminal value of your pension fund and the current or future annuity rate offered by insurance companies. At least 75% of your terminal fund must be used to buy an annuity at the going rate for annuities either on the date of your retirement or later.

If you work for a large company running an occupational pension scheme it is theoretically possible for you to opt out of the company scheme and set up your own personal pension plan. This is rarely the better option since you will lose the many free 'perks' that are usually made available within a company based pension scheme. You may also lose your employer's contribution to your pension fund.

It is essential for every self-employed person to set up a secure and adequate pension fund and to set this fund up as early in life as possible. The British government provides generous tax concessions to the self-employed to encourage them to adopt just such a course of action. It would be foolish to look such a gift horse in the mouth.

5. What benefits will your dependants receive from your pension scheme?

If you die in service or, more probably, die after your retirement, before the death of your spouse, most company pension schemes provide a partial pension, usually at least one-half of the full pension, for your spouse. The maximum pension allowed to a spouse is usually $\frac{6}{9}$ of the pension that you would have received if you had been employed until the normal retirement age. Your dependent children may also receive a fractional pension for some years after your death until they reach maturity.

Most company pension schemes incorporate a life assurance policy which is set up for the benefit of your spouse or other beneficiary of your estate. This will only be paid out if you die before the date of your retirement. In other words it is a term policy.

You can buy additional term cover costing up to 5% of your 'pensionable' salary to compensate for an inadequate pension for your spouse. Few employees take advantage of this useful tax concession.

It is important to check that the pension rights built into your pension scheme are sufficient to provide an adequate income for dependants following your decease. If the income available is not adequate then you should 'top up' the financial provisions by buying term insurance as above or buying in additional voluntary contributions which will be discussed later in the chapter.[7]

If you are responsible for looking after a handicapped child or an elderly parent then even further additions to your pension provision may be needed. In all such cases additional pension or insurance provision may need to be arranged over and above that provided by the basic company or personal pension scheme.

MAJOR PROBLEMS IN PENSION PLANNING

Pension planning throws up a number of difficult problems. We will now discuss some of the more important of these problems and how to cope with them.

1. Preserving the 'real' value of your pension

Inflation is the traditional enemy of the pensioner. If your pension is fixed in money terms then the real value of your pension will diminish year by year as inflation grinds down its value. Exhibit 2.9 illustrates the annual rate of inflation in the UK over the last 80 years. Note the bursts of high inflation that occurred between 1971 and 1981, this decade alone would have reduced the value of a fixed value pension by almost 75% in real terms! As illustrated in Exhibit 5.4, an annual inflation rate as low as 5% will half the value of a fixed value pension in only 14 years, an inflation rate of 7% a year will half the value of your pension in only 10 years.

The State pension scheme is regularly adjusted upwards to allow for inflation and all government pensions make an almost complete upward adjustment for inflation each year. Most final-salary-based pension schemes run by large companies increase the pension annually to allow for inflation but only up to some upper 'capped' limit, say 5%. Many of the pension schemes run by smaller companies, the so-called 'money purchase' schemes (MPS), make inadequate allowance for future inflation. Where the future pension is based on a fixed-value annuity, no allowance whatsoever is made for future inflation.

You must ensure that your pension scheme is designed to provide at least a partial compensation for the falling value of money. However within money purchase or personal pension schemes the cost of guaranteeing full compensation on your pension for the impact of future inflation is exceedingly high. The cost of any given level of pension may be doubled! As noted in the previous paragraph, the best you can afford may be that your pension will be increased to compensate for inflation up to an upper 'cap' of, say, 5% per annum. Inflation-adjusted government stock can be used to ensure that your pension income keeps up with inflation but this type of stock pays out a very low rate of interest and so a great deal of the stock would need to be bought to provide you with an adequate income.[8] Inflation-indexed annuities are another possibility but as we noted in Chapter 4 these can cost almost double the cost of a normal 'flat rate' annuity paying the same initial income.

In Chapter 2 we pointed out that, in the long term, equity shares provide the best buffer against inflation. So equity-based pension funds provide the best security against inflation.

If you are of the opinion that your pension fund is inadequately proofed against future inflation then one solution is to arrange for *additional voluntary pension contributions* (AVCs) to be bought as a back-up. Additional voluntary contributions are allowed against tax at your highest marginal rate of tax, so, in effect, the government contributes towards the cost of your AVC. The contributions into an AVC can be placed within an existing occupational scheme or can be used to create an independent 'free standing' personal pension, called a *free-standing additional voluntary contribution* scheme (FSAVC), but only if you are an employee. We shall expand on this topic later.

Initial nominal value of pension = £10 000 per year.

Inflation rate (%)		1	3	5	7	10
Years after retirement	Year			Pension value (£)		
0	1997	**10 000**	**10 000**	**10 000**	**10 000**	**10 000**
1	1998	9901	9709	9525	9346	9091
2	1999	9803	9426	9070	8734	8264
3	2000	9706	9151	8638	8163	7513
4	2001	9610	8885	8227	7629	6830
5	2002	9515	8626	7835	7130	6209
6	2003	9420	8375	7462	6663	5645
7	2004	9327	8131	7107	6227	5132
8	2005	9235	7894	6768	5820	4665
9	2006	9143	7664	6446	5439	4241
10	2007	9053	7441	6139	5083	3855
11	2008	8963	7224	5847	4751	3505
12	2009	8874	7014	5568	4440	3186
13	2010	8787	6810	5303	4150	2897
14	2011	8700	6611	5051	3878	2633
15	2012	8613	6419	4810	3624	2394
16	2013	8528	6232	4581	3387	2176
17	2014	8444	6050	4363	3166	1978
18	2015	8360	5874	4155	2959	1799
19	2016	8277	5703	3957	2765	1635
20	2017	8195	5537	3769	2584	1486
21	2018	8114	5375	3589	2415	1351
22	2019	8034	5219	3418	2257	1228
23	2020	7954	5067	3256	2109	1117
24	2021	7876	4919	3101	1971	1015
25	2022	7798	4776	2953	1842	923

The table shows the diminishing real value of a pension over 25 years. The real value is the nominal value adjusted for inflation.

On average a woman retiring at the age of 60 lives for 22 years after retirement. A man retiring at 65 lives for 14 years. The average rate of inflation in the UK over the last 70 years has been around 5% per year.

The table emphasizes the need to ensure that you have made ample provision for inflation in any future pension plan. Note how many years it takes to half the value of your pension in real terms at these various rates of inflation. The relevant years are boxed in the table.

EXHIBIT 5.4: How inflation can reduce the value of your pension

2. Predicting the date of your retirement

Unless you are self-employed it is likely that you work in an industry where there is a 'traditional' age for retirement. This retirement age is usually either 60 or 65 years. In recent years executives, and particularly senior executives, have been retiring (or are being retired!) at a younger age than in the past. This trend may not continue and may even be reversed if a scarcity of executive talent should arise in the future, but if the trend does continue it could pose a serious financial problem for the retiring executive. The value of your pension is often determined by the number of years you have contributed to your pension fund; if you retire early the impact on the value of your pension can be severe. This fact is often overlooked by a retiring employee until it is too late to retrieve the situation.

Most companies provide some kind of compensation to employees who retire early but the value of this compensation is usually much less generous than the employee supposes. A typical situation is illustrated in Exhibit 5.5 The early date of retirement in the example not only cuts the value of the pension by 16% but the final calculations are almost certainly based on a lower nominal wage than if the employee had retired five years later. In addition, unless the retiree finds another job after retirement, then five years additional savings are lost. Finally, as also illustrated in Exhibit 5.5, if inflation is not compensated for in the pension, or only partly compensated for, the cost of early retirement will be increased even more.

Every offer of early retirement should have a notice attached to the effect that 'Early retirement can do serious damage to your financial health!'

On the other hand if you can find another lucrative job after 'retirement' and so save the pension until the original expected date of retirement arrives, then you may, in the end, find yourself richer than if you had retired on the original date. However, experience suggests that jobs, lucrative or otherwise, are hard to come by over the age of 55 and almost impossible to find beyond the age of 60.

If your early retirement is truly voluntary we would strongly advise you to think very seriously about it and to ensure you know all the facts before accepting this option. Early retirement should be avoided if at all possible.

3. How can you check out the security of your pension fund?

As we noted above, government pensions are safe and pensions paid out by large, well-established companies are reasonably safe. The management of the 'core' pension fund run by companies is now tightly controlled and protected by government legislation. The law requires that actuarial valuations of the pension fund, testing its ability to meet its obligations, be made every few years by a qualified actuary. Any surplus

Most final-salary-based pension schemes are based on a formula such as

$$\frac{n}{80} \times \text{final salary}$$

where n is the number of years the pensioner has contributed to the fund. For example:

Final salary   = £36 000 gross
No. of years' contribution   = 32
Expected age at retirement   = 65

Normal pension is therefore (32 ÷ 80) × 36 000 = £14 400.

Suppose this individual is retired at 60 years of age. What effect does this have on his pension?

$$\frac{27}{80} \times 36000 = £12\,150 \text{ at age 60.}$$

The pension is cut by (12 150 ÷ 14 400) × 100 = 16%.

However, the pensioner is paid this pension for 5 more years than if he were to retire at 65. If he can find another job for the 5 years, which pays more, net of tax, than the difference between the old salary and his new pension, he is better off than he would have been between the ages of 60 to 65 but worse off thereafter.

We have assumed that the real value of the wage is the same on both retirement dates. However, retirement on the earlier date is very likely to be at a lower wage. If the salary is inflation-indexed and the pension is not fully indexed this could very well be the case. Salaries also tend to rise by 2% per year faster than inflation; pensions seldom do.

So what about the effects of inflation? As we noted above, the pension might not be fully inflation-indexed. If the pension is increased by 5% per year to compensate for inflation, which is actually 7% per year over the period, the real value of the pension will fall by approximately 2% per year. Over 5 years, calculating the value in year 0 money, this amounts to $(£12\,150 \div (1+0.02))^5 = £11\,005$, compared with £14 400 in year 0 money for retirement 5 years later, if we assume that the salary is fully inflation-indexed at 7% over the period. The retiree will have lost £3395 per year (24% of his £14 400 real value pension) by early retirement. If the company pension plan is not inflation-indexed at all, or indexed by less than 5%, the situation would be much worse.

Most government pensions are fully inflation indexed. Most company schemes are not. It might be necessary to arrange an additional 'top up' pension to compensate for inflation (or convert a level pension to a lower initial level pension that increases at *x* % per year to compensate for inflation).

A warning notice should be added to every pension plan: 'Early retirement can damage your financial health!'

EXHIBIT 5.5: By how much is a pension cut in real terms by early retirement?

must be removed. This can possibly be done by paying the surplus back to the contributors.

Most pensions are paid out of a fund held by trustees for the benefit of present and future pensioners. In many cases these pension funds have a market value running into many hundreds of millions of pounds.

The company running the pension scheme pays the monthly contributions into this trust fund and the fund managers invest this money on behalf of the contributors. The fund may be managed by a team of professional investment managers employed by the company itself or the company may delegate the running of the pension fund to an outside organization which specializes in managing investment funds.

The fund manager, whether internal or external, will invest the regular pension-fund contributions into a wide range of securities. Most UK pension funds are permitted by law to invest their funds into a wide range of both financial and real assets. This latitude is not available to fund managers in many other countries in the European Union where the law requires that pension-fund money be invested in a very restrictive set of securities. These restrictions may have important future implications for UK pension funds. So far the UK has always adapted to the EU and not vice versa.

How secure is your pension fund? How easily can the funds be raided by an unscrupulous management board? As we stated above recent legislation has greatly tightened the control and supervision of pension funds but the employees contributing to the pension fund still have far too little say in the running of their own fund, which will in time provide their future pension. The notorious Robert Maxwell case shocked the financial community because of the ease with which Maxwell, a trustee, was able to plunder the fund. Further legislation is under way to protect pension funds against misuse by unscrupulous directors but at the time of writing this legislation is still not on the statute book.

The large financial institutions, which hold the majority of pension funds, are monitored by several watchdogs such as the SIB, the PIA, IMRO and the recently created Pension Fund regulator. Several organizations in the private sector, for example Standard & Poor's, measure the performance of externally managed pension funds on a regular basis.[9]

The computer-based financial system called MICROPAL measures the performance of a wide range of invested funds on a regular basis.

If you are a contributor to a pension fund you should obtain a copy of the document setting out your rights in the pension fund. The law requires that this information must be provided to every contributor to a pension fund. You may also obtain the latest accounts of your pension fund. If these are not available you should enquire why not. The latest actuarial report on your pension fund is another useful document that can be used to check the financial security of the future demands on the fund. The method of valuation is sometimes a little obscure to the non-expert on pension funding but a professional actuary will provide an opinion for a small fee.

Most contributors to pension funds possess only a very sketchy knowledge of their pension rights. Your pension rights should be audited by you or your adviser on a regular basis to ensure that no unusual conditions are attached to these rights. You need to check that your pension will provide yourself and spouse with an adequate income after retirement and that other important features of pension schemes, such as adequate life assurance, the consequences of failing health and the rights of dependants, are adequately covered.

4. How portable is your pension?

The 'portability' of pension rights has always been a contentious subject. In the not too distant past an employee could leave a company after many years of contributing to a company pension scheme and his rights in the fund would be 'frozen' until he reached retirement age. Thus an employee who held many jobs over a working life could finish up with a bundle of frozen pension rights which might provide a rather inadequate income on retirement. This would be especially serious if the frozen pensions were not inflation-indexed. As an ex-employee of many companies you might not know how much your various pensions were actually worth until the date of your retirement!

Recently the situation with regard to the portability of pension rights in the UK has been much improved thanks to government legislation.[10]

If you leave one company and join another then the accumulated value of all your guaranteed pension rights to date from that company must be evaluated by an actuary and you will be notified of the *transfer value* of your pension fund. You are thus able to transfer the value of your prior pension rights into the pension fund of your new company. In other words the accumulated pension funds of every employee are now portable. You can now accumulate a pension income as you move from one company to another and can calculate with a fair degree of accuracy where you stand with regard to your future pension at any time.

If you do not wish to place the transfer value of your pension fund into the pension fund of your new company you have other options open to you. You could transfer the fund into your own personal pension fund. The company for whom you now work can be asked to deduct the requisite pension contribution from your salary each month and pay this contribution into your personal pension fund.[11]

The issue of *portability* is no longer a problem. When you next move from one company to another the new company continues to place your regular pension contributions into your existing personal pension fund. However, note that you have lost the company contribution to your pension fund, a substantial loss.

Another alternative is to invest the transfer value of your pension fund into a single premium policy with an insurance company, a buy-out bond or an annuity. This is known in the trade as a *Section 32 buy out* or a *S 32 buy out*. An S 32 buy out is a useful staging post between an occupational pension scheme and a personal pension plan (see below). You can convert the S 32 fund into a personal pension plan later if you should wish to do so.

Finally you can simply leave your pension fund with the company from which you are departing. The company must upvalue your fund each year by 5%, or the retail price index increase for that year, whichever is lower, until you retire. This tactic is not recommended.

Unless you are approaching retirement age your best policy, almost invariably, is to join the pension fund of your new company and invest your transfer value into this fund.

TYPES OF PENSION

Pensions in the UK can be segregated into three types. First, there are the State-run pension schemes organized and financed by the British government. There are two State pension schemes. The first scheme consists of the basic State pension, available to all who have contributed to the scheme for the requisite number of years. The second scheme consists of the earnings-related pension scheme (SERPS), but many employees have been opted out of SERPS and into a company fund by their employers.

A second type of pension scheme is an *occupational pension scheme*. There are two kinds of occupational pension scheme. The first, based on the final salary of the employee, is called, appropriately enough, a *final salary scheme*. These pension schemes are mainly provided by public institutions such as the Civil Service, local government authorities, the universities and by the larger companies in the private sector.

The other kind of occupational pension is called a *money purchase scheme*. This type of pension scheme is favoured by smaller companies since no pension value is guaranteed by the company. The pension you receive under such a scheme will depend on the terminal value of your pension fund and the annuity rates offered at that time.

The third type of pension scheme is called a *personal pension scheme*. These schemes can be set up by any working individual whether employed or self-employed. Most personal pension schemes are set up by the self-employed, this is their only option, but in recent years many employees have opted out of their company pension scheme and set up their own personal pension schemes . . . and almost certainly rue the day they did so. The serious financial consequences of the mis-selling of personal pensions in the UK after 1988 is now a global legend.[12]

Let us now examine each of these pension schemes in more detail.

THE STATE PENSION SCHEMES

In the UK the State runs two pension schemes. The first and primary scheme is the basic State pension scheme, which is available to all who contribute to the scheme for the requisite number of years. There are four categories of State pension named A,B,C and D.[13]

A pensioner must have contributed to the scheme for at least 41 years to obtain the maximum State pension. To obtain the minimum basic State pension, which is currently 25% of the maximum, you must have worked in the UK for at least nine years in total.

The rules regarding the receipt of a State pension in the UK are exceptionally complicated. Note that a State pension in the UK is not the right of every citizen. You must have worked in the UK for the requisite number of years to obtain a State pension.[14]

A wife can claim a State pension based on her husband's contributions. She will get around 60% of what her husband would have received if he had lived.

The second State-sponsored pension scheme is the State Earnings-Related Pension Scheme or SERPS, which is currently being reduced in importance, but can still provide a significant addition to your basic pension if you have contributed to the scheme for a good number of years in the past.[15]

There is no minimum contribution period for SERPS: the pension builds from the first contribution.

Many employees (15 million by 1997) have been taken out of the SERPS scheme in favour of a pension scheme run by their employer or have set up a personal pension scheme for themselves. If you are not contributing to a company or other pension plan you are automatically enrolled into the SERPS scheme.

If you are contributing to the SERPS scheme and work for an employer you have the option of increasing the future value of your SERPS pension by paying Class 1 National Insurance contributions at the maximum rate rather than the normal lower rate. I estimate that an employee on the *average* wage in the UK who is dependent on the SERPS scheme for a pension will receive an average additional pension of about £60 a week (in 1996 values) from SERPS if he or she retires in the year 2010.

The SERPS pension is based on lifetime earnings, not final salary; there is no 25% lump sum option as with an occupational scheme and SERPS can only be taken at the statutory retirement age. These conditions make SERPS much inferior to all occupational and most personal pension schemes, but if you have no other pension to look forward to SERPS is better than nothing.

Should you stay in the SERPS scheme or opt out of it? The experts on pensions have calculated that older people over 40 and those on low incomes, say less than £10 000 per year, should stay in the SERPS scheme. Otherwise you might consider leaving. The government is encouraging people to leave by giving some financial incentives to those who opt out.

You are allowed to opt out and then opt back in again. The experts have calculated that a man should opt in again (if he has opted out) if he is over the age of 40. A woman, if she has been opted out, should opt back in again when she reaches the age of 35.[16]

There was a great deal of concern at one time that those who had been persuaded to convert from SERPS to a private pension between 1989 and 1993 had been mis-sold the private pension since they would have fared better in SERPS. A recent government report concludes that this is not so. Only around 150 000 of the five million who converted from SERPS to a private pension are likely to be worse off from the move. The government has persuaded the insurance companies to compensate these unfortunate individuals.

The basic State pension in the UK, even including SERPS, is quite inadequate to sustain the lifestyle of a professional person. In fact the State pension provision fails to keep any pensioner with no other income above subsistence level. When measured as a percentage of the average industrial wage, the UK State pension is amongst the lowest in the industrialized world. This statement is supported by the fact that most pensioners in the UK whose sole income comes from their State pension, receive supplementary benefits.

The above analysis suggests that no-one should rely simply on the basic State pension, even including SERPS, to provide their sole source of income on retirement and certainly no-one in the professional class. The basic State pension in the UK, which is currently received at age 65 for a male and 60 for a female,[17] can be considered to be no more than a useful supplement to other pension provisions built up over a working life.

If you postpone taking your State pension until after the age of 60 or 65 the pension is increased by about 7.5% a year until you reach 65 or 70. The maximum increase flowing from this delay is around 40%. This is not a sensible option unless you are working in the meanwhile.

If you decide to live abroad after retirement this could affect the future value of your State pension. State pensions are frozen at their existing value when you leave the UK unless the country to which you transfer your residence has entered into some reciprocal agreement with the UK. Your pension will continue to be upgraded with UK inflation if you live in the European Union or a few other mainly commonwealth countries (Canada and Australia are noted exceptions) but not elsewhere.[18]

FINDING OUT ABOUT YOUR FUTURE STATE PENSION

The above discussion should have persuaded the reader, particularly if the reader is female, that it is difficult to calculate the future value of the State pension you will receive when you reach pension age. For this reason the government has set up a pensions forecast service to provide you with an estimate of your likely pension when you reach pension age.

You can enquire about your likely future pension by telephoning the DSS and asking for either form BR19 or form NP38. Once you have received the form you fill it in and send it back to the DSS. Around six weeks later you will receive a calculation that will provide you with an estimate of your future basic pension at pension age and any additions (BR19) or simply your estimated SERPS pension (NP38).

You are warned that these estimates are likely to be lower than you expect!

OCCUPATIONAL PENSION SCHEMES:
(A) FINAL-SALARY-BASED SCHEMES

The law does not require all companies to run a pension scheme on behalf of their staff but most companies do provide some kind of pension provision for their employees. In April 1988 legislation was passed stating that no employee in the UK can be forced to join a company pension scheme; the employee can choose to set up his or her own personal pension scheme. If such a scheme is set up by an employee the employer is obliged to pay the monthly contributions towards the employee's pension into the employee's personal scheme rather than into the company scheme.

Pension contributions to salaried employees are awarded several important tax concessions. For example pension contributions are allowable as a charge against income at your highest marginal rate for the purpose of calculating your income tax, thereby reducing the cost to you of building up a pension fund. The government, in effect, contributes towards the cost of your pension.

In addition the income on the pension fund which is cumulating year by year and from which your pension will eventually be paid is not subject to income or capital gains tax. This is a remarkable concession by the Inland Revenue.

The most common form of occupational pension scheme operated in the UK is the *final-salary-based scheme*. Under this type of scheme the value of your pension when you retire is based on two factors (a) a factor based on the value of your final annual salary[19] before retirement plus (b) a factor based on the number of years you have contributed to the scheme. Normally you will receive a pension on retirement equal to $\frac{n}{60}$ or $\frac{n}{80}$ of your final salary where n equals the number of years you have contributed to the pension scheme. An illustration of this type of calculation is provided in Exhibit 5.6. Many companies use the $\frac{n}{60}$ formula but only compensate partly for future inflation. Most government schemes use the $\frac{n}{80}$ formula but compensate fully for future inflation. Which is the better scheme depends on the future rate of inflation. The $\frac{n}{80}$ schemes, which compensate fully for inflation, are the safer schemes but are likely to provide a lower average income to the retiree, especially in the early years after retirement.

In addition to the monthly pension as calculated above the employee will usually be offered in addition a capital sum equal to two to three years salary on retirement. This amount is not usually subject to tax.

A typical employee in a company pension fund will contribute 5% to 8% of gross monthly salary into the scheme and the employer will contribute an equal or greater amount. If you are working in the public service and have not worked for a sufficient number of years to gain the

Mr John Tyrrel retires as managing director of Bradford Manufacturing PLC on 31 December 1997. His final salary is £42 000 and he earned an additional £3000 in commission. He has worked for the company for 26 years and 8 months.

Bradford Manufacturing runs a final-salary-based scheme that provides the retiree with $n \div 60$ of his final salary on retiral, where n represents the number of years the employee has worked for the company. Commission does not count towards the pension.

The pension partially compensates for inflation. If inflation is 5% or less in any year, the annual inflation will be fully compensated in the next year's pension. If inflation is more than 5% then a 5% increase in the pension will be allowed in the following year.

A capital sum equal to three times the final year's salary will also be paid to Mr Tyrrel on retirement.

Since Mr Tyrrel earned £42 000 in his final year and since he has worked for the company for 26 years and 8 months, he will earn a pension of $(26.66 \div 60) \times £42\ 000 = £18\ 662$. He will also receive a lump sum of £126 000.

Final-salary-based schemes may base the pension not on the final salary but on the highest salary ever received by the retiree when past salary levels are adjusted for inflation. Another possibility is to average the best three or five years in the past.

EXHIBIT 5.6: A typical final-salary-based scheme

---

maximum possible pension under the scheme you may be able to 'buy in' additional years of contribution in a very tax-efficient manner. This 'additional years' option' may well prove to be an efficient investment for any surplus funds you may have accumulated before retirement. You should, at the very least, evaluate this option and compare it with the return you can achieve on an alternative investment of your surplus funds at that time.

If you are employed by a company in the private sector you can supplement your future pension by making *additional voluntary contributions*, (AVCs). We will explain how AVCs operate later in the chapter.

As an employee you may be paying only 5% to 8% of your gross salary into your pension scheme but the tax authorities allow you to pay a much higher percentage of your gross annual salary into your occupational pension scheme if you should so wish. You are allowed to pay up to 15% of your gross salary into the scheme. For high earners a maximum cap is placed on 'relevant earnings' by the tax authorities to limit the tax allowances available to 'fat cats'. This cap was £82 200 in the tax year 1995–96. This limitation on contributions to a pension fund only refers to tax allowances; there is nothing to stop a company setting up an 'unapproved' pension scheme for highly paid staff but the contributions will not be allowed against the tax bill of the 'fat cats'.

Since investing to obtain a higher pension is a very tax efficient form of investment you should always include this option in any review of your investment strategy.

If you are contributing to a final-salary-based scheme you are likely to retire with a pension equal to between 35% and 60% of your final year's gross salary but between 45% and 75% of your final year's net salary after all deductions have been made. It is the percentage of *net* salary that is the relevant figure to consider in pension planning since this is the amount that is available to you for spending out of the gross salary. This net figure is the one to use when preparing a post-retirement income and expenditure account such as the one set out in Exhibit 5.3.

If you intend to stay with your company for a long period of time then a final-salary-based scheme provides excellent value for money. Final-salary-based pension schemes usually provide many valuable advantages that would be very expensive to purchase under a personal pension plan. In fact the high cost of these advantages is persuading some larger companies to move away from final-salary-based schemes to the less expensive 'group pension' schemes that are run by insurance companies.

ADDITIONAL VOLUNTARY CONTRIBUTIONS

If you consider that a pension based on your employer's scheme will not provide you with the standard of living you would hope to enjoy in retirement, probably because you will not have been able to contribute to the scheme for a sufficient number of years to generate an adequate pension, you may consider 'topping up' your company pension rather than leaving the scheme. You can do this in one of two ways, both of which are very tax-efficient.

If you are working within the public sector you may, as we noted above, be able to 'buy-in' additional years of contribution to your pension scheme. If you are working in the private sector you can choose to make additional voluntary contributions (AVCs) to your company scheme. A further alternative is to set up an independent free standing AVC (FSAVC) pension with an insurance company.[20] A free standing AVC scheme can be kept confidential between you, the contributor, and the insurance company so long as the contributions do not exceed some upper limit (£2400 per annum in 1996). Funds can be deposited into an AVC through a regular savings plan or in a lump sum.

The tax authorities set limits on the amounts you are allowed to contribute to a pension scheme but the contributions, if allowed, are allowed against tax at your highest marginal rate. Since the income earned from the pension fund in the hands of the trustees is not subject to income or capital gains tax, the fund grows year-on-year gross of tax. Thus the AVC and FSAVC schemes are exceptionally tax-efficient forms of investment.

One disadvantage of placing your AVC into a company-sponsored scheme is that, if you should switch companies, the transfer value of your AVC will be added to the total transfer value of your pension fund. Some experts on pensions claim that the AVC transfer value might be lower, perhaps significantly lower, than the value of the fund if you had accumulated the fund under an independent FSAVC scheme. You will need to check on the formula used to calculate the transfer value of your AVC fund by the company you are leaving to answer this question. Some knowledge of the experience of other employees who have left the company and organized a transfer value would be useful here. Your trade union can assist you in this matter.

On the other hand the costs of setting up a FSAVC are about double the costs of setting up an AVC (for example, more commission is involved). It might be worth while checking out the priority of AVC funds in a company liquidation. They may rank below normal pension funding claims.

The AVC and FSAVC schemes are run in a very similar manner to the 'money purchase' schemes to be discussed in the next section of this chapter. All of these schemes can only be converted into a pension by buying an annuity on or after retirement. The minimum age of retirement for an AVC scheme is 50. The conversion of part, usually 25%, of the terminal value of your pension fund into cash on retirement is not available under either an AVC or an FSAVC scheme.

The AVC and FSAVC are useful pension-planning tools that are used less often than they might be: only 11% of those eligible for either scheme are taking them up in 1997. The tax efficiency of such schemes are seldom appreciated by employees with surplus funds to invest.

OCCUPATIONAL PENSION SCHEMES:
(B) MONEY PURCHASE SCHEMES

Many smaller companies in the UK prefer to run either a 'money purchase' pension scheme for their employees or a 'group' pension scheme rather than a final-salary-based scheme. A final-salary-based scheme is likely to prove to be beyond the resources of a small company. The recent Pensions Act is likely to accelerate the trend from final-salary-based schemes to money purchase schemes. The new regulations on final salary (designated benefit) schemes are very onerous.

In the case of a final-salary-based scheme the risk of under-performance by the pension fund is borne by the company; in the case of a money purchase scheme the risk of underperformance is borne by the employee. By 'underperformance' we mean that the income from the pension fund over the years is lower than expected so that the future pension is lower than expected.

A money purchase pension scheme is financed by both the employee and the employer contributing an agreed amount each month into the pension fund, usually each party contributes around 5% to 8% of the employee's gross monthly salary into the fund.[21]

In addition to the basic pension contribution it is usual for both the employee and the employer to pay a lower rate of National Insurance contribution. This 'saving' on NI is invested in a protected pension for the benefit of the employee.

The total contributions are placed into a fund which is managed for the benefit of you, the employee, and your spouse. The pension fund accumulates, with annual income added gross of both income and capital gains tax, until you retire. On retirement the amount accumulated in your fund is used to buy an annuity. The income from this annuity will provide you with a pension for the rest of your life. This type of annuity is called a 'compulsory purchase' annuity.

Under this type of pension scheme the value of your pension on retirement will depend on two factors: the terminal value of your pension fund on the date of your retirement and the annuity rates offered by insurance companies on that date.[22] A minimum pension is sometimes guaranteed by the company managing the scheme, usually an insurance company, but this amount is likely to be based on a very conservative estimate.

Money purchase schemes are less common than final salary schemes but they are becoming more popular even with larger companies since they are less expensive to run and less risky for the company. These schemes tend to be used by smaller companies as an economical way of providing a pension for their employees at a known, relatively low, cost. The funds are usually administered by an external agency, such as an insurance company, investment trust or unit trust, on behalf of the company. Money purchase pension schemes are unlikely to have many free 'perks' attached to the scheme.

Under a money purchase scheme you may have a choice as to the type of investment into which your contributions are placed. The usual choice is between a unit trust, an investment trust, a 'with-profits' scheme, or a simple cash deposit at fixed interest. You can mix these choices. It is useful to have the right to switch between investment types if you should wish to do so, at a low or zero cost. These same remarks apply to the FSAVC schemes discussed above.

The problem with a 'money purchase' pension scheme is that such a scheme is a 'defined contribution' plan rather than a 'defined benefit' plan. As an employee you will know exactly how much you need to pay into the pension fund but you will not know how much your pension will be worth on retirement.

As we explained above the value of your pension will be based on two factors: on the value of your terminal fund in the pension scheme and the annuity returns offered by insurance companies on the date of your retirement. You will not know either of these figures until you retire. A further problem concerns your age on retirement. Annuities do not pay out substantial returns until an annuitant reaches the age of 65 or above. Thus if you are forced to retire early, say at age 57, you can be left with an inadequate pension income.[23] Another factor to consider is that few 'money purchase' schemes make adequate allowance for future inflation.[24]

We conclude that salary-based pension schemes are almost invariably much superior to money-purchase-based pension schemes. Salary based schemes are 'defined benefit' schemes; in other words you know in advance the value of the pension you will receive on retirement since it is a defined proportion of your final salary.

DRAWDOWN VERSUS A PHASED ANNUITY PLAN

If you have a personal pension then you do not need to convert it into an annuity on retirement after the age of 59. You can 'drawdown' an amount of income from your pension fund up to an amount between 35% to 100% of what could be earned on a 15-year government stock with this fund. The value remaining in the pension fund is still protected from tax.

The perceptive reader will notice the resemblance between this option and the 'phased annuity' option discussed in Chapter 4. You need expert advice on choosing between these two methods of avoiding having to convert all of your pension fund to an annuity on your retirement.[25]

HOW MUCH WILL YOU AND YOUR EMPLOYER CONTRIBUTE TO YOUR PENSION FUND?

If you are working in a profession that has a retirement age of 60 or 65 then your contribution to your pension scheme is likely to be around 5% to 8% of your gross monthly salary. Your employer will make an equal or greater contribution. If you work in a profession where you retire at a younger age, for example if you work in the fire service, the police service or the military, you may have to pay a higher proportion of your monthly salary into your pension fund. Early retirement will increase the percentage that you need to contribute to your pension fund monthly by a substantial amount if it can be foreseen. In some cases you may be required to contribute as much as 15% of your gross monthly salary into your pension fund to provide yourself with an adequate pension on your comparatively youthful retirement.

Some companies, particularly companies operating final-salary-based schemes, require a contribution of less than 5% of your monthly gross salary to finance your future pension. A few companies, particularly companies with their head office resident abroad, make no deduction from your salary towards the company pension scheme. This latter approach might create tax complications for UK employees.[26]

If your pension fund is found to have a surplus during one of the periodic actuarial evaluations of the fund then contributions to the fund may be waived for several months or even years.

ADVANTAGES OFTEN ATTACHED TO OCCUPATIONAL PENSION SCHEMES OF LARGE ORGANIZATIONS

If you are contributing to a pension scheme run by a large organization certain advantages may be offered to you at no additional cost, or at a very low cost, from within the scheme. Such advantages are not likely to be offered by pension schemes run by smaller companies or by personal pension schemes.

Examples of some of these advantages are listed below. It is curious how few employees contributing to company pension schemes are aware of the value of these advantages or even of their existence. Buying such advantages from outside a company scheme can be a very expensive business. These advantages are therefore equivalent to an untaxed increase in your salary. If you are contributing to a final-salary-based company pension scheme you ought to identify and value these perks before you compare your salary to another salary offered outside the company by another company with no final-salary-based scheme.

Compensation for inflation

Most government-run pension schemes and schemes within the public sector compensate pensioners 100% for inflation. This is a very expensive advantage to incorporate into a pension scheme. The cost of compensating every present and future employee 100% for the fall in the value of the pension due to inflation is so great that only governments can afford take on this risk. Presumably governments can afford to take on this degree of risk because they have easy access to other people's money!

Few, if any, private company schemes guarantee 100% compensation to their pensioners for inflation. Non-government pension schemes are now required to provide some limited form of 'cap' on inflation compensation. For example the scheme might guarantee compensation for inflation up to a maximum of 5% increase in the pension in any one year or the previous year's annual increase in the RPI, whichever is the *lower* figure.

Money purchase schemes and personal pension schemes may not be fully inflation indexed unless you opt to pay for the indexation yourself. This is an expensive option. The cost of building 100% compensation for inflation into your personal pension scheme will increase the monthly cost of the scheme by 50% to 100%. The actual cost depends on current expectations about future inflation rates in the UK.[27]

Early retirement provisions

Many company pension schemes provide remarkably generous terms for early retirement including topping up the number of years worked to the maximum possible as if you had stayed in work to 60 or 65. For example if you retire at 58, and you could have worked until you were 65, you could be awarded an additional seven years of contributions to your pension scheme and treated for the purpose of calculating your pension as though you had actually retired at age 65 *with your present level of salary.*

Other early retirement perks are provided by occupational schemes. For example, life insurance and even health insurance may be provided to you and your family free of charge after retirement up to your 'normal' retirement age (you pay tax on this benefit after retirement).

The early retirement situation under other types of pension scheme is likely to be very different. A personal pension scheme may provide you with no compensation whatsoever for early retirement and cut your pension substantially since the annuity rate offered to you on retirement will be much lower because of your youth. Any early retirement benefits, if offered, will have to be paid for by you. The costs of providing such additional benefits, probably in the form of an insurance policy, are likely to be high.

If you have a personal pension be careful about your choice of insurance company. Some companies offer a good deal of flexibility on your retirement date at low cost, others charge heavy penalties for early retirement. For example if you take an initial 25 year policy and retire after 15 years you can lose 20% of your pension.[28]

Ill-health provisions

Suppose you are off work for an extended period because of ill health. Will your pension contributions be paid on your behalf by your company while you are off work?

If you are in a company scheme the company is likely to take a sympathetic view of your situation and pay your pension contributions even if your salary is temporarily cut or suspended while you are off work. The same company may be less sympathetic if you have set up your own personal pension scheme which is independent of the company scheme. You need to check on this. In the latter case you may need to take out insurance to cover your pension contributions if you are off ill for an extended period.

Some company schemes incorporate critical illness insurance and income replacement insurance. See Chapter 7 for a full discussion of these forms of insurance. If you do not benefit from a company scheme you will need to pay for these useful forms of insurance yourself.

What is the financial situation of your spouse and children on your death?

If you should die while still at work or after retirement what portion of your pension, if any, will be paid to your spouse and children? Under most, but not all, company schemes the spouse, usually the wife, receives around 50% of the pension rights her husband would have enjoyed until her death or occasionally her remarriage. The maximum figure allowed is two-thirds. The calculation of the precise amount can be complicated depending on the age of the deceased and the presumed retirement date. In addition an amount, often set at 25% of the pension rights of the deceased, might be available for each child until the child reaches the age of 16. The precise details vary a great deal between schemes.

You must check out the precise terms of your pension contract to ensure that your spouse and children are financially protected in the case of your death. If they are not protected you must set up insurance contracts sufficient to plug this gap in your financial shield.

Money purchase and personal pension schemes are likely to be much less generous to spouse and children on the death of the contributor to the scheme. Benefits will be offered to dependants on the death of the contributor but they will have to be paid for as an additional cost in your personal pension plan. The benefits will not be offered as free 'perks' as they are in the case of most final-salary-based company schemes.

A substantial term life-insurance policy is also attached to most pension schemes to protect the financial solvency of the spouse and children of the deceased. The maximum insurance value allowed is a tax-free sum equal to four times salary. You should check the value for your scheme; it could be much less than four times salary on the date of decease but the sum is tax free. A refund of pension contributions plus interest is also permitted by the tax authorities. These amounts (four times salary and refund of contributions plus interest) are maximum amounts); few schemes are this generous. Such policies are term policies that usually terminate on retirement.

What is the transfer value of your pension?

If you are in a final-salary-based scheme or a money purchase scheme and you switch employment from one company to another, the company which you are leaving must work out a 'transfer value' on your pension rights. This is one of the few situations where a personal pension scheme may offer an advantage over a company scheme. The current value of your personal pension is independent of the company you are leaving.

What will you do with this transfer value? You cannot take it out and spend it.[29] You have several options:

- You can place the transfer value of your pension into the pension fund of the company you are joining. This is the usual procedure.

- You can use the transfer value to buy a single premium insurance policy, a buy-out bond or an annuity from an insurance company, which can accumulate value until you retire and which retains some of your previous pension rights. In the trade this is called a *Section 32 buy out*. It is seldom used but it is a useful option in certain situations. The Section 32 bond can be converted into personal pension later. This option might be useful if you are approaching retirement.

- You can place the transfer value into a personal pension plan run by an insurance company or some other financial institution.

- You can leave the pension 'frozen' in the pension fund of the company you are leaving. It will be 'topped up' by the RPI index or 5% each year, whichever is the lower figure. Eventually, when you retire, you will get a mini-pension or its discounted equivalent. This is not a good idea unless the company you are leaving runs a very generous pension fund that provides benefits to departed employees, something that is most unlikely.

The first option is almost invariably the better option. But if you are moving abroad or are now unemployed another of these options may have to be selected. If you are now self-employed you will choose a personal pension.

The calculation of the transfer value is a problem. Some pension experts claim that the transfer value of your pension rights may be much less after this transfer than they would have been if you had remained with your previous employer. It has been claimed by some actuaries that the transfer value of your pension rights may be worth no more than 50% to 80% of the value which would have accrued to you if you had stayed with your previous employer. These are serious allegations which need to be checked out by independent experts.

If you transfer your pension fund several times during your working life these moves can seriously deplete its total value. Such problems do not arise if you have set up your own personal pension fund which is independent of any company scheme. There is no question of a transfer value here since the new employer, like the previous employer, simply places your pension contributions into the existing personal pension fund, which is run by an independent insurance company.

If your pension is based on a series of salary-based schemes added together, the value of your pension will be reduced every time you move to another company. Your pension is made up of the terminal value of your salary in each job multiplied by the number of years you worked in that job. Your final job will only pay you a pension based on your final salary *multiplied by the number of years you worked for that company*. The pensions due from the other prior jobs might be much lower. This point is often overlooked when final pension is being estimated.

Other potential benefits

Many other benefits may be attached to a company pension scheme. For example in some schemes you may be allowed to take over the payment of term assurance premiums, previously paid by your employer, if you retire early. Death while at work on company business sometimes results in a doubling of insurance benefits paid to your beneficiaries. As we noted above, special forms of insurance such as medical insurance for yourself and your family or critical illness insurance or income-replacement insurance may be built into your company pension scheme.

Most of these benefits are rarely triggered but such benefits are very valuable to you or your dependants if the unusual event that triggers the payment should occur. It is most important that you take the trouble to identify and evaluate each of these advantages attached to your company pension scheme. You will find all of these benefits listed in your pension scheme rule book which must be supplied to you by law.

PERSONAL PENSION SCHEMES

We have discussed salary-based schemes and money purchase schemes. This leaves personal pension schemes as a last resort if salary based or money purchase schemes are not available to you. If you are self-employed or work for a company with no pension plan or a company operating what seems to you to be a financially inadequate pension plan you can set up your own personal pension plan in association with a financial institution.

A personal pension plan works as follows:

- You contact an insurance company or some other financial institution that sells and manages personal pension plans.

- You find out maximum proportion of your gross annual wage that you are allowed to contribute to your personal pension plan. This depends on your age. The proportion varies from 17.5% to 40% of gross salary.

- You estimate how much of a pension you will need when you retire.

- You calculate how much you must contribute into your personal pension plan over the years before retirement to achieve this level of pension.

- You may find that you cannot afford to pay this level of contribution and so you must compromise by selecting a level of contribution you can afford.

- You may decide to buy your pension with a single lump sum rather than with a series of monthly contributions over many years. Both methods are tax efficient.

The insurance company selling you the plan or a pension advisory service can provide you with an approximate estimate of the value of your pension at 60 or 65 years of age for various levels of monthly contribution. A study by the *Financial Times* found that the growth in the value of pension funds was around 7% to 8% per annum.

Your pension contributions are placed into an investment fund that is managed by the financial institution you have chosen, which is usually an insurance company. The current regulations on pension fund investment allow your monthly contributions to be invested in a wide range of securities. You may be offered a choice as to the particular type of security into which your pension fund is invested. If you are in an 'umbrella' fund you can switch between different funds if you wish. This allows you to switch your funds into a deposit account in the last few years before retirement and so avoid a dip in the stock market.

A personal pension plan is a very tax-efficient vehicle for saving and investment. The income from your pension fund, which is reinvested in the fund, is not subject to income tax or capital gains tax. Moreover, the monthly contributions to your pension fund that are deducted from your salary are allowed against your income tax bill at your highest marginal rate of tax. Thus the higher your marginal rate of tax the more the government contributes towards your pension. Your employer's contribution towards your pension is not taxed as your income, a truly remarkable set of tax concessions by the Inland Revenue.

The pension fund is used to buy you a pension on the date of your retirement. At least 75% of your personal pension fund must be used to buy an annuity although this need not be done immediately on your retirement. The return from this annuity will generate your pension. The remaining 25% of your pension fund can be taken in the form of cash if you wish. You should take advantage of this. The money so obtained can be placed, *over time*, in a PEP or TESSA or some other tax-free investment vehicle. This option provides you with useful future liquidity.

As we have noted, the value of your personal pension on retirement is thus dependent on two unknown factors:

- the rate of interest offered on annuities on or after the date of your retirement and

- the terminal value of your pension fund

when you decide to convert it into an annuity. Neither of these values can be forecast on the date when you set up your pension plan. Remember that you may set up your pension plan some 40 years before you retire! Thus it is very important that you monitor the value of your personal pension fund every few years and 'top-up' the fund if it seems for any reason that it will not generate the income you expected on retirement.

Several monthly publications on personal finance publish the predicted value of externally managed pension funds on a regular basis. See Chapter 12 for the names of these publications.

IN WHAT TYPE OF SECURITY SHOULD YOU INVEST YOUR PERSONAL PENSION FUND?

We noted above that you may be given a choice as to the type of security into which your monthly pension contributions will be invested. You may be offered, say, a choice between a 'with-profits' endowment insurance policy, a unit trust fund, or a high interest deposit account. The risk-return profiles of each of these three types of investment are very different. Equity investment has, in the past, provided the best return while, at the same time, providing a stout shield against inflation. The value of equity-based funds can, however, fall quite drastically during an economic downturn in the economy. The 'with-profits' endowment policy provides greater stability to the value of your pension fund while also being mainly equity based. The nominal returns from high-interest deposit funds are more stable and have, historically, provided higher returns than equities during periods of economic stability.

If, in the mid 1990s, we look at the terminal value of managed pension funds accumulated over the previous 20 years, we find that the value of the best managed fund is some 40% higher than the value of the worst managed fund. This fact is not very comforting if we do not know how to choose a reliable fund.

Exhibit 5.7 shows that there is a substantial difference between current estimates of the projected value of unit linked pension funds for 5, 15 and 25 years into the future.

Statistics such as those set out in Exhibit 5.7 are somewhat misleading since they ignore the changing value of money. Money fell in value in the UK by about 80% between 1973 and 1993 and is likely to fall in value by 50% to 70% over the next 25 years. We need to adjust the projected value of pension funds, such as those shown in Exhibit 5.7, to the present day value of the pound to make the projections meaningful. Few pension-fund projections make this adjustment.

I would go for a fund with low charges, a stable rather than an outstanding performance over the last five years and which is mainly invested in a wide range of equities. I would not go for 'top of the league' funds. Research has shown that these tend to move towards the bottom of the league as time passes.

We conclude that it not easy to estimate the value of the pension that you will eventually receive from your personal pension plan.[30] The best strategy is to ensure that a substantial part of your pension fund is invested in equities and build conservative assumptions into your estimate of the future value of your pension.

PERSONAL PENSION PLANS FOR EMPLOYEES

Personal pension plans were designed for the self-employed. In July 1988 the UK government introduced new regulations that allowed an employee to set up a personal pension plan if she or he did not wish to enter into the employer's plan.

This alternative approach to pension planning is now available to all employees who wish to leave their company scheme and establish their own. Insurance companies are only too happy to arrange private pension plans for employees wishing to leave their company scheme.

The advantage of setting up a personal pension scheme rather than using the company scheme is that your pension scheme is now independent of any particular company. You own your own pension. In the past many employees felt that they were 'locked in' to lifetime employment with one company because of the value of their accumulated pension benefits. They feared that if they left the company they might lose a substantial part of their future pension rights. Even if the accumulated pension rights were not lost, they might be 'frozen' until the date of retirement by which time inflation might have reduced the real value of the pension by a substantial margin.

This situation has now changed quite dramatically. The government has introduced legislation forcing all company pensions to be 'portable'. The employee who leaves a scheme is given a transfer value that he or she can use as described above. There can be no doubt that the introduction of the 'portability' of company pension values plus the introduction of additional voluntary contributions to company pension schemes has reduced the comparative advantage of personal pension schemes for employees. It is now generally agreed by pension experts that the introduction of legislation allowing employees to set up their own personal pension plans has proved to be a mixed blessing for employees.

There is no problem if you are self-employed. The majority of contributors to personal pension schemes are self-employed. The government has provided generous tax benefits to the self-employed to encourage them to set up their own personal pension schemes to provide an adequate income on retirement. These tax benefits are so generous that the self-employed would be foolish not to take full advantage of them.

The situation is quite different for any employee who opts out of a company pension scheme, particularly a final-salary-based scheme, into a personal pension plan. Few employees are likely to benefit from such a move.

The many valuable 'perks' attached to company schemes, which we outlined above, will be lost or will have to be paid for by increased contributions from the employee. Such additional benefits are costly to fund if they are not provided within a group scheme.

A further negative factor relates to the terminal value of the personal pension fund. Pension experts have calculated that personal pension plans entered into during the period 1988 to 1994 did not provide a very good return on the money invested in them. It is possible that this poor performance may well prove to be a short-run phenomenon caused by the peculiar financial conditions of this seven-year period but we cannot be sure about this.

We conclude that if you are an employee contributing to a company pension scheme, particularly to a final-salary-based scheme, then it is most unlikely that you will benefit financially by transferring your funds into a personal pension plan. If you are self-employed you must set up a personal pension plan; you have no other choice.

Funds available from pension contributions

Personal pension fund: with-profits policy

Sex	Male
Age	65
Premium	£200 per month
Date of retirement	1993

Value of open-market option pension funds

Years paid in	5	10	15	25
Performance of fund	£	£	£	£
Highest	16 000	60 000	160 000	440 000
Average	15 000	52 000	136 000	302 000
Lowest	13 000	40 000	90 000	160 000

Personal pension funds: unit-linked pensions

Sex	**Male**	**Male**	**Male**
Age	40	50	60
Monthly premium	£200	£200	£200
Date of retirement	2018	2008	1998

Projected future value of fund

Years to retirement	25	15	5
Projected performance of fund	£	£	£
Highest	208 000	71 000	14 300
Average	190 000	66 000	13 500
Lowest	167 000	59 000	11 700

The first table illustrates the performance of the best, average and worst pension funds resulting from investing in a 'with-profits' policy over 5, 10, 15 and 20 years. The tables are based on a monthly contribution of £200. The second table shows the projected payouts on a unit-trust-linked pension fund. The table estimates the likely best, average and worst terminal payouts for a male who will pay in £200 a month for the next 5, 15 and 20 years. It is assumed that the contributor will retire at age 65. The projections are based on the actual performance to date of the fund.

It is most important to be aware of the impact of the changing value of money in these estimates. For example a monthly payment of £200 in 1976 pounds would be worth £1143 in 1996 pounds. Could you have afforded £1143 a month in 1996? The future projections will have to be reduced to allow for your estimate of future inflation. The reader may care to refer to the chapter on annuities to see the value of pension that these terminal values would buy for a male retiree aged 65 years.

EXHIBIT 5.7: Actual and estimated terminal value of personal pension funds

HOW MUCH CAN YOU INVEST IN YOUR PERSONAL PENSION SCHEME?

You can invest as much as you like in a personal pension scheme but not all of your contributions will be allowable against tax if you exceed the limits set down by the Inland Revenue authorities.

The limits set down for the tax year 1995–96 are given in the table below:

Age at start of tax year	Percentage of net relevant earnings
35 or less	17.5%
36–45	20.0%
46–50	25.0%
51–55	30.0%
56–60	35.0%
61–74	40.0%
Over 75	0.0%

If you are an employee you pay contributions net of tax at the basic rate and reclaim any higher tax relief at the end of the tax year. An 'earnings' cap is placed on the 'net relevant earnings' figure to limit excessive tax benefit going to fat cats. This cap was £82 200 for the 1996–97 tax year. This amount is inflation indexed.

Up to 5% of your contribution limit can be used to buy life assurance. This is, in effect, allowable against tax at your highest marginal tax rate. Thus a 47-year-old employee on £50 000 a year could pay a premium of 25% × £50 000 × 5% = £625 and have it allowed against tax at his or her highest marginal rate. A £625 annual premium on a healthy male would provide level term 25-year insurance cover of around £135 000.

CARRY FORWARD AND CARRY BACK TAX RELIEF

Another advantage for personal pension holders is the 'carry forward' and 'carry back' tax relief granted on personal pension contributions. Since maximum pension contributions allowed by the tax authorities are seldom fully utilized the Inland Revenue allow personal pension holders to apply unused relief to any earnings they have had while self-employed or while employed but not accruing retirement benefits under an employer's pension scheme. The unused allowances can be accumulated for up to six years back and used to reduce your income tax bill in the current year. The contributions paid in any year must not exceed the 'net relevant earnings' limit for that year. This is a very useful concession if you are near retirement and want to buy a pension in several lump sums. An example is shown in Exhibit 5.8.

A 'carry back' facility is also available. Your contributions to a personal pension in any year can be treated for tax purposes as if they had been made in the previous year when you may have been paying tax at a higher marginal rate. The normal 'carry back' is for one year; the maximum period of 'carry back' is two years if you were self-employed at the time.[31] The claim is made using tax forms PP42 and PP120.

TAX ASPECTS OF PENSION SCHEMES

We have referred to tax aspects of pension schemes many times in this chapter. Let us try to summarize this material in this last section. Tax concessions by the Inland Revenue are a most important part of pension planning.

In recent years the government in the UK have tried to encourage the growth of private pension plans in order to reduce the burden on the State pension scheme in the future. This encouragement has taken the form of providing substantial tax concessions to every employee in a company scheme or to the self-employed person, or others who set up a private pension plan.

The basic tax philosophy of the government is to allow the contributions into your pension scheme to be set off against your income tax bill at your highest marginal rate of tax. If you pay tax at 40% the contributions will be allowed against tax at 40%. The income from the investments cumulating in your pension fund portfolio are also not subject to income tax nor capital gains tax (the tax on pension income is now refunded to the trust at the 75% rate, not 100% as in the past). This is a major tax concession by the Inland Revenue and it makes pension fund investment exceedingly tax efficient. It is difficult to find any alternative investments which are as tax efficient as investing in a well-run pension fund.

If you, as an income earner, decide to set up a future pension with a single lump sum payment then, so long as you enjoy access to a sufficient level of *net relevant earnings*, the consequent reduction in income tax can cut the cost of your pension very considerably. Some of the current cost of your pension can be set off against unused pension relief in previous years up to six years back. Note that this relief is given at the current year's rate of tax. You can also carry back pension contributions for one year but in this case the relief is given at last year's tax rate.

Your employer's contributions to your pension fund are not taxed as your income and the 25% lump sum paid out of a pension fund on retirement[32] is not subject to tax up to a given limit.

Your pension income itself, if sourced from an annuity bought with money from a fund receiving all these tax concessions, is, understandably, taxed as normal income. If your pension income comes from a 'purchased' annuity bought out of income already subject to tax then special tax rules apply to this income. The average rate of tax paid on the income from a 'purchased' annuity is likely to be well below the basic rate. See Chapter 3 on the taxation of annuities.

We conclude that tax aspects of pensions are a very important part of pension planning.

If you set up a personal pension plan your maximum contribution to the plan in any one year that can benefit from tax concessions is restricted as follows in the 1996–97 tax year.

Age	Percentage of net relevant earnings
Under 30	17.5
36–45	20
46–50	25
51–55	30
56–60	35
61 or older	40

However, the Inland Revenue allows an important concession in that the pension premiums need not be paid in the income tax year during which they qualify for tax relief. Suppose that the net relevant earnings over 8 years were as follows:

Age	Year	Net relevant earnings	Max. contri- bution %	Max. contri- bution (amount)	Actual contri- bution	Unused relief
54	1990	40 000	30%	12 000	5 600	6 400
55	1991	40 000	30%	12 000	5 600	6 400
56	1992	40 000	35%	14 000	5 600	8 400
57	1993	45 000	35%	15 750	6 300	9 450
58	1994	50 000	35%	17 500	7 000	10 500
59	1995	55 000	35%	19 250	7 700	11 550
60	1996	60 000	35%	21 000	8 400	12 600
61	1997	65 000	40%	26 000	9 100	16 900

A self-employed director who wishes to arrange a pension in the year 1997 will be allowed to set up a pension based on the maximum percentage for 1997, that is 40% of £65 000 plus the unused relief from the years 1992 to 1996 namely £52 000.

An amount of £69 400. In addition the director can add 40% of whatever he earns up to the date of his retirement to this sum. A cap is placed on the maximum net relevant earnings that can qualify for tax relief in any one year. In 1996/97 this cap was £82 200.

There is no limit to the amount that can be invested in the pension fund but only £82 200 will be given tax relief in any one year. The Inland Revenue also allows you to elect to carry a pension premium back to the preceding tax year or to the year before that if you had no income in the preceding tax year.

The government makes generous provision for allowing individuals to set up pension plans for themselves. The astute individual will take full advantage of these provisions.

EXHIBIT 5.6: Contributions allowed to a pension plan

THE PENSION MORTGAGE

One particularly efficient tax-saving scheme involves the pension mortgage. Combining a mortgage with a pension plan can provide a particularly tax-efficient investment vehicle. A pension plan is set up as described above but the cost of the monthly contribution to the plan is much greater than that needed to achieve the required pension. Under this combined plan an interest-only mortgage is provided by a building society or a bank to buy a house. The mortgage is granted on the security of the endowment insurance policy attached to the pension scheme. On the date of your retirement the 25% lump sum, which can be taken in cash from the pension fund on retirement, is used to repay the mortgage and the balance is used to buy an annuity that provides you with a pension.

The advantage of such a scheme is that all of the contributions to the pension plan are allowed against tax at your highest marginal rate of tax, currently 40%. The sum of £1000 a month paid into such a pension plan only costs the contributor on a 40% marginal rate of tax £600 per month net of tax.

Naturally the various limitations imposed by the tax authorities on pension contributions will apply to such a scheme. For example the maximum contribution to the pension plan is limited to between 17.5% and 40% of net relevant earnings depending on your age. However the pension mortgage overcomes the strict limitations now imposed on charging mortgage interest against your tax bill. Currently the interest allowed against tax is limited to a maximum £30 000 mortgage and this interest is only allowed to reduce your tax bill at a 15% tax rate.[33]

If you are worried about losing your 25% lump sum from the pension fund conversion you can, perhaps, if you are in a company scheme, take out an FSAVC sufficient to compensate for this loss. The FSAVC contributions are allowable against tax at your highest marginal rate of income tax up to the contribution limit. Your upper contribution limit to pension funding may prevent this course of action being taken unless you have a very high salary.

The tax treatment of pension planning is an extensive and complex subject in its own right. This is one area where expert advice can provide a useful return. The problem lies in finding the expert. Many financial advisers have only a limited knowledge of tax aspects of personal pensions.

PROTECTING YOUR PENSION AGAINST ILLNESS

If you should fall seriously ill for an extended period you might find difficulty in keeping up your pension payments. Within a company scheme this is less of a problem. The company usually pays your premiums. The situation is different with a personal pension. This problem of non-payment can be ameliorated by taking out an insurance policy which provides a 'waiver of premium option'. Such an option is offered by most insurance companies at relatively low cost but seldom publicized.

A waiver of premium option comes into effect if the contributor to the pension fund falls ill for an extended period, usually for more than six months. Under these circumstances the insurance company pays the pension contributions until the contributor is fit enough to return to work or until the contributor reaches his or her retirement age at 60 or 65.

The cost of a waiver premium is typically 2% of the value of the monthly contribution but it can vary between 0.5% and 8% depending on circumstances. The contributor to the pension will need to submit to a medical inspection before the policy is accepted by the insurance company.

You need to choose your insurance company carefully since very stringent conditions can be placed on 'waiver of premium' policies. Some companies insert so many exclusion clauses into the policy that it is difficult to make a claim. It is important to check the insurer's definition of 'disability'. Will the premiums be paid if you are unable to perform your 'own' work or 'any' work? It is also important to ensure that the company will pay the full but uncertain premium value at the time of your illness which could be many years in the future when premiums are higher than they are now.

KEY DATES

The above discussion refers to the pension situation in the UK in 1997. If your pension plan was set up some time ago then different rules might apply. The key dates are plans set up before 17 March 1987, plans set up between 17 March 1987 and 31 May 1989 and plans set up on or after 1 June 1989. If your plan was set up before 1 June 1989 you should refer to a specialist text on pensions, for example Harrison (1995), to see what the differences in your situation are compared to the current situation.

THE PENSIONS ACT OF 1995

The Pensions Act of 1995 will come into force in April 1997. The full consequences of this Act are not yet known and will only become clear after some time has elapsed. The Act is obviously important for the pension world. Indeed, it has been described as 'arguably the most radical piece of pension legislation ever'.[34]

The most important points in this legislation from the point of view of the pensioner are as follows:

- An Occupational Pensions Regulatory Authority (OPRA) has been set up to monitor the pensions industry.

- A Pensions Compensation Board will be set up to recompense contributors to occupational (but not personal) pensions for up to 90% of any losses incurred through fraud, theft or misappropriation. Notice that this protection does not cover management incompetence!

- A third of pension trustees will be appointed by fund members. Certain powers and responsibilities of the trustees, specified in the statute, will override the rules set by the individual schemes.

- Professional advisers to the pension fund such as actuaries and accountants must report on unsatisfactory matters to the trustees, members and elsewhere if need be.

- Pensions in respect of service completed or contributions paid after April 1997 must be increased by the current retail price index or 5%, whichever is lower. This will apply to all occupational schemes and some personal pension schemes. The rule does not apply to AVC schemes. It will add another 1.5% to the salary bill of companies.

- Age-related National Insurance rebates are introduced for contracted-out money purchase schemes and personal pensions.

- Under a personal pension scheme a 'drawdown' is allowed from the pension fund rather than converting it to an annuity between the ages of 60 and 75. The amount withdrawn can vary from 35% to 100% of what would be available on a 15-year government stock of this value.

- State pensions for men and women will be equalized by the year 2020 so that both men and women will receive their State pension at 65 years of age. The scheme will be phased in between 2010 and 2020.

- Pension rights can be included in divorce settlements, although the law here is still not clear.

- If you are a member of an occupational scheme and you apply to the trustees of your pension fund for a 'transfer value', a value must be given to you and guaranteed for a three-month period.

Much else is included in the Bill, especially on the financing and running of funds but the points highlighted above are the more important ones so far as the contributors and beneficiaries of the fund are concerned.

SUMMARY

1. You are likely to spend the last quarter of your life in retirement. Pension planning is thus a key component of personal financial planning.

2. It takes at least 25 years to build up sufficient funds to provide yourself with a decent pension (unless you are seriously rich). It is much better and less financially onerous to build up a pension fund over 30 to 35 years.

3. The 'ageing' of the British population, linked to the earlier age for retirement in the UK, makes the funding of adequate pensions a major national problem. In future the value of the State pension, already very low, is likely to decrease in real terms. An increasing responsibility will thus be placed on you to fund your own pension and that of your spouse after retirement.

4. You must ask yourself six key questions when designing your pension plan. When will I retire? How much of an income will I need when I retire? How much of a pension am I likely to receive from my current pension plan? How secure is my current pension plan? If I am employed should I arrange an additional pension to supplement my current company plan by adding an AVC or FSAVC to my existing pension plan? If I should die before my dependants what will be their financial situation? Should I set up additional insurance to cover their needs?

5. For those resident in the UK there are three basic sources of pension. There is the basic State pension, including SERPS. There are the occupational pension schemes run by public sector organizations and companies in the private sector. These can be further divided into final-salary-based schemes and money purchase schemes. Finally we have personal pension plans.

6. Most pension schemes run by public organizations and large companies base the value of your pension on your final salary. These are called *designated benefit* schemes. Smaller companies offer *money purchase* pension schemes to their employees where the value of the pension depends on the terminal value of the pension fund and the annuity rates prevailing at that time. These are called *designated contribution* schemes. The self-employed are encouraged by the Government to set up very tax-efficient personal pension plans to provide themselves with a pension when they retire.

7. All pension schemes in the UK are now 'portable'. This means that you can, if you wish, carry the current transfer value of your pension fund from one company to another when you change employer.

8. You have a range of choices as to what to do with the transfer value of your pension. You can place it into the pension fund of the new company, buy a single premium insurance policy, buy an annuity, or use it to set up a personal pension. If you have worked for the company for less than two years you can cash it in.

9. If you are already in an occupational pension scheme run by a large organization it is most unlikely that you will be better off opting for a personal pension plan. The advantages provided by large companies within their pension schemes are very expensive to buy in the open market. Examples of such advantages are early retirement options, cover for dependants and ill-health benefits.

10. The generous tax benefits provided by the Government to encourage people to set up pensions outside the State scheme are a very important part of pension planning. The Inland Revenue provides generous tax allowances to encourage individuals to set up proper pensions for themselves after retirement. The regular contributions to your pension fund are allowable against your income tax bill and the dividends on the investments paid into your pension fund are not subject to income or capital gains tax. The 25% of your terminal pension fund that can be encashed on retirement does not incur a tax penalty. However in consequence of these tax benefits the pension you receive after retirement is treated just like any other *earned* income so far as tax is concerned.

11. If your pension is based on a 'purchased' annuity bought from taxed income, the capital portion of the income provided by the purchased annuity is exempt from tax. In other words you pay a much lower rate of income tax on the income from a purchased annuity.

12. If you have a 'money purchase' or personal pension that buys an annuity, at least 75% of the terminal value of your pension fund must be converted into an annuity to create your retirement pension. Many types of annuity are on offer. These were outlined in Chapter 4.

13. The Pensions Act coming into force in 1997 will change pension planning quite radically. The full implications of this are not yet clear.

TEST YOUR KNOWLEDGE

1. If you are a 45-year-old female and are expected to live to the age of 83, for how many years are you likely to be retired? For how many years will you be working?

2. Some Government Ministers have said that the State pension in the UK will be a much lower proportion of the average industrial wage in 2020 than it was in 1997 when it was 15%. Since our national income is growing year on year, why do think this is so, if it is so?

3. Suppose you are sitting down to work out a pension plan for yourself. What are the five key questions you must ask and answer before you can begin your planning process?

4. If you are in a salary-based pension plan it is relatively easy to work out your future pension, at least as a proportion of your final wage. If you are contributing to a pension plan that is based on buying an annuity with your pension fund on retirement the value of your pension is much more difficult to predict. Why is this?

5. Which kind of pension plan are you in? What advantages and disadvantages attach to this kind of pension plan compared to other types of pension plan?

6. What benefits will accrue to your dependants in your current pension plan?

7. A higher-than-average rate of inflation can cause problems in pension planning. Explain what these problems are. How can a pension plan be designed so as to hedge against the risk of higher-than expected inflation?

8. How much money do you think you will need when you retire? In other words, how much money will you need after all deductions including tax and contracted costs like mortgage payments have been paid out?

9. What rights of portability are attached to an occupational pension?

10. Women used to retire and claim their State pension at the age of 60. This age will be gradually increased until both men and women receive their pension at age 65. How much do you think a woman of 38 years of age would have to invest today (1997) to compensate for this loss of income between the ages of 60 and 65 in future?

11. If you are in an occupational pension scheme your pension can be increased by setting up an AVC or a FSAVC. What is the difference between an AVC and a FSAVC? Who can set up an FSAVC?

12. Salary-based occupational pension schemes often provide 'perks' to employees free of charge which would have to be paid for under a personal pension plan. Provide three examples. How could you set up similar benefits when contributing to a personal pension plan?

13. Assume that your pension fund is being managed by a financial institution. How can you measure the relative performance of your pension fund?

14. The return on inflation-indexed bonds suggests that the market expects the rate of inflation from 1 January 1997 to 31 December 2006 to average around 4% per annum. If inflation averages not 4% but 5% per annum from 1997 to 2006 how much will an unindexed

pension of £20 000 a year starting on 1 January 1997 be worth on 31 December 2006 in 1997 pounds sterling?

15. Why do some companies prefer to run a *money purchase* type of pension scheme? Does this type of pension provide any advantages to an employee over a personal pension scheme?

16. Why are annuity rates offered by insurance companies closely tied to the return on medium-term government bonds?

17. An inflation-indexed annuity protects the pensioner against the ravages of inflation. Why don't all pensioners convert their pension fund into an inflation-indexed annuity. How long does it take for the income from an inflation indexed annuity to catch up with the return from a simple level term annuity?

18. Why is there such a wide difference between the annuity rates offered by different insurance companies on a particular date?

19. A 70-year-old woman, Mrs Black, purchases a £100 000 annuity from taxed income which pays her £12 000 a year for life. Her life expectancy is 156 months. How much tax will she pay on each monthly payment of £1000? Assume her marginal rate of tax is currently 23%.

20. The cost of living in Malta is said to be only 70% of the cost in the UK. If you have a pension of £1000 per month after tax in the UK how much would this be worth in Malta? Will you receive annual inflation-based increases in your UK pension if you live in Malta?

NOTES

1. In 1950 the average life expectancy of a man was 72 and that of a woman was 74. By 1994 this expectancy had increased to 78 and 82 respectively.

2. The government has announced a plan to equalize the retirement age between men and women in the UK at 65 in accordance with EU regulations, but this legislation is likely to have a very limited effect on the actual retirement age of women in the UK. It will only affect the date on which the State pension is available to women. In 1994 a 38-year-old woman would need to have made a one-off payment of £10 850 into her pension fund to compensate for equalization of the State scheme. See *Which Pension*, January 1994. Women born after 6 April 1950 are affected to some degree. Women born after 6 April 1955 will only receive a State pension when they reach 65.

3. Mr Michael Portillo, a senior member of the British Treasury team at that time, put forward this view in the TV programme 'House to House' on 14 December 1993.

4. The ability to raid a pension fund has been much reduced by recent legislation following from the Goode report on pensions published in 1993. The members of a pension fund can now insist on adequate representation on the board of trustees of any pension fund with more than 50 members. Funds that are calculated to be 'surplus to requirements' must be reduced.

5. The telephone number is 0191 225 6414.

6. Or some variation of this such as the highest salary you have ever received over n years after your past salary has been adjusted for inflation. There is also an 'earnings cap' providing an upper limit on contributions that receive tax benefits.

7. For example, an employee can currently make voluntary contributions up to the 5% limit noted earlier to increase the value of a life-assurance policy up to a value of 2.5 times salary. This fact is little publicized.

8. For example index-linked certificates currently pay 3% plus the rate of inflation eight months back.

9. Standard & Poor's (S & P) provide a regular grading system for measuring the security of 'with profits' funds, grading them from AAA to DDD. These gradings are available to the general public in a regular publication by Standard & Poor's. *Money Management* and *Money Observer* publish regular listings of the value of managed pension funds, including rankings of the performance of the funds.

10. Portable pensions were introduced into the UK by government legislation on the 1 July 1988.

11. . . . or not as the case may be. You may prefer to keep your private pension fund secret. This can be arranged by an insurance company under certain circumstances.

12. If you think you have been deliberately sold an inappropriate personal pension, telephone the Pension Unit of the PIA (the number is 0171 417 7001). They will tell you how to proceed against the person or firm that mis-sold you the pension.

13. Category A is for workers who have built up a pension from their own contributions. Category B is for those persons who claim a

pension from the contributions of a spouse. Category C is for those who reached pensionable age before July 1948 (any left?). Category D is for non-contributors to the scheme who have reached the age of 80.

14. See Harrison (1995) *Pension Power.* John Wiley, Chichester, Section 2, for a detailed explanation of the current eligibility for a State pension in the UK.

15. At the time of writing, in 1996, the maximum to be earned from SERPS is £94 per week but few contributors will receive as much as this because of their limited number of past contributions.

16. These are very rough calculations. The precise amount is uncertain but there is one thing of which you can be sure: you will not live fat on a SERPS pension!

17. The age at which a woman in the UK receives a State pension will be raised from 60 to 65 in 2010. The retirement age for a woman will be gradually increased from 60 to 65 over the years 2010 to 2020.

18. Apart from the EU and some West Indian islands the most interesting countries where UK pensions are upgraded are Cyprus, Israel, Mauritius, Philippines and the United States. A useful leaflet on the subject is available from BAPA 605 Royal York Road, Toronto, M6Y 4 OS, Canada. Note that, at the time of writing, pensions are not upgraded for inflation if you are living in Australia, Canada or South Africa.

19. Or on the highest annual salary ever received after past annual salaries are adjusted for inflation (or some variant of this).

20. The *Financial Times* prints a list of 'top-up' providers in the 1996 pamphlet *Top-Up Pension Plans,* which is available from the *Financial Times.*

21. Actually at the time of writing 47% of companies are said to be paying nothing into their pension schemes since excess past payments allow them to enjoy a 'contribution holiday'.

22. Under recent UK legislation passed in 1995 the terminal fund from a *personal* but not occupational pension need not be converted into an annuity immediately. The conversion process can be delayed until a later date when annuity rates have improved. The fund must be converted before the pensioner reaches 75 years of age. The fund will still accrue income free of tax until it is converted. This is called the *income drawdown* option. You can withdraw income directly from the personal pension fund up to a given annual limit.

23. Readers are referred to Chapter 4 on annuities for a fuller discussion.

24. Annuities are available that make annual adjustments to the pension to allow for inflation but these are very expensive, sometimes costing almost twice as much as a non-inflation indexed annuity. This means that the *initial* value of the pension might be only about one-half to two-thirds the value of a non-inflation indexed pension. Recent pension legislation is requiring some adjustments to be made for inflation on future pensions. This will come into effect in July 1997.

25. An excellent article which discusses the main issues involved can be found in Ainscough M. (1995) Change for the better. *Money Management.* February, pp. 62–4.

26. In such cases your pension may not be protected by UK pension legislation.

27. Current market expectations about future inflation for a given period ahead can be estimated from the difference between the return on normal and inflation-indexed government bonds for that number of years ahead. The figure is currently around 4% for 10-year stock.

28. See Skypala, Pauline (1996) Watch your step: early retirement penalties. *Money Management* (January) pp. 46–52.

29. Unless you have been in the scheme for less than two years when a cash payment is allowed.

30. Several pension review services are offered in the UK that will work out the likely value of your future pension from your current pension investment mix. Carr Shepard is one company that runs such a service for private individuals.

31. The Scottish Provident Institution, 6 St Andrews Square, Edinburgh, provide a useful pamphlet setting out the precise conditions on 'carry forward' and 'carry back' in some detail. You will need this document. The precise provisions are complicated.

32. When a pension fund is converted into an annuity, 25% of the terminal value of the fund can be taken in the form of cash. This amount is not subject to tax up to a given figure.

33. Some tax experts consider that the tax concessions currently available on pension mortgages may be withdrawn in the not-too-distant future.

34. Moss, Bruce (1995) Countdown to April 1997. *Money Management,* (October) p. 43.

Financing and investing in your home

6

INTRODUCTION

A home is probably the most important investment you will make in your entire life. Accommodation is essential for everyone and the ownership of a home lays the foundations for a secure life. Public opinion polls have found that most individuals in the UK prefer to own their home rather than to rent it. A recent Gallup poll, funded by the Sun Alliance insurance company, found that no less than 84% of the general public in the UK would like to own their home.[1] We will argue later in this chapter that this preference may not be a wise one for certain people.

If we examine the wealth portfolios of families in the UK we find that the value of the family home makes up a very substantial proportion of the total wealth of most families, often exceeding 80% of the total family wealth. The breakdown of the total wealth portfolio of all individuals in the UK is shown in Exhibit 6.1. The figures, which are taken from the CSO Blue Book series, show that, in the UK, the value of houses owned by individuals accounted for some 42% of the total value of all assets owned by individuals in 1995 and, in addition, accounted for some 58% of the value of 'accessible' assets.[2]

In this chapter we will examine four aspects of housing. First we will study the problem of financing the acquisition of a home. Secondly we will ask the question 'is housing is a good investment?' Thirdly we will compare the cost of buying a home with the cost of renting a home. Finally we will discuss the oft-neglected topic of the costs associated with maintaining a home in good condition.

RENT OR BUY?

We will examine the economic aspects of renting versus buying a home later in the chapter. The question of whether to rent or buy a home is, however, of such importance that before we launch into a discussion of the various methods of buying a home perhaps we should pause for a moment to consider this issue.

Real assets	%	%	%
Housing		42	
Other real assets		5	
Total real assets			47
Financial assets			
Insurance and pension rights	27		
Building society deposits	7		
Equity shares	7		
Bank deposits and			
National Savings	8		
Other financial assets	4		
Total financial assets			53
			100

Note that investment in housing makes up over 40% of the value of assets owned by individuals in the UK. Insurance and pension rights are the other major assets they owned. The proportion of personal wealth held in the form of building society deposits is roughly equal to the value held in the form of equity shares.

EXHIBIT 6.1: Where did UK citizens invest their personal assets in 1995

Between 1984 and 1989 in the UK the issue of whether to rent or buy a home was easy to resolve. The answer was 'buy'. During this five-year period houses in the UK almost doubled in value in money terms and the value of the mortgage used to finance the acquisition of the home was reduced by 50% in real terms by the high inflation suffered during this period. Even after allowing for inflation, the real value of houses in most parts of the UK rose by more than 20% over the period 1984 to 1989. Several useful tax benefits were also attached to buying rather than renting a home during this period.

Between 1989 and 1995, however, house prices fell in money terms by 15% to 25% and in real terms, after allowing for inflation, by 25% to 35%. Most of the capital gains of the period 1984–89 were lost between 1989 and 1995. During this six-year period it paid to rent a home rather than to buy one.[3]

The myth that housing is a profitable form of investment was created during the period between 1970 and 1990. It *is* a myth. As we shall explain later in the chapter, housing is a mediocre investment choice compared to many other alternative forms of investment. Renting, for many people, is likely to be the better *economic* option. Renting offers a lower, more steady cash outflow and removes many of the burdens of ownership. We shall expand on this topic later in the chapter.

We discuss the question now to emphasize the fact that the period between 1970 and 1990 was a most unusual period for the housing market in the UK. A set of circumstances existed which are unlikely to be repeated for many decades, if ever. Strategies for house acquisition that developed during the 1970 to 1990 period are no longer valid.

THE IMPORTANCE OF OWNING A HOME

Renting may be the better option on purely economic grounds but 84% of the British people would like to own their own home. Why?

Most of the benefits flowing from owning one's home are not concerned with economics. The first benefit is security. You cannot be thrown out of your home so long as you keep up the regular mortgage payments. This is a major psychological benefit. Second, there is the indefinable thing called 'status'. Owning one's own home seems to confer a higher status on the individual compared to renting. A third benefit is 'independence'. You have a much wider choice of what you can do with your home if you own it. Landlords place strict limits on using or altering a rented home. Finally there is the benefit of increased 'creditworthiness'. Lenders regard a borrower who owns his own home more favourably than one who rents it. This can reduce the cost of credit quite substantially. For all of these reasons cost may not be the prime consideration when deciding whether to rent or buy a home.

TAX AND HOME OWNERSHIP

Until 1992, the Conservative government in the UK tried to encourage home ownership by offering various tax incentives to the home-owner. Mortgage interest was allowed against tax, initially up to any amount, at the home owner's highest marginal rate of tax. There was also no capital gains tax to be paid on the profits arising from the sale of a first home. You need not pay tax on the rental value of your home.

These substantial tax perks have been gradually whittled away in recent years. The tax benefit on interest paid on a mortgage is now limited to a maximum of the first £30 000 of the mortgage and the tax relief itself has gradually been reduced from the owner's highest marginal rate of tax to the 15% rate.[4]

It is possible that in the not-too-distant future mortgage interest will no longer be allowed against tax. Maybe we should all begin to budget for a zero rate of tax relief on our mortgages?

Tax relief on mortgage interest is provided through a scheme called mortgage interest relief at source (MIRAS). It is available to all mortgage holders, not simply to those who pay income tax. Thus mortgage interest is paid net of relief for income tax at the 15% rate.[5]

Mortgage interest is even allowed against the income of home owners living abroad or in another part of the country for up to four years after departure but only if they can prove that they intend to return to the UK at the end of their period abroad. Note that this relief may not be allowed under MIRAS: you may have to reclaim the tax from the inland revenue at the end of the year.

It seems unlikely that any British government, of whatever political hue, will ever subject the profits on the sale of a first home to capital gains tax.

When a first home is bequeathed by a spouse to the other spouse the value of the home is not subject to inheritance tax.[6]

We conclude that the tax benefits attached to home ownership have been much reduced in recent years.

FINANCING THE ACQUISITION OF A HOME

The average value of a home in the UK in 1996 was approximately £60 000.[7] In the Central London region the average price was £75 000. The cost of the average home represents a very substantial investment for the average wage-earner in the UK. The average house value in the UK in 1996 stands at 2.9 times the average wage. Professional workers, such as lawyers, doctors or accountants, will tend to aim to acquire more expensive properties costing in the region of £150 000 to £400 000 – possibly four to six times their annual salary.

Few individuals in any class of society have sufficient wealth to buy a house outright with cash. Most individual buyers in the UK need to borrow a substantial proportion of the cost of their new home from a lender such as a building society or bank.

If it were not for the existence of financial institutions that specialize in providing housing loans (mortgages) to individuals to acquire property, home buyers would have to save up for half a lifetime before they could hope to acquire a home of their own. This is the current situation in Japan where the financing of privately owned housing is underdeveloped.

Financial institutions in the UK pioneered the process of providing cheap loans to individuals to buy their own homes. The UK system of providing mortgage finance to individuals is still the most advanced in the world. In no other country of the world is it so easy for an individual on a moderate wage to buy a home.

Building societies are still the main providers of housing loans to UK citizens but, in recent years, commercial banks, insurance companies and mortgage corporations from the USA have made a determined effort to enter the UK housing loan market. Some foreign financial institutions also offer housing loans to UK citizens, possibly denominated in a foreign currency. The range of institutions offering finance for house purchase in the UK is now so varied that the individual house purchaser is spoilt for choice.

We have also witnessed a dramatic increase in the number of financial products and mortgages on offer. Forty years ago a potential home buyer would be offered only one type of loan: a simple repayment mortgage. Today the potential borrower will still be offered a repayment mortgage but in addition the borrower is likely to be offered any one of a range of different kinds of mortgages. These will include the simple endowment mortgage, the unit trust mortgage, the PEP mortgage or even the very tax-efficient pension mortgage.

You might be offered a mortgage at a fixed rate of interest for a fixed number of years or at a variable rate. You might be asked if you wish to repay the mortgage over 25 years, the usual period, or over a shorter period, say 10 or 15 years. You might be offered an interest-only mortgage, with the capital repaid at the end of the mortgage period, or a rolled-up interest or deferred mortgage. You might even be asked if you wish to have your mortgage denominated in pound sterling or in some other foreign currency such as Swiss Francs.

Your objective must be to match your particular needs and financial circumstances to the widening pool of financing opportunities offered to you in today's housing market. To benefit from these opportunities you need to understand the various characteristics of the different kinds of mortgage offered to you in the current mortgage market.

SHOULD YOU BORROW IF YOU CAN BUY?

As we noted above, few individuals can afford to purchase a home out of current wealth, but a few can. Suppose you have sufficient funds to buy the property for cash, or put down a substantial deposit, say 50% of the cost of your chosen house. Given the choice should you use up your own funds or borrow the funds from a lender?

There are two aspects to this problem. First you need to compare the net of tax returns from the two options. Secondly, you need to consider your liquidity position.

Suppose you own financial assets having a net worth of £120 000 and the house you are hoping to buy costs £120 000. You might either put down a deposit of £20 000 and borrow £100 000 from a lender or sell your financial assets and buy the house with the resulting £120 000. The option you choose can be decided by comparing the net of tax return on the £100 000 of financial assets you will need to sell with the net of tax cost of the £100 000 mortgage.

It is an easy matter to calculate the net returns on both options for the coming year but the mortgage might well run for 25 years. You need not make estimates for 25 years ahead but you do need to estimate the likely returns and costs for the next few years ahead.

This calculation is thus not as easy to make as it might seem at first glance. If the funds are wisely invested they should generate a net of tax and net of inflation return of about 5% to 7% per annum (see the chapter on investment). If you take out a fixed rate mortgage for, say, five years then a straight comparison is possible. If the cost of the mortgage net of tax and inflation exceeds the return from your investments the better option is to buy the house with the £120 000. This will generate a higher income than taking out the mortgage.

Much depends on the cost of the mortgage. Both the nominal rate of interest charged and the real rate, net of tax and inflation, has varied a great deal in recent years as is shown in Exhibit 6.2.

Until around 1990 the best option would almost certainly have been to take the mortgage since the net of tax and inflation cost of mortgage finance was substantially lower than the return on equities. Since the real

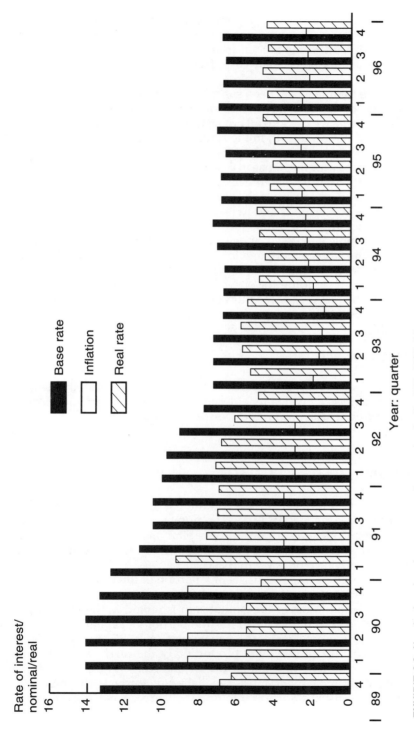

EXHIBIT 6.2: Nominal and real average mortgage rates in the UK, 1989–96

cost of mortgage finance (adjusted for inflation) has risen in recent years and the net of tax return on equities is gradually falling the decision is now more difficult to make than in the past. The matter is likely to be decided by factors other than cost. This brings us to the question of liquidity.

From time to time we all need substantial sums of money to deal with emergencies or to take advantage of financial opportunities. In the previous example we used up all our spare funds to buy the house. In real life we would not do this. If, in the future, the need arises for additional funds then mortgage funds are by far the cheapest funds available. We can, of course, pay for the house in cash now and then raise a mortgage on the house in the future when the need for funds arises, but the entry and exit costs of mortgaging are high. The more sensible policy is to estimate your future need for funds and to take out a mortgage sufficient to leave you with adequate liquid funds for the future.

In the example discussed above you might put down a deposit of £50 000 and take out a mortgage for £70 000, thus leaving yourself with an invested fund of £70 000 to cover future emergencies.

The key factor deciding the size of your mortgage, if you have funds available, is the real cost of the mortgage versus the estimated net return from the investment of the funds *not* invested in the property.

TYPES OF MORTGAGE

House mortgages can be divided into two basic types: the simple *repayment mortgage* which is repaid over the life of the loan and *interest-only mortgages* which pay interest on the loan but repay none of the capital until the end of the mortgage period.

THE REPAYMENT MORTGAGE

The repayment mortgage is the traditional form of mortgage. The borrower repays the loan over a given number of years in instalments, each instalment includes a portion of capital and a portion of interest. The payments are usually made once a month but the interest charge is calculated in advance on a yearly basis.[8]

Although each payment consists of a portion of interest and a portion of capital, very little capital is repaid during the first two-thirds of the repayment period. Most of the capital sum is repaid in the last third of the loan period. Exhibit 6.3 illustrates the portion of capital and interest repaid in each year during the repayment of a 25-year repayment mortgage. Note that a very high proportion of the early payments on a repayment mortgage are made up of interest. When mortgagees terminate their repayment mortgage half-way through the mortgage period they are usually surprised to find that such a small portion of the capital has been repaid.

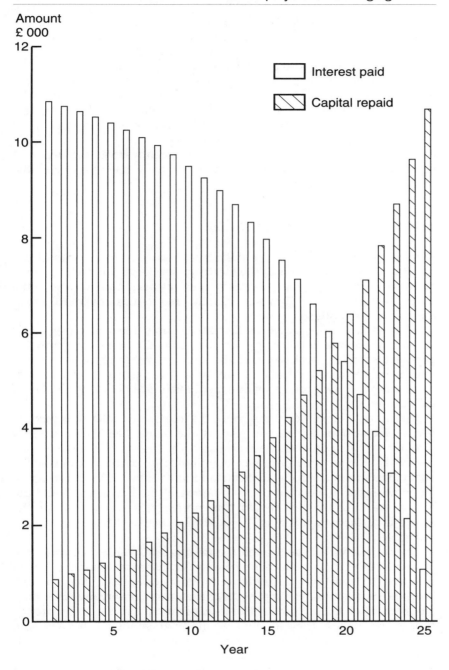

Data for a £100 000 repayment mortgage repaid over 25 years.

EXHIBIT 6.3: Capital and income repayment

Mortgage lenders like to lend for long periods and often do not emphasize the benefits of short repayment periods even if the borrower can afford the higher monthly payments this would entail.

The lender will insist that the house, which provides the security for the loan, is insured for the full cost of rebuilding the house. The lender is likely to insist that a 'reducing' term insurance policy be taken out on the life of the borrower for the benefit of the lender to cover the risk that if the borrower dies within the mortgage period his beneficiaries might not be able to repay the mortgage out of his estate.

Note that if you move your home frequently then the series of repayment mortgages that you will need to borrow may repay very little of the capital between each move.

THE ENDOWMENT MORTGAGE

With an interest-only mortgage the capital borrowed from the lender is not repaid over the period of the mortgage but instead a capital sum is built up from the regular payments made by the mortgagee to some third party. This capital sum is eventually used to repay the mortgage at the end of the mortgage period.

The best-known example of the interest-only form of mortgage is called an *endowment mortgage*. In this case the monthly mortgage payment is made up of two parts. The first part, as before, consists of the interest payment on the loan, the second part consists of an endowment premium on a 'with profits' endowment insurance policy on the life of the borrower.

No capital is repaid over the life of the loan – only interest is paid. A part of the insurance premium paid by the mortgagee is invested in a fund managed by an insurance company. The insurance company must ensure that the monthly insurance premium is sufficient to cover the life policy plus enough surplus to create a terminal fund sufficient to repay the mortgage at the end of the loan period. If the borrower should die before the loan is fully repaid the mortgage is repaid out of the proceeds of the life policy as it would have been with the repayment mortgage.

The company that has loaned the mortgage to you expects that the proceeds of the endowment fund held by the insurance company will be sufficient to repay your mortgage at the end of the loan period. Insurance companies, in the past, have been very conservative in setting the amount of the monthly insurance premium on the 'with profits' endowment policy. They set the premium high enough to be very sure that sufficient funds would be available at the end of the loan period to repay the mortgage out of these funds. In fact, in the past, the 'with profits' policy premium was usually fixed at so conservative a level that a substantial additional sum was likely to be available to the borrower at the end of the mortgage period. In other words a sum, often a substantial sum, would be available to you in addition to the amount needed to repay your mortgage. Thus an endowment mortgage was both a home-financing plan and a savings and investment plan.

The perceptive reader will have noticed the use of the past tense in much of the previous paragraph. Endowment mortgages have come under a cloud in recent years.[9] The return on the investment in endowment policies has been much reduced in recent years and in some cases the terminal fund has proved to be insufficient to repay the mortgage at the end of the mortgage period. Several insurance companies have written to mortgagees informing them that they must increase their monthly mortgage payments over the remainder of the loan period to ensure that the terminal fund is sufficient to repay their mortgage at the terminal date.

An endowment mortgage is what is called in the trade a *bundled financial product*. You are buying two financial plans at the same time: a house financing plan plus a savings and investment plan.

Which of these two options, the repayment mortgage or the endowment mortgage, is the better option for the house buyer? The answer to this question depends on the definition of 'better' and the particular circumstances of the borrower.

REPAYMENT OR ENDOWMENT MORTGAGE?

The first factor to consider when comparing the two options is the net cost of both options. Since the endowment mortgage is both a financing package and an investment package it is usually more expensive per month than the simple repayment mortgage, although not as expensive as it might seem at first sight since there are tax factors to consider.[10]

In the UK the interest paid on a house mortgage by an owner occupier[11] is allowable against tax[12] up to a certain amount, currently up to the first £30 000 of the mortgage which is allowable against tax at the 15% rate of tax. Since a part of the monthly payment on a *repayment* mortgage is a repayment of capital, this part of the monthly payment is not allowable against tax. This restriction can make a difference to the net monthly cost of the two types of mortgage once the mortgage is around two thirds of the way through the repayment period. All of the interest paid on an endowment mortgage is allowable against tax at the 15% rate (up to a limit of £30 000 as noted above). The second part of the monthly payment on the endowment mortgage is made up of the life insurance premium. The holder of a repayment mortgage must also pay for a reducing term insurance but this is much cheaper.

At most times in the past the repayment mortgage has imposed a lower monthly cash outflow on the borrower than the endowment mortgage. The net monthly cash outflow can be important since if you have a limited cash inflow you may not be able to afford the more expensive endowment mortgage even if you believe it to be the better option.

As we noted above, the endowment mortgage provides you with both the finance to buy a house and a savings and investment plan that will provide you with an unknown amount of money at the end of the mortgage period. You may well ask the question: 'Is it worthwhile paying out the additional cost of the endowment mortgage over the cost of the repayment mortgage for an unknown amount of money at the end of the mortgage period?'

The key point is that you, as an investor, do not know how much you will receive at the end of the mortgage period. The amount you will receive depends on the investment skills of the insurance company investing the funds on your behalf.[13] This stricture, however, also applies to most other investment schemes.

An alternative investment strategy open to you would be to take out a repayment mortgage and invest the difference between the cost of the repayment and endowment mortgage in a suitable investment scheme. For example you could invest the difference in a personal equity plan (PEP) which is free of tax to the investor and gives you a wider choice of investment (see Chapter 2). Another alternative is to take out a PEP unit trust mortgage (see below).

The choice thus boils down to answering the question: 'How good are the insurance companies at investment?' Until recently the insurance companies had a good record on investing the proceeds from endowment policies; they provided excellent returns on their endowment funds. Recently some doubt has been cast on the efficient investment of these funds and it has been suggested that the capital sums received at the end of the mortgage policy period might be quite low compared to alternative investment options available to the mortgagee. In extreme cases, as we noted above, the proceeds from the 'with profit' fund may not be sufficient to provide sufficient funds to cover the mortgage debt due to be repaid at the end of the mortgage period.[14]

DISADVANTAGES OF THE ENDOWMENT MORTGAGE

Since only interest is repaid and no capital, endowment mortgages are more sensitive to changes in interest rates than repayment mortgages.

If you run into financial difficulties you can extend a repayment mortgage and so reduce the monthly payment. This does not work with an endowment mortgage. You are often allowed to stop repayment mortgage payments for a few months if you have financial problems. It is not likely that you will be allowed to do this with an endowment mortgage.

One final comment on endowment mortgages. Be careful when cashing-in these policies, if you cash them in early the surrender value can be low relative to what you have paid into the scheme over the years. If you are short of money, take out a loan based on the current surrender value of the policy but do not cash it in. The amount paid out by the insurance company in surrender values, even one year before the terminal date, can be low, and it varies a great deal between societies. For example in 1996 one society offered a mere 47% of the value that mortgagees would have received if they had held the policy until the terminal date only one year later! Another society offered a respectable 90% of what holders would have received if they had not surrendered the policy one year early.

ALTERNATIVE MORTGAGE SCHEMES

If you wish to take out an investment-type interest-only mortgage, but are not happy about leaving the investment of your funds to an insurance company, you might consider taking out a *unit-linked endowment policy*. Under this mortgage scheme a part of the regular mortgage payment is invested by the insurance company in a unit trust selected by the borrower from a list provided by the insurance company. The units are bought on a regular basis from the insurance part of the mortgage premium. In the case of a unit-linked policy the current value of the fund to repay your mortgage is known[15] and you, as the borrower, accept responsibility for repaying the mortgage out of the unit trust fund at the end of the loan period. A similar arrangement can be set up for a tax-efficient PEP unit-trust-based mortgage. You can contribute an annual amount up to the annual PEP limit allowed by the tax authorities (£750 a month in 1997). You need to beware of the high initial and management charges attached to some unit-linked funds, but some are quite cheap; check out the charges out before you buy.

The advantage of a unit-linked mortgage is that you have more control over where your funds are invested; you can repay your mortgage early if you so wish and you also know the current value of your fund. You save tax if you set up a PEP fund. The one major disadvantage of a unit-linked fund is that the value of your repayment fund is subject to the fluctuations in Stock Exchange values. The value of a 'with profits' fund run by an insurance company is much more stable since reversionary bonuses cannot be clawed back. You can solve this problem by investing in an 'umbrella' fund which allows you to switch funds at low or zero cost within the 'umbrella' scheme. As you approach the repayment date on your mortgage, you switch your funds into a safer fund such as a 'gilt edged' fund or a 'bond' fund.

Many other variants of the interest only mortgage are on offer. For example there is the *low cost endowment policy* which is cheaper than a conventional endowment policy but provides a much smaller 'nest-egg' at the end of the mortgage period and the *low-cost start policy* for young people taking on their first house purchase. In this case during the first two or three years the borrower pays a significantly lower monthly mortgage payment which is compensated by higher payments in later years when the income of the borrower, hopefully, is rising, at least in nominal terms.[16]

THE PENSION MORTGAGE

An endowment mortgage can be arranged in association with a pension. Under a *pension mortgage* a single monthly payment provides the funding for a pension on retirement and also finances the purchase of your home (plus life insurance). The scheme is only open to those running personal pension plans. Such a scheme is only really viable for those with high incomes – say those earning over £50 000 a year.

The tax laws allow 25% of a pension fund available on retirement to be taken in the form of cash. This 25% in cash can be used to repay your mortgage.

The regular monthly payments into a tax-approved pension fund are allowable against tax at your highest marginal rate of tax. With mortgage interest only the interest on the first £30 000 is allowed against tax and this only at the 15% rate. Thus under a pension mortgage all of the payments on your mortgage are allowed against tax at your highest marginal rate, 40% in the case of a salary of £50 000 per year.

You need to ensure that the 75% of the value remaining in the pension fund is sufficient to buy you an annuity that can provide you with an adequate pension. This should be so if the 25% of your terminal fund covers a mortgage of, say, £100 000. This implies a fund of £300 000 for a pension, giving you a £30 000 to £35 000 per year level pension.

If you move from a personal pension to an occupational pension then you will have to find some other way of paying off your mortgage. Thus if you adopt such a scheme you are probably stuck with a personal pension during the period of the mortgage.[17]

THE QUESTION OF 'BUNDLING'

It is a matter of controversy whether the 'bundling' of two or more financial products, such as a home loan plan and a saving and investment plan or a home loan plan and a pension plan, is a wise strategy. The bundling process may provide you with some tax advantages which are not otherwise available or the provider of the bundled plan may provide you with a special discount if the products are 'bundled'. Otherwise it is probably more efficient financially to structure each financial need into a separate plan. This approach is likely to provide you with a greater degree of flexibility within each plan.

THE DEFERRED MORTGAGE

One type of mortgage that we would not advise you to take out is the *deferred mortgage*. Under this type of mortgage the regular interest payments are 'rolled up' and added to the capital sum. This might seem like a good idea until you come to repay the mortgage and learn about the awesome power of compound interest. The interest is added to the previous sum of interest 'rolled up' so the size of the loan escalates at an alarming rate after a time. For example a deferred mortgage on a £100 000 8% per annum loan with interest rolled up amounts to £147 000 after 5 years and to £216 000 after 10 years. If the mortgage were an 83% mortgage on a house worth £120 000 the mortgagee would soon be in trouble. Don't touch deferred mortgages. If you do, you might soon join the 'negative equity' club.

SHOULD YOU USE A MORTGAGE BROKER?

A professional service called *mortgage broking* is available to the general public. There is a charge of around one-half of one per cent of the value of the mortgage chosen for seeking this service but it might be well worthwhile paying this fee since the broker has access to so much current information about mortgages.

It is odd that so few home buyers seek the advice of a mortgage broker. The broker is expert on all of the many different types of mortgage on the market and can fit a particular type of mortgage to the needs of a particular client.

So many new products have been introduced onto the mortgage market in recent years that it would seem to be money well spent to seek the advice of a broker. You need not take his advice if you don't like it.

The broker is likely to have access to information on the mortgages offered by 300 to 500 different lenders with each lender offering several different products including 'covered' foreign currency mortgages.

Brokers will offer advice over the phone and send you details of the mortgages they suggest. Mortgage brokers provide a useful and much underutilized service to mortgage seekers.[18]

HOME INCOME AND REVERSION PLANS

A home-income plan is not a plan for buying a home but for raising income. In many ways home-income plans, if poorly structured, have the same defects as deferred mortgages. They can be expensive. However, if they are well structured, they can solve a problem faced by many retired people.

It often happens that a retired person or couple owns a valuable home on which the mortgage has been paid off. The home may have a market value of, say, £120 000. This same retired person or couple have an annual joint income, net of tax, of say £1000 a month. It is not easy for a retired professional couple to live well on a net £1000 a month.

The home could be sold and a smaller home bought. This is an inconvenient solution for many elderly people who wish to continue living in the home they have known for so many years. Lodgers could be taken in who will pay a tax-free room rental but this is an even more inconvenient solution for most elderly people.

The couple discussed above have an income problem but they do not have a wealth problem. They own an asset worth £120 000 – their home. The problem is how to convert this wealth of £120 000 into an additional income.

A home income plan or *home reversion plan,* if properly structured, can solve this problem.

There are several types of plans on the market, some safer than others. The least safe is a home income plan that raises a mortgage on the property and then invests the value of the mortgage in the stock market. If the income from the stock market investment, net of tax, exceeds the cost of the mortgage, net of tax, then the income of the home owner is increased by the difference. Unfortunately the reverse also applies: if the income from the stock market investment is less than the cost of the mortgage then the home owner is worse off than before. The home owner may even lose his or her home to the mortgage lender. This horror story was played out many time in the early 1990s. In 1993 the City Regulator, the SIB, banned such schemes and required that the companies who had run these schemes pay £22 million compensation to the unfortunate participants. An alternative format of these plans is now permitted, but subject to regulation.

Fortunately, safer plans for generating additional income from your home are now available to the home owner. Two popular schemes currently on offer are the *mortgage annuity* plan and the *home reversion* plan. These are normally taken out by home-owners over the age 70.

The mortgage annuity plan is not unlike the equity plan noted above but it is much safer. A fixed-interest mortgage is taken out on a proportion of the value of your property, say 25% of the value. The funds forthcoming from this mortgage are invested in an annuity. The income from this annuity depends on the age and sex of the annuitant. Men and older people gain a higher income than women or younger people. A joint annuity on the life of both partners provides a lower income than the income received from an annuity based on the life of a single person. See Chapter 4 for a fuller explanation of the reasons for this apparent anomaly. The mortgage is repaid out of the proceeds from the house sale on the death of the annuitant, or the death of the second party if it is a joint annuity.

The income from an annuity is almost certain to be higher than the cost of the interest on the fixed-interest mortgage since the annuity income includes a partial repayment of capital. This difference between additional income and additional cost provides the added income to the home owner. The scheme is much safer than the equity scheme because the annuity income is fixed and guaranteed by an insurance company until the death of the annuitant(s). Since the income is very safe the additional income may not be very substantial: possibly £300 to £500 a year for each £10 000 of mortgage taken out. Thus the retired couple mentioned above might expect an additional income of some £1050 a year gross on a £30 000 mortgage based on 25% of the value of their home (£350 x 3) in addition to their current net of tax income of, for example, £12 000 a year. The schemes are usually limited to a maximum £30 000 mortgage for tax reasons. One important point is that all of the interest on the mortgage is allowable against tax at the standard rate. The allowance is not restricted to the 15% rate band as with normal mortgages.

The income from the plan is taxed like the income on ordinary purchased annuities (see Chapter 4). Note that this additional income could effect means-tested social security benefits.

If the annuitant dies within four years of taking out the annuity, some value from the annuity will revert back into his or her estate. Otherwise the annuity has no value to the benefactors from the annuitant's estate.

An alternative plan for generating income from your home is called a *home reversion plan*. Under this type of scheme an insurance company buys the rights to the ownership of your property or, more probably, the ownership of a proportion of the value of your property. The right will be exercised on your death. The lump sum paid for this right is given to you and you can do what you like with the money but the wisest course of action is to invest the lump sum into an annuity as was the case with the *mortgage annuity* scheme above. The maximum proportion of the value of your home that can be handed over to the insurance company varies with your age but is usually around 40% to 50% of the market value of your home.

Some reversion plan operators base the return you will receive on current property prices. We would not recommend entering such a scheme; property prices are volatile. Note that there is no £30 000 limit on home reversion plan schemes as there usually is on mortgage annuity schemes.

In our opinion home reversion schemes are a little dangerous since they assume that the home owner will use the large influx of funds received from the scheme in a responsible way.

An association called Safe Home Income Plans (SHIP) provides advice on home income plans and offers three guarantees to scheme members:

- the right to live in your home for life;

- the right to move house if you wish;

- a small but secure regular income until death or a cash sum in lieu.[19]

FIXED OR VARIABLE INTEREST?

Fixed interest loans on property have always been on offer to the public in the UK but, in the past, they were offered by a rather limited range of sources. Until quite recently most of the housing mortgages on offer were of the *variable* interest type.

A variable interest mortgage allows the lender to alter the rate of interest paid by the borrower on the mortgage at any time. The variable mortgage rate is related to the open market rate of interest at that time. If the market rate of interest, as defined by the bank rate, or Libor, moves up or down, the variable mortgage rate is likely to move up or down soon afterwards. This is even more true now than it was in the past since the building societies have begun to raise substantial funds from the wholesale money market.

A mortgage based on a variable rate of interest provides more security to the *lender*, since, as the market rate of interest changes, so the rate charged to borrowers also changes. The lender's profit margin on existing loans is secure, although the lender may sell fewer mortgages at the new, higher rate of interest. Exhibit 6.2 (above) showed that the mortgage rate, which is heavily influenced by government policy, changes quite frequently in the UK. Between 1982 and 1995 the mortgage rate varied between a high of 15.4% in 1990 to a low of 7.7% in 1993.

In recent years, fixed-interest mortgages have come on stream. Fixed-interest mortgages are being offered by most mortgage lenders to the housing market in the UK. Thus you can now choose between a variable-rate loan and a fixed-rate loan to finance your house purchase. The fixed-rate mortgage is usually offered for a shorter period of time than a variable-rate mortgage, although there are exceptions to this rule.

A fixed-rate home mortgage is seldom offered for the full 25 years offered on the conventional variable rate mortgage. Usually the fixed-rate mortgage is offered for a period of two, three or five years and is renewable, as another fixed-rate mortgage, at a new rate of interest at the end of this period. The level of the interest rate on offer at the end of the initial loan period is decided by the mortgage lender at that time. The borrower need not accept this offer of a new fixed-rate loan at the end of the loan period since he or she can negotiate a new loan, fixed or variable, with another lending company.

House mortgage providers now raise money in the wholesale money market so the level of the fixed rate of interest on offer depends on the rate the mortgage lender has had to pay for two-, three- or five-year money in that market.

Should you take out a variable or fixed rate mortgage to finance the purchase of your home?

The decision depends on the level of the fixed rate of interest offered on the loan compared to expectations as to the trend of future interest rates on the open market over the mortgage period. The expectations as to the trend of future open market rates, in its turn, is much influenced by expectations as to the trend of future inflation. The decision is not an easy one to make.

The average nominal rate of interest, gross of tax and inflation, on variable interest mortgage loans over the period from 1970 to 1995 in the UK was around 9%. If this rate can be taken as a guide to the future average rate then if a fixed rate loan is offered to you which costs significantly below 9% per annum it might seem prudent to take the fixed rate mortgage rather than the variable rate. Unfortunately the past 25 years is no sure guide to the financial future and the long-term rate of interest seems to be stabilizing in the UK at a lower rate than in the past. However the *real* rate of interest, the nominal rate you pay less inflation, is actually moving to a higher rate than in the past.

Accepting a fixed rate loan for a good number of years ahead, say five years, at a gross rate below 7%, would seem to be a safe strategy unless the market rate of interest should collapse, which is most unlikely. Accepting a fixed rate mortgage above 9% per annum would seem to be unwise. At a fixed rate between 7% and 9% per annum, whichever you choose is a gamble.

The decision will be influenced by your expectations about future inflation rates and also, to a minor extent, by the marginal tax rate at which your mortgage interest can be charged against tax. Market expectations as to the future rate of inflation over various periods ahead can be estimated from the difference between the current return on inflation indexed bonds for a given period ahead compared to the current return on unindexed bonds of the same type for the same period. If the dragon of inflation should once again raise its ugly head in the UK then variable interest mortgage rates will most surely rise; fixed rates will not.

A fixed-rate loan provides you with one considerable advantage. You will know exactly how much cash you will need to pay the fixed-rate loan over the fixed period of the loan. This allows for accurate cash budgeting. This is important when we consider that the nominal cost of a variable-rate mortgage has swung between a low of 6% per annum and a high of 16% per annum over the period between 1970 to 1995 and that even the real rate, the nominal rate less inflation, has swung between 5.5% and 8.5% during the short period between 1989 and 1993. See Exhibit 6.2 (above) for the annual variation.

If a fixed-rate loan comes on offer at a suitable rate you should take it. Note that the value of the fixed rate loan may be limited to 75% of the value of the house you are purchasing. A higher percentage loan may entail you in taking out an expensive *mortgage indemnity guarantee* (MIG) policy.

The rate you pay on the fixed rate mortgage may depend on the proportion of the house value represented by the mortgage. For example if the rate charged is 8% per annum when you put down a 15% deposit the rate may rise to 8.25% per annum if you can only afford to put down a 10% deposit. The rate charged on a mortgage with a zero deposit, a 100% mortgage, would be substantially higher, if such a mortgage were obtainable.

HOW MUCH SHOULD I BORROW?

One of the key questions in mortgage finance is how much you should borrow. A higher mortgage means a better home but a higher mortgage might also lead to a financial nightmare. This conundrum can be best solved by working out an accurate cash budget for the years ahead.

Cash budgeting is a key activity in financial planning. The regular monthly payment you make on your mortgage is likely to be the largest single regular payment you make. The amount of the monthly mortgage payment is determined by several factors: the amount of the loan, the type of loan (repayment or interest only), the interest rate on the loan, the tax deduction allowed on the interest payment on the loan, and the length of the repayment period of the loan.

On a variable rate mortgage the proportion of your income paid out each month can vary a great deal over the life of the mortgage. The Council of Mortgage Lenders calculated that the fraction of income paid out on a mortgage for the average income earner was 11.1% of income in 1969 rising to 26.4% of income in 1990 and then falling back to 12% of income in 1996.

You need to ensure that the regular payment on your mortgage will not cause you financial distress when the loan is taken out *or at some point in the future.* Thus you need to calculate the monthly net of tax cost of the mortgage under various assumptions and ensure that your future income can cope with this level of mortgage payment. For example, what will be the impact on the family cash flow if your wife becomes pregnant and gives up work or if your husband loses his job or becomes incapacitated?

Exhibit 6.4 sets out the annual repayment costs on a £100 000 repayment mortgage under various assumptions regarding interest rates and repayment period. These figures take no account of the fact that the interest on a mortgage of up to £30 000 is currently allowed to be charged against your tax bill at the 15% tax rate. This allowance may well be phased out in the future.[20] Figures such as these can be used to calculate what proportion of your regular monthly net cash flow can be safely committed to mortgage repayment.

The lenders themselves limit the size of the mortgage they are prepared to offer you to a multiple of your individual or family annual gross income. Twenty years ago this multiple was two and it was only applied to the income of the main breadwinner. The years following 1976 witnessed a dramatic increase in the multiple offered by lenders. In some cases the mortgage lenders offered three times the income of the breadwinner plus another fraction of a multiple for the spouse if he or she was a wage-earner.

These multiples subsequently proved to be unsafe and many who borrowed in the late 1980s on these terms ran into severe financial difficulties in the early 1990s because of the foolish largesse of the building societies and others. The ratio of average house price to average earnings reached 4.65 in June 1989[21] against a long-term average of 3.

It is wrong to use the gross earnings of the breadwinner as the measure of income when calculating how much you can afford to borrow. The correct measure of income to use is the net monthly cash flow from all sources of the breadwinner and spouse after tax and other compulsory deductions have been subtracted. The family should not commit more than one third of this net cash flow towards mortgage

Repayment period (years)	Value of mortgage loan	Interest rate % p.a.	Monthly payment	Total amount paid	Additional interest paid (beyond 5 years)
5	£100 000	12	£2 224	£133 467	
10	£100 000	12	£1 435	£172 165	£38 698
15	£100 000	12	£1 200	£216 030	£82 564
20	£100 000	12	£1 101	£264 261	£130 794
25	£100 000	12	£1 053	£315 967	£182 501

Repayment period (years)	Value of mortgage loan	Interest rate % p.a.	Monthly payment	Total amount paid	Additional interest saved (below 15%)
25	£100 000	15	£1 281	£384 249	
25	£100 000	12	£1 053	£315 967	(£68 282)
25	£100 000	10	£909	£272 610	(£111 639)
25	£100 000	8	£772	£231 545	(£152 704)
25	£100 000	6	£644	£193 290	(£190 959)

The normal repayment period for a mortgage in the UK is 25 years. When inflation was high, say above 8%, it made financial sense to repay a mortgage over a long period and allow inflation to destroy the real value of your debt. Under current conditions, when inflation in the UK is under 4%, it is worth considering repaying a mortgage over a much shorter period of 20 or 15 years if your finances can make this possible.

Note from the top table that the additional interest saved on a mortgage of £100 000 repaid over 15 rather than 25 years is close to £100 000!

The rate of interest also has a powerful influence on the total lifetime cost of the mortgage. A drop in the rate from 12% to 6% on a 25-year £100 000 mortgage saves around £122 000 over the 25-year period.

Note that the above figures do not take account of the fact that mortgage interest on a loan up to £30 000 can be charged against personal income tax at the 15% rate.

EXHIBIT 6.4: Monthly cost of a £100 000 repayment mortgage under various repayment schemes

payment unless there is strong evidence that the cash flow will increase in the near future.

If the borrower is in the top quartile of professional earners this percentage can, perhaps, be increased to 40%. The current level of house prices is also a key factor here (see below). If it is well below the long-term trend line the percentage might be increased somewhat but it is not wise to commit yourself to an excessive mortgage. The 'one third of monthly net cash flow' rule is a sound basis for decision. Obviously a much lower figure is better still. One-third is the *maximum* to which you should commit yourself.

The estimated *future* net cash flow of your family over the next decade is another important factor in the decision as is the level of job security of the breadwinner and spouse.

How much will one third of net cash flow allow you to borrow at an average gross rate of interest of 9%? A gross family income of £30 000 per year, a substantial income which would place the household in the top 10% of family incomes in the UK in 1997, will only allow you to take out a loan of £70 000 over 25 years using this rule. The average value of a new mortgage taken out in 1996 in the UK was £60 000.

Another limitation on your borrowing power arises from the fact that mortgage lenders will seldom provide a mortgage equal to 100% of the value of the house you are about to buy.[22] If they do they will charge you extortionate rates for insurance cover through a mortgage indemnity guarantee policy. These policies do not protect you from having your house repossessed: they protect the lender against the possibility that your house, if sold on default, will bring in less money than the value of the mortgage. We will return to mortgage indemnity guarantee policies later in the chapter (they are not what they seem) but for the present we should note that if the value of your mortgage exceeds 75% of the value of the house you are about to buy then the mortgage may well have an MIG premium attached which might cost you as much as the mortgage.[23]

In the late 1980s it became fashionable to take out a mortgage costing much more than one could afford in order to buy an expensive home as an *investment* which would appreciate in value in the future. The value of the mortgage, it was assumed, would be destroyed by inflation as it had been in the past.[24] Between 1989 and 1995 nominal house prices in the UK *dropped* in value on average by 20% and inflation fell to an annual rate well below 4%.

Two million households in the UK were enjoying the fruits of 'negative equity' by the end of 1993. Negative equity occurs when the value of a mortgage on a house exceeds the current market value of the house. There should be a notice on all house-sale contracts warning the buyer that house prices can go down as well as up.

You should buy property at a price you can afford. Inflation no longer destroys the value of a mortgage and housing, as we shall see later in this chapter, has proved to be a rather poor investment at most times in the past in most of the countries of the world.

THE DOUBLE MORTGAGE TRAP

A final caution on limits to borrowing. If you are selling your home and find a new 'dream home' before your first home is sold you may be tempted to negotiate a temporary 'bridging' loan from a bank that allows you to own both homes until your first home is sold. Don't! This is a very dangerous course of action to pursue. In some sad cases it has led to the bankruptcy of the dual home owner. The problem of the double mortgage is often not obvious to the house seller who lacks financial sophistication.

The problem is that you, as a dual owner, are paying the interest on your original mortgage plus the interest, usually at a higher rate, on a loan covering the entire cost of your new home. This monthly joint interest bill can easily exceed your entire monthly cash flow. The interest will certainly eat up a good fraction of your monthly cash flow unless you are very rich indeed! See Exhibit 6.5.

If you succeed in selling your original home within a reasonable period, say within three months, you can roll up the additional interest charges to the bank and, with luck, pay the amount off out of the proceeds of the surplus on the house you are selling.

But suppose you fail to sell within three months, or six months, or a year? A financial catastrophe is building up month by month! This scenario was played out many times during the 1989–92 period in the UK when the bottom fell out of the housing market. Amateur house speculators found themselves saddled with a rapidly depreciating and unsaleable asset, their old home, and an exponentially mounting debt burden on the new one.

The moral of this cautionary tale is this: 'Don't buy a new home until you have sold the old one.' Sophisticated legal methods are available for holding on to the right to purchase the new home until the old home is definitely sold.[25]

OVER HOW MANY YEARS SHOULD YOU REPAY YOUR MORTGAGE?

The conventional period for repaying a mortgage on a home in the UK is 25 years. Most borrowers accept this period of repayment without question, but a mortgage can, within reason, be repaid over any period the borrower wishes, although the maximum period offered is likely to be 30 years.

Twenty-five years need not be the optimal repayment period for you. Three important factors to be considered in choosing a repayment period are the number of years to your retirement, your monthly net cash flow, as discussed above, and the real rate of interest on the loan.

In many circumstances there are good reasons for choosing a period of repayment of much less than 25 years. If you enjoy a sufficiently large regular cash inflow and the real rate of interest is well above the

Loans	Repayment period (years)	Value of mortgage loans	Interest rate % p.a.	Monthly payment £
Loan 1	25	30 000	6	193
Loan 2	25	100 000	8	772
Total		130 000		965

During the late 1980s many house buyers were caught by the mortgage nutcracker. They found a new house before they had finalized the sale of the old. They bought the second home with an additional 'bridging' mortgage and then the sale on the first home fell through. They were thus left with a substantial double mortgage which sometimes exceeded their entire monthly cash flow.

EXHIBIT 6.5: The double mortgage nutcracker

---

long-term trend you should consider making a higher regular repayment on your loan over a shorter period. When the annual rate of inflation is high, say over 8% per annum, it is likely that the *real* rate of interest will be relatively low[26] and sometimes even negative after allowing for inflation and tax. Under such circumstances, which existed in the UK between 1973 and 1981, a long repayment period allows inflation to destroy the real value of your mortgage. On the other hand, when the real rate of interest is high, as in the UK in the 1990s, you should consider repaying your mortgage over a much shorter period to save on interest charges. Table 6.1 shows the cost of repaying a £100 000 mortgage when it is repaid over 25, 20, 15, 10 and five years respectively. Note the substantial saving in interest charges that can be effected by early repayment. Even a small increase in repayment can have a dramatic impact on reducing the number of years to full repayment. If a sufficient regular cash flow is available you should consider choosing, or switching to, a shorter repayment period, especially when the real rate of interest is well above the average historical real rate of 4%.[27]

Most mortgage lenders offer schemes for speeding up loan repayment. However lump sum repayments are not usually credited to the account until the end of the year, so these payments should be paid in near the year end. You should check with your lender as to the precise terms as they apply to early repayments. Companies such as MARPRO offer an accelerator facility for repaying mortgages. The monthly repayments are paid to MARPRO and kept in a separate deposit account. The money is paid to the lender at the best time to maximize the repayment of your loan.[28] Mortgage repayment systems of 13 or 26 payments a year rather than the usual 12 monthly payments can speed up repayment of a loan by up to five years on a 25 year mortgage without undue financial pain.

The general rule should be that the higher the real rate of interest and therefore, quite probably, the lower the rate of current and expected inflation, the quicker the mortgage should be repaid if your net cash flow can take the strain.

SHOULD YOU REPAY YOUR MORTGAGE EARLY IF FUNDS BECOME AVAILABLE ?

It often happens that, quite unexpectedly, you find that you have access to considerable funds, possibly inherited funds on the death of some relative. Should you use these funds to repay all, or part, of an existing mortgage?

This is a singularly difficult question to answer. It depends on so many factors.

Interest on mortgage finance on a first home up to £30 000 is still allowable against your tax bill at the 15% rate. This is a cheap source of funds. Even that portion of a mortgage above £30 000 is still one of the cheapest forms of finance available to an individual borrower because of the excellent quality of the security offered, namely the house.

If you believe that you will need to borrow further finance in the future it would be foolish to repay the mortgage and then subsequently have to seek additional funding at a cost substantially above the net of tax cost of the current mortgage finance. Your estimated future funding needs will decide the issue here.

If the mortgage is a repayment mortgage then most of the payments made near the end of the loan period consists of capital repayment which is not allowed against tax. For this reason it has been advocated by some financial advisers that repayment mortgages should be repaid a few years early, if the funds are available, since the tax benefits attached to a repayment mortgage can diminish rapidly over the last few years of the repayment period.[29]

Note that this advice does not apply to an endowment mortgage. This type of mortgage should not be repaid early if it entails closing out the endowment policy since the surrender value of the endowment policy will be low. Early repayment of *part* of an endowment mortgage will reduce the debt due and so reduce the monthly interest paid but it will not reduce the mortgage period or affect the endowment policy.

Another somewhat arcane factor effecting early repayment of a mortgage relates to health. If, while you were healthy, you took out a life policy to cover repayment of the mortgage on your death and you have subsequently developed a serious health condition such as cancer or a bad heart, then the mortgage should not be repaid early since the benefit of the life policy may be lost. The precise conditions differ between policies but if the loan were repaid thus terminating the life policy you would be likely to find that another life policy of equivalent value would either be very expensive or impossible to obtain.

The ultimate deciding factor on early repayment of a mortgage is what economists call the *opportunity cost* of the interest payments on the mortgage. What would the inherited funds earn for you if they were not used to repay the mortgage? In other words, what net cash flow is foregone if the inherited money is used to repay the mortgage rather than being invested in some other form of investment? If the net cash inflow, net of tax, on the alternative investment is likely to be higher than the net cash outflow, net of tax, on the mortgage, then do not repay the mortgage. You can generate a higher income for yourself by investing the money elsewhere. If you are a higher-rate taxpayer it might be quite difficult to find an investment which generates a higher return net of tax than the mortgage net of tax.

The final factor to consider is a psychological one. Some people do not like to owe large sums of money. The mortgage hangs like an albatross around their necks making their lives a misery. If you fall into this class of borrower, even if your future financial position is sound and better investment opportunities exist elsewhere, it might be wise to repay a substantial part of the mortgage, no matter what the opportunity cost of this decision might be. It will enable you to sleep at nights.

TECHNICAL ASPECTS OF EARLY REPAYMENT

Mortgage lenders place strict conditions on early repayment of a mortgage. There may be a penalty of three or even six months interest to pay if the mortgage is repaid early, particularly if the mortgage is a fixed interest mortgage or if you have been awarded a special discount mortgage. If you are considering repaying your mortgage early check on the exit costs with your lender first. It usually pays to speed up payment rather than to pay the mortgage off in its entirety. As noted above schemes are offered by most lenders that allow you to speed up the repayment of your mortgage.

SWITCHING MORTGAGES

Should you switch your mortgage to another lender if an alternative form of mortgage with more suitable terms becomes available? During the late 1980s it became fashionable in some quarters to switch home mortgages from one company to another as new, more flexible, more predictable or less expensive mortgages came onto the market. Is it sensible to follow this course of action if the opportunity should present itself?

There can be no doubt that financial circumstances change. The best mortgage deal available at the time you took out your mortgage may not be the best deal now. Your personal situation may change; for example you may become divorced or move abroad and rent property in a foreign country or, if you have taken out a variable-interest mortgage, you may decide that a fixed-rate mortgage best suits your future circumstances.

In principle it is a sensible strategy to review your mortgage situation at least once a year. New mortgage products do come onto the market and the outlook for the financial markets are in a constant state of flux.

The trouble with switching mortgages is the cost of the switch. Your home will have to be re-surveyed to satisfy the new lender as to its current value and there will be additional legal costs and a land registry fee. These costs alone can exceed £1000 per switch. There is likely to be a loan arrangement fee that is paid to the lender costing, perhaps, £250. If the existing loan is a fixed-interest loan there are possible early loan repayment penalties of three to six months' interest due to be paid to the existing lender. The costs of a 'mortgage indemnity guarantee' policy to cover the lender's risk on mortgages which make up a high percentage of the house value is another possible cost. The benefits derived from switching to a new mortgage that better matches your needs are thus often cancelled out by the switching costs of £2000 to £5000. It may be, however, that the new lender will pay some of these switching costs on your behalf.

You will need to work out the 'break-even point' of switching mortgages. The break-even point is calculated in months and it tells you how many months must pass after the switch before the savings from the switch repays the switching costs. Some mortgage brokers will work out this break-even point for you.[30]

If you employ a personal financial adviser on a regular basis he or she can keep you up to date on new financial products and if some new mortgage product comes onto the market which better suits your needs then during the annual financial audit of your affairs the PFA should carry out a cost-benefit analysis on the net benefit to you of switching to a more suitable type of mortgage.

Certainly the assumption, popular prior to 1985, that a mortgage taken out with one company is a mortgage for life is no longer valid. If a mortgage provider becomes uncompetitive the mortgage should be switched to another lender just as a car owner switches from one unsatisfactory model to a better one. The increase in mortgage switching after 1985 has greatly improved the competitiveness and therefore the efficiency of the mortgage market in the UK.

The decision to switch depends on the net benefit or cost of the switch to you and whether you are willing, or can afford, to wait long enough for the switching costs to be repaid by the new mortgage. An illustration is provided in Exhibit 6.6.

RAISING A MORTGAGE IN A FOREIGN CURRENCY

In recent years the mortgage market in the UK has become more international. The abolition of exchange control regulations in the UK in October 1979 opened up the UK mortgage market to foreign competition.

Few foreign institutions have taken advantage of this opportunity. Those that have entered the UK market are mainly offering pound sterling mortgages. Foreign currency mortgages make up a very small part of the total mortgage market in Europe: in 1996 less than 0.5% of mortgages were in a foreign currency. However, in the future, as the countries within the EU draw closer together, the option of taking out a

What is the cost of a £2700 loan to be repaid over 18 months? Will the new lender help with these costs? Such questions need to be asked if you are considering switching out of a fixed period mortgage into any other form of mortgage

Suppose you have a 5-year fixed-interest mortgage of £120 000, which is costing you £800 per month. An alternative 5-year fixed-interest mortgage comes onto the market that will only cost you £650 per month. Should you switch to the new fixed-interest mortgage?

It all depends on the cost of the switch. If you switched to the new mortgage, the associated costs would be:

	£
Penalty for early repayment of the first mortgage:	
2-months interest	1600
Legal costs of new mortgage	650
Land registry	100
Loan arrangement fee to broker	350
Total costs of switching	2700
Monthly saving on the new mortgage (£800 – 650)	150
Number of months to the break-even point (£2 700 ÷ 150)	18

The mortgagee can save £150 per month by switching to a cheaper fixed-interest mortgage but the switch is expensive. The borrower must wait for 18 months to recover the cost of the switch. However, since the mortgage has three years to run the switch will save £150 × 36 = £5 400 – 2700 =£2700 over the next 3 years. Can the borrower afford the £2 700 he or she will need to make the switch.

EXHIBIT 6.6: Calculating the break-even point when switching mortgages

mortgage denominated in a currency other than the home currency must be considered. The introduction of a single European currency, the Euro, would simplify matters. This would truly open up the entire EU mortgage market to any financial institution operating within it.

If you peruse the statistical pages of the *Financial Times* you will see that the rate of interest charged on identical loans denominated in different currencies is not the same. Substantial differences in interest rates exist at any one time. Exhibit 6.7 illustrates a typical spread of base interest rates in different currencies at one point in time.

The financially naive homeowner might consider reducing his interest burden by taking out a fixed rate mortgage denominated in that currency offering the lowest rate of interest. From Exhibit 6.7 we see that this currency would have been the Japanese yen in September 1996. This minimum cost strategy suffers from one serious defect. If the loan is taken out in Japanese yen the loan and the interest on the loan will have to be repaid in Japanese yen. This raises the question: 'What will the cost of Japanese yen be in terms of the pound sterling in one year's time, or five years' time, or 20 years' time?' The truth is that no-one knows the answer to this question.

Unless you have access to the foreign currency concerned from some foreign source of income you might be faced with a loan and interest repayment in terms of pound sterling which is 10% or 30% or even 50% higher than if the loan had been taken out in pounds sterling. (See Exhibit 6.8 which compares the cost of a Swiss franc loan with a loan in pound sterling of the same initial value (£100 000).) Initially the Swiss

	Rate of interest %	Cost % difference
Greek drachma	12.85	6.10
Italian lire	10.75	4.00
Spanish pesetas	9.25	2.50
US $	8.25	1.50
Portuguese escudos	7.12	0.37
Belgian francs	7.00	0.25
UK £	**6.75**	0.00
French francs	6.75	0.00
Swedish krone	6.50	−0.25
Danish krone	6.00	−0.75
German Deutschmarks	5.50	−1.25
Dutch guilders	4.25	−2.50
Swiss francs	3.50	−3.25
Japanese yen	1.63	−5.12

Exchange controls were abolished in the UK on 19 October 1979. From that date, UK residents have been able to raise loans in any foreign currency they choose so long as the Central Bank in the foreign country approves the removal of funds for investment in a foreign country. The nominal cost of funds varies a great deal between countries. The difference between the highest and lowest cost in the above table is 11.22%.

The difference in cost represents the markets estimate of the likely future rate of inflation in the two countries. In other words the markets believe that over the next few years the difference in the rate of inflation between Greece and Japan will be 11.22% per year.

The cost of housing loans are likely to be 2% to 9% above the base rates quoted. Whether a UK house buyer should take out a loan in a 'cheaper', or 'more expensive', foreign currency depends on the buyer's estimate of future inflation rates in the two countries. This is a financial decision that is best left to the experts. Foreign interest payments can be hedged using derivatives called 'futures' and 'options' but these only apply over short periods of a few years.

EXHIBIT 6.7: The base rate of interest in 14 countries on 28 September 1996

franc loan is cheaper but later in the loan period the sterling loan becomes cheaper because of changes in the exchange rate between the pound and the Swiss franc.

Loans denominated in a foreign currency are subject to what is called *foreign exchange exposure risk.* Loans denominated in the local currency, that is the currency in which the borrower receives his income, are not subject to foreign exchange exposure risk. The difference in interest rates between otherwise identical loans denominated in different currencies represents the capital markets' best guess as to the likely changes in future exchange rates between the two currencies in the months and years ahead.[31]

Further discussion of this subject would lead us into the choppy waters of international finance, an area that is much too complex to be pursued here.[32]

Financial products called *derivatives*, devices such as forwards, futures and options, are available for hedging the exchange rate risk attached to foreign loans but only experts on derivatives are qualified to advise on the use of these devices. Unless you know of a personal financial adviser who has set himself up as a foreign mortgage expert it is advisable to steer clear of foreign currency loans. Savings can be made by taking out mortgages in a foreign currency and hedging the exposure risk via derivatives but you really need to know what you are doing if you go

Assumed rate of exchange 10 September 19X7		£1 = 2 Swiss francs
Value of mortgage loan in pound sterling	£	100 000
Value of mortgage loan in Swiss francs	swf	200 000
Fixed rate of interest in pound sterling	(% p.a.)	8
Fixed rate of interest in Swiss francs	(% p.a.)	3
Term of loan		10 years

Year	(a) Annual cost of Swiss franc loan in Swiss francs	(b) Assumed actual rate of exchange between SWF and £	(c) Annual cost of Swiss franc loan in £ sterling (a)/(b)
1	23 446	2.0000	£11 723
2	23 446	1.9048	£12 309
3	23 446	1.8032	£13 002
4	23 446	1.7000	£13 792
5	23 446	1.6034	£14 623
6	23 446	1.5129	£15 497
7	23 446	1.4178	£16 537
8	23 446	1.3342	£17 573
9	23 446	1.2557	£18 672
10	23 446	1.1054	£21 210
Total cost	234 460		£154 938

Year	Annual costs of loan in £ sterling
1	14 903
2	14 903
3	14 903
4	14 903
5	14 903
6	14 903
7	14 903
8	14 903
9	14 903
10	14 903
	£149 030

At the beginning of the loan period the Swiss franc loan is cheaper in terms of pounds, but as the rate of exchange between the pound sterling and the Swiss franc changes (the Swiss franc gets stronger against the pound) the balance of advantage switches to the pound sterling loan. The initial interest rate advantage is cancelled out by the fall in the value of the pound against the Swiss franc. Remember that the Swiss franc loan must be repaid in Swiss francs.

EXHIBIT 6.8: The comparative cost of a mortgage taken out in pounds sterling and Swiss francs at current exchange rates

down this path. If you are thinking of buying a property abroad a foreign currency mortgage might be a good buy since financing the purchase of foreign property with pound sterling loans can be expensive.

There is also a further question as to whether the interest on a foreign currency mortgage would be allowed against your UK income tax bill.

If in the future a single European currency becomes a reality, the year 2002 is the projected date, then opportunities might exist prior to this changeover to gain access to cheap mortgage money from currencies offering rates of interest lower than that obtainable in sterling.[33]

IS HOUSING A GOOD INVESTMENT?

We all need a home to live in but is a house a good investment? A home provides us with accommodation but it also provides the owner of the home with a substantial investment together with some other useful benefits; for example a home can be a powerful prestige symbol as well as an index of creditworthiness.

The traditional argument supporting investment in housing is that housing is a *levered* investment. It is easy to raise a loan of, say, 80% on the value of the house you wish to purchase and so if the return on the property exceeds the cost of the mortgage the return, or profit on the eventual sale, is 'levered' upwards. An example is provided in Exhibit 6.9. What the advocates of levered finance forget is that this operation can work in reverse. If the market value of the property falls below the cost of the mortgage you now owe more money to the building society than the value of your home. The state of the housing market in the last decade of the twentieth century does not support the case for using housing as a 'levered' investment.

In Chapter 3 we discussed the role played by real assets in the portfolio of an investor. We commented at the time that most real assets are acquired for reasons other than cash flow. This comment applies to an investment in a house just as much as it does to any other real asset. A house is bought primarily to provide adequate accommodation for the owner and family; the investment aspect of house purchase is usually a secondary consideration. At least it was a secondary consideration prior to 1982 when an important change took place in the attitude of owner-occupiers in the UK. Home owners in the UK began to look upon their owner-occupied homes as an important component in their overall wealth portfolio.

One consequence of this change in our attitude to housing, a change which began to treat housing as an investment, was the spending spree on consumer goods that occurred in the late 1980s. Many home owners, seeing their homes double in value in nominal terms over a two year period, saw no need to save and began to spend a much higher proportion of their income.

As shown in Exhibit 6.10, over the period from 1974 to 1989 the real, inflation-adjusted value of houses rose by anything from 50% in the East

	No mortgage	80% mortgage
The cost of your home	£100 000	£100 000
The sale price of your home	£135 000	£135 000
The profit on the sale	£35 000	£20 000
You invest in your home	£100 000	£35 000
You borrow from a mortgage lender	£0	£80 000
Total amount invested in your home	£100 000	£100 000

The percentage gain on your initial investment is thus

$$\frac{£35\ 000}{£100\ 000} \qquad \frac{£35\ 000}{£20\ 000} \qquad 35\% \qquad 175\%$$

The loan allows you to lever your income in order to buy a more expensive home and also to lever the capital gain on any profit on the sale of that home over the cost price. These figures ignore the effect of inflation and the cost of mortgage interest versus the return you can achieve with the £80 000 you are not investing in your home.

If the sale price of your home should fall below the cost price then the result reverses the above situation. If the sales price is, say, £70 000 then we have what is called a *negative equity* situation. The market value of your home has a value below the repayment value of your mortgage. You will need to find another £10 000 to repay your mortgage if you sell your home.

EXHIBIT 6.9: The leverage effect of using a loan to assist in buying your home

---

Midlands to 100% in Greater London. This rise in value was followed by an equally dramatic fall. House prices in the UK fell, on average, by 25% in real terms between 1989 and 1995. In Cambridge, for example, even nominal house prices fell by a dramatic 30% over this six-year period. So much for the well-known aphorism 'safe as houses'.

We now return to the original question posed at the beginning of this section, namely: 'Is a house a good investment?' We need to look at house prices in the UK over a much longer period of time to answer this question. The boom in house prices in the UK between 1971–74, 1976–78 and 1984–89 and the busts in the intervening years are no basis for a logical discussion of this question.

The first thing to understand when discussing changes in house prices is that it is not the house that alters in price but the land on which the house is built. House prices act as a proxy for land prices. In July 1989 the average house price in London cost 2.3 times as much as the same size of house in Yorkshire yet the cost of building the house in London was only 30% more than the cost of building the same house in Yorkshire.[34] The real difference lay in the cost of buying the land on which the house was built. It is a sudden scarcity of building land that drives up house prices, not the cost of building houses.[35]

Exhibit 6.11 shows the selling price of the average house in London and Yorkshire over the period from 1973 to 1996. It shows why so many home owners in the UK believed themselves to be seriously rich by 1989. The nominal value of their homes had risen by a factor of 12 over the period. However, this belief was based on an illusion. The increase

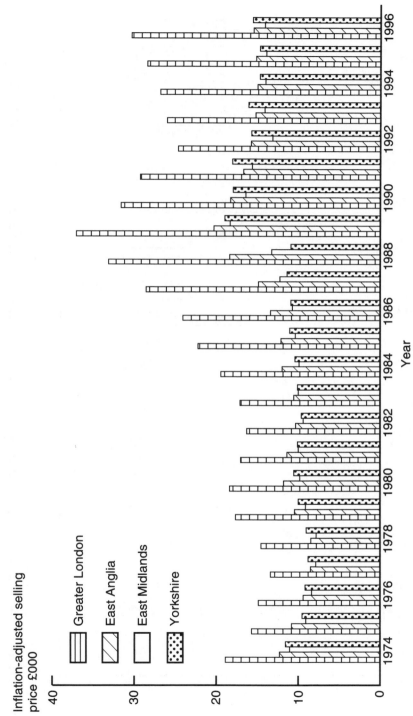

Inflation-adjusted selling price £000

Legend:
- Greater London
- East Anglia
- East Midlands
- Yorkshire

Year

EXHIBIT 6.10: The movement of inflation - adjusted average house prices in four regions of the UK, 1974–96

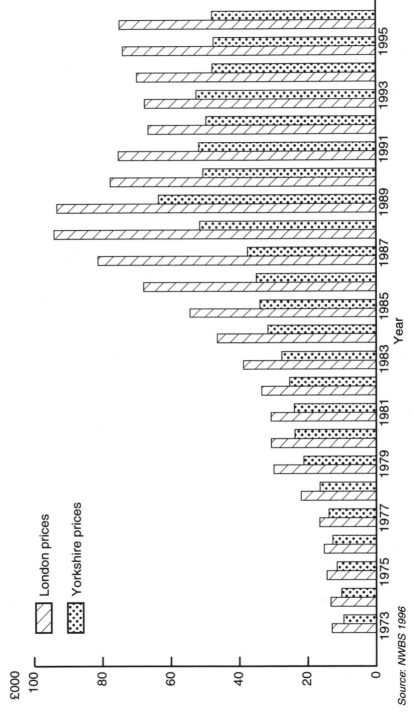

Source: NWBS 1996

EXHIBIT 6.11: The average market value of house prices in the London region and Yorkshire, 1973–95

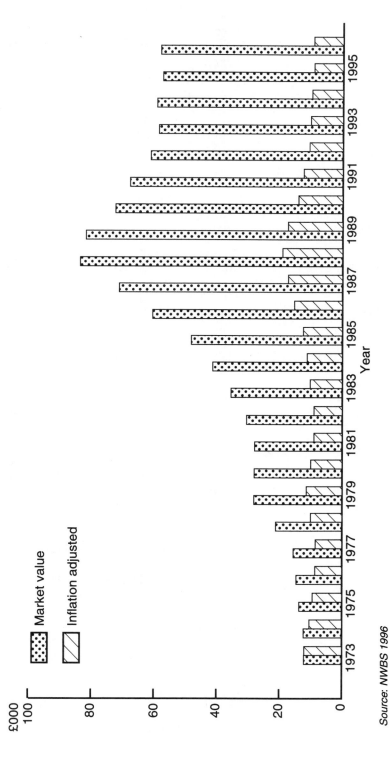

Source: NWBS 1996

EXHIBIT 6.12: The market value versus the inflation-adjusted value of home prices (mordern properties) in London, 1973–96

	£200 000 5 bedroom house	£100 000 3 bedroom house	£50 000 2 bedroom flat
Monthly costs (£)			
Maintenance cost	167	100	63
Mortgage cost	1 561	781	390
Renting agency cost	120	72	48
Total monthly cost (£)	1 848	953	501
Monthly capital at 7%	1 167	583	292
appreciation (in at 3%	500	250	125
nominal terms) at 0%	0	0	0
Assumed monthly rent £	1 000	600	400
Total monthly income (£) (rent plus capital appreciation)			
Appreciation: at 7%	2 167	1 183	692
at 3%	1 500	850	525
at 0%	1 000	600	400
Monthly surplus			
at 7%	319	231	191
capital at 3%	−348	−103	24
at 0%	−848	−353	−101
Nominal return (% per **annum)**	%	%	%
at 7%	1.9	2.8	4.6
at 3%	−2.1	−1.2	0.6
at 0%	−5.1	−4.2	−2.4

The return on rented accommodation is highly sensitive to the current rate of interest on the mortgage used to finance the purchase. However, the above figures show that it is difficult to make an adequate return on rented accommodation compared to the other forms of investment discussed in Chapter 2.

Note that rent is not a constant proportion of the market value of the house. Small value flats and houses can be rented for a proportionately much higher rent than expensive houses except in the centre of large cities.

EXHIBIT 6.13: The nominal return on rented accommodation

mostly reflected a fall in the value of money over the period. The average real value of a house in both London and Yorkshire in 1993 was actually below the real value in 1973.

An important factor in understanding the true trend in house price change is to understand the impact of inflation, the falling value of money, on house values. Exhibit 6.12 shows the nominal value of the average house in London over the period 1973 to 1996 and compares this value to the real, inflation adjusted, value in the same years. Note that the nominal value of the average house rose from £3000 in 1970 to £52 000 in 1990, a rise of almost 17 times the 1970 value yet once the figures are adjusted for inflation the rise is a mere 30% and by 1993 this rise in real value had fallen to 20% and, as previously noted, was actually below the 1973 value.

Inflation in recent years has done much to propagate the myth of housing as a golden investment. In fact the real benefit to house owners in Britain during the 1970s and 1980s was not the rise in house values but the destruction by inflation of the value of the mortgage which had financed the purchase of the house in the first place. The ratio of the nominal value of housing in the UK to the nominal value of UK mortgages financing those houses rose dramatically between 1970 and 1990 because of the fall by over 80% in the real, inflation-adjusted, value of the mortgages over the period. This rise was not compensated for by higher interest rates.

We have already discussed the impact of high inflation on interest rates. Mortgage interest rates fail to compensate fully for inflation during periods of high inflation so the real interest rate tends to fall in inflationary periods, dragging down the real value of the mortgage with it. The capital gains generated by home ownership have been much exaggerated.

CALCULATING THE RETURN ON HOUSING AS AN INVESTMENT

The best way to evaluate housing as an investment is to look at the return on a house that is rented out and yet continuously maintained in its original prime condition by the owner.

Exhibit 6.13 sets out the estimated return on renting out a series of homes of various size. The return on the home is calculated by estimating the rent received from the tenant plus or minus the capital increase or decrease in the value of the home during the year. In this case we also consider the cost of maintaining the home in good condition and the fee to the renting agent.

Exhibit 6.13 shows that if we ignore the capital appreciation on the value of the house then the return on a large house, treated simply as an investment, is very poor. In other words a large house in the UK is only a worthwhile investment if it is expected to attract a substantial tax free capital gain during the period of ownership. Over the long period from

1945 to 1993 the average increase in detached house prices in the UK was just under 2% per annum in real terms.[36]

Even when the net return on renting the house is added to this figure the return is still far short of the return of 7% to 9% gross of tax achieved by ordinary shares over the same period. Only the small two bedroomed flat provided an adequate return. The return on the small flat is superior because rental returns show that a small flat can be rented at a higher fraction of its market value than can a larger detached house in most regions of the UK.

We conclude that, so far as financial return is concerned, housing is a poor investment easily surpassed by many other types of financial and real assets.

OTHER ATTRIBUTES OF HOUSING AS AN INVESTMENT

What about all of those other characteristics of investment that we discussed in Chapter 2? How does housing shape up? Not too well, I think.

Housing is illiquid, it generates high buying and selling costs, and the protection and maintenance costs of housing are high except for the basic insurance cost which is low relative to the value invested. A house is not normally transportable, it is geographically fixed on one site. We conclude that these other attributes of a house, except for basic insurance cost, are all negative. The only positive characteristics associated with housing as an investment are the many, but diminishing, tax advantages attached to housing plus the possibility of a stable cash flow if, and only if, the owner finds that prize beyond price, a good tenant.

We conclude that housing is a poor investment. This opinion is shared by financial analysts in most other countries of the world. There are a few exceptions to this rule, such as property sited in some city centres and property on islands with limited space available for housing (Singapore and Hong Kong spring to mind) but such prime housing sites are few and far between.

The ownership of a house can provide the owner with several useful advantages but investment is not one of them. Housing should be avoided if it is to be used solely as an investment. The acquisition of a house for the purpose of accommodation is obviously essential, but the house need not be bought – it could be rented.

BUY OR RENT? A SECOND LOOK

The proportion of people who own their own homes in the UK, at 67% in 1995, is higher than in almost all the other countries of the world. There are several reasons for this high proportion of home ownership in the UK but the limited availability of rented accommodation is, without doubt, a major contributing factor. The lack of private rented accommodation in the UK (only 10% of homes in the UK are privately rented) stems from the poor legal treatment of those who own and rent property and the poor image presented of such persons by the media. If we add to these negative aspects of renting the fact that housing is a poor investment compared to the many alternative investment outlets available then it is not surprising that so few houses are privately rented in the UK compared to other countries. The fault lies with the limited supply of rented property rather than with the lack of demand for such property.

The lack of rented accommodation in the UK is unfortunate since many of us find ourselves in situations where renting a home would be a much better option than buying a home. If a person moves job location frequently, particularly if he moves abroad, renting is the better option. If a house-seeker lacks sufficient capital to buy a home then acquiring a rented property is a simple alternative. Many older people would benefit financially if they could release capital by selling their home and renting a similar property. A high proportion of the wealth of many retired persons is tied up in their homes. Such people can be wealthy but with a poor regular cash flow. Asset rich, cash poor.

The major advantage of renting a home is that you do not need to invest such a high proportion of your total wealth in a single asset, your home. In Chapter 2 we noted the financial advantages which can flow from diversifying your wealth portfolio between different kinds of assets. By diversifying your wealth over many different kinds of assets you remove the specific risk attached to holding one particular asset.

Another major advantage of renting is that it transfers the cost of maintaining the property away from the occupier and onto the owner of the property.

We noted above that investment in property provides a poor return to the investor unless substantial profits can be made from capital gains. If we return to Exhibit 6.10, which illustrates the rise in real house prices in four regions of the UK between 1974 to 1995, we find that capital gains on house values in the UK are less spectacular than is popularly supposed. If the opportunity cost of the investment in property is taken into account (what can you earn with the money in alternative investments?) then renting is the cheaper option in many cases. What we mean by this is that if the return on the money the renter is *not* investing in the property he or she occupies is deducted from the rent paid to the owner of the property then the renter-occupier is paying remarkably little for the privilege of living in the property. The current levels of rent charged in many regions of the UK do not include a proper charge for the cost of the funds invested by the owner in the home he is renting out.

All of these curious anomalies in the UK housing market stem from the unsubstantiated belief that housing values in the UK are sure to outpace inflation in future years. All of the evidence available at present in the late 1990s suggests the contrary to be the case. The proportion of young people in the population, those who buy homes, is falling and, as shown by Exhibit 5.2(a) in Chapter 5, the proportion of older people in the population, that is those who sell homes, is rising. A study by the Joseph Rowntree foundation published in July 1994 found that by the year 1999 around 200 000 homes a year will be coming onto the UK housing market, sold by the inheritors of property from deceased parents. The value of these homes will be in the region of £20 billion per year. Consumption will rise, house prices will fall.

We appear to be facing a diminishing demand for homes and an increasing supply of homes in the future. This is not a recipe for rising prices.

Renting should not be automatically dismissed as an inferior option to buying. In every case where home acquisition is being considered the cost of renting should be compared with the cost of buying in the context of your particular situation. Most house-seekers will probably continue to buy their homes because of the security it provides but many more should rent than do so at present. The economics of the case currently favours renting over buying.

PROPERTY AND CREDIT

In Chapter 9 we will be discussing the question of raising short-term credit from lenders. The ownership of a home is a most important determinant of creditworthiness. In order to gain access to credit you will need to persuade the lender that you are a good credit risk. If you own rather than rent your home then credit is easier to obtain. The cost of credit based on the security of a house or flat is likely to be much cheaper than credit loaned without such sound security.

This is one of the benefits flowing from home ownership that is often overlooked. The value of this advantage depends on how much credit you are seeking and how often. If you never borrow to buy then it is of no benefit to you. If you borrow consumer loans, on average, of £10 000 per year, your improved creditworthiness might be worth £600 to £800 a year to you.

BUY–RENT SWITCHING

As we noted above, there were some wild oscillations in both the nominal and real value of houses in the UK between 1970 and 1996. These swings in house value have persuaded some sophisticated investors to switch from renting to buying and then back again every few years. This technique is called rent–buy switching.

If house prices are depressed, as in 1994, these investors buy. When house prices move above the long-term trend, as in 1989, they sell at a profit and rent until the housing cycle hits bottom in 1994 when they again buy.

We suspect that few householders, particularly the married variety, would be willing to take this trouble just to maximize their property income. The cost of switching can be quite high – some £3000 to £7000 a switch. These switching costs may well cancel out the capital profits arising from the switch. However it is claimed that substantial profits *can* be made by following a rent–buy switching strategy.

We suspect that the strategy worked between 1970 and 1995 because of the wild gyration in UK house prices over this period but that this strategy is now redundant. The future house-price cycle is likely to be much flatter than in the past.

THE COST OF MAINTAINING THE HOME

So far our discussion of housing economics has been confined to buying or renting a home but there is another aspect of housing economics that is just as important but is rarely discussed, namely the cost of maintaining your home in pristine condition once you have acquired it.

We noted in Chapter 3 that the maintenance and protection cost of an asset may be an important attribute of that asset when viewed as an investment.

The major components of house maintenance are insurance, structural repairs, interior decoration, drainage and the dreaded subsidence. The annual cost of insuring a house against fire and structural damage excluding subsidence is very low: normally the annual premium is well below 1% of the current market value of the house. The geographical differences in the cost of insuring these risks are much less than they are with contents insurance. Insuring for landslip is normally low but the cost can be very high if your house is sited in an area that is notorious for subsidence. Insurance companies now target subsidence all the way down to the right hand digits in your postal code.

If you own a house which was built in Edwardian times or before with much ornamental decoration you may find that the insurance company insists on insuring the house for a value well in excess of its current market value. The insurance company has to cover itself against the high cost of replacing these stone filaments and Dutch mouldings which give so much character to your home.

Estimates of the cost of rebuilding your home are prepared annually by the Royal Institute of Chartered Surveyors for the ABI. The estimates take into account the age, size and type of your home and its geographical location in the UK.

Exhibit 6.14 provides a sample of the data provided in these estimates. This particular Table allows a home-owner to estimate the current cost of rebuilding a detached house in various parts of the country if it should, for example, be destroyed by fire. The cost of *contents insurance* varies quite dramatically between different regions of the country (see Exhibit 7.2 in Chapter 7). In some areas of the country burglary is such a frequent event that contents insurance cannot be obtained at any cost.

In addition to property and contents insurance, a mortgage lender who provides a repayment-style loan will require that the mortgagee takes out a *mortgage protection policy* to cover the risk of the borrower dying before the loan is repaid. This might cost you around £20 to £80 a month in addition to your mortgage costs. The insurance will be of the decreasing-term type. This is relatively cheap and protects your dependants.

Another more recent type of mortgage insurance is called *payment protection insurance*. This insures you against the risk that you cannot pay your monthly mortgage payments because of illness or loss of job. Since income support on mortgage payments is now held back for several months by government edict you would be wise to take out this form of insurance unless you are seriously rich. The cost is around £6 a month for each £100 of interest payment.

Mortgage indemnity guarantee insurance (MIG) is another form of mortgage insurance that is often misunderstood. If you apply for a mortgage of a value above 75% of the value of the house you are buying then the lender may well insist that you take out a mortgage indemnity guarantee insurance policy. This insurance policy protects the *lender* against the risk that you may not be able to repay the mortgage loan out of the proceeds of the sale of your home. It does not protect you from having your home repossessed. You still have to repay the balance of the mortgage if the sale value of your home falls below the value of your mortgage when you sell your home. In recent years, after the house price fall of 1989 to 1995, many homeowners were shocked to find this fact out only after they sold their home for less than the outstanding value of the mortgage secured on the home. They found themselves liable for the unpaid balance.

The annual cost of an MIG policy can rise to £6 per £100 of the excess of the mortgage value over 75% of the house value. For example the cost of an MIG policy for a £90 000 mortgage on a £100 000 house could be £75 a month, ((£90 000 − 75 000) x 0.06) ÷ 12. The MIG cost on a 100% mortgage on the same house might rise as high as £230 a month.

Repairs and maintenance

The cost of maintaining a house in good condition is very high relative to the cost of maintaining most other assets in good condition. It is determined by many factors: climate, the type of soil on which the house is built, the behaviour of the occupants, pollution levels, neighbourhood characteristics and so forth. However even with a good climate, soil, behaviour and other factors the average annual cost of repairs and maintenance is likely to be much higher than the owner believes it to be.

The cost of maintaining your house in good condition is generally overlooked when personal financial budgets are being constructed. These costs are irregular but very substantial when they do arise.

The best way to finance house maintenance is to set up a *maintenance equalization fund* into which a regular payment is made and out of which

Detached house	Region	Large (£)	%	Percent cost of post-1980 house	Medium	Percent cost of post-1980 house	Small	Average
Pre-1920	London	74	100	128	79	139	80	78
	SE England	65	88		70		70	68
	East Anglia	62	84		66		66	65
	Other	59	80		63		64	62
1920–45	London	71	100	122	74	130	76	74
	SE England	62	87		65		67	65
	East Anglia	49	83		83		63	61
	Other	47	80		51		52	50
1946–79	London	59	100	102	64	112	65	63
	SE England	52	88		56		57	55
	East Anglia	49	83		53		54	52
	Other	47	80		51		52	50
1980 onwards	London	58	100	100	57	100	62	59
	SE England	51	88		50		54	52
	East Anglia	48	83		48		51	49
	Other	46	79		46		49	47

Rebuilding cost per square foot

Note that the cost of rebuilding a house in the South-East of England is about 25% more than in other parts of the UK. The cost of buying a house in South-England is usually substantially more than 25% above that for a similar house elsewhere in the UK. The difference is accounted for by the cost of land. Land suitable for building is much more expensive per hectare in the South-East of England.

To use the table, measure the length and breadth of your house from the outside. Multiply these figures together to find the area of the ground floor. If there are two storeys multiply the figure by two. For a three-storey house you need only add $\frac{3}{4}$ of the area of the third story.

Consider, for example, the case of a two-storey medium-sized house in London built in 1960.

Ground area: 25 × 25 = 625 square feet
Multiply this by two: 625 × 2 = 1250 square feet
Multiply this square footage by £64: 1250 × £64 = £80 000.

This is the estimated cost of rebuilding the house, not the value you would receive if you tried to sell the house. The selling price includes the value of the land on which the house is built.

This sample of costs is taken from tables prepared by the Building Cost information service.

EXHIBIT 6.14: Estimate of the cost of rebuilding a detached house in various regions of the UK (1995)

the maintenance costs will be paid. If you do not regularly maintain your house in a systematic way the quality of the fabric can deteriorate to a point where a second mortgage may have to be raised to bring the fabric back up to good condition.

What is the annual cost of maintaining your house in as good a condition as when you bought it? You might like to make a guess before you read the next paragraph. A realistic figure is very substantial and will shock many home owners. The figure for regular annual maintenance cannot be expressed as a percentage of current market value of the house since, as we noted above, this figure varies a great deal from year to year while the cost of maintenance rises steadily with inflation. An approximate estimate of the annual cost of maintaining an older house or flat with in good condition in 1996 is given below:[37]

5 bedrooms	£2 000 per annum
4 bedrooms	£1 500
3 bedrooms	£1 200
2 bedrooms	£750
1 bedroom	£500

From this table you will see that if you own a four-bedroomed house and you wish to set up a maintenance fund to ensure that you can afford to pay out the irregular maintenance costs when they become due you need to accumulate a fund that will produce £1500, net of tax, each year. If you are paying tax at a marginal rate of 25% on your investment income the fund needs to earn £2000 a year gross of tax to generate £1500 a year net of tax. If the fund can earn 8% gross of tax the level value of the fund would need to be 2000 ÷ 0.08 = £25 000 to meet these requirements – and we are ignoring the impact of inflation on repair costs.

We suspect that most owners of four bedroomed houses would be shocked if they realized that after buying and financing the house and contents for, say, £150 000 they need to set aside an additional amount of this magnitude just for maintenance but this is the only safe policy, otherwise financial pressures are likely to persuade them to let the fabric of the house deteriorate – which, in the long run, will cost them a good deal more than the annual £1500 cost of maintaining the fund intact.

Note that if the house is rented the landlord, not the tenant, must meet the cost of setting up the equalization fund.

CONCLUSIONS ABOUT ACQUIRING A HOME

The prime consideration in acquiring accommodation is to find a suitable home at a price you can afford without putting undue strain on your financial resources. This means that you need to select a financing plan suited to your estimated future cash flow.

Investment considerations, that is the risk-return mix on your house treated as an investment, should be awarded a secondary role in your analysis. You should avoid tying up too high a proportion of your total wealth (equity) in this one asset. A lopsided wealth portfolio will breach the diversification principle discussed in Chapter 2. You can initially reduce the proportion of your total wealth that is invested in housing by taking on a substantial mortgage, but later, as the mortgage is repaid, the proportion of your wealth invested in housing will increase.

Contrary to popular belief, housing is a poor investment. The returns available on housing in the UK over the last 50 years or so, despite it being a levered investment, do not justify the risks involved in investing in housing. Renting out a second home is simply not an economic proposition. There may be some excellent reasons for you owning a second home, but investment is not one of them.

Investment in housing has proved to be a reasonably good hedge against inflation over the years but no better than many other investments such as equity shares. It would be unwise to assume that substantial capital profits can be made on an investment in housing in the future. Current socio-economic trends do not support such a strategy. An ageing population will be selling houses, net, rather than buying them. Current socio-economic trends suggest relatively stable house prices in real inflation-adjusted terms for many years ahead.

Renting a home should not be automatically dismissed as an inferior option to buying. At current levels of rent, renting a home is a cheap option if the return on the capital *not* invested in the rented home is taken into the calculation. Renting is only an inferior option if the large capital profits flowing to house owners in the 1980s are repeated in the future. This is most improbable.

Whether you should rent or buy depends primarily on your likely future lifestyle and your desire for security. The investment return on the purchase of a house should be treated as a secondary consideration.

Renting is the favoured option in Europe and may well be adopted as the favoured option in the UK if housing law in the EU is standardized.

In the recent past the only real economic advantage accruing to housing as an investment has arisen from the very favourable tax benefits attached to owner-occupation. Benefits such as the fact that the interest on housing loans on the first home up to £30 000 is paid net of tax at 15% and that capital gains on the sale of a first home are not subject to tax. How many of these benefits will survive a more integrated EU tax system remains to be seen. The tax allowance on mortgage interest is being gradually phased out.

A house provides many benefits to the owner of the house such as security, prestige and creditworthiness, but a good investment return is not high on this list of benefits.

SUMMARY

1. The investment in your home is likely to be by far the most important investment you will ever make in your life. It is therefore worthwhile expending some thought on the maximum price you can afford to pay for your home and the method you should use to finance the purchase – if you decide to purchase.

2. Since the value of housing has fluctuated widely in every region of the UK in recent years we should abandon the expression 'safe as houses'.

3. If you decide to buy a house it is likely to be financed by a mortgage. Many different kinds of mortgage are offered to the house buyer. Traditionally the two basic types offered have been the repayment mortgage and the interest-only mortgage. The repayment mortgage is simple to understand and relatively safe. The endowment mortgage form of the interest-only mortgage 'bundles' house financing together with a saving and investment plan. Whether or not 'bundling' of financial products is a financially efficient technique is a matter of some controversy. The 'with-profits' endowment mortgage has fallen out of favour in recent years although it is still the most popular form of mortgage. Many other types of tax-efficient interest-only mortgages are now on offer, such as PEP mortgages and pension mortgages.

4. In the past most loan providers charged the borrower a variable rate of interest linked to the current market rate of interest. Today many loan providers are offering mortgages at a fixed rate of interest for shorter periods of time in addition to the long-term variable rate mortgage. If the current market rate of interest is well below the historical trend line for interest rates then the fixed-rate mortgage might be the cheaper option. We should always remember that a fixed-rate mortgage allows for accurate cash budgeting.

5. In the past, high inflation rates in the UK have destroyed the real value of mortgages over a few years. This fact, together with the many tax advantages linked to housing finance, encouraged many house buyers to take on a housing loan well in excess of what they could really afford. This situation has now changed dramatically. The rate of inflation and expectations about inflation in the UK have now fallen to a much lower figure than in the past. You should not take on a mortgage which exceeds a third of your monthly net cash flow.

6. Many of the traditional approaches to housing finance are changing. The conventional period of 25 years to repay a mortgage may today be much too long a period considering current financial conditions.

Fixed interest mortgages are now widely available and may often be preferable to variable rate mortgages. Switching mortgages from one lender to another in mid-term is quite a common practice and 'covered' mortgages denominated in a foreign currency are now used by some house buyers in the UK. Housing finance has become much more sophisticated in recent years providing opportunities for you to cut your housing costs but you must know what you are doing in each and every case or you could lose heavily.

7. Housing has seldom proved to be a good investment in the long term in the UK or elsewhere, although there have been periods when spectacular profits have been made by house trading, an example being in the UK between 1984 and 1989. If, in the future, the rise in house prices simply matches inflation then renting rather than buying a home may become as fashionable in the UK as it was in nineteenth century England and is currently in Continental Europe. Renting is probably cheaper than buying in the UK in the 1990s but ownership of a house provides other benefits apart from it being an investment. These benefits include security, status and greater creditworthiness.

8. The cost of maintaining a house in good condition is much higher than most owners think. The full cost of maintaining a house in good condition over many years is often overlooked until the owner wishes to sell it. Rather than be financially embarrassed by sudden large expenditures on home maintenance it is wise to set up a *maintenance equalization fund* to equalize the annual cost of maintaining your home over the years.

TEST YOUR KNOWLEDGE

1. If your house is financed by a 20-year endowment mortgage, approximately what percentage of the mortgage will be repaid after 10 years?

2. *With-profits* endowment mortgages have become somewhat less popular in recent years. Why do you think this is?

3. What is a *bundled* financial product? Give an example. Why do financial institutions sell bundled products? Why might you find a bundled product to be less efficient than if each product were bought separately?

4. What is a *unit-trust linked* endowment mortgage? How does it work? Are there any advantages associated with holding a unit trust linked mortgage compared to holding a conventional *with-profits* endowment mortgage?

5. Why do lenders usually prefer to offer you a variable-rate mortgage rather than a fixed-rate mortgage? Why do you think it is that fixed-rate mortgages are usually offered for much shorter periods than variable-rate mortgages?

6. Can you think of any advantages that a fixed-rate mortgage might offer you over a variable (floating) rate mortgage?

7. In the early 1990s the newspapers were constantly talking about the 'negative equity situation' in the housing market? What is 'negative equity'? Why do you think it was that, in the UK in December 1993, 2 000 000 house owners were in a 'negative equity situation'? Why is it so difficult to get out of such a situation?

8. Why does the expected future rate of inflation affect the variable mortgage rate of interest? Why might the expected future inflation rate also affect your decision as to the period over which a mortgage should be repaid?

9. Suppose you have been paying off a 25-year repayment mortgage with a variable interest rate over the last 10 years. An offer of a five-year fixed rate mortgage comes on the market at a lower rate than you are currently paying on the variable rate mortgage. How do you calculate whether or not you should switch to the fixed rate mortgage?

10. Investment in housing may offer you certain tax advantages over investing in many other types of assets. What are these advantages?

11. Suppose you are moving house to Leeds in Yorkshire from Bristol. You can sell your Bristol house for £220 000 leaving you £100 000 after the mortgage and other expenses are paid off. An estate agent in Leeds offers you a house costing £220 000 in Leeds. However this unfurnished house can also be rented by you for three years at £900 per month plus rates. You know that, on average, you are moved every three years in your job. Would you buy the house in Leeds or rent it for the three years?

12. Your gross family income is approximately £30 000 a year. Net of all deductions such as tax and pension contribution this income provides, on average, a net cash flow of £21 000 a year. You would like to buy a house for £150 000. You have a deposit of £15 000 available. Can you afford to take out a £135 000 repayment mortgage to buy the house if the current cost of the mortgage is £9000 per year net of tax?

13. You are 33 years old, unmarried and work in selling bonds in the City of London. You have a gross of tax income of £60 000 per year.

Your net cash flow after deductions is £40 000 per year. You would like to buy an up-market two-bedroomed flat in Islington, London for £200 000. You will need an £180 000 mortgage to buy the flat. You calculate that the interest on this mortgage, net of tax on the first £30 000, plus life insurance, is £1800 a month. You tell the Boomtime Property Company, which is selling the flat, that you cannot afford it at the present price. The Boomtime Property Company, which is having difficulty selling these new hi-tech flats, makes you the following offer: 'You pay half the flat cost now and take half the equity. In three years time you buy the remaining half as valued by an independent valuer. Meanwhile you pay us £500 per month rent for the half of the flat we own.' Discuss the merits and risks of this deal. Would you take it on?

14. Do you think that housing will be a good investment over the next 20 years? If so, why? If not, why not?

15. We noted in the above chapter that over the last 15 years or so some 'city types' have moved between buying and renting property in the City of London every few years. If you decided to follow this strategy what criteria would you use for deciding when to sell and move to rented property and when to buy back?

16. If the cost of building a detached house in London is only 30% higher than the cost of building the same detached house in Yorkshire, why is the cost of the detached house in London 75% higher than the identical detached house in Yorkshire?

17. Let us suppose that you bought a five-bedroomed detached house in Yorkshire in 1971 for £20 000. The purchase was financed with a 100% mortgage. In 1989 this house was sold for £200 000. If the value of money fell by 80% over this period what was the ratio of house value to mortgage value in 1971 and 1989? What was the nominal and real profit on the sale of the house?

18. Suppose that you own a house in Cambridge that cost you £200 000 in 1985 and is now worth £250 000. It was valued at £350 000 in 1989. You have taken out a £150 000 variable interest repayment mortgage on this house the current cost of which is 8% per annum gross of tax.

    You read in the *Investor's Chronicle* that 10-year fixed-interest mortgages in Swiss Francs are now offered to UK residents by a Swiss Bank in Zurich at a gross rate of only 4% per annum. The interest, up to a limit of £30 000, would still be allowable against your income tax as with the UK loan.

    Do you think it would be wise to switch from the current variable interest sterling loan at 8% to the 10-year Swiss Franc fixed rate loan at 4%. What precautions would you need to take?

19. You are offered a choice between investing £200 000 in a house in London that can be rented for £1500 a month or investing it in a fixed-interest government stock paying 8% per annum. The stock is due to be repaid at par in the year 2010. Which do you consider to be the better investment?

20. You would like a 100% mortgage to buy a house costing £100 000. You are told by the lender that you must take out a mortgage indemnity insurance (MIG) policy covering 25% of the mortgage value before the loan is granted. What is an MIG policy and why must you beware of such policies?

21. What would be the approximate value of a maintenance equalization fund, the income from which would be used to keep a two-bedroomed flat worth £100 000 in mint condition? Assume that you pay tax at a marginal rate of 40% and that the fund can earn 5% per annum.

NOTES

1. See the *Sunday Telegraph*, 13 November 1994.

2. An *accessible asset* is an asset that can be sold if a buyer can be found for it. Examples of such assets might include houses, company shares and jewellery. The current value of an employee's pension rights and many whole of life assurance policies are not 'accessible' assets under this definition. It might be more correct to say that these assets are only accessible to the owner at an unacceptably high cost.

3. Between 31 March 1994 and 2 October 1995 the annual cost net of tax of the average house mortgage rose by £900 or 27%, from £3400 per year to £4300 per year because of tax benefit reduction, rising interest rates and increased cost of insurance cover.

4. In 1993 a home owner with a mortgage of £30 000 would have saved around £50 a month in income tax. By 1995 this amount had been reduced to only £30 a month.

5. Tax relief for mortgage interest arose because, at one time, home owners were charged an imputed income for owning a home. They were presumed to be renting the home to themselves! It seemed logical to allow mortgage interest as tax relief against this imputed income. When tax on home ownership was abolished, the government should really have abolished tax relief on mortgage interest at the same time. It did not. The government feared the political repercussions.

6. Take legal advice on whether the home should be 'held in common' between husband and wife or 'shared'. This has inheritance tax implications.

7. *Nationwide Anglia Quarterly Housing Report,* March 1996.

8. There are two kinds of repayment mortgage. The first type is called a *gross profile mortgage* and the second a *constant repayment mortgage.* With the second you pay the same amount over the entire period of the mortgage unless the interest rate or tax rate changes. You probably have a constant repayment mortgage.

9. Yet 60% of mortgages in the UK in 1996 were still of the endowment type whereas 30% were of the repayment type.

10. The endowment mortgage could result in a lower cash flow when the interest rate is very low. However the tax advantages of the endowment mortgage are being gradually whittled away by the Government.

11. But not, normally, to an owner who is not occupying the premises or to the owner of a second home that is not rented.

12. Even if the borrower lacks sufficient income to receive the tax allowance the payment is still reduced by an amount equivalent to the tax allowance under a system called MIRAS (Mortgage Interest Relief At Source). Otherwise, it is claimed, the situation would be inequitable between high-income earners, low-income earners and non-income earners.

13. The performance of 'with profits' funds have varied a great deal between insurance companies. In 1996 the best fund on both 25-year and 10-year funds were 50% higher than the worst. See *Money Marketing* for regular updates on endowment fund performance. *Money Marketing* covers around 80% of the market.

14. The insurance company will sometimes guarantee to repay the mortgage even if the terminal fund is not sufficient, but under these circumstances the borrower would have found it cheaper overall to have taken out a repayment mortgage in the first place.

15. The value of the insurance fund is also known, or can be estimated, but the value is very dependent on the performance of the fund during last few years before the endowment policy terminates.

16. It may not be wise for a newly married couple to take out such a policy since the initial mortgage may be based on the wages of both parties and if the wife becomes pregnant and has to leave work the

mortgage payment begins to rise just as family income falls. The popular press have dubbed such policies *kamikaze* policies.

17. You can get out of a pension mortgage but it may prove to be an expensive move.

18. Three of the better-known mortgage brokers are John Charcol, Blyth McKenna and Chase de Vere.

19. At the time of writing the members were Allchurches Life Assurance, Carlyle Life, Stalwart Assurance and Home and Capital Trust.

20. Budget speech by the Chancellor of the Exchequer, Kenneth Clarke, November 1993.

21. Nationwide Anglia Building Society house price index, June 1989.

22. In 1989 no less than 22% of all mortgages in the UK were 100% mortgages. By 1993 this figure had fallen to 11%. (BSA figures.)

23. Currently up to £6 per £100 of mortgage in excess of 75% of the value of the house.

24. The rate of increase in the variable mortgage rate has not compensated the lender for inflation in the past. It might do so in the future. Lenders can learn too.

25. The keys of the old home should never be released to the buyer until you have confirmed from your solicitor that the cash from the old home is sitting safely in the solicitor's bank account. (And do you hold insurance against your solicitor going bankrupt?)

26. The real rate of interest is the nominal rate adjusted for inflation. For example, if the nominal rate is 12% after tax and the rate of inflation is 5% the real rate is approximately 7.4%. Academic studies have shown that over long periods of time the nominal rate has not risen sufficiently to compensate for *unexpected* bursts of inflation, therefore the real rate tends to fall when inflation is high.

27. The real rate is the nominal rate you pay minus the rate of inflation. If the nominal rate is 8% and the rate of inflation is 3% the real rate is:

$$(1 + 0.08) \div (1 + 0.03) - 1 = 0.0485 = 4.85\%.$$

28. This scheme currently has an entry cost of £195 plus an annual management fee of £6.

29. It depends on the kind of repayment mortgage.

30. For example Blyth McKenna, the mortgage brokers, will provide you with a computer printout giving the future date when the break-even point occurs (if it occurs).

31. See McRae T. (1996) *International Business Finance,* John Wiley, Chichester, Chapter 3 for a discussion of the problem.

32. A correct analysis of the loan discussed here would involve discounting the amounts to be paid to the beginning of year one, a discussion of the tax situation and a calculation of the cost of derivative cover.

33. We assume that the mortgage repayment period would extend far beyond the date of the introduction of the single currency. This potential saving will not be available if financial markets are efficient since the benefit would be discounted into the current rates.

34. Source: *Nationwide Building Society Quarterly Bulletin,* December 1989.

35. In 1989 the average price of land in England was £426 000 per hectare. By 1992 this value had fallen to £337 000 a hectare, a fall of 23% in only 4 years. See figures from *Estates Gazette,* 13 August 1994.

36. Calculated by the author, in association with Ms Fang Dong, from data supplied by the Nationwide Anglia Building Society.

37. The figures were approximated by a large estate agent that manages many houses for rent while their owners are abroad.

Managing the hazards of life: insurance

7

MANAGING RISK

Life is a risky business. We all face many hazards every day: death or serious illness, the loss of a well-paid job, the destruction of the family home by fire or flood or subsidence, the theft of valuable possessions plus a host of less serious calamities face us at all times. Fortunately these events rarely affect most of us. The question we will attempt to answer in this chapter is: 'How should we handle these risks that are ever present in our everyday life?'

Risk management is currently *the* major concern of the business world. In 1996 over five trillion US dollars passed through the world's swap and derivatives markets. All of this money was expended on reducing business risk.

Reducing the risks attached to future events is as important to the individual as it is to directors of companies. A well-designed personal financial plan must aim to reduce personal risk to a minimum and in certain cases to eliminate the risk altogether. The basic idea in risk management, whether the technique is applied in a business context or by an individual, is to identify the key risks and *hedge* them.

THE CONCEPT OF HEDGING

The meaning of the expression 'avoiding a risk' is obvious to everyone but the precise meaning of the expression 'hedging a risk' is less well understood. Let us suppose that you have identified a future event that is likely to cause you a financial loss if it occurs. Examples of such events might include a collapse in the market value of a company share that you own or your house burning down. Such an event can be avoided by not investing in shares or not owning a house, but this passes up the considerable benefits which can be derived from investing in shares (see Chapter 2) or owning a house (see Chapter 6).

The potential loss resulting from a fall in the value of a share can be avoided by buying a financial product called a *traded put option* on the share options market. This option gives you the right to sell the share at a fixed price at some date in the future. If the value of the share should collapse during the option period then the value of the put option rises by a roughly equivalent amount thus 'hedging' the potential loss on your share. The total value of the share plus the put option on the share remains relatively constant through time. You have hedged your bet by buying the option.

Now it is true that this traded put option has a cost, but this cost is a fixed cost that you know in advance. You have swapped an uncertain future event of unknown cost for a certain event of known cost.

The above example illustrates the key idea behind hedging risk. If an event might occur that threatens you with a potential future loss then the solution is to set up a hedge that is triggered by the same event and that provides a gain of approximately equal value. In the above example the traded option costs money, but this cost is usually only a small proportion, a few per cent, of the current value of the product hedged.

The same principle can be applied to a potential loss resulting from your house burning down. A loss such as this can be covered by the well known hedging device called *insurance*. Insurance substitutes a small certain payment, the annual premium, for the small probability of the very large loss that would occur if your house burned down.

HOW DOES INSURANCE WORK?

Let us suppose that one million people own their own homes that are worth £100 000 each. From past records the insurance company knows that on average approximately 100 of these one million homes will burn down in a given year. If no insurance market existed then each year one hundred of these one million home owners would face a catastrophic loss of £100 000 when their house burned down. Their whole financial future could be ruined.

The total loss is £100 000 × 100 = £10 000 000. Thus if each of the one million home owners is willing to place £10 into an insurance fund each year the total fund will be equal to £10 000 000. When the 100 homes burn down during the year the insurance company can afford to pay £100 000 to each home owner to rebuild their home. All one million home owners are protected against a financial calamity by paying a mere £10 a year into the insurance fund. Naturally the insurance company must cover its running costs so the premium will be slightly above £10, say £11 a year. It is still a very good bargain.

WHEN SHOULD YOU USE INSURANCE AS A HEDGE?

Exhibit 7.1 illustrates a suggested approach to handling risk. In the diagram the importance of a loss-inducing event is defined by two factors. The first factor is defined as the significance of the loss. The amount of the potential loss is either significant relative to your wealth

Type of event causing loss	Rate of occurrence	
	Frequent	Rare
Low-cost events	Change system	Ignore (self-insure)
High-cost events	Get out of system	Insure

The method of handling risk depends on the frequency of occurrence of an event and the value of the loss flowing from this event compared to the wealth of the individual.

Rare low-cost losses can be ignored. If frequent high-cost losses occur the individual involved should remove himself or herself from the system in which they occur. Frequent low cost losses should be countered by changing the system. Insurance is used to hedge against rare events that result in a high loss compared to the wealth of the individual.

EXHIBIT 7.1: How to handle risk

---

or it is not. Your house burning down imposes a significant loss, the loss of a plastic comb does not.

The second factor relates to the probability that the event will actually occur. By placing a future hazard in one of these boxes you can decide whether to hedge the risk and whether or not to use insurance to hedge the risk.

When should you use insurance to hedge a risk? Insurance is the appropriate hedging technique to use for handling those risks which fall into the lower right hand box in the diagram. This is the box containing all of those events that occur only rarely but that result in a significant loss when they do occur.

Returning to Exhibit 7.1 we note that there are three other boxes to consider that are not covered by the hedging technique called insurance.

Frequent, low-cost losses fall into the top left-hand box. Minor damage to electrical appliances is a good example of such a loss. The correct strategy to use here is to change your system. Restrict the use of such equipment to responsible users. Insurance would prove to be an expensive way of covering this kind of risk since insurance companies dislike having to process frequent claims that incur heavy administrative costs.

The events falling into the top-right hand box, rare low cost losses, can be ignored. Events that fall into the bottom left hand box, frequent high-cost losses, cannot be endured. You must move out of such a system, and quickly. Insurance is much too expensive a remedy in such cases and is probably unobtainable. If you continue to operate within such a system you will soon face bankruptcy or worse. An example of the kind of event that falls into this particular box is burglary in certain districts of certain towns in England. The losses from burglary are so frequent and so expensive in certain regions that the insurance companies have either increased the contents insurance premiums to prohibitive levels or have ceased insuring the contents of houses located in certain postal districts in these regions. The only option available to the unfortunate householder in such postal districts is to sell their home at whatever value it will fetch and move elsewhere.

The remainder of this chapter is devoted to discussing events that fall into the bottom right hand box, namely those events with a low probability of occurrence but which will impose a high loss on the individual concerned if they should occur.

INSURANCE AND GAMBLING

It is not possible to insure against all negative events. The person taking out the insurance must have an 'insurable' interest in the particular event. In other words if the event occurs it must inflict some kind of a loss on the individual before an insurance company will insure against the occurrence of the event.

Insurance would be form of gambling if this were not so: if an acquaintance was looking a bit seedy you would be able to take out an insurance policy on his life in the hope of making a quick profit on his demise.

However, the odds offered by bookmakers can be used as a form of insurance, particularly where insurance companies do not provide insurance against the particular event you wish to insure against. For example if you enjoy a very high income and are worried about a Left-Wing party winning the next election and putting up taxes you can make a bet on this Left-Wing party winning the election. If it does win the election, the winnings on the bet will compensate for the additional tax you expect to pay. Bookmakers pride themselves on taking bets on the outcome of almost any future event, and this includes economic events. You do not need to have an 'insurable interest' to place a bet.

In theory you cannot make a profit on insurance since you can only recover what you have already lost.

A PERSONAL RISK AUDIT

It makes good sense to conduct a regular *risk audit* of your personal affairs. In conducting such a risk audit the first thing you need to do is to identify those future events which, if they should occur, would impose a significant cost on your future wealth or income.

Those for whom you are responsible		Negative event incurring loss
Self	Richard William	Death, illness, loss of job
Wife	Alexis	Death, illness
Children		
	Sarah Jane	Illness
	John Symon	Illness

Assets owned

House	Burglary, fire, landslip, storm damage
House contents	Burglary, fire, breakage, loss
Car	Crash, theft, fire
Caravan	Crash, theft, fire
Jewellery	Theft, loss, fire

Other events incurring loss

Libel, slander	Legal costs, damages
Third party injury	Legal costs, damages
Divorce	Legal costs, alimony

A well-designed risk analysis questionnaire, which is available from many insurance companies, can alert you to impending problems that you might have overlooked. Once the risk has been identified it is not difficult to find some way to hedge the risk. Insurance can be used to hedge those risks that are rare events but cost you, or your family, a great deal of money if they should occur.

EXHIBIT 7.2: A risk analysis questionnaire

Many insurance companies are only too happy to assist in this task. They may offer to provide you, a potential customer, with a *risk questionnaire* that reminds you of the many risks you may face in the future along with information as to which of these risks can be hedged by buying insurance and how much this insurance will cost. A section of such a questionnaire is shown in Exhibit 7.2. This questionnaire examines life and health, personal property and speciality insurance products.

In carrying out a risk audit on your personal affairs the first step is to identify those persons for whom you are responsible and then to identify the risks to life and health faced by them and by yourself. The second step is to list all of the possessions you own that are at risk and that are of sufficient value to be worth insuring: your house, your car, your household goods, your jewellery and so forth. The third step is to identify any other future negative events that might cause you significant loss in terms of your income or your wealth if they should occur. Examples in the last category range from serious matters such as losing your job or the costs of a libel action to holiday insurance and insuring against rain on your daughter's wedding day.

The next step is to ascertain the minimum cost of insuring against these risks and then to assess whether or not it is worth taking out insurance to hedge them. Certain types of insurance are available, as we shall see later in this chapter, but can be very expensive to acquire. You may not be able to afford this depth of cover. If you cannot afford to hedge against all of the risks you have identified in the initial phase of your risk audit you may have to ignore the less important risks.

WHAT TYPES OF INSURANCE ARE AVAILABLE?

Insurance is conventionally divided into three classes called personal insurance, property insurance and other forms of insurance. The last two are sometimes lumped together and called *general insurance.*

PERSONAL INSURANCE

Personal insurance covers all of those risks to life and health faced by the individual, or by those people for whom the individual is responsible. Personal insurance policies are mostly concerned with death and with health. Various types of life assurance policies are offered[1] that pay out an agreed sum to the beneficiaries of the assured on the death of the assured. The more common forms of life policy are the *whole of life with profits* policy, the *whole of life without profits* policy (the so-called 'bare' policy), term insurance for fixed periods of time and endowment insurance which is really a form of investment plan and is often tied to a mortgage repayment scheme. Accidental death benefit and family income benefit are other policies that might fall into this category.

Health insurance offers an even more varied range of policies than life assurance. The more common of these are private medical insurance (PMI), permanent health insurance (PHI) more correctly called income replacement insurance, long-term care insurance, critical illness insurance (CII), personal accident and sickness insurance and injury to third party insurance. These health insurance policies hedge the additional costs involved, or the income lost, if you, or those for whom you are responsible, have the misfortune to suffer illness or disability while the policy is in force.

You can use these policies to build an almost completely protective shield against the costs of the many health hazards faced by yourself and your family but we will find later in the chapter that providing *complete* protection is a very expensive business indeed that few can afford. You need to be selective in the choice of which risks to hedge.

PROPERTY INSURANCE

This type of insurance covers the risk of loss or damage to property owned by, or under the protection of, the insured. Almost everything you own can be insured: your house, your household contents, your motor car, your jewellery, your collectibles and so on, but not under all circumstances. You may find difficulty in insuring your house if it is rented out to a tenant, for example.

All contents can be covered against fire, damage or theft at a relatively low insurance cost unless you have the misfortune to live in a postal district prone to burglary or theft. The qualification 'but not under all circumstances' is important. You would be wise to read the small print in property insurance contracts. The insurance company underwriting the risk often lays down strict rules on the safekeeping and protection of the property insured in the contract. For example jewellery may have to be stored in a bank vault and only worn for a given number of days in each year. A householder may be required to install a certified burglar-alarm system before the house contents are accepted for insurance cover. If the given conditions are breached the contract is void.

UNUSUAL HAZARDS

So long as you have an insurable interest in a potential loss it is likely that you can insure against the hazard concerned. Some unusual hazards that you can be insured against are: lawsuits for libel or slander, the additional costs associated with holiday cancellation through illness, the bankruptcy of a personal financial adviser or solicitor, the additional costs resulting from rain on a wedding day, the additional costs incurred if a mother has twins, veterinary fees, being hijacked in an airliner, the costs of divorce (but the claim is only allowable after two years from initiating the policy!), redundancy and so forth.

Whether it is worthwhile taking out cover against such rare events depends on your lifestyle, your income and, most crucial of all, your attitude to taking risk.

Some people take a 'belt-and-braces' attitude towards risk. They like to cover all risks that can be identified even if this strategy reduces their income substantially in the meanwhile. Others prefer to concentrate on covering only the major risks they face like death, ill health, job loss, and loss of home.

The most important hazards to be insured against, so far as the individual is concerned, are death, health problems, loss or damage to house and car and the financial consequences of loss of employment.

In the next section we will examine life and health insurance in more detail. A more exact description of these forms of insurance would be death and ill-health insurance.

WHOLE LIFE 'WITH PROFITS' ASSURANCE

This form of life insurance, as the name suggests, covers you for life no matter how ill you may become in the future. If you die while the policy is in force the insurance company will pay a fixed amount of money into your estate plus an additional amount depending on the income earned from the investment portfolio (life fund) of the insurance company over the period during which the policy is in force.

A part of your monthly insurance premium is paid into a life fund managed by the insurance company and this fund is invested in a range of assets, usually financial assets like gilts and ordinary shares. The assets earn an income and a share of this income is added to your fund each year. Thus a 'with-profits' policy can pay out considerably more than the bare amount of life cover guaranteed in the event of your death.

Insurance companies place a substantial part of their life fund into government gilts and ordinary shares. The gilts provide a steady income and research has shown that ordinary shares provide a good bulwark against inflation. Thus a whole of life 'with-profits' life assurance policy provides a relatively safe harbour for your funds since they are less volatile than unit and investment trusts, because of the gilt element, while providing a good bulwark against inflation through the ordinary shares.

A 'with profits' insurance policy provides a good example of a 'bundled' financial product. The policy covers your dependants against the financial consequences of your early death while at the same time building up an investment fund for them.

So long as the insurance company pursues a wise investment policy and so long as you wish to build up an investment fund for your dependants this is a useful financial product. However, you might prefer to keep your life insurance plan and your savings and investment plan in separate boxes. In this case a *term* insurance policy can be used to provide protection against an early death and a PEP or TESSA can be built up to provide a tax-efficient saving and investment plan. This 'unbundling' injects more flexibility into your personal financial planning.

Some life policies raise the annual premium by a percentage equal to the rate of inflation each year. This keeps the insured amount of the life policy roughly in line with inflation and so keeps the real value of the policy constant over its life. Alternatively you could take out another policy, possibly with another insurance company, to keep up the real value of your life cover.

Whole life 'with profits' policies top up the value of your policy fund with a *reversionary bonus* each year. The reversionary bonus is declared and credited to your policy fund. Once a reversionary bonus is declared it cannot be taken back: the money is yours but only your heirs will benefit!

UNIT-LINKED WHOLE LIFE ASSURANCE

Under a 'with profits' policy your money is invested in the insurance company life fund. Under a unit-linked whole life policy your money is invested in one or other of the unit trusts run by the insurance company. The investment situation is very similar to investing in a conventional unit trust. The main difference is that a minimum guarantee is provided as to the payout from the policy on your decease.

A part of your insurance premium is used to buy units in a unit trust. A wide range of unit trusts are offered by most insurance companies. You choose; you can invest in ordinary shares, gilts, even in property. This kind of investment decision is discussed in Chapter 2.

Unit-linked whole life policies are more volatile and so more risky than 'with-profits' policies where the reversionary bonuses cannot be taken back once declared. The potential return on unit-linked policies is much higher, however, because a substantial proportion of 'with-profits' life funds are invested in gilts, which provide very limited access to capital gains.

These policies are really investment schemes masquerading as insurance schemes. You can vary the proportion of your premium that goes into investment and insurance. The higher your insurance cover the lower your regular investment. The charges on unit-linked schemes can be high so you should check this out and choose a scheme with relatively low charges.

If you want to invest in unit trusts we would advise you to do so directly rather than going through a unit-linked insurance policy.

INSURANCE BONDS

A wide range of investment products are sold with insurance policies attached to them. The insurance connection is mainly to gain tax benefits. These products, which include such things as guaranteed income bonds, guaranteed growth bonds and investment bonds, are basically investment products, not insurance products. We discussed these products in Chapter 2 on investment.

IMPAIRED LIFE ASSURANCE

If, when you take out a simple life policy, you suffer from some potentially serious illness such as a heart condition or cancer, death arising from these conditions will normally be excluded from your life policy. In other words if you die from the disease you were suffering from when you took out the policy, the *pre-existing condition,* the policy has no value and no money is due to be paid by the insurance company into your estate.

There are, however, some insurance policies that are designed to cover just this situation. After a rigorous medical check-up by doctors acting for the insurance company, an individual suffering from such a condition may be offered an *impaired life policy.*

Obviously these policies cost a good deal more than a similar policy offered to a healthy person of the same age. It all depends on the medical report, but an individual suffering from ill health should be aware that such policies are available. Some people assume that if they suffer from a serious pre-existing condition then no life policy can be obtained covering death from this condition. Some insurance brokers specialize in finding life insurance cover for clients with potentially serious medical conditions.

TERM INSURANCE

The cheapest life cover is provided by term insurance. If you wish to protect your dependants against the financial consequences of your death but cannot afford the high monthly cost of a whole-of-life 'with-profits' or 'unit linked' policy, a term policy provides you with a solution to your problem. Exhibit 7.3 shows an example of the costs of level term insurance of £50 000 cover for a fixed period for a male at various ages.

A term policy pays out a fixed sum of money into your estate if you should die during the fixed term of the policy. If you are young, under the age of 40, and in good health, the probability of your death before the age of 50 is quite low (around 5%). If such a person takes out a 15-year term policy at the age of 35 the insurance company issuing the term policy will expect to pay out nothing on the policy. For this reason term insurance is very cheap for the relatively young person compared to the cost of 'whole of life' assurance.

A married man aged 35 with a wife and three young children might consider taking out a 'term' policy worth £100 000 for a period of 15 years at a cost of £12 a month. If he dies during this period his estate will receive £100 000. If he dies after he has reached the age of 50 his estate will receive nothing but his widow and family will have been protected against the financial consequences of his death over the 15-year period. Beyond the age of 50 we presume that his family will be in a better position to look after themselves and an investment fund should have been built up by this time.

'Term' insurance is the ideal way to protect your family against the financial consequences of your early death. It is a great pity that so few breadwinners take advantage of this relatively cheap protective device. As shown in Table 7.1, the cost of substantial term cover can be bought at a cost of no more than a few pounds a week.

'Term' insurance can also be used to cover the cost of school fees or other future expenditures that could not be met by the family if the breadwinner were to die suddenly and unexpectedly. A *convertible term insurance policy* allows you to convert your term insurance into a whole life or endowment policy *without a medical examination*. This could be a useful advantage if your health deteriorates in the meanwhile.

A *renewable term insurance policy* allows you to take out another term insurance policy when the current one terminates *without a medical examination*. The terms of the new policy will not be the same as the old but it is still a useful advantage if your health deteriorates. The cost is again around 10% above the cost of a simple term policy.

Reducing term insurance (RTI) is an even cheaper form of life insurance. In this case the value of the life policy is reduced as the liability it covers is reduced. For example, future school fees are reduced by each year the pupil completes at school and so the cover reduces proportionately. Reducing term insurance is also used to cover the repayment of repayment mortgage which reduces in value year by year as the capital is repaid.

The annual cost of various types of insurance

The insured: male in good health

	Whole life	Endowment	Low cost endowment	Level term	Mortgage protection	Income benefit
Term	Life	25 years	25 years	25 years	25 years	25 years
Value	£50 000	£50 000	£50 000	£50 000	£50 000	£20 000 p.a.
Age	£	£	£	£	£	£
30	1 032	1 962	978	92	65	300
40	1 428	2 046	1 050	230	165	667
50	2 022	2 310	1 302	608	455	2 011
55	2 442	2 562	Not available	974	729	3 365

The above table shows the costs of various types of life insurance in July 1994. The rates vary a great deal from time to time and between companies. These figures show the better rates quoted.

The costs for a woman will be about 20% less than for a man, but it varies with age. The cost of a joint policy on the life of a man and a woman will be around 60% to 80% more than for a man insuring himself.

Note how cheap term and mortgage-protection insurance are compared to whole life or endowment. The latter two are investment schemes masquerading as insurance schemes.

The requirements regarding medical inspections are set out in the Stone and Cox insurance handbook, which is available in many public libraries.

EXHIBIT 7.3: The costs of various types of life insurance

Term insurance policies are *qualifying policies* and so no income or capital gains tax is usually paid on payouts or benefits from these policies. This is useful if the recipient is a high-rate taxpayer.

FAMILY INCOME BENEFIT

This form of insurance pays out an agreed monthly or annual income, free of tax, to the family of the insured for a fixed number of years after the death of the insured.

Family income benefit is similar in structure to 'term' insurance in the sense that the payments are limited to a fixed number of years ahead. The regular payments on family income benefit are often increased each year by the rate of inflation. This ensures that the real income from the policy remains constant over the life of the policy.

Family income benefit insurance, like term insurance, is relatively cheap to buy since in most cases the insurance company pays out nothing on the policy. The costs of one such scheme are set out in Exhibit 7.3 above.

ENDOWMENT INSURANCE

An endowment insurance policy is another example of a 'bundled' financial product. The endowment insurance contract incorporates both a term life policy and a savings and investment scheme. Endowment policies are normally tied to mortgage schemes for buying homes. The proceeds from the endowment policy payout is used to repay the mortgage at the end of the loan period. The term life policy ensures that the loan will be repaid out of the proceeds of the life policy if the borrower should die before the end of the loan period.

For example suppose you are considering taking out a mortgage to buy a house. The purchase price of £120 000 is to be financed by taking £20 000 from your personal savings and by borrowing a mortgage of £100 000 from a building society, the loan to be repaid over 20 years. You can take out an endowment insurance policy to assist in raising the initial finance of £100 000 from the building society. The proceeds from the endowment policy will repay the £100 000 loan at the end of the 20-year period. The endowment policy also ensures that if you should die before the 20 years are up the loan will be repaid out of the proceeds of the term insurance policy on your life.

The monthly premiums you pay on the endowment policy are calculated to be sufficient to cover the life insurance part of the package while leaving a substantial surplus which is invested in the life fund of the insurance company. This surplus is invested to produce 'bonuses' which accumulate in an endowment fund which, hopefully, repays the £100 000 loan at the end of the 20-year period.

In the past insurance companies have been very conservative in calculating the value of the monthly endowment premium. The insurance company needs to ensure that the premium is large enough to build up a fund sufficient to repay the loan at the end of the loan period. Until quite recently the surplus built up in the insurance fund was large enough to repay your mortgage loan at the end of the loan period and leave a substantial surplus to provide a nest-egg for you, the policy holder.

In effect an endowment insurance scheme constructed to repay a mortgage incorporates a home financing scheme, a loan repayment scheme, a life insurance scheme and a savings and investment scheme. It is a very complex financial product indeed.

These endowment mortgage schemes worked well until quite recently. Since 1993 it seems that, in some cases, the accumulated 'bonuses' on the invested fund have been insufficient to repay the building society mortgage at the end of the plan. As a result of this shortfall some endowment policy holders have been advised by their insurers to increase their monthly payments into the insurance fund by a small amount each month to ensure that there will be sufficient funds available to repay their mortgage at the end of the loan period.

This failure of the insurance companies to generate sufficient profits from their insurance funds to repay the underlying mortgage loans has cast something of a cloud over endowment insurance policies. Many financial advisers are now recommending that the various financial plans bundled within an endowment mortgage policy, plans such as home financing, life insurance and saving and investment plans, should be 'unbundled' so that the house buyer has a clearer picture of each individual plan. For example the endowment mortgage can be replaced by a simple repayment mortgage, the whole-life policy can be replaced with a term policy and the savings scheme can be replaced by a regular investment into a 'pepped' unit trust.

A 'terminal' bonus is paid into the endowment fund right at the end of the plan. This terminal bonus can make up a substantial proportion of the total bonus, perhaps 30% to 50% of the total sum. This is why you must not terminate a 'with profits' policy in midstream. You can lose your very large terminal bonus.

An endowment policy should not be surrendered or paid up before termination if you can possibly avoid this course of action. If you are short of funds your best plan is to take out a loan based on the security of the policy to pay the premiums or alternatively to make a 'partial surrender' of the policy which allows you to cash-in the 'reversionary' bonuses earned to date to pay the future premiums until your financial position is stabilized. In the last resort, if your policy has run for some time, it is better to sell your endowment policy to a buyer of traded endowment policies rather than to simply surrender it to the insurance company. The trader will give you 5% to 15% more than the insurance company would for your policy. The costs of an endowment policy taken out by a male at various ages are set out in Exhibit 7.3.

ACCIDENTAL DEATH INSURANCE

As the name implies, this form of insurance pays out a fixed sum on the death of the insured in an accident. The normal policy conditions exclude death in dangerous sports such as gliding or rock-climbing.

Accidental death insurance is very cheap since few claims are made on such policies, but it is invaluable to the family of the deceased if the unfortunate event occurs. These policies are so cheap that everyone with dependants should take out an accidental death policy for an amount equal to around four times gross annual salary.

LONG-TERM CARE INSURANCE (LTCI)

Long-term care insurance is a variant on medical care insurance. It is intended to cover, or at least reduce, the cost of looking after the elderly if they are unable to look after themselves. An LTCI plan may offer to cover residential fees or home care help. There has been a great deal of fuss about LTCI in recent times since the Government introduced a scheme to reduce the cost of this kind of insurance. The Government claims that it wishes to encourage people to look after themselves financially in old age.

We noted in Chapter 5 that the proportion of the elderly among the general population is rising rapidly in the UK and that the cost of looking after this section of the population is becoming a serious economic and social problem. Around 5% of the population over the age of 65 and 20% over the age of 80 suffer from some form of senile dementia.

The annual cost of placing an elderly relative in a residential or nursing home is around £15 000 to £20 000 at present and the cost is rising by 5% a year. Nursing homes for the mentally ill cost much more. The average length of time a resident spends in a home in the UK is under three years and only 5% of residents remain in the home for more than five years.[2]

In order to claim under an LTCI policy the claimant must be unable to perform certain basic activities such as eating, washing or going to the lavatory by him or herself. These activities are called ADLs in the trade. You normally need at least three ADLs to claim although the conditions vary between companies.

The State will not pay for your stay in a nursing home if you have assets in excess of £8000 including your home,[3] so if you do not wish to see your hard-earned wealth flowing into the coffers of the nursing home industry you will need to take out some kind of LTCI insurance.

There are two types of scheme:

- prepayment plans where you pay a regular premium or a lump sum in advance of needing care and

- immediate care plans which are created at the point of needing care. You fund this type of scheme with a lump sum.

Since the cost of being cared for in a nursing home is currently £15 000 a year what is the cost of a policy that will provide you with £15 000 a year in income? It is very high even with the government's new scheme that involves the government sharing the cost. The cost depends on your sex and age when you take out the policy but a 60-year-old woman would have to pay around £100 per month and a 70-year-old man around £140 a month. Not many elderly people can afford sums like these. Exhibit 7.4 sets out a range of costs on prefunded schemes.

You can fund immediate care schemes by buying an impaired annuity, a simulated annuity or a pure endowment policy. These schemes are structured to be very tax efficient. The cost of an immediate care scheme lies between £30 000 to £40 000. This provides care fees of £1000 to £1500 per month. Management charges by the provider can be rather high on these schemes so check them out.

There is no tax relief on LTCI premiums but the income from the policies is free of tax.

Only a very small fraction of the population will go into a home[4] and an even tinier fraction of these will remain in care for more than five years, thus it might be wiser to invest your £100 a month in a PEP or TESSA and hope for the best. An investment fund of £50 000 or so should see you through a terminal stay in a home unless you are very unlucky.

PERSONAL ACCIDENT AND SICKNESS INSURANCE

This is an inferior form of PMI. If you suffer an accident and cannot earn your normal livelihood for a given period you are paid a lump sum or possibly a small income for a given period. A life policy will be attached.

PERMANENT HEALTH INSURANCE (PHI) (INCOME REPLACEMENT INSURANCE)

This type of insurance is incorrectly named. Permanent health insurance does not insure your health in perpetuity but provides you with an income if you should fall ill and become unable to work. The correct name is *income replacement insurance.*

Permanent health insurance normally comes into play once the insured has been ill and off work for a fixed period of time, say three months. The longer the period before PHI comes into effect, the less it costs as can be seen from Exhibit 7.5.

Permanent health insurance can provide you with an income until the age of 60 or 65 or up to the date when you expect to retire. The sooner the termination date of the policy is, the lower the cost will be. The maximum amount to be paid is usually restricted to 75% of your current earnings taking into account any State benefits that you may receive. Permanent health insurance benefits are not taxed, which is helpful. It is very expensive to buy full 75% cover. Most workers choose a much lower amount – just enough to keep the wolf from the door in a time of financial stringency.

Many companies pay for such policies on behalf of their senior employees. You will have to pay tax on this advantage if you receive it. If it has not been offered you might suggest to your employer that it be provided. Half of all PHI policies are currently sponsored by employers.

Naturally the insurance company underwriting the policy will require regular medical evidence of continuing physical impairment while you are making a claim. Mental illness may not be covered by your PHI policy. Self-induced injury or drug abuse are not covered.

In recent years some of those who have claimed under PHI policies have complained that the definition of *physical impairment* has been applied much too strictly by the insurance companies. For example can

Critical illness insurance: £50 000

Cost per month

Person insured	Age	40	50
		£	£
Male	Non-smoker	61	107
Female	Non-smoker	44	86
Male	Smoker	92	158
Female	Smoker	64	122

The table shows the monthly cost of critical illness insurance cover. A sum of money is paid to the insured on medical diagnosis of one of the insured conditions. The value is £50 000. These rates will only apply if the claim is made before the retirement of a male aged up to 65 or a female aged up to 60.

Long-term care insurance

Cost per month

Age	55	60	65
Person insured	£	£	£
Male	54	65	78
Female	77	93	115

This table shows the cost of insuring for long-term care of up to £1000 per month. The value is inflation-indexed at 5% per annum. In 1996 this would cover the cost of a residential home in the north of England but not in the London area. Cover for a London home would cost around 50% more than this per month.

These forms of insurance are expensive, especially when you become older. Few families can afford to take out both critical illness insurance and long-term care insurance. The annual cost of placing an elderly person in a nursing home is around £15 000 per year and this cost is increasing by around 5% per year. These are serious concerns that require careful consideration, but remember that only a small fraction of the population ever need to go into a nursing home and that those who do move into a nursing home stay there, on average, for less than three years.

EXHIBIT 7.4: The cost of criticial illness and long-term care insurance

---

you claim under PHI if you are too ill to perform your chosen profession but well enough to perform another less demanding job requiring lesser skill and receiving a much lower wage? Doubts on this score may be the reason why PHI policies have not sold well in the United Kingdom. This is a pity since PHI policies hedge the very real risk that the physical impairment of the breadwinner in a family could play havoc with the family finances. Personal health insurance provides very useful cover.

Personal health insurance is best suited to the needs of the middle aged – that is those between the age of 35 and 50. Currently in the UK the average age of those who make PHI claims is 40.

Before taking out a PHI policy it would be advisable to obtain a very clear statement from the insurance company as to the precise conditions under which a claim can be made. How ill or disabled must you be before you can make a claim?

If an inflation-indexed PHI option is available, take it. Over the long term inflation is a major risk to those who depend on fixed incomes no matter how low inflation might be at present.

CRITICAL ILLNESS INSURANCE (CII)

The sudden and unexpected illness of a family member, not necessarily the breadwinner, can impose heavy costs on the finances of a family. Critical illness insurance is designed to hedge this risk. If you fall ill with one of the critical illnesses designated in your CII policy, a substantial single sum is paid to you so long as you survive for around 30 days. You could use this money to pay off your mortgage or business loans.

Only illness of a very serious nature is covered by CII. The usual illnesses covered are cancer, heart attack and by-pass surgery, stroke and kidney failure and total and permanent disability. Some other conditions that occur less commonly may be covered by some policies but most policies do not cover either AIDS or mental illness.

The insured must be prepared to undergo a detailed medical examination before taking out a CII policy and pre-existing medical conditions are not likely to be covered. Critical illness insurance can be taken out for the whole of your life or for a fixed term. It is often attached as an option to another insurance policy such as a PMI policy.

Critical illness insurance is expensive and is usually taken out by senior executives who enjoy a substantial income and need the money to buy expensive medical and other treatment to get themselves back to work as quickly as possible. The cost is often covered or at least subsidized by an employer as part of a remuneration package. A guide to the cost of CII policies are set out in Exhibit 7.4 above. The premiums are seldom fixed for the duration of the policy. They are reviewed upwards every few years. Much depends on the performance of the underlying fund managed by the CII provider.

One positive feature of CII is that there is much less emphasis here on the insurance company checking out the 'degree' of your disability before paying out, as there is with a PHI policy. You are diagnosed as either having the condition or not having it. If you wish to continue to work after receiving the proceeds from a CII policy you may do so.

Critics of CII point out that you must fall ill with one of the specific illnesses set down in the policy to receive payment whereas with PHI you will receive your replacement income no matter what the illness so long as you can prove you are sufficiently disabled to justify payment.

Critical illness insurance payments are almost all tax free. Some policies are non-qualifying but it is unlikely that a higher-rate taxpayer will have to pay tax on the receipts.

£10 000 per year cover to age 65 for a man or woman

Monthly cost (£ per month)

Age		Cover deferred for 13 weeks			Cover deferred for 26 weeks		
		30	40	50	30	40	50
Two company quotes							
A	Man	15	19	31	13	17	26
	Woman	17	28	45	15	22	37
B	Man	11	18	30	10	11	20
	Woman	19	31	50	11	18	32
Inflation-indexed							
C	Man	16	27	61	14	19	44
	Woman	22	40	93	16	27	66
D	Man	15	22	35	12	16	29
	Woman	22	35	60	15	22	42

Permanent health insurance insures a worker's income against the possibility of serious long-term illness. It provides the insured with a long-term income of an agreed amount until the age of 60 or 65. Since women live rather longer than men, the premium for women is rather higher than for men at any given age. If payment is deferred from the usual 13 weeks to 26 weeks, a substantial discount is available to the insured. Some PHI policies are index-linked to the retail price index. Indexation is advised to cover future bursts of inflation.

EXHIBIT 7.5: The cost of permanent health insurance (income replacement insurance)

If you have a fair idea of what illness you are likely to suffer from, take out CII. Otherwise take out PHI.

PRIVATE MEDICAL INSURANCE

The National Health Service in the UK provides a good service for acute medical conditions but the treatment of chronic conditions by the service has been much criticized. Despite much effort by governments and the hospital service waiting lists for consulting services are long and the delay in receiving prophylactic treatment is a painful process for many patients. One solution to this problem is to take out private medical insurance to finance treatment in the private sector.

A wide range of medical insurance schemes are on offer in the UK. The cost of medical insurance varies a great deal between the different schemes. Charges vary from around £30 per month per person for very basic schemes to over £200 per month for an extremely high quality scheme. Exhibit 7.6 sets out the cost of several schemes.

Medical insurance aims to cover hospital bills for surgery and hospitalization but some portion of consultancy services and other medicinal costs may also be covered. Few types of insurance require a more careful perusal of the small print in the contract than does a private medical insurance policy. These policies are very carefully drafted by legal experts and it often happens that the cover is much less than the insured person believes it to be. The expectations gap is not usually revealed until you make a claim. Tight limits are placed on total costs to be refunded within each year and annual thresholds that must be paid by the insured before any refund can be claimed are often high: a £250 threshold in any one year is common.

Medical insurance is useful for speeding up treatment for chronic illness and for covering the cost of major operations for the elderly but it is of limited value in covering acute conditions or minor illness. You should take care to select a policy that covers your essential needs, but make sure that it provides no 'frills'. The 'frills' in medical insurance can be very expensive. As private medical insurance becomes very expensive when you get older it may become unaffordable beyond 65 years of age, even if the premiums are allowed against tax at the basic rate.

One might question the wisdom of investing in private medical insurance unless your company pays the premiums for you.[5] You might consider investing the premium you would pay for private medical insurance into a tax-free PEP or TESSA and use this fund to pay for private medicine directly. A £10 000 fund can be built up in around 10 years and few single treatments in the private sector cost more than £10 000.

PERSONAL INJURY INSURANCE

This form of insurance is similar to personal accident. It provides compensation if the insured suffers some serious injury such as the loss of, or use of, some body part such as an eye or leg or hand. Each body part is allocated a specific sum.

This type of insurance can be critical if you use a specific body part, such as both hands, to perform your job. The critical body part can be insured for a substantial sum.

INJURY TO THIRD PARTY INSURANCE

If you accidentally injure or even kill a third party or damage someone's property then third-party insurance can be useful. Third-party insurance is usually incorporated into 'general' household insurance policies but if you do not hold such a policy third party insurance may be overlooked.

A lack of third party insurance can be a serious matter since, although claims by third parties are rare, if they do occur they can be for a very substantial sum indeed, running to many thousands of pounds.

It is worth checking out your general insurance policies to ensure that you are covered against third party claims.

PROPERTY INSURANCE

All property owned by you or under your protection should be insured against fire, theft or other kinds of damage. The cost of property and contents insurance is not high, unless you have the misfortune to live in a district prone to burglary. General contents insurance covers all of your moveable possessions but limits claims on specific items to a fixed amount. Your moveable possessions are insured even when they are taken out of the home, unless it can be proved that you were careless in protecting them. The more important items of property that need to be insured are your home, your home contents and your car.

INSURING YOUR HOME

Most home owners are forced to take out adequate insurance on their home since a building society or other lender is unlikely to loan funds to buy a house unless the house is adequately insured. Once your mortgage is paid off the situation changes and you must make your own arrangements for insuring your home. Some home owners forget to do this with potentially catastrophic consequences if their home should burn down or be otherwise damaged.

The value for which a home should be insured is a matter of some controversy. If your house was built in the nineteenth century or earlier then rebuilding the house to the exact nineteenth-century specifications can cost a good deal more than the current market value of your home. This means that the insurance value on which the insurance premiums are based can be well above the current market value of your home. House buyers should bear this fact in mind when contemplating buying an older house.

The land on which a house is built is not destroyed in a fire. The value of a home is made up of the value of rebuilding the home plus the cost of the land on which the home is built. Thus the value of the home, by itself, has a lower value than the value of the home plus the value of the land on which it is built.

In the past most insurance companies based the value of house insurance on the total value of rebuilding the house plus the value of the land. This is an incorrect valuation since the value of the land is not affected by the fire. The house owner might find himself paying a higher

Exhibit 7.6: The costs and benefits of some private medical insurance policies in the UK

Plan A

	Age	Cost (monthly) £	
Single person	30–34	56	Band A hospitals
		33	Band B hospitals
		28	Band C hospitals
Family group (Age of oldest person in group.)	40–44	144	Band A
		84	Band B
		71	Band C

Full refund within hospital band for in-patients.

Other benefits

1. Includes overseas travel cover at no extra cost.

2. No policy limits on cost of specific treatments.

3. 'No-claims discount' can reduce premiums by up to 60%.

4. Low-cost option with lower benefits provides a 15% reduction in premiums.

5. The rates can rise quite steeply for the over 60s. Special schemes are offered.

Limitations

1. Will not cover prior or existing medical conditions.

2. Normally will not cover AIDS, alcoholism, drug abuse, regular kidney dialysis, chronic long-term illness or psychiatric illness.

3. Some payment are imposed on out-patient care.

Plan B

	Age	Cost (monthly)	
Single person	31–35	34	Private hospital. Private bed in NHS hospital; 100 selected private hospitals. Extra benefits.
Family (Age of oldest person in group)	41–45	87	As above.

Plan C

	Age	Cost	
	£	£	
Single person	30–41	33	Various bands of hospital offered.
Family (age of oldest person in group)	42–50	71	Various bands

Other benefits and limitations

Similar to above. Many discounts offered to professional workers. If insured chooses a hospital above the selected band the company makes a contribution to the cost.

A large number of schemes are on offer. BUPA has taken 50% of the UK market, PPP has 28%, WPA 6% and BCWA 4%. The above figures are taken from schemes offered by some of the smaller companies. The benefits provided are very complex. The above tables simply provide a rough guide to the available services and the costs involved.

---

premium for house insurance than is justified by the value of the house alone. In recent years the insurance companies have rectified this error by basing the value of the annual house insurance premium on the rebuilding cost of the home alone but a wise house owner will check that this is so.

In a few cases the value of the land has been overestimated by the insurance company so that the house is now *underinsured*. A regular check to verify that the insurance value of your home is approximately equal to the rebuilding cost of your home is a wise precaution that should be taken by every house owner. A table indicating the rebuilding cost of stand-alone houses was provided in Exhibit 6.14 in Chapter 6.

SUBSIDENCE

Subsidence is a key factor in house insurance. Since around 1990 insurance companies have become very wary of insuring houses built on soil liable to subsidence or houses built near old mine workings. Subsidence is a very serious matter which can make a house difficult to sell since the potential new owner can find it difficult to obtain house insurance at a reasonable cost. Estate agents are now required to tell potential house buyers about the possibility of this problem in the area of a house for sale. Insurance claims for subsidence can drag on for years.

The conventional house insurance policy makes the home owner liable for part of the cost of rectifying subsidence. The first £500 or £1000 of the cost must be paid by the home owner.

Before signing the contract to buy a house you would be well advised to check out that signs of subsidence do not exist in the area around the house. The simplest way to do this is to employ the services of a reputable qualified surveyor who knows the area. The structural survey should be a full survey, not the limited variety, and the surveyor should be asked a specific question about the possibility of subsidence in the area of the house.

HOME CONTENTS INSURANCE

The contents of a home are not covered by normal house insurance. House insurance only covers losses arising from damage to the fabric of the house and outbuildings. The conventional house contents insurance policy covers all of the moveable items stored in the house. The specific hazards covered are losses caused by theft, fire, flood, accidental damage, spoilage or breakage and so forth.

Your home contents insurance policy may well cover the loss or damage to these items even if they are taken out of the house, but you should always check up on the precise conditions imposed by the insurance contract in this regard. For example household goods stolen from a car or a garage may not be covered by your contents policy.

It is unusual for a house to burn down and for its contents to be destroyed. The more common situation is for individual items to be stolen or damaged. Thus an important value inserted into every household contents insurance policy is the individual item claims limit. The contents of a home may be insured for £30 000 but the highest claim which can be made for any individual item may be as low as £500, which is not a high value by today's standards. Many hi-fi systems, antiques, microcomputers and jewellery have an individual item value well in excess of £500.

It is therefore essential for you to insure all your possessions with a value above the individual value limit as a separate item with a specific value attached. Most householders will already follow this procedure for insuring antiques and jewellery but many other household items such as washing machines and sophisticated hi-fi and video systems can breach the upper limit on individual value. Items should be insured at replacement value rather than at current value.

A WARNING ABOUT CONDITIONAL CLAUSES

Claims made on household contents insurance policies are particularly prone to be at risk from abstruse conditional clauses in the insurance contract. For example claims under a house contents insurance policy might only be met if the house is fitted with an *accredited* burglar alarm system: any old alarm system will not do. The lock on the external doors of a house may have to be a 'dead' lock before a claim is acknowledged. The policy may state that the property insured must not be left untenanted for more than a month in any one year for a claim to be met. The property must not be rented without the insurance company being informed. Even tenants in an occupied house may breach the contract conditions. The contract may state that jewellery has to be stored in the safe deposit box of a bank and can only be worn for an agreed number of days each year. The potential for restrictive conditional clauses in insurance contracts are legion.

The only safe remedy is to read the insurance contract very carefully. However the full insurance contract is often forwarded to the insured person long after the insurance is taken out. This means that the careful reading of the contract is often overlooked until a claim arises. This is much too late to be of any value in arguing a disputed claim.

In the writer's opinion insurance law should be changed so that the onus is on the seller of the insurance to point out any *important* conditional clauses in the insurance contract that might affect a claim by the buyer of the insurance. The restrictions should be pointed out before the insurance is taken up. Simply providing a list of conditions to the buyer in small, often very small, print is just not good enough. *Caveat emptor* should not apply between the parties to a contract when one party has very limited access to key facts about such contracts.

SHOULD YOU TAKE HOUSE AND CONTENTS INSURANCE WITH SAME COMPANY?

Some financial advisers suggest that house insurance and household contents insurance should be taken out with the same insurance company. The reason for this recommendation is that some untoward event such as a burst water pipe or flooding can damage both the fabric of the house and the contents in the house. If the house and contents are insured with two different insurance companies there might be argument between these companies as to who is responsible for each part of the total claim. This cannot arise if both the house and contents are insured with the same company.

On the other hand if the insurer of the property believes that it has the home owner in its pocket for both types of insurance it might overcharge for the contents insurance. The home owner should check out competitive rates before assigning both house and contents insurance to the same insurance company.

As shown in Exhibit 7.7, the cost of household contents insurance varies widely between different parts of the country and even between different parts of the same town. The insurance companies have allocated a 'risk of claim' coefficient to every postal district code in the UK. If you are unfortunate enough to live in one of the high risk areas the annual cost of contents insurance of a given value can be 10 times the cost in a low risk area. Check on the insurance category of your new postal address before buying your new home.

SPECIAL TYPES OF INSURANCE

Most of the hazards in life can be insured against so long as one has an insurable interest. Insurance will be taken out to cover these specific hazards on an *ad hoc* basis as they arise.

One of the more popular forms of insurance taken out under this heading is insurance to cover legal costs, particularly the costs that can be incurred by committing libel or slander. There is some evidence that the UK has become more litigious of late.

Insurance can be taken out to cover any loss incurred by reason of the bankruptcy or defalcation of an adviser, such as a personal financial adviser, a solicitor or an accountant. Insurance is offered against the costs of divorce. Holiday insurance is a fast growing sector of the market. You can insure against the costs incurred by cancelling a holiday because of illness, the loss of luggage or, most important, against medical costs incurred during a holiday abroad. Insurance is offered against the cost of veterinary fees for your pets and a whole host of minor or improbable hazards such as postponement of a wedding, hijack, being mugged, having twins and so forth. You can even insure against the risk of redundancy unless you work in an area where redundancy is a common occurrence.

But beware! An excessive concern with hedging every conceivable risk that might face you in the future is likely to lead to either paranoia or bankruptcy . . . whichever comes first.

THE COST OF INSURANCE

Insurance is not an expensive commodity relative to the potential benefits it provides. Most annual insurance premiums cost only a tiny fraction of the value insured during the period of the insurance, often less than one per cent of the value insured.

The insurance industry allows a group of people facing a common risk to pool the risk and share the total cost of that risk between themselves. The annual cost of the insurance premium depends on the claims made in past years by that particular pool of customers. The administrative cost and profits made by the insurance company adds only a very small percentage to the premium cost.

If the value of the year-on-year claims should rise in a particular category, the insurance company increases the annual premiums proportionately. It is the past claims record, not the insurance company, that fixes the cost of the insurance premiums charged to cover a given risk. For example, the increase in the claims from

Annual cost of premiums

Town	Buildings cover (£100 000)		Contents cover (£20 000)	
	Cheapest	Most expensive	Cheapest	Most expensive
	£	£	£	£
Aberdeen	132	190	55	80
Newcastle	132	218	136	320
Belfast	140	190	70	114
Ipswich	147	280	56	82
Cardiff	147	245	107	190
Brighton	160	280	107	148
Liverpool	160	280	268	450
London	235	400	216	400

The table illustrates the lowest and highest annual premiums offered for insuring houses and the contents of these houses in various parts of the UK. Note the wide variation in cost. Some insurance companies will not insure the contents in various towns such as Liverpool, London and Newcastle.

EXHIBIT 7.7: The cost of insuring buildings and their contents in various parts of the UK

burglaries in recent years in the UK has greatly increased the annual cost of house contents insurance in certain districts of the country.

Cross-subsidy between the customers in a given pool used to be a common practice in UK insurance. A group of people in the pool who were at high risk were subsidized by others in the same pool who were at low risk. This situation is changing rapidly. The insurance companies are targeting high risk groups much more precisely than they were able to do in the past. This targeting is gradually redistributing the total cost of the annual insurance bill between the participants in each pool.

If you are at high risk of burglary, car accident or catching some particular disease you are likely to be targeted as such by the insurance company and will find your insurance premiums rising rapidly as a consequence if the premiums are not fixed premiums.

The possibility of using genetic fingerprinting to identify those at risk of developing some serious disease in later life will raise a major social problem in the future. Some individuals could find themselves uninsurable as a consequence of these developments. This fact, the inability to find insurance, could affect their ability to raise loans, particularly mortgage loans.

The ending of cross-subsidy and the more precise targeting of those at risk are important enough questions to require a political solution. As the tools become available to identify high-risk applicants for certain types of insurance the insurance companies will most certainly use them to fix their premiums more precisely. It is up to governments to forbid such a practice if society decides that these practices will impose an unfair burden on certain social groups. This has now become a European problem by reason of recent legislation regarding competition among insurance companies in the European Union.

For the present our advice would be to take out all relevant insurance now before such practices become commonplace and the targeting of applicants at risk becomes more precise.

REDUCING THE COST OF INSURANCE

Various stratagems are available for reducing the annual cost of insurance. Let us now examine some of these stratagems.

Shop around

If you study the current cost of insurance charged by the various insurance companies for providing the same type and degree of insurance protection you will be amazed at the huge variation in cost. In no other competitive market do we find such a wide variation in the pricing of identical products. How can sellers in a free market charge different amounts for providing an identical service?

The answer to this conundrum lies in the inefficiency of the information processing system within the insurance market. Customers just do not know how to find out for themselves the cost of the products offered by the various insurance companies operating in the insurance market.

The buyer of an insurance product cannot 'shop around' to find the lowest premium on the market since there are simply too many products on the market. You must approach an intermediary, such as an insurance broker or a bank representative, to find the comparative costs of the insurance product you want to buy.

There is a particularly wide variation between the premiums charged in the PHI and critical illness markets. The highest annual premium cost in these markets can be a remarkable 40% above the lowest cost for what is almost identical cover.

There are three other reasons for this variation in the cost of providing an almost identical benefit. First, the claims record of all insurance companies on a particular risk are not identical, thus the premium charged will vary depending on the pattern of past claims. Second, some insurance companies have chosen to pay a high rate of commission to agents to encourage sales rather than to cut the cost of the end-product to the customer. This practice is fast diminishing but it is not yet dead. The third reason for the wide variation in premium costs is that all insurance companies do not wish to participate in all insurance markets. Certain insurance products are sold at an uncompetitive price to discourage sales.

From the point of view of the buyer, the important thing is to find the cheapest policy that suits your needs. The buyer of an insurance product needs to be able to search among the various policies available to find that insurance policy which best meets his needs at a reasonable cost. At present the individual buyer of insurance is too much at the mercy of his intermediary adviser. Most intermediaries are competent and honest, but some are not.

The recent development of telephone insurance services, personal financial fact services like Money-facts and *Which?*[6] magazine, 'on-line' computer-based insurance databases and insurance information services are allowing the determined individual insurance buyer to make a direct search of the cost and terms of the current policies available. These information services allow buyers to discover for themselves the relative cost of the premiums charged by the insurance companies for a particular insurance product[7] and the conditions attached.

The 'best' policy need not be the one offering the lowest annual premium since there is a small risk involved in the safety of payout by the insurance company (the insurance company might go bankrupt; this occasionally happens with small insurance companies). Some insurance companies are safer than others. In fact an excessively low premium, that is a premium cost well below the cost offered by other companies, might excite suspicion in the mind of a cautious buyer.

We will return to the security of the insurance company underwriting the policy later in this chapter. For the moment let us emphasize that the insurance market is not very efficient at diffusing information about costs of insurance to customers and so by shopping around you should be able to reduce your annual insurance bill by a substantial margin.

Make full use of 'deductibles'

If you are prepared to pay a proportion of the cost of the loss incurred yourself then the insurance company will almost certainly offer you a substantial discount on the annual insurance premium. The reason for this reduction in the cost of insurance is that fewer claims from customers are likely be made to the insurance company and this fall in the number of claims will reduce the administrative costs to the insurance company. The annual reduction in the cost of the premium will almost certainly be greater than the value of the small claims you do not make.

Seek out any premium-reducing attributes you may possess

Insurance companies do a great deal of research on the nature of claims. They often find certain attributes in their customers that are associated with a low (and high) claims record. You may possess some attribute that the insurance company associates with low claims. The company will thus charge you a lower-than-average premium if you inform it that you possess this particular attribute.

Elderly persons, for example, are often offered substantial discounts on motor insurance because elderly drivers are involved in fewer accidents. The annual cost of house contents insurance is reduced for those with *accredited* burglar alarm systems. Non-smokers are offered substantial discounts on life and PHI policies compared to smokers. Professional workers are offered substantial discounts on certain health policies compared to manual workers and, most important of all, insured persons making no insurance claims for several years are offered very large discounts called no-claims bonuses by most insurance companies. Note that 'no-claims bonuses' are often transferable from one insurance company to another company that offers an even larger discount.

Not all insurance companies offer the same discounts. Once you have established that you possess a cost-saving attribute you need to seek out the insurance company that offers the highest special discount to those customers possessing the particular attribute.

The special discounts offered on specific attributes vary a great deal between insurance companies and the rates of discount are changed quite frequently. Finding the right company is a job for your insurance broker, and most do an excellent job, but sometimes, despite the stringent regulations of the profession, some financial intermediaries are not as assiduous as they might be in finding the cheapest policy!

Insure through a trade association or professional body

Favourable rates of insurance are offered by insurance companies to 'block' insurance schemes bought by professional associations, trade associations and similar organizations. You may be able to obtain a substantial discount on your annual insurance premiums by taking out insurance through a group scheme if you are a member of such an association. For example, the cost of private medical insurance can be much reduced if the policy is taken out under a group scheme.

Beware of undervaluing the items insured

One way of reducing your insurance costs that does not work is to undervalue the item insured. If the insurance company concludes that the current market value of the item insured exceeds the insured value the company will simply reduce the claim proportionately. Since the replacement value of most insured items will rise as time passes, particularly in inflationary times, it pays you to insure at replacement cost rather than at historical cost. This is the more expensive option but insuring at replacement cost provides assured cover for the replacement of the item if it is lost or destroyed.

The same advice will apply to life and health insurance. The value of a life or health policy should be adjusted upwards annually by a current cost-of-living index such as the retail prices index to keep the payout in line with real, inflation adjusted, costs and values. Many insurance policies offer you the option of revising your annual premium upwards to adjust the payout value by the current cost-of-living index. You should accept this option if it is offered.

The cost of most insurance policies is quite reasonable relative to the benefits offered but this should not inhibit you from seeking out the many ways of cutting your insurance costs to a minimum.

WHERE SHOULD YOU BUY INSURANCE?

Insurance can be bought from a wide range of outlets. Some of these outlets employ more efficient pricing methods than others. As we advised above one needs to shop around to find the best buy.

It might be thought that the obvious way to buy insurance is to approach an insurance company directly, so eliminating the cost of an intermediary. Certainly this can be done very easily in the case of direct-selling organizations. A phone call to the direct seller of insurance can obtain a quote and the insurance contract can be concluded immediately.

The direct sellers of insurance have cut out the heavy costs of high street offices and so tend to quote below the rates of the older insurance companies, but this is not always so. It has been claimed that direct sellers quote low by 'cherry picking' customers who are at low risk of making a claim. In other words if you are thought by the direct insurer to be a higher-than-average risk in a particular category you may find the premium quoted by a direct insurer to be uncompetitive.

Checking out the rates quoted by many insurance companies for covering a particular risk is a tedious approach to choosing your insurer. Many hundreds of companies sell insurance in the UK and the list of companies is expanding rapidly as the insurance market becomes more internationalized.

The most economical approach to finding the best quotation among the many policies on offer is to consult an *insurance broker* who has immediate access, via a computer terminal, to the current rates and discounts quoted by hundreds of insurance companies. Brokers have a sound knowledge of the insurance market and can use this knowledge to tailor policies to your specific needs. Insurance brokers are strictly regulated and most brokers are reliable but some may put you automatically into the cheapest policy which, as we noted above, may entail a modicum of risk.

Insurance brokers make their money by selling insurance, not by advising their clients, so they have a tendency to put a new client into a new policy even if the old policy was quite adequate. Alternatively a broker may choose an insurance company that pays a high commission rather than one that offers a low cost despite the fact that this is against the statutory SRO regulations (unless the agent is a tied agent with access to a restrictive set of options). If the broker is independent, he or she must give you 'best advice'. We shall expand on this in Chapter 11.

When dealing with a broker the best strategy is to ask the broker for a list of the five cheapest policies on offer which meet the specific requirements you have put forward and then choose the most suitable from amongst these. This cuts down the time of search, leaves you with the final choice and reduces the leverage of the broker.

If you have unusual insurance needs, such as an 'impaired life', then a specialist broker is essential to find a company willing to take you on as a customer at a reasonable price. The British Insurance and Investment Brokers Association will put you in touch with a list of brokers who deal with unusual insurance needs.

Insurance companies claim that the same insurance from the same insurance company will always cost the same wherever it is bought. There appears to be exceptions to this rule.

Insurance can be bought through financial institutions other than insurance companies. Banks and building societies, for example, sell insurance on behalf of insurance companies. In some cases the two institutions have some kind of business relationship so that a loan from a bank is linked to an insurance policy from the associated company.

It is unlikely that policies sold in this way are the cheapest on the market although they may offer other non-financial benefits. Just because you are dealing with a financial institution on one transaction, say a bank loan, this does not mean that you can be forced into buying insurance from the company recommended by that institution. Some institutions conceal this fact from their customers.

Again it is seldom a wise policy to buy insurance on a product or service from the seller of that product or service. For example buying insurance cover on a hi-fi system from the seller of the hi-fi system is not a good idea. Recent research by the Office of Fair Trading has shown that many insurance policies sold in this way are extremely expensive. The seller of an item cannot force you to buy insurance from him on that item although the seller tries to give the naive buyer the impression that he can do this. We might also question why you would want to insure the item since it will have a guarantee attached re performance and it will be covered by your normal house policy against theft.

There are a few exceptions to this rule. Occasionally the seller of an unusual or foreign product does offer to sell you certain kinds of insurance at a lower cost than that charged on the open market. The seller adopts this policy as a marketing ploy to encourage sales. The saving on the insurance of the product is really a form of discount on the purchase price. This mainly applies to motor cars.

HOW SAFE IS INSURANCE?

The safety of an insurance policy depends on two factors: the precise terms of the insurance contract and the reliability of the insurance company underwriting the contract.

Conditional clauses

We have already referred to the dangers inherent in conditional clauses when we discussed household contents insurance. Most insurance contracts contain many pages of small print. These pages need to be read with some care. Research by the insurance companies themselves suggests that this is seldom done. An insurance claim will only be honoured by the insurance company if you, the buyer of the insurance, have complied precisely with the terms of the insurance contract. Conditional clauses, some of them quite abstruse, are not emphasized by the insurance company when the insurance contract is signed. They are emphasized quite strongly when the insurance claims come in.

Conditional clauses in insurance contracts set many limitations on the liability of the insurance company underwriting the contract. For example a life contract requires a precise statement about the state of health of the client at the time the contract is entered into; any obfuscation on the part of the client when filling in medical details can void the contract. An annual travel insurance contract requires a statement as to the number of months the insured individual will spend out of the UK during the period when the insurance is in force. If the buyer stays abroad for one day more than the contract stipulates the contract is void. The insurance of valuable jewellery will invariably require information about where the jewellery is to be stored and how many days it will be worn in a given year. If the jewellery is stored in some other place or worn for more days than stipulated the contract is void.

Honesty and accuracy are essential requirements when filling in the requested information on an insurance contract. The insurance company will not pay up if any of these carefully drafted questions are incorrectly answered. The number of insurance claims that are disallowed because of incorrect information being supplied by the insured when entering into the contract is much greater than the public realizes. It is unwise to assume that some minor infringement of the terms will be overlooked by the insurer. Experience suggests otherwise.

You should not enter into an insurance contract without first reading the conditions in the contract very carefully and abiding by them.

The reliability of the insurance company

The security of payment from an insurance contract also depends on the reliability of the insurance company underwriting the contract. In recent years a substantial amount of legislation, such as the Insurance Act of 1982, has been passed by the UK parliament to protect the interests of the insured. However from time to time insurance companies *do* fail and customers finds themselves unprotected.

You can take out insurance at low cost to protect yourself against losses incurred because of the failure of your insurance company. Naturally this policy is taken out with another company.

The credit rating of an insurance company can be checked out before placing a contract with that company. Chapter 12 provides a list of some insurance related data bases that contain this type of information. Credit rating agencies, such as Standard & Poors, also provide useful information on the credit ratings of insurance companies on a regular basis.

The large insurance companies are very safe. The risk lies with the smaller companies, which may charge lower premiums but take on unusual risks in order to obtain rapid premium growth. There can also be problems with insurance companies resident offshore: the protective legislation applying to the customers of those companies can be very different to the that in the UK.

COMPLAINING ABOUT YOUR INSURANCE PROVIDER

In Chapter 11 we will examine the self-regulatory framework that has been set up by the UK government to protect those who buy personal financial products and services. Several government sponsored but independent regulatory bodies have been established to protect the buyer of insurance products. We will explain the operation of the complaints mechanism and the various compensation schemes available to insured persons in more detail in Chapter 11.

Until the Personal Investment Authority (PIA) was set up in 1995 most personal life assurance came under the aegis of the Life Assurance and Unit Trust Regulatory Organization (LAUTRO). In 1995 the PIA subsumed LAUTRO and its sister organization, FIMBRA. You should always check that the insurance company or agent with which you are dealing is a registered member of a regulatory organization such as the Securities and Investment Board (SIB), the senior regulator, the PIA, the Investment Manager's Regulatory Organization (IMRO) or some other regulatory organization that vets the quality of its entrants and sets strict standards for the behaviour of its registered members. The fact of membership must be stated on the entity's notepaper.

Information on the membership of a regulatory organization can be accessed through any TV system equipped with CEEFAX terminals. You can also enquire about membership of an SRO directly to the regulatory organization by phone. The relevant phone numbers and CEEFAX codes are listed at the end of this book. Most central libraries hold listings of registered members of self-regulating organizations.

You should also check that any insurance broker involved in setting up a policy for you is a member of the British Insurance and Investment

Brokers Association (BIIBA). This association lays down strict rules as to how its members should conduct their business. A listing of these rules will be sent to you by BIIBA on request.

The insurance company itself should be a member of the Association of British Insurers (ABI), which sets down strict standards of conduct for members of the association. Note that many foreign insurance companies are not members of the ABI.

Complaints against insurers in the UK can be lodged with the Personal Insurance Arbitration Service, the Association of British Insurers or, last but by no means least, the insurance ombudsman. Note that the complaints procedure of the insurance company against which you have lodged a complaint must be exhausted before these secondary complaints authorities will take up your case. A listing of the addresses and telephone numbers of all of these organizations is set out at the end of this book.

Finally, and only as a very last resort, you can institute legal proceedings against the defective party. This is a very expensive procedure and not to be recommended unless you are both seriously rich and very determined. If you are penniless you may be able to get legal aid . . . but don't bank on it.

As we noted above, the domicile of the insurance company underwriting the insurance contract is important where complaints are concerned. If the company is domiciled abroad then the law of the foreign country may apply to any insurance claim arising. Care must be taken when placing contracts with insurance companies domiciled in small principalities, such as small off-shore islands. The quality of protection varies: some are excellent, some less so. You must check before you buy. In recent years several of these off-shore insurance companies have gone bankrupt leaving their customers in the lurch.

TAX AND INSURANCE

The general rule regarding the taxation of the proceeds from insurance policies is that the proceeds are not taxed. Income from insurance policies is not subject to income tax and lump sum payments are not subject to capital gains tax if you pay the premium out of a taxed income. There are few exceptions to this rule such as PMI where, if a female is aged 60 or over or a male is aged 65 or over, the premium is allowed against tax and yet the payout on claim is not taxed.

Thus family income benefit, income replacement payments under PHI, the lump sum from CII, long term care payments, accident compensation and so on are not subject to tax. Such policies are called 'qualifying' policies.

Non-qualifying policies, the proceeds from which are subject to tax, are mostly investment products masquerading as insurance products: products such as growth bonds, investment bonds and so forth. In these cases the income or capital gain is usually subject to income or capital gains tax. These matters are covered in Chapter 2 on investment. In certain cases you can take out 5% of the initial lump-sum insurance premium each year over the life of the policy and pay no tax so long as you are a basic rate taxpayer. Higher rate taxpayers can 'top-slice' the proceeds from their 'non-qualifying' policies to reduce tax but this is too complex an issue to pursue here.

Most of the income on insurance company funds is taxed at 20% except for capital gains which are taxed at 25%. Non-taxpaying holders of financial products whose income comes from such funds should note that they cannot reclaim the 20% or 25% tax deducted as they can if they hold normal investments such as unit or investment trusts. Taxpayers who do not use up their capital gains allowance each year are in the same position. Non-taxpayers should steer clear of investing in insurance-based funds. Higher-rate taxpayers benefit from investing in such funds, however, since they pay tax at only 20% rather than the 40% they would pay if they had invested the money in a non-pepped unit or investment trust.

SUMMARY

1. Risk management is concerned with hedging the many hazards that face the individual and family during their passage through life.

2. Risks may be hedged by substituting a small certain payment, such as an option or insurance premium, for a much larger uncertain loss.

3. Insurance works when a group of people facing an identical risk decide to pool the risk so that everyone in the pool pays for, or shares, the loss incurred by a few members of the pool.

4. Insurance is only a suitable vehicle for handling risk if the event to be insured against is a rare occurrence that will result in a substantial loss if it does occur.

5. Insuring against a potential loss is not gambling as a profit cannot be made. Insured individuals can only recover what they have already lost. They must have an *insurable interest* in the event insured.

6. The first step in building an insurance shield around your future is to conduct an *insurance audit* to identify the more important hazards faced by yourself and your family in the future.

7. Once the hazards have been listed, the next step is to find out the cost of insuring against the potential losses arising from these hazards. It is likely that a complete insurance shield will prove to be much too expensive so the lesser risks will have to be left.

8. A wide range of insurance products are offered by the insurance market. The more important categories are life assurance, health insurance, property insurance and various special types of insurance such as insuring against legal costs and the costs of divorce.

9. *Whole of life 'with profits' insurance* builds up a savings fund and protects against the financial consequences of early death. Whole life policies should protect the terminal fund against inflation by reason of the equity content in the life fund. Endowment insurance is really an investment product masquerading as insurance.

10. *Term insurance* is a cheap and very effective form of insurance that can protect a family against the financial consequences of the early death of the breadwinner.

11. A wide range of *health insurance products* are on offer. Products such as private medical insurance to cover hospital and associated costs, permanent health insurance to cover for lost income, critical illness insurance to cover for the heavy costs of sudden serious illness and long-term care insurance to assist with the cost of home and residential care. It is also possible to insure against personal injury and injury to a third party.

12. *Property insurance* is essential for every home owner. Check the current cost of rebuilding your home regularly. The buyer of a home must be aware of the possibility of existing or future subsidence.

13. If you insure the contents of your home, check that valuable individual items are insured for their current worth. Insurance companies usually place an upper limit on the value of the individual items covered under the policy. This upper limit may not be high enough to cover valuable items. It may make sense to insure your home and contents with the same company to avoid disputes between insurance companies.

14. Insurance is not expensive relative to the benefits it provides, but there are a few simple strategies that can reduce the cost even further. The major strategies available are to shop around, to take advantage of *deductibles*, to take advantage of any premium-reducing attributes you may possess and to insure through a composite body like a trade association or professional group. The increasing ability and willingness of insurance companies to target high risk customers more precisely will lead to a major social problem in the future since some people may find themselves allocated to an uninsurable category.

15. The simplest way to find the cheapest insurance on the market is to go to an insurance broker. If you think you can do better yourself, or

you want to check up on the insurance policy recommended, then many databases listing insurance costs are now accessible to the layman. It is doubtful whether insurance provided by the sellers of a product is the cheapest insurance available for that product.

16. Insurance bought in the UK from a UK company is very safe. A great deal of government legislation was passed with this object in view. However, insurance companies occasionally go bankrupt with unfortunate consequences for their customers. Credit-rating agencies examine the creditworthiness of insurance companies. Moreover, the self-regulation apparatus in the UK financial industry is now formidable. Complaints can be placed before insurance industry watchdogs and compensation will be provided if the complaint is found to be justified. Always check that the company or adviser you are dealing with is a member of the relevant regulatory organization.

TEST YOUR KNOWLEDGE

1. What is meant by *hedging* a risk? Suppose you own £25 000 worth of shares in Glaxo PLC. The shares are standing near an all-time high. You will need to sell these shares in one year's time to finance the purchase of a new car. How can you hedge the risk that the shares will fall substantially in value over the next year?

2. Which of the following events can be insured against and which cannot? What special conditions might be attached to these specific policies if insurance is available?

   a. The death of a friend

   b. Rain on a wedding day.

   c. Ordinary wear-and-tear costs on car.

   d. Failing to pass a university exam.

   e. The costs of a divorce.

   f. Being sued for something you said at a party.

   g. Loss of a hand if you are a professional footballer.

   h. A heart attack.

   i. Being hijacked in an airliner.

   j. Losing your job.

3. What is meant by having an *insurable interest* in the outcome of a future event?

4. In relation to both insurance and gambling you bet a fixed amount of money now which opens up the possibility of receiving a much larger amount in the future. Is there any difference between insurance and gambling?

5. You can hedge against the following list of potential losses in the future by (a) using insurance, (b) changing the system, (c) getting out of the system or (d) self-insuring. Suggest which of these four approaches is best suited to hedging the risks attached to the following events:

   a. A fire in your house has been caused by electrical wiring being very old.

   b. The cancellation of a holiday because a child of the family catches chickenpox.

   c. Your house being damaged by an earthquake.

   d. A chimney pot falls off of the roof of your house in a gale injuring a passer-by.

   e. The cost of replacing the windows of your house that are being smashed frequently by footballs kicked by boys in an adjoining field.

   f. Six months off work caused by a serious unexpected illness.

   g. Losing your contact lenses several times a year

   h. A series of burglaries, running at three burglaries a year, over the last five years

6. What are the three major hazards facing you and/or your family at the present time? How have you hedged the risk of these hazards occurring?

7. Set out the four basic steps required to conduct a *risk audit* of your affairs.

8. What are the two major types of life insurance? What conditions favour taking out one type rather than the other?

9. 'Use insurance to invest in your good health.' Explain what this means?

10. What is meant by the term 'bundling' of financial products. Explain how an endowment mortgage policy is a bundled product. How could this product be unbundled to give the house buyer a wider range of choice in planning his or her financial affairs?

11. Why is the annual premium on life insurance sometimes raised each year in line with inflation? How does this increase in premium benefit the beneficiary?

12. What is an *impaired* life policy? Who would need such a policy?

13. Why is *term* insurance for a fixed amount so cheap compared to the cost of a *whole life* assurance policy for the same amount?

14. A cursory examination of any listing of the costs of insurance cover against a specific loss will show a wide variation in the costs of almost identical insurance cover offered by the various insurance companies. How can this be? Surely the companies with the higher charges will sell no insurance within this category?

15. What is permanent health insurance? What kind of benefit does it provide? Why is it misnamed?

16. Your company offers you permanent health insurance cover or critical illness cover, but not both. Which would you accept? Why?

17. You are making enquiries about taking out accident insurance on your new car. The General Insurance company quotes you an annual premium of £840 for full cover. You are shocked that the premium is so high. Discuss the steps which are open to you to reduce the cost of this annual premium.

18. Why is it that some advisers suggest that a house and the contents of the house should be insured with the same insurance company?

19. Suggest some conditional clauses that might be applied by an insurance company to policies covering: (a) jewellery; (b) items left in a car; (c) damage to a house caused by the roots of a nearby tree; (d) a car accident; (e) the costs of divorce; (f) medical insurance; (g) having twins.

20. What is meant by *cross-subsidy* in insurance? Why is cross-subsidy much less common today than it was a few years ago? Why is this fact of great importance to you?

21. Why might the use by insurance companies of genetic analysis create a new 'under-class' in society?

22. If you buy a product from a trader can the trader insist that you buy insurance on the product from him?

23. How can you check on the reliability of an insurance company?

24. You have taken out an insurance policy on damage to your home. The premium is £400 a year. Three years after you start this insurance some drunken youths start a fire in your home during a party while you are away from home. The fire causes £15 000 worth of damage to your house. The insurance company refuses to meet the insurance claim because they counter-claim that the youths were invited into your home by one of your children and you have been negligent in protecting your own property. What procedures are open to you in complaining about your treatment by the insurance company?

NOTES

1. If an event, like death, is certain to occur the word *assurance* is used; if an event might occur but is not certain, the word *insurance* is used.

2. There is little point in being mealy-mouthed about this: the reason they 'leave' the home is because they die.

3. If you share your home with a spouse or other elderly relative this rule may not apply.

4. Approximately 7% of the over 75s and 30% of the over 85s lived in care in 1995 in the UK.

5. If the company pays your PMI premiums for you this advantage will be taxable.

6. *Which?* magazine is a particularly useful source of information on all kinds of insurance products. Comparative tables of key conditions, costs and policy limitations are often provided.

7. For example you can search through on-line databases such as TELESURE and FINIS which are accessible to the individual enquirer through a home computer through a modem connection.

Managing your personal credit

8

A SURFEIT OF CREDIT

The trouble with short-term credit in the UK is that there is far too much of it around. The letter columns of the newspapers frequently carry complaints that the correspondent has received a red printed demand note for final payment on an overdue debt, including blood-curdling threats as to what the credit provider will do if the debt is not paid immediately, while at the same time receiving a further offer of credit for several thousand pounds from the same credit source. The current culture of short-term credit provision in the UK encourages an irresponsible attitude on the part of the borrower.

The reason for the plethora of short-term credit providers in the UK is the very high level of profitability associated with this business activity. The credit provider can borrow money in the wholesale money market at, say, 12% per annum and sell it to his customers at anything between 17% per annum and 34% per annum.

Such a wide variation in the cost of credit from many suppliers suggests that the UK credit market is not very efficient. The customer does not seem to have access to sufficient information to compare the various sources of credit and pick the cheapest source. We will return to this topic later in the chapter.

As things stand at the moment lending institutions spend vast sums of money offering credit to potential borrowers about whom they know very little. This can lead to problems for both the borrower and the lender.

'Getting into debt' is now a major social problem in the UK. Several organizations exist with the sole purpose of providing individuals who have a serious debt problem with free advice on how to get out of debt with a minimum of suffering.

It is very easy for a borrower in the UK to take on an excess of personal debt because there is a lack of symmetry between the generous lending policies pursued by many financial institutions and their tough pursuit of borrowers who fail to pay on time. The law in the UK should be altered to force some kind of symmetry between the lending policy of a credit provider and its debt-recovery policy. If a credit provider pursues an irresponsible lending policy a brake should be imposed on the powers of that credit provider when it comes to recovering debt.

The way to avoid the 'debt trap' is to limit the credit you take on to some fraction of your income or wealth. We will discuss this approach later in the chapter. Psychologists tell us that taking on additional credit beyond your capacity to repay can become just as much of an addiction as gambling or alcohol.

CREDITWORTHINESS

A good credit rating is a valuable asset. Many borrowers do not take advantage of certain attributes they possess that can be used to reduce the cost of their credit. Certain lenders will appreciate these attributes and offer credit to you at a rate of interest significantly lower than for other borrowers.

Many sources of short-term credit are available in the UK and the difference between the cost of credit offered by the cheapest and most expensive of these sources can be very substantial. You will find that with a good credit rating you can borrow at an annual rate of interest that is often 10% p.a. or more below the rate charged to a borrower with a poor credit rating.

A good credit rating is determined by many factors. Some lenders use a purely subjective form of assessment when offering credit. Other lenders use a technical device called a 'credit rating scale' to determine the creditworthiness of a potential borrower. Some of these credit rating scales are quite sophisticated and apply statistical techniques such as discriminant analysis to process information about the payment record of past customers to identify those factors that make up a sound borrower. If you score sufficiently well on the credit scale you will be offered credit; you may even be offered cheaper credit if you build up a high enough credit score. It is therefore sensible for you to find out the 'key factors' that make you a safe bet so far as the credit provider is concerned.

Some of the key attributes which appear to differentiate a good credit risk from a poor one are:

- your past credit record;

- your current income level;

- age;

- state of health;

- current job security;

- owning your own home;

- the length of time you have spent in your present job and home;

- your marital status.

Various points are awarded for each of these factors depending on the answer you give to the question. The points are then added up to arrive at your credit score. If you possess a good past credit payment record, if you are the recipient of a high regular income, if you are married and middle aged with good job security and you own your own home you will enjoy a high degree of creditworthiness with any lender.

You should use this valuable asset of high creditworthiness to find a lender who will appreciate these attributes and, in consequence, provide you with relatively cheap short term credit funds. Oddly enough, many borrowers fail to follow this course of action and accept the first source of credit offered to them. This first offer usually comes from the seller of the goods they are about to buy. Such a source is almost certainly the most expensive form of credit on the market.

CREDIT RATING AGENCIES

A *credit rating agency* provides information to those who sell goods on credit about the creditworthiness of the buyer of those goods. Most sellers of consumer goods who sell on credit subscribe to one or more of the five large credit rating agencies in the UK that offer a credit evaluation service. These agencies hold the court records of individuals who default on their credit repayments on a computer database. Once you find yourself on the books of one these credit rating agencies it can be difficult to find further credit or, at best, the credit offered to you will cost more than it otherwise would.

If you find that your name is listed on a credit rating agency database as having a poor credit record it is a serious matter, requiring immediate attention. Examples of incorrect entries in credit record databases are legion.

Some credit databases hold a formidable amount of information. The credit agency INFOLINK, for example, keeps 44 million records in its database and can be accessed by on-line computer 80 hours a week.

What do you do if a mistake is made? If an individual is refused credit he or she is permitted by law (Consumer Credit Act 1978, S157 (1)) to ask if a credit rating agency has been consulted. If the answer is 'yes' then the individual can ask for the name of the agency. The person refused credit can then write to the agency within twenty eight days enclosing a fee of £1 and asking for a copy of the relevant credit rating report. This must be provided by the agency on request. If the file is incorrect or misleading in some respect the individual whose creditworthiness is being assessed can force the agency either to make a correction or to include an explanation of the reasons for the credit default in the file which will be sent to future enquirers.[1] This useful legislation prevents sloppy work by the credit rating agency resulting in credit withdrawal from innocent parties.[2]

SOURCES OF CREDIT IN THE UK

There are many sources of short-term credit in the UK. The business of lending money is very profitable and not too difficult to organize. As we said above, you borrow on the wholesale money market and sell on the retail market. Advertising, book-keeping and credit recovery are the main costs involved. The ease of entry to the short-term credit market opens the market up to credit sharks so the government has set up some fairly tight controls on participants in this market.

Sources of short-term credit can be either *open-ended* or *specific*. The provider of an *open-ended* source of credit will initially agree some upper credit limit with you, the borrower. Most open-ended sources of credit are provided by banks. The loan can be a personal loan for a fixed number of years or a revolving credit account. You are now allowed to borrow money and repay the loan within your credit limit. Your credit limit will be a multiple of the amount of money you pay into the account each month. This multiple varies between banks.

The lender does not keep a record of how you spend your money; the lender simply checks that the upper spending limit on the credit line has not been exceeded. The rate of interest you are charged depends on the amount you borrow. Small loans attract a higher interest rate. If you wish to terminate the loan agreement before the fixed period agreed at the outset you may be fined several months' interest (usually two or three months' interest).

A *specific* source of credit is usually targeted at individuals who wish to acquire some specific asset such a car or a dishwasher. The value of the loan is related to the value of the asset to be acquired. A specific loan will have a fixed repayment term attached to it.

A fixed rate of interest will normally be charged on the loan and various other quite strict loan conditions, such as default conditions, will be incorporated into the loan agreement. These conditions must be strictly adhered to by the borrower. Specific credit loans are much less flexible than open-ended credit loans.

Some of the more common forms of open-ended credit loans are the traditional bank overdraft, a personal or rolling credit loan for a fixed number of years, loans from an insurance company that are secured on a life assurance policy, the credit offered under most credit card and some charge card schemes and the revolving credit schemes offered by large stores. Common forms of specific credit loans include bank loans for a specific purpose and the ubiquitous hire-purchase agreements.

Bank credit tends to be cheaper than the other sources of credit listed above but, in recent years, the gap between the cost of bank credit and other forms of credit has narrowed dramatically as all credit providers draw their funds from the same pot. The providers of bank credit and credit based on 'gold' credit cards tend to pay more attention to the creditworthiness of their borrower than do the other sources of credit listed above. Thus if you consider yourself to be a creditworthy borrower you would be well advised to seek short-term credit from these discriminating sources since the cost of credit from these cautious lenders will tend to be much less than from other less-discriminating lenders.

Most insurance companies will, if asked, provide you with a loan secured on your life-assurance policy. The maximum value of a loan available from this source depends on the paid-up value of your life policy. This cheap source of credit is not advertised and is often overlooked by individuals with substantial life policies. Since the loan is secured on the life policy it is a very secure loan and so the cost of credit from this source should be relatively low compared to other sources.

Hire-purchase credit is easy to come by and for that very reason is usually the most expensive form of credit on offer.

CREDIT FROM CREDIT CARDS

If there is too much credit around there are certainly too many credit cards around. It seems that every conceivable organization is trying to persuade the public to adopt its credit card. Most of these cards cost a few pounds per year although some are free. There is no point in paying for a credit card if you can get one free. There is an upper limit to the amount you can charge to a credit card in a month. This upper limit can be negotiated with the provider of the card.

The cost of credit from a credit card lies at either end of the credit cost spectrum. If you pay your credit card bill on time you get 'free' credit for 30 to 50 days. I am sceptical of the value of this credit since it is only of value if you keep all your surplus funds in a high interest account. Most of us don't.

At the other end of the spectrum, if you don't pay on time, credit cards are, for the most part, a very expensive source of credit. The interest charge can vary from 17% to 34% on an annual basis. Don't take your credit from this source if you can avoid it; a bank loan is much cheaper. However credit card credit is instantly available: you do not have to consult your bank manager.

There are other forms of plastic available that substitute for cash. *Charge cards* like American Express cards allow you to buy goods or services with no upper limit to the charge. This is very useful if you want to buy a £10 000 pearl necklace for your girlfriend in Lugano. Charge cards must be paid off at the end of each month or you will face horrendous costs. This fact is a useful discipline that appeals to many card holders but charge cards are really for the seriously rich who need fast access to substantial amounts of money in various parts of the world. The annual cost of a charge card is quite high at £40 to £70 per year.

Another form of plastic payment is the *debit card*. You present your debit card to the shopkeeper who swipes it through a machine and the money is instantly electronically transferred from your account to that of the shopkeeper. No credit is involved.

One form of debit card has a specific value entered into the card when you buy it from your bank; the value is debited to your bank account. When you pass this kind of card to the shopkeeper she again swipes it through the machine but this time the cost is debited to your card (not to your bank account) which falls in value by the given amount. In this case you are loaning money to your bank.

The most advanced form of plastic card is the *chip card*, which has been introduced in the USA. This card is a tiny personal data bank which knows more about you than you do yourself. When you place this card into an ATM or 'swipe machine' it will allow you to debit and credit values between your accounts, pay bills and find out about your current financial status on all fronts.

THE COST OF CREDIT

There is a wide variation between the cost of credit offered by the various credit providers in the UK. It is not uncommon for the cost of the most expensive credit on offer to be two to three times the cost of the cheapest credit available.

Unless the loan you require is very small it should be worth your while to shop around among these various credit providers to find the cheapest source of credit on offer. We pointed out above that to accept credit from the first source of credit offered is a foolish and expensive practice.[3]

Secured loans from insurance companies will normally prove to be the cheapest source of credit. If you have a 'whole of life' assurance policy or something similar it is likely that you will be able to borrow at relatively low cost against the security of the current value of this policy.

The key point to keep in mind is that the more discriminating the lender is in accepting borrowers, the cheaper is the credit provided by that lender. A lender who loans money indiscriminately takes on many poor credit risks who fail to repay their loans and so run up heavy legal costs for the lender. Thus the interest rate charged by such a lender must be increased *to all borrowers* to cover these debt recovery costs. The discriminating lender does not bear these costs and so can provide cheaper credit to his or her high-quality customers. The astute borrower needs to find the most discriminating lender who will accept him as a client.

CALCULATING THE TRUE COST OF CREDIT: THE APR

Until quite recently it was very difficult for a borrower to calculate the true rate of interest he or she was paying on a loan. Many loans were set up in a complicated fashion that included initial costs which were not included in the interest charge. The repayment schedule could also be complex. Most borrowers were paying rates of interest way above what was stated in the loan agreement.

This situation has been much improved by the introduction of the Consumer Credit Act 1978. Since the consumer credit regulations were introduced the true rate of interest on a loan, called the *annual percentage rate* (APR), must be stated in advertisements by lenders offering loans in addition to any other interest rate advertised. In other words whatever rate is advertised must be converted to its APR equivalent for the period of the loan and the APR must be published in addition to the other rate. The APR on a loan allows you to compare the true interest cost of various loans offered to you before you decide which loan to accept.

In the past the rate of interest advertised as the cost of a loan could be very misleading to a naive borrower. A good example of this misrepresentation is the calculation of the *flat add-on* rate of interest much favoured by the sellers of consumer goods who offer loans to their customers to buy these goods on hire purchase.

Suppose, for example, that you want to buy an expensive hi-fi system for £1000. You cannot afford to pay cash so the seller offers you a £1000 loan to buy the item with a repayment period of four years at a 'flat rate of interest' of 20% a year. The lender makes the calculation as follows:

20% a year = £200 a year for four years = £800.

The total you are being asked to pay is thus £1000 + £800 = £1800 and if this is repaid over 48 monthly instalments the monthly instalment is 1800/48 = £37.50 a month. The rate of interest is stated to be 20% p.a. but the true rate, the APR, is close to double this rate at 38% per annum. The reason for the discrepancy is that the capital of £1000 is being continuously repaid over the four-year period of the loan repayment so the average value of the loan outstanding over the four years is not £1000 but just over £500. The Consumer Credit Act was introduced to prevent lenders from misleading borrowers in this way.

The calculation of the APR can be a rather complex process in certain cases but this is not a problem for you. All you have to do is to compare the APR printed on the various sources of credit offered to you. The UK government has published a booklet on the subject.[4]

As we noted above, the calculation of the true APR can be rather complex. However a simple method of approximating the APR is available in some, but not all, cases. An illustration of this simpler method is provided in Exhibit 8.1. This provides a formula for making a rough estimate of the APR. The method is applied to calculating the APR on a *flat-rate add-on* interest loan of £2000 at a flat rate of 10% per annum.

The government has placed a powerful tool in the hands of the borrower by forcing lenders to publish an APR on all loans and credit offered. Unfortunately this useful cost-saving device is not used by borrowers as often as it might be. There is disturbing evidence that many

The precise calculation of the APR is rather complicated but the following formula provides a good approximation of the true APR in some cases.

Let us suppose that a merchant offers to sell a microcomputer costing £2000 sterling. The credit terms involve a loan of £2000 over 2 years at a flat rate of interest of 10% per year. Payments are to be made monthly.

The seller makes the following calculation:

$$£2000 \times 10\% = £200$$

The borrower is to repay

$$£2000 + (2 \times 200) = £2400$$

over the two years. So the monthly payment is $\frac{£2400}{24} = £100$.

Thus the capital $= £2000$. Finance charges $= £400$.

What is the true rate of interest, APR, on this loan?

Let:

APR = annual percentage rate
P = number of loan repayments per year
N = number of loan payments to be made over the entire life of the loan
C = finance charges
L = loan amount

The formula for approximating the APR is:

$$\frac{P \times ((95 \times N) + 9) \times C}{12 \times N \times (N + 1) \times ((4 \times L) + C)}$$

Substitute in numbers:

$$\frac{12 \times ((95 \times 24) + 9) \times 400}{12 \times 24 \times (24 + 1) \times ((4 \times 2000) + 400)}$$

Therefore APR = 18.17%

Since:

P = 12 periods
N = 24 periods
C = £400
L = £2000

The true rate of interest is not 10% per year but 18.17% per year.

EXHIBIT 8.1: A method to calculate the approximate APR

Annual %	Quarterly %	Monthly %	Weekly %	Daily %	Continuous %
5.00	5.09	5.11	5.12	5.12	5.13
10.00	10.38	10.47	10.50	10.51	10.51
15.00	15.86	16.07	16.15	16.17	16.18
20.00	21.55	21.93	22.09	22.13	22.14
30.00	33.54	34.48	34.86	34.96	34.98
40.00	46.41	48.21	48.95	49.14	49.18
50.00	60.18	63.20	64.47	64.81	64.87
75.00	98.85	106.98	110.56	111.53	111.70
100.00	144.14	161.30	169.25	171.45	171.82

The table illustrates the effect of compounding the rate of interest more than once per year. For example, if the annual rate is stated to be 20% but if it is compounded monthly, not annually, then the true annual rate is 21.93%. The final column shows the cost of continuous compounding.

The difference is quite small until the rate exceeds about 20% per year. So long as a rate compounded more than once per year is expressed as an APR, the difference will be brought to the notice of the debtor.

If you want to make your own calculation, the equation is

$$(1 + \frac{j}{m})^m) - 1$$

where j is the nominal annual rate and m the number of times the rate is compounded each year.

EXHIBIT 8.2: The effect of compounding the annual interest rate more than once per year

---

borrowers ignore the APR when raising credit since they do not understand the concept.

ADJUSTING THE NOMINAL RATE OF INTEREST

When calculating the cost of a loan it is sometimes necessary to convert the rate to a different time base or to differentiate between the *nominal* interest cost of the loan and the *real* interest cost of the loan. For example you may wish to convert a rate of interest based on a period of less than a year, say, three months, to an annual rate to arrive at the true interest cost of the loan for the year. Alternatively you may wish to convert an annual rate to a rate based on a period of less than a year. Another possibility is that you may wish to adjust a nominal rate of interest to a real rate after adjusting for the effects of past or expected inflation.

Exhibit 8.2 shows the sensitivity of the interest rate to the compounding period used. It shows the true rate of interest if a loan is compounded, not once a year, but several times a year by the borrower.

Exhibit 8.2 shows the effect of compounding quarterly, monthly, weekly and so forth. Notice that the difference is small in absolute terms at low rates of interest but quite significant at high rates of interest.

When inflation is high, say above 6% per annum, the difference between the nominal rate of interest you are paying and the real rate after adjusting the rate downward for inflation can be significant. The real rate is what counts so long as your income, after tax, rises to compensate for inflation.

MEASURING YOUR DEBT CAPACITY

We stated in the opening section of this chapter that it is important to ensure that the total debt you take on at any one time is within your debt capacity, otherwise you are likely to fall into the 'debt trap' that has been much publicized by the media in recent years. Your debt capacity is determined by several factors the more important of which are

- the amount and stability of your periodic income;

- the value remaining from this periodic income after deducting all legally committed and essential expenditures (we shall call this latter figure your 'discretionary' income);

- your expected *future* income; and

- the market value and composition of your existing wealth portfolio with particular regard being paid to the liquidity of your wealth portfolio (how quickly it can be converted into cash).

Calculating your debt capacity is thus not a simple matter as several of these factors are not easy to measure accurately. You would be wise always to err on the side of caution when making this calculation.

Estimating your debt capacity from your income and expenditure account

New debt will add an additional expenditure to your spending commitments. You should ensure that you can really afford this. You cannot give yourself this assurance unless you have provided yourself with a regular monthly income and expenditure account. We discuss the preparation of such a document in Chapter 10.

Ranking your expenditures

The left hand column of Exhibit 8.3 illustrates a typical personal expenditure account of a professional family.

Name: John Wilson
Marital status: Widower
Assumed inflation (1997–2007) (%): 4% per annum

Occupation: Shop manager
No. of children: 2
Currency unit: £

Age: 45
Year: 1997

Date of birth: 10 July 1952
Actuarial life expectation: 34 years

Income	Classified ranking			Ranked by importance
Salary	24 500			24 500
Dividends	4 000			4 000
Other income	400			400
Total income	28 900			28 900
Less:				
Tax	5 780			5 780
Other deductions	920			920
Total deductions	6 700			6 700
Gross cash flow	22 200			22 200

Expenditure		Ranked expenditure	
Classification		Essential expenditures	8 370
Accommodation	550	Accommodation	550
Clothing	1500	Food	1 000
Food	2200	Gas and electricity	1 200
Gas and electricity	1700	House insurance	340
House insurance	340	Medical and health	480
Medical and health	480	Rates	1 100
Children	500	Telephone	200
Rates	1 100	Transport	1 000
Recreation	1 500	Clothing	1 100
Repairs	1 200	Repairs	900
Subs and gifts	500	Children	500
Telephone	330		
Transport	1 900	Important expenditure	1700
Other	1 200		
		Food	500
		Gas and electricity	300
		Telephone	100
		Transport	500
		Repairs	300
		Discretionary expenditure	4930
		Food (meals out)	700
		Gas and electricity	200
		Telephone	30
		Transport	400
		Recreation	1 500
		Subs and gifts	500
		Clothing	400
		Other	1 200
Total expenditure	15 000	Total expenditure	15 000
Surplus for saving	7 200	Surplus for saving	7 200

The left-hand columns show a conventional expenditure account. The right-hand column ranks the expenditures into three categories with respect to their importance. Each item of expenditure is allocated to the 'essential', 'important' or 'discretionary' category. This classification allows the 'opportunity cost' of additional credit to be calculated. Note that some expenditures are split between the important and discretionary categories.

EXHIBIT 8.3: A ranked expenditure account

An alternative way to present the expenditure account is to allocate all items of family expenditure into one of three classes. First we identify *essential* expenditure – sums that must be paid come what may such as the monthly mortgage payment and the food bill. Second we identify the *important* expenditures that can be avoided but only at some cost (school fees for example). The third category, the remaining expenditures, consist of what we will call *discretionary* expenditures. These costs are not essential and can be avoided without undue sacrifice. They include theatre tickets, expensive meals out, the costs of a second car, holidays abroad and all the other various luxuries that make life worth living but are not absolutely essential for survival.

The total of these expenditures can now be compared to the total net income of the family. If the total income, net of tax and other regular deductions, exceeds the total expenditure, we create a fourth category of cash outflow called *saving.*

We are now in a position to assess what economists call the *opportunity cost* of taking on more debt. The cost of the additional debt will first be set against savings, if a surplus is available. If a surplus is not available the debt will have to be substituted for some part of the discretionary spending. If the cost of the new debt exceeds all of the saving plus the discretionary spending then the opportunity cost of the new debt is quite severe since it will entail curtailing some 'important' expenditures.

At this point in your analysis you may well decide that the opportunity cost of the new debt is too high, or you may not, as the case may be. The important point is that by setting out your income and expenditure account in this way you can calculate, in advance, the items of spending that must be curtailed if you are to take on the additional debt. The opportunity cost of the additional debt is now known and can be evaluated and compared with the value of the item to be acquired with the debt.

The key to measuring future debt capacity is to calculate what additional expenditure can be undertaken on top of existing expenditures without encroaching on your important or essential expenditures.

If a loan is taken out at £200 per month for 24 months it is possible to calculate the effect of this repayment on the pattern of current spending and saving. It might be that the monthly cost of this loan will simply reduce *involuntary saving* for the period of the loan. Alternatively it might reduce voluntary saving and cash available for inessential expenditures like theatre and holidays. Once the cost of the new debt has eliminated the discretionary expenditure, the opportunity cost becomes very significant. The new debt may now force you to make a choice between reducing important but non-essential household expenses such as school fees and private medical provision. This provides the upper limit to your debt capacity since you will not wish to cut into your important contractual monthly expenses like mortgage payments.

Ranking expenditures in this way allows you to gauge both the opportunity cost and the degree of risk you are taking when you enter into a consumer finance contract involving regular additional cash outlays for a given period ahead. The degree to which you put other expenditures at risk is up to you. You must compare the benefits derived from the object acquired with the loan against what you have to give up to repay the loan. The above procedure provides a numerical framework within which this choice can be made.

There is also the possibility that your current net cash flow might decline suddenly and unexpectedly by reason of unemployment, illness or pregnancy. As we noted in Chapter 7, permanent health insurance (PHI) (income replacement) and critical illness insurance (CII) can be used to hedge against such risks, or a loan protection policy can be taken out to cover the risk of debt default by reason of illness or unemployment.

THE VALUE AND LIQUIDITY OF YOUR ASSET PORTFOLIO

Another important factor in determining your debt capacity is the value and composition of your existing wealth. Your marketable assets will provide security to a lender which may increase your potential debt capacity well beyond the debt capacity supported by your cash flow. Lenders will usually provide credit up to a value equal to about two-thirds of the market value of your assets pledged in security for the loan.

The potential may be there but it is not wise to raise debt based on your existing assets for the purpose of excess consumption. Remember that we are discussing short-term credit here, not long-term loans. If the interest on a short-term loan cannot be paid out of current income, you are eating into your capital base and this is seldom a wise move unless you are quite old. It is not wise, under normal circumstances, for a borrower to pledge marketable assets as cover for an inadequate cash flow to finance short-term consumption.

Thus an income-and-expenditure statement highlighting your *discretionary* expenditures provides the best framework for deciding on the *safe* level of personal debt that you can raise. However the ultimate decision on a personal credit *ceiling* is determined by balancing your attitude to accepting the financial risk of default against the strength of your desire to acquire the good or service in question. The ultimate decision on debt level, as always, is yours.

CONSUMER CREDIT AND THE LAW

Since the consumer credit industry is such a profitable industry and since it is not too difficult to enter the industry, consumer credit has attracted more than its fair share of loan sharks and confidence tricksters. For this reason the Government has taken a great deal of interest in this area of business activity in recent years and has passed detailed credit legislation. The Government department responsible for supervising consumer credit is the Office of Fair Trading.

The legal constraints placed on those providing consumer credit have been tightened up in recent years. The most important Act aimed at controlling credit operations in the UK is the Consumer Credit Act 1974. Some of the more important constraints placed on the behaviour of companies providing and monitoring consumer credit are listed below:

1. As we have noted, those credit rating agencies that provide personal information about potential borrowers to potential lenders must, if asked, send a copy of the credit report supplied to the lender to any individual who believes he or she has been denied credit because of the contents of the report. If, on enquiry, you find that you have been denied credit because of a negative credit agency report you can contact the Credit Agency concerned and ask for the requisite enquiry form and instruction sheet on how to fill in the enquiry form. You fill in the form and send it, together with a sum of £1, to the credit rating agency. A copy of the credit report is then sent back to you. If you think that the report is misleading you are allowed to write an explanation and insist that this explanation be included with your credit report if the report is supplied to another customer of the agency in the future. Severe penalties are imposed by the Office of Fair Trading on any credit agency that fails to follow these procedures.

2. Several strict rules apply to the signing of a consumer credit contract. For example, if the contract is signed on the premises of the seller the contract has immediate effect unless fraud or deception can be proved. However the potential buyer might have a *face-to-face* chat with the seller of the good in question and then take the contract away from the premises of the seller before signing it. If a copy of the signed contract is then sent back by the seller to the buyer the buyer has a right to cancel the contract within five days from receipt of the contract.

   Contract law is complex and if you feel that you have been misled by the seller as to the terms of a credit contract offered to you it is advisable to seek legal advice. The solicitor will give you an estimate regarding the cost of pursuing the case. This cost may be recoverable.

3. If you find that your current cash flow is insufficient to service your current debts, and this can happen to the best of us, you have three options:

   - try to do a deal with your creditors;

   - apply for an *administration order;* or

   - file for bankruptcy.

The last two options only apply in England and Wales, not in Scotland. If you have any choice in the matter the first of these three options is by far the best since the other two options, and particularly the third, can blight your creditworthiness for years to come.

Since the second and third options will entail the entry of a third party, the courts, into the dispute, many lenders are willing to renegotiate a deal if you can persuade them that you can repay the debt due over a longer period of time. At this point the lenders may agree to suspend any further interest charges on the debt since the courts will probably enforce this condition anyway if the matter goes to law.

If you wish to apply for an *award of administration* you must fill in a form (form N92) detailing your various debts and current income and expenditure. The debts must total less than £5000 and a judgment by the County Court must already have been made against you. Under these circumstances the courts will take it upon themselves to administer the debt repayment. The court will write to all the creditors involved checking that your debt schedule is accurate and then fix an amount that you will be required to pay to the courts each month. Any additional interest payments will be stopped. The court will decide how to distribute the monthly payment between your various creditors.

If your total debt amounts to less than £5000 but the court believes that it is still too large, relative to your current and expected income, to ever be repaid you can apply to the courts for *composition* which means that the courts may set aside a substantial part of the debt. This procedure is sailing very close to bankruptcy but is not actual bankruptcy, thus you can still, with luck, obtain credit in the future.

If your total debt exceeds £5000 you can file for *bankruptcy*. However if you still have substantial assets the courts might refuse to grant you bankruptcy and force you to set up an *individual voluntary arrangement* whereby you must sell your assets and distribute them *pro rata* to the debts owing to your creditors.

You should be aware that the financial consequences of bankruptcy are severe. As a bankrupt you would have to declare yourself to be a discharged bankrupt for the rest of your life when applying for credit (if you remain in the UK). You will find any form of credit extremely hard to obtain in the future. The law of bankruptcy is very complex and legal advice is essential. A debtor who mishandles bankruptcy can face imprisonment for a long term.[5]

You would be well advised to avoid bankruptcy at all costs. Less drastic alternatives are usually available.

It should be noted that mortgage and tax arrears are not written off by bankruptcy proceedings. Homeowners in a 'negative equity' situation cannot cancel their mortgage debt by simply handing their home back to the building society which granted them the loan (which now exceeds the market value of the home). The building society will simply sell the property for what it can get, deduct this amount from the outstanding value of the mortgage, and bill the homeowner for the balance! The homeowner is then worse off than before: he still owes money but has no home!

If you think you are heading for trouble on the debt front you should contact National Debtline (0121 359 8501), the Consumer Credit Counselling Service (0345 697 301), or the Bankruptcy Association of Great Britain and Ireland (01482 658 701). These organizations are there to help people in financial difficulties.

4. The law provides some useful backup cover for credit card holders who buy goods or services with their credit card. If the goods cost more than £100 and are not delivered to the buyer, or do not come up to scratch, or the seller goes bankrupt, the credit card holder can proceed against the credit card company in addition to the seller of the good. This 'joint liability' is a useful and free additional benefit provided to the users of credit cards.

5. The law regarding disclosure of the annual percentage rate (APR) on loans offered to borrowers was discussed earlier in this chapter. Note that the APR must be clearly displayed on the offer of the loan and must be displayed using the same *size* of type as the other rates quoted (but a *different* type of the same size may be used for representing the two rates).

SUMMARY

1. Short-term credit is too easy to obtain in the UK at present. This can lead you into a severe financial crisis if you are not careful. You must be as aware of your debt capacity as you are of your liquor capacity.

2. If you possess several of the characteristics associated with being a 'good credit risk' you are *creditworthy*. A high level of credit-worthiness is a valuable asset that you should exploit when seeking credit. Borrowers with a good credit rating can obtain substantially cheaper credit than those who do not enjoy such creditable attributes.

3. You are likely to be awarded a good credit rating if you enjoy a high regular income, if you are in a steady job that you have held for a reasonable length of time, if you have a stable marriage, if you own your own home, if you are in good health and if you have an excellent record of past credit payments.

4. Credit-rating agencies are organizations that keep records on borrowers with poor past payment records. If you are denied

credit by a seller you can ask why; if the reason given is a negative report from a credit-rating agency you have a legal right to ask for the name of the agency involved. You can write to it and demand to see a copy of your credit record, which must be corrected if wrong.

5. Credit can be supplied to you on open account up to a set limit, as with bank overdrafts, or credit can be provided for a specific purpose. The former type of credit is usually cheaper than the latter.

6. There is a remarkable variation in the cost of credit offered by credit providers in the UK. Rates of interest varying from 12% p.a. to 35% p.a. are not uncommon. You should shop around. The more discriminating the supplier of credit, the cheaper is the credit provided by that supplier since he carries fewer bad debts.

7. When credit is advertised, the cost of the credit must be expressed as an annual percentage rate (APR) in addition to any other expression of the interest rate. This APR rate is consistent between the different forms of charging credit. You can use the APR to compare the true cost of each source of credit offered.

8. You ought to attempt to estimate your debt capacity. Your debt capacity is influenced by many factors but the size and regularity of your income is obviously an important factor. You need to structure your expenditure account to bring out the value of your 'discretionary' expenditure and involuntary saving. The value and composition of your wealth portfolio will allow you access to short term consumption credit but this temptation should be resisted. Your aim must be to calculate the true opportunity cost of any additional credit you take on board.

9. Since short-term credit is a favoured habitat of fraudsters, government regulations and the common law have imposed strict rules on the industry. Credit rating agencies must disclose copies of their files to persons listed on these files if asked to do so. The law also provides some protection to individuals against the machinations of unscrupulous credit providers.

10. If you borrow money and cannot fulfil your financial obligations you have several choices as to how to proceed. You can try to do a deal with your creditors, apply for an award of administration, or apply for bankruptcy proceedings to be brought against you. Bankruptcy is a very serious business and should be avoided if at all possible. A bankrupt person will find it difficult to raise future credit in the UK.

11. If you purchase goods or services with a credit card from a UK-based seller rather than using cash, you have some useful additional protection against default by the seller and some other benefits.

TEST YOUR KNOWLEDGE

1. You hope to buy a hi-fi system costing £1000 but do not have the £1000. A dealer offers to sell you the system with a loan to repay the cost over 24 months at £60 a month. The annual rate of interest is claimed to be 20%. A set-up contract charge of £40 is also added to the cost. The calculation of the monthly charge is made up as follows: £1000 + (£1000 × 20% × 2) + 40 = £1440. $\frac{£1440}{24}$ = £60. What is the true annual rate of interest, the APR, on this loan?

2. 'The astute borrower needs to find the most discriminating lender who will accept him as a client.' Explain.

3. You apply for credit from a dealer to buy a dish-washer costing £800. The dealer offers to sell you the machine for cash but declines to extend credit to you. You ask why. The dealer declines to explain why. You ask if he has consulted a credit-rating agency. He refuses to answer. What action is open to you to resolve this problem?

4. Suppose that, following on the last question, the dealer tells you that he has consulted a credit rating agency and your credit rating is inadequate. He gives you the name and address of the agency. What should you do now if you believe that your credit rating is good and some sort of mistake must have been made by the rating agency?

5. What advantages does an *open-ended* source of credit enjoy over a *specific* source of credit?

6. Why is bank credit and credit from a 'gold card' credit source usually cheaper than the cost of credit from other sources?

7. A loan that is obtained from an insurance company, and which is secured against a whole life assurance policy, is usually a cheap source of credit. Why is this the case? Why is hire-purchase credit so expensive?

8. All advertisements offering credit in the UK must state the APR on the credit. What is this APR? How can you use the APR when selecting credit sources?

9. A lender charges you 20% interest on a loan; the interest is charged annually but you pay the interest monthly. What is the real rate of interest you pay on the loan? (See Exhibit 8.2.)

10. Rearrange your monthly income and expenditure account so as to bring out your essential expenditure, your important expenditure and your discretionary expenditure each month. What percentage of your total expenditure is discretionary?

11. What aspect of your asset portfolio will be of particular interest to a potential lender?

12. What is the name of the government department to which you should write if you think that you have been deceived in a consumer credit transaction?

13. Under what conditions can you withdraw from a credit contract that you have signed?

14. If you find that you cannot pay your debts, what are the three options open to you?

15. 'Bankruptcy can take a great weight off your mind. You are free of debt at last.' Why then is it that most solicitors advise their clients to avoid bankruptcy at all costs?

16. Name two forms of debt not cancelled by bankruptcy proceedings.

17. If you purchase a microcomputer using a credit card, what additional benefits do you enjoy that you would not enjoy if you had paid by cheque?

NOTES

1. See the leaflet entitled *No credit? Your Right to Know What Credit Rating Agencies are Saying about You.* This can be obtained from the Office of Fair Trading, Field House, 15 Breams Buildings, London EC4A 1PR, telephone 0171 242 2858.

2 . An interesting example of the type of problem that can occur is when one person in a block of flats becomes a poor credit risk and all the other people in the same block are blacklisted.

3. It might be argued that the 'opportunity cost' of the time spent in searching for the cheapest source of credit could outweigh the benefit in finding the cheapest source. This is unlikely to be the case. The current cost of credit can be checked with a few phone calls to banks, insurance and credit card companies or by surveying such publications as *Money Observer* or *Moneyfacts*.

4. See the 1982 government publication *Calculating the APR*, London, HMSO.

5. For a short introduction to bankruptcy proceedings see the booklet entitled *The Insolvency Act 1986: A Guide to Bankruptcy Law*, from the Insolvency Service Organization 2 Burnhill Row, London EC1Y 8LL.

Managing your personal tax

9

THE TAIL THAT WAGS THE DOG

No-one can doubt that taxation is an important issue in personal financial planning but tax must never be allowed to dominate your personal financial plan. Every year the tax rules and tax allowances are changed in the national budget and so a personal financial plan based on a tax stratagem may be made redundant by the Inland Revenue within a few months. Few taxpayers realize just how vulnerable tax-based personal financial plans are to changes in the Government's annual budget.

The return you will receive from any investment should always be calculated net of tax. First you need to work out a financial plan suited to your particular circumstances; then you must fine-tune this plan for tax. The tax tail must not be allowed to wag the financial dog. This said, your current financial plans may need to be regularly modified in the light of changes introduced by the Chancellor of the Exchequer in the annual budget.

Tax is important because the income from certain types of investment is either untaxed, taxed at a reduced rate, or can be organized in such a way as to delay the date when you are due to pay the tax until your marginal tax rate is lower than your current rate.

The Government uses tax to entice you to do certain things such as set up a pension for yourself, set up a saving scheme or take out insurance to cover your financial position if some misfortune should befall. The wise man or woman will take full advantage of these tax concessions.

TYPES OF TAX

In the UK the individual taxpayer is subject to three types of personal tax: income tax, capital gains tax and inheritance tax. *Income tax* is paid on all types of income, both earned and unearned. *Capital gains tax* is charged on any profit you make in excess of the inflation-adjusted cost when you sell an asset. *Inheritance tax* is based on the value of gifts or the estate you leave to others on your death, but you only pay inheritance tax if the total value of your estate exceeds a given quite substantial amount.

PAYING INCOME TAX

If your annual income exceeds a certain amount you will be required to pay income tax. Most taxpayers in the UK pay income tax through a payment system called Pay-As-You-Earn (PAYE). Under a PAYE system, which was introduced in the UK but is now used as a tax-collection device by most developed countries in the world, the employer is given a tax code for each employee and this allows the employer to deduct the requisite amount of income tax from the employee's pay each month using a set of PAYE tables.

This makes life easy for you, if you are an employee, since at the end of the year, at worst, only a small amount of tax needs to be paid by you to the Inland Revenue tax collector. If it were not for PAYE you would need to pay a large amount of tax to the Inland Revenue out of your income at the end of each year, just like a self-employed person has to do. You would also need to employ the expensive services of a tax accountant.[1]

If you are self-employed you will be required by the Inland Revenue to prepare a set of annual accounts which must be submitted to the tax authorities each year. The Inland Revenue works out your tax assessment based on these accounts and sends you a tax assessment which you can appeal against if you are not happy about the amount of tax you are required to pay.

If you pay tax under PAYE you are assessed under a tax regime called 'Schedule E'; if you are self employed you pay tax under 'Schedule D'. As we will see later in the chapter certain advantages accrue to you if you are assessed under Schedule D rather than Schedule E.

REDUCING PERSONAL TAX

The government, through the tax authority, grants you certain 'allowances' and 'reliefs' against your income which reduce your tax bill. Examples of 'allowances' are the married couples' allowance and the blind person's allowance. Examples of 'reliefs' are certain expenses that you can set against your income and so reduce your personal tax bill, such as the interest paid on a mortgage on your first home and your contribution to a pension fund. In such cases the government, in effect, contributes towards the cost of the good or service bought.

Once your net taxable income has been calculated by the Inland Revenue this net income is taxed in 'slices' with a different rate being applied to each slice. Certain types of income are not taxed or are zero rated. This variation in the rate of personal tax means that if you can alter your income tax situation so that a lower rate of tax is applied to your marginal income, substantial tax savings can be effected. The current rates of tax applied to personal income in the UK vary between 15% and 40% of income received, so by altering the rate that is applied to your income you can reduce your tax bill by a substantial margin. By taking full advantage of all tax allowances available to you, by identifying any tax reliefs that can be used to reduce your expenses, and by switching income from a higher to a lower or even a zero tax band you can effect a substantial reduction in your total tax bill. This activity is called *tax planning*.

SOME EXAMPLES OF TAX PLANNING

Suppose you have £100 000 to invest and you decide to invest the money in government stock providing a return of 9% per annum for 10 years, at which point you hope to retire. Your income from this investment is £9000 a year, gross of tax. If, however, you invest the £100 000 in a lump sum pension fund in such a way that the £100 000 can be charged against income which would otherwise be taxed at the highest, 40%, rate of tax then you can receive a tax refund of £100 000 x 40% = £40 000. This rebate of tax reduces the cost of your investment to only £60 000. The gross income from the investment is still £9000 so the annual rate of return is increased from 9% to $\frac{9\ 000}{60\ 000}$ = 15%. A substantial increase in return on the original 9%.

Let us take another example. Suppose you are a male and married. You will leave an estate worth approximately £500 000 to your wife on your death. In such a case probably no inheritance tax is due to be paid to the tax authorities since assets passed from a husband to a wife normally give rise to no inheritance tax or other tax. However, suppose your wife dies soon after yourself and leaves her estate to your children. At that point £(500 000 − 200 000) × 40% = £120 000 tax is payable in inheritance tax from your wife's estate. The children inherit £380 000. If, on the other hand, you, on your death, were to leave £200 000 of your estate to your children and the balance of £300 000 to your wife then no death duties are payable on your death but when your wife dies only

$$£(300\ 000 - 200\ 000) \times 40\% = £40\ 000$$

is due to be paid in inheritance tax by your children. The children inherit £460 000 between them. This is a saving of £80 000 in tax compared to the first option.

Tax *avoidance*, that is minimizing your tax bill, is perfectly legal but tax *evasion*, concealing income from the Inland Revenue, is not. There is a grey area between tax avoidance and tax evasion which tax professionals call tax *avoision*. Quite a number of personal tax plans spill over into this grey area and you need to beware that you are not caught up in a tax evasion scheme masquerading as a tax avoidance scheme. Only a fool or a saint will pay more tax than he or she needs to pay. By utilizing the various tax allowances and tax benefits that are offered by the tax authorities you can save yourself a great deal of money. So tax planning is an important facet of personal financial planning, although it must not drive personal financial planning.

THE COMPLEXITY OF TAX LEGISLATION

Tax legislation and tax rules are in a perpetual state of flux and even tax specialists have difficulty in keeping up to date with all the latest changes in the various tax laws, allowances and regulations, especially in an international context.

The rules of personal (and company) taxation reflect an eternal battle between the tax inspectors and the tax consultants. The government of the day introduces some new tax legislation, often to plug loopholes in the existing tax law, and the tax consultants immediately get to work on this new legislation to design ingenious new loopholes to save their clients' money.

It is difficult for anyone who does not devote their full time and energy to tax matters to keep up to date with all these ramifications. Fortunately the basic rules of personal tax are relatively simple and it is to these basic rules that we shall now turn. If your tax problem becomes complicated you have no alternative but to turn for advice to a tax expert. The Inland Revenue itself will supply free advice; unfortunately your problem is likely to involve a disagreement with this very authority. It is not difficult to find a personal tax expert: every major accounting firm runs a personal tax department, but advice on personal tax does not come cheap. Personal tax advice from a competent adviser will cost you at least £100 per hour.

Spending a little of your time learning the basic rules of personal tax can therefore save you a great deal of money. You will be able to extract more information from your tax adviser in a shorter period of time since you will understand what he or she is saying and will be able to ask the right questions.

Some personal financial advisers will design a set of personal financial plans for a client, including basic tax optimization, and then hand these plans over to a personal tax specialist to fine tune them for maximum tax efficiency. The question the tax consultant needs to ask himself is: 'Can the same planning objectives be achieved at lower cost by utilizing a more subtle tax strategy?' Whether you, as the client, have to pay for this 'fine-tuning' depends on the charging policy of your personal financial adviser.

We will now take a more detailed look at the three personal tax systems operating in the UK.

A	Income from lands and buildings, including rents.
B	Abolished in 1988.
C	Income from government securities.
D	This schedule is divided into 6 cases.

Case 1:	Trades
Case 2:	Professions and vocations.
Case 3:	Interest received, annuity payments, annual payments.
Case 4 and 5:	Overseas income from invesments and business income.
Case 6:	Any other profits not included in other cases.

E	Wages and salaries.

Case 1:	Work done in UK by UK resident.
Case 2:	Work done abroad by non-resident. Income paid in UK.

F	Dividends and other distributions paid by companies.

The schedule under which income is taxed is important since the allowances and concessions differ between schedules. Items allowed against tax under Schedule D may not be allowed against tax under Schedule E.

EXHIBIT 9.1: Classes of income as defined by the Inland Revenue

---

INCOME TAX

Almost all income in the UK is subject to tax of one sort or another. The Inland Revenue allocates personal income into several classes or 'schedules', the income received under each schedule being treated rather differently by the tax authorities. The various schedules of income are set out in Exhibit 9.1. Some schedules are further subdivided into 'cases'.

The schedule to which a source of income is allocated can be a matter of some importance. For example earned income is given more tax concessions than unearned income.

Certain types of income are not subject to any form of tax. These types, which are few, are listed in Exhibit 9.2. The reasons why these sources of income are exempt from tax are varied. In the case of PEPs, TESSAs, SAYE[2] and pension lump sums the government exempts these sources of income from tax because it wishes to encourage share ownership or saving by people with lower incomes or the setting up of a pension plan. Most of the other cases would either involve double-taxation of the same income (alimony for example) or tax being charged on persons with very low incomes who would pay little or no tax in any case.

Some benefits received by employees from their employers are also tax free, for example contributions to the employee's pension fund, if it was an approved scheme, and life assurance.

Once the total income[3] of an individual from all sources throughout the world has been calculated, certain tax 'allowances' are available that can be set off against this total to arrive at 'taxable' income. A list of the allowances for tax year 1996–97 that can be offset against income is given in Exhibit 9.3. Not all of these allowances can be offset against your highest marginal rate of tax. Some, which are listed in the table, can only be offset at the 15% rate of tax. These tax allowances are frequently changed in the budget presented in November each year by the Chancellor of the Exchequer, so do not plan on the assumption that they will remain the same for ever.

1. Compensation for loss of office up to £30 000.

2. Covenanted payments made under a voluntary non-charitable deed of covenant (but many restrictions apply).

3. Dividends paid out of personal equity plans (PEPs).

4. Interest earned on tax-exempt saving schemes (TESSAs).

5. Interest on National Saving Certificates.

6. National Savings Bank interest up to £70 per annum on an ordinary account.

7. Rent received from a tenant under the 'rent-a-room tax free' scheme.

8. Payments in kind so long as the employee is earning less than £8500 per annum.

9. Interest paid under a tax-exempt save-as-you earn scheme.

10. Maintenance payments such as alimony paid under a court order.

11. Scholarship income while studying.

12. Most social security benefits.

13. Proceeds from most life assurance policies.

14. Winnings from premium bonds.

The table lists most of the important types of income that are not subject to tax or are zero-rated in the UK. The reasons for the exemptions are either that the Government wishes to encourage this type of investment, or that the income has been taxed already, or that the money is paid to poor people by the Government to ensure a reasonable standard of living and that to tax this income would not be sensible.

EXHIBIT 9.2: Income not subject to tax in the UK

Value of the tax benefit

	Amount	Value at 15% rate	Value at 20% rate	Value at 24% rate	Value at 40% rate
Personal allowances					
	£	£	£	£	£
Age below 65 years	3 765	565	753	904	1 506
Age 65–74 *	4 910	737	982	1 178	1 964
Age 75 and over *	5 090	764	1 018	1 222	2 036
Married couples allowance					
Age of elder spouse below 65 **	1 790	269			
Age of elder spouse 65–74 **	3 115	467			
Age of elder spouse 75 and over **	3 155	473			
Other allowances					
Widow's bereavement allowance **	1 790	269			
Single parent allowance **	1 790	269			
Blind person's allowance	1 250	188	250	300	500

* Excess above the basic personal allowance is reduced by 50% of income above £15 200 until the reduction equals the normal personal allowance. Thus the age benefit is of no value to you if your total income exceeds £17 490 in the 1996–97 tax year.

** Tax relief is restricted to the 15% tax band for several allowances in the 1996–97 tax year.

The table shows some of the allowances that can be set off against the income of the individual for the 1996–97 tax year. That is the year from 6 April 1996 to 5 April 1997.

Note that many of these allowances only provide relief at the level of the 15% tax band, not the 24% or 40% tax band as in the past.

EXHIBIT 9.3: Some income tax allowances for tax year, 1996–97

Note that the age allowance is reduced if your income exceeds a given figure. For example in the tax year 1996–97 the age allowance is reduced to zero if you are between the ages of 65 and 74 and earn more than £17 490.[4]

After your taxable income has been calculated by the Inland Revenue the tax authorities apply various rates of tax to each ascending 'slice' of this 'taxable income'. These rates are changed quite frequently, at the time of writing the 1996–97 tax year rates are as follows:

- a rate of 20% is charged on the first £3900;

- a rate of 24% is charged on the next £21 600;

- a top rate of 40% is charged on the remainder.

These rates will be likely to change in the future. The top rate of tax paid by a taxpayer is important. This rate is called the taxpayer's *marginal* rate. Many tax allowances can be set off against income at this top 'marginal' rate. At one time in the distant past mortgage interest on any size of loan was allowed as a charge against income tax at the taxpayer's marginal rate. Thus when the top rate of income tax was 60%, as it was at one time in the past in the UK, a mortgage costing 10% per annum cost the taxpayer on a high income only 10% x 0.4 = 4% per annum! Some single payment pension plans allow the lump sum premium to be charged against your current income tax at the highest 40% marginal rate.

A personal tax computation for the tax year 1995–96 is set out in Exhibit 9.4. Mr John Mee earns an annual salary of £20 000 plus a bonus of £4500. He receives £1600 of dividends from UK companies paid net of tax at 20% and interest on National Saving Certificates of £960 in the year. The Mee family receive £2000 a year from a rent-a-room scheme from a student at the local university. Mrs Mee's only income is the £1200 she received from a building society account. Mr Mee's income for the year which is subject to tax is thus £26 500. The interest on the national savings certificates and the rent are tax free. He is permitted to deduct a personal allowance of £3525 from this total and a married couples allowance of £1720 but the latter can only be charged at the 15% rate. Mr Mee is also allowed to charge the interest paid on his mortgage against his taxable income but only on the first £30 000at the 15% rate. The total payable after all allowances and reliefs is thus £4746. This figure represents 18% of his income subject to tax. His marginal rate is 25% in tax year 1995–96.

Mrs Mee pays no income tax as the £1200 she receives from the building society is well below her personal allowance of £3525 for the 1995–96 tax year. Mr Mee should transfer some income to Mrs Mee to allow her to use up her total personal allowance.

The taxable income is taxed in three slices at increasingly higher rates. The first £3200 is taxed at 20% the remainder of £17 775 at 25%. The dividends are already taxed at 20%. Most of the tax due has already been paid to the Inland Revenue. The salary and bonus will have been taxed under PAYE and the dividends have had 20% deducted by the company before Mr Mee receives them.

BASIC, MARGINAL AND AVERAGE RATES OF TAX

The *basic rate* of tax is the standard rate of tax charged on normal incomes. Currently in the UK this rate is 24% in the tax year 1996–97.

Personal tax computation for John Mee, 1995–96

Mr John Mee works as a business executive with the Arcadia Engineering Company. John is 46 years old and married to Shirley Mee. They have three children, Julie (12), Paul (10) and Cathleen (7). Mrs Mee is not employed. They have let out a room in their home to a student at £2000 for the year. Mr Mee currently earns a salary of £20 000 per year from Arcadia Engineering. He has earned a bonus on company profits of £4500 for the year to February 1995, paid in July 1995. He received dividends from UK companies of £1600 for the year to 5 April 1996 plus interest on National Savings Certificates of £960 for the same year.

The only income received by Mrs Mee is building society interest of £1200 for the year to 5 April 1996. The Mee children have no income.

Mr Mee has taken out a mortgage on his house for £40 000. He paid £2720 interest under the MIRAS scheme during the year.

Income	Tax schedule	£
Salary for year to 5 April 1996	E	20 000
Bonus (paid in year 1995–96)	E	4 500
Dividends from UK companies (£1600 + £400)	F	2 000
Income subject to tax		26 500
Less:		
Personal allowance		3 525

Taxable income

Tax to be paid thereon:	Amount	Rate	
Tax on non-dividend income	3 200	at 20%	640
	17 775	at 25%	4 444
Tax on dividends	2 000	at 20%	400
	£22 975		5 484
Less: married couples allowance	1 720	at 15%	258
			5 226
Less: tax deducted at source on mortgage interest	3 200	at 15%	480
Total tax payable			**4 746**
Average tax rate paid	£4 746 / £26 500		18%
Marginal tax rate paid			24%

Mr Mee pays £4746 of income tax. The tax on his salary will be deducted by his employer under PAYE and forwarded monthly to the Inland Revenue. The income from the National Savings certificates and room rental is free of tax. Mr Mee can claim a personal allowance and a married couple's allowance. He also benefits from the fact that mortgage interest can be charged against his tax bill at the 15% rate.

There is no income tax to pay on Mrs Mee's income from her building society account since her personal allowance of £3525 eliminates this income. She is not utilizing her full personal allowance. Mr Mee should transfer some income to his wife to allow her to use up her full allowance.

EXHIBIT 9.4: Example of a personal tax computation

This is the rate paid on most of the income earned by most people in the UK who are on average incomes.

The *marginal rate* of tax, as we noted above, is the rate charged on the 'top slice' of income. Currently in the UK the highest marginal rate that can be applied to income by the tax authorities is 40%.

The *average rate* of tax is the total income tax paid by the taxpayer divided by the total income subject to tax. This was 18% in the case of Mr Mee.

THE INCOME TAX SCHEDULES

We noted above that the tax authorities allocate different kinds of personal income to one or other of various classes. These classes are called *schedules*. Most earned personal income is allocated to Schedule D and Schedule E. These will become more important under the new self-assessment schemes.

Self-employed persons working in a trade or profession are taxed under Schedule D. Thus anyone who runs their own business is taxed under Schedule D. Some interest and annuities are also taxed under schedule D. Many items of expenditure that can be offset against income taxed under Schedule D cannot be offset against income taxed under Schedule E. Therefore, if it is possible to choose between schedules, it is better to arrange matters so that you are taxed under Schedule D rather than under Schedule E.

A self-employed person who pays tax under Schedule D will need to arrange for business accounts to be prepared once a year. These accounts will be sent to the Inland Revenue but unless the firm has a revenue in excess of £90 000 the accounts need not be audited. The tax inspectorate works out the tax bill for the year and sends the bill, the tax assessment, to the self- employed person after the end of the year.

Employees, that is persons who work for someone other than themselves, are taxed under Schedule E. Normally Schedule E tax is deducted by an employer on a regular basis under the tax payment scheme called PAYE which we discussed above. Very few deductions are allowed against income assessed under Schedule E therefore it is difficult to use tax stratagems to reduce a Schedule E tax bill. As we noted above Schedule D income offers much more scope for legal reduction of the tax bill.

Company distributions of income, such as dividends, are taxed under Schedule F. Income from land and property is taxed under Schedule A.

PERSONAL TAX IN THE UK: CAPITAL GAINS TAX (CGT)

If you sell an asset for more than you paid for it then you may be liable for capital gains tax. The tax rate charged on a capital gain depends on your marginal tax rate *before* you calculate your liability to CGT. The capital profit, net of allowances, is added to your other income to arrive at your CGT liability. Husbands and wives are taxed separately for CGT purposes. This can provide much scope for reducing the total CGT liability on your family.

A CGT allowance is available. For example in the tax year 1996-97 the first £6300 of your capital gains was exempt from CGT. This is a substantial sum and it means that, in the great majority of cases, profits on asset sales are not subject to CGT. Note that any unused capital gains allowance cannot be carried forward to be offset against your capital gains in future years. However capital losses on the sale of your assets *can* be carried forward and offset against capital gains tax due in future years.

Any capital profit in excess of £6300 in any one year is subject to tax at a rate depending on your marginal tax rate in that year. If the marginal tax rate on the top slice of your other income in that year is already being assessed at the 40% tax rate then the capital gains tax rate will be 40%. If the marginal tax rate on the top slice of your other income in that year is 24% the CGT rate is 24%, but if you have used up only part of one band, say the £3900–£21 600 24% tax band, you can use up the remainder of the band on the balance of your capital gains tax liability. Once this is used up the balance of capital profit will be taxed at the next higher band which is currently 40%.

You do not need to be a tax expert to see that organizing your sale of assets to minimize your CGT is not too difficult an exercise. You can sell off your assets in parts, each sale netting a £6300 profit; you can delay selling profitable assets until later in life when your marginal tax rate is at the lower 24% band (after you retire?) or you can sell a profitable asset in the same year as a loss-making asset, or you can split your assets with your wife and both can now claim the maximum CGT allowance on sale in any one year.[5]

An example of a CGT assessment is set out in Exhibit 9.5. From this we see that Mrs Soames made an ostensible capital gain of £120 000–£50 000 = £70 000 on the sale of her Lalique bowl in the 1994–95 tax year, however the calculation of the capital gains tax payable is not as simple as this. First, something called an *indexation allowance,* see Exhibit 9.7 (below) needs to be worked out. Second the capital loss on another sale during the same tax year needs to be allowed for. Third the annual exemption of £5800 on capital profits for tax year 1994–95 needs to be deducted and finally the marginal rate of tax of Mrs Soames needs to be calculated. The calculation of CGT tax liability is complicated!

Exhibit 9.5 shows the indexation allowance, which allows for inflation, to be £15 367. The capital loss of £5000 on the sale of ceramics in the same tax year is deducted, then the £5800 annual CGT exemption is deducted, and finally the marginal rate of tax is calculated.

Mrs Soames' lowest 20% tax band of £3200 has been fully used against her earned income of £20 500 and £17 300 of the 25% tax band (1994–95 tax year) has also been used against her earned income so there is only

Mrs Judith Soames bought a nineteenth-century Lalique bowl for £50 000 in December 1988. She found herself short of money in 1994 and so she sold the bowl for £120 000 on 25 April 1994. The costs incurred on the sale were £9700.

In January 1995, Mrs Soames incurred a capital loss of £5000, adjusted for inflation, on the sale of some Chinese ceramics.

Mrs Soames works as an auctioneer. Her taxable income after all tax allowances, is £20 500 for the year to 5 April 1995. What is her liability for capital gains tax for the year to 5 April 1995?

Calculations

	£	£
Revenue for sale of Lalique bowl		
Gross revenue		120 000
Less: costs of sale		9 700
Net revenue		110 300
Original cost of asset sold	50 000	
Indexation allowance		
$((144.2 - 110.3) \div 110.3) \times 50\ 000$	15 367	65 367
Chargeable gain on sale of bowl		44 933
Capital loss on sale of ceramics		5 000
Computation of capital gains tax payable		
Chargeable gain on sale of bowl		44 933
Less: capital loss on sale of ceramics		5 000
Net chargeable gain		39 933
Less: CGT exempt amount allowed in 1994–95		5 800
CGT chargeable		34 133

The tax rate applied to the CGT charge depends on the marginal rate of tax paid by Mrs Soames on her other income. In this case Mrs Soames' taxable income is £20 500 after all allowances have been deducted. Mrs Soames has therefore used up the lowest 20% tax rate and £17 500 of the 25% band (1994–95 tax years). She therefore has £20 700 – £17 500 = £3200 of the 25% rate band left to use up before paying 40% on the balance due for CGT. Her CGT is thus:

	£
£3200 charged at the 25% rate	800
£30 933 charged at the 40% rate	12 373
£34 133	
Total CGT on sale of Lalique bowl	£13 173

The CGT charge is reduced first by the capital loss that was incurred during this period and then by the indexation allowance, then by the exempt allowance of £5800 for the 1994–95 tax year.

The charge of £34 133 is treated like normal income. Since the 20% band has been used up, the balance is charged at the 25% rate up to £23 700 and the remainder is charged at the 40% rate.

Losses caused by indexation can no longer be carried forward against future capital gains. Other normal losses can be carried forward.

The tax rates and allowances in this example apply to the 1994–95 tax year. Different rates and allowances apply in earlier and later years.

EXHIBIT 9.5: Calculation of a capital gains tax charge

£(20 500 – 17 300) = £3200 of the 25% band left to tax the capital gain of £34 133 at the basic tax rate of 25%. So the first £3200 of the capital gain of £34 133 is taxed at 25% and the balance £(34 133 – 3200) = £30 933 is taxed at the highest 40% tax rate, a charge of £12 373. The total CGT payable is thus £13 173.

ASSETS EXEMPT FROM CGT

Certain assets are exempt from CGT, the most important of these being the family home. The family home can be sold at a considerable profit and yet no CGT is payable on this profit. This exemption only applies to your first home; the profit on the sale of a second home is not exempt from CGT. Other assets exempt from CGT are listed in Exhibit 9.6. The most important of these other exempt assets are the proceeds of life-assurance policies and assets passed into your estate at the time of your death. The latter may be subject to inheritance tax.

INDEXATION OF THE COST VALUE OF AN ASSET SUBJECT TO CGT

If you sell an asset the original cost of the asset can be increased to allow for inflation between buying and selling of the asset before CGT on any profit on the sale is calculated. This a major concession by the Inland Revenue. The cost value of the asset is indexed to allow for the impact of inflation. In other words the amount of tax payable under CGT is reduced by an indexation allowance which is applied to the cost value of the asset.

This inflation allowance is designed to compensate for the fact that the purchasing power of money tends to fall over time by reason of general price inflation. If it were not for this indexation allowance CGT would be paid on any 'increase' in the value of an asset due to the falling value of money itself. Such an increase in money value does not reflect a real increase in value; it simply reflects a fall in the value of money.

An example showing how to index an asset for the purpose of calculating CGT due is provided in Exhibit 9.7.

Mrs Julie Siani buys 10 000 shares in LCI PLC for £12 000 in 1988. She sells them for £25 000 in February 1993. However part of this £13 000 'profit' simply reflects a 34% fall in the value of money between 1988 and 1993. Once the indexation allowance is applied to the 'profit' the profit falls from £13 000 to £8938, and the first £5800 of this capital profit is exempt from CGT in tax year 1992–93. So Mrs Siani only has to pay CGT on £3138. This is £3138 at her marginal rate of income tax. If her marginal rate is 25% she pays 3138 × 0.25 = £784.50.

Capital profits on the sale of the following assets are exempt from CGT:

Primary private residences (first home if more than one owned)

National Savings certificates

Premium savings bonds

Proceeds of Life Assurance Policies

Government securities

Securities issued by public corporations

Most fixed interest stocks

Most 'private chattels' such as motor cars or furniture (not antiques)

Investments in PEPs, enterprise schemes and venture capital trusts

Assets held at the time of the owner's death

Assets given to a charity

Assets given to a national institution

Assets given to a spouse unless the couple are living apart

Retirement relief on the disposal of a business: 100% of profit on sale eliminated up to £250 000; 50% of profit exempt up to £750 000.

The profits on the sale of many assets sold by an individual taxpayer are exempt from capital gains tax. The most important of these exemptions is the private residence, the primary home, of an owner occupier. The proceeds from most life assurance policies are also exempt from CGT.

A concession by the Inland Revenue allows the cost of an asset to be indexed for inflation. This prevents the owner of the asset having to pay CGT on an increase in the value of an asset caused solely by the falling value of money relative to other goods.

EXHIBIT 9.6: Assets exempt from capital gains tax

RETIREMENT RELIEF

Retirement relief from CGT on profits of up to £250 000 arising from the disposal of a business on the retirement of its owner is a very important concession by the Inland Revenue. The matter is, however, too complex to be pursued here.

Other somewhat complex CGT provisions apply to gifts and profits on assets sold which are held in trust. See Slevin (1993) and Mellows (1992) for a more detailed discussion of these provisions.

INHERITANCE TAX

Inheritance tax is charged on the value of assets transferred by you to others, either during your lifetime as a gift or, more usually, on your

An asset can rise in value because of the fall in the real value of money. Thus, when the asset is sold, the 'profit', that is the excess of the selling price over the cost, is not a real profit but is simply a reflection of the fall in the value of money over the period.

Taxing such an unreal profit would be unfair so the Inland Revenue allows the seller of the asset to adjust the cost price upwards by an indexation allowance. The indexation is based on the retail price index (RPI). The Government publishes a RPI every month.

Let us suppose that Mrs Julie Siani bought 10 000 shares in LCI PLC on 3 February 1988. The net cost of the shares was £12 000. On 18 February 1993, Mrs Siani sold the shares for £25 000. How can the indexation allowance reduce the CGT that Mrs Siani must pay on the profit from the sale? Assume that Mrs Siani sells no other chargeable assets during the year. The key statistics are:

RPI for February 1988	103.7
RPI for February 1993	138.8

The indexation allowed on the cost price is therefore:

$((138.8 - 103.7) \div 103.7 \times 100$	33.85%
Cost price	£12 000
$12\ 000 \times 33.85\% =$	£4 062

The CGT due on the sale is therefore:

Proceeds of the sale	£25 000
Less: cost of the shares on 3 February 1988	£12 000
Net unadjusted proceeds	£13 000
Less: indexation allowance	£4 062
Chargeable to CGT	£8 938
Exemption allowance for year 1992–93	£5 800
CGT to be paid	£3 138

EXHIBIT 9.7: Calculation of indexation allowance to reduce CGT

death through a will. Only 4% of estates in the UK pay inheritance tax. Only the seriously rich need read the following section.

The following discussion assumes that the deceased is resident and domiciled in the UK at the date of death. If residence or domicile is uncertain the inheritance tax situation can be somewhat complicated and a legal expert will be needed to sort it out.[6]

REMEMBER TO MAKE A WILL

Perhaps this is as good a point as any to emphasize the importance of making a will. If you do not make a will your estate passes in the following order: in the first instance it passes to your spouse; failing this it passes to your children; next in line are your parents, then your grandparents, then your brothers and sisters, then finally your uncles and aunts. In the absence of all of these your estate passes into the grateful hands of the Chancellor of the Exchequer. If you make a will you can decide for yourself who will inherit all or part of your estate after you die. If your heirs think you are unreasonable in the terms of your will and *if they all agree* the terms of the will can be changed by mutual agreement. In the tax year 1996–97 the rate of inheritance tax payable is as follows:

- On the first £200 000 of value transferred: NIL.

- On the remainder: 40% of the value of the estate at date of death.

TRANSFER OF ASSETS

Transfer of assets on death is called a 'deemed transfer'. 'Chargeable' transfers (gifted up to seven years before death) are added to the deemed transfer to arrive at the value of the estate for the purpose of calculating the liability to inheritance tax.

The transfer of any asset between a husband and wife is exempt from inheritance tax no matter how large the estate may be. For example, if the family home is in the name of the husband and it is left to the wife on the death of the husband, no inheritance tax is payable on the transfer value.

EXEMPT TRANSFERS FROM PENSION SCHEMES

If a lump sum is paid into your estate from an occupational or personal pension scheme on your death, this amount is not normally subject to inheritance tax. The trustees must have some discretion as to who receives the fund.

If you make a gift during your lifetime the gift may be subject to inheritance tax as a *potentially exempt transfer* even if you die up to seven years after the gift is made. The gift will be valued at it's value on the date of transfer for the purpose of inheritance tax.[7]

Not all gifts that you make are subject to inheritance tax. For example, gifts to your spouse, wedding gifts to one of your children up to a market value of £5000 and many other forms of gift are exempt. Gifts up to £6000 in total made by one person over a two-year period are exempt from inheritance tax.

POTENTIALLY EXEMPT TRANSFERS

The current rules of inheritance tax state that if an individual dies within seven years of making a substantial gift that is not exempt from inheritance tax, the inheritance tax to be paid on the gift by the recipient of the gift will be as follows:

Years before death	Inheritance tax rate (%)	Effective tax rate (%)
1–3	100%	40%
4	80%	32%
5	60%	24%
6	40%	16%
7	20%	8%
8	0	0

The tax must be paid by the recipient of the gift. If you wish to hedge the risk that the recipient may have to pay this tax if you die within the seven-year period you can take out a *stepped* term insurance policy on your life (or some alternative) at a relatively low cost.

Similar provisions apply to gifts made to various types of trust but the inheritance tax rules regarding the tax to be paid on the transfer of business assets to trusts and the tax liability of trustees for assets held on behalf of beneficiaries are much too complex to be pursued here. See Mellows (1992) for a detailed discussion of the subject.

One useful concession made by the Inland Revenue is to allow unquoted shares held for at least two years to be passed on to beneficiaries free of inheritance tax. The idea here is to prevent private companies being crippled with inheritance tax charges on the death of a major shareholder. So many stratagems are available for avoiding inheritance tax that it is really a voluntary tax unless the estate is very large.

SELF-ASSESSMENT FOR TAX

As from 6 April 1997 the government is introducing a new system of tax assessment for over nine million UK taxpayers. The system is called *self-assessment*. In theory this will save the government money by reducing the number of people employed in the Inland Revenue.

The new system will not affect you if you are an employee and you receive all of your income from a single employer who deducts tax from your salary under a PAYE system. The same exclusion applies if you are receiving your sole income from an occupational pension scheme.

The individuals who will be affected include the self-employed and employees or pensioners who receive income from several sources, company directors, and people with substantial investment income.

The new scheme requires that you fill in a detailed set of schedules, one for salary, one for investment income, and so forth, which will be sent to you in due course. You can work out the amount of net tax due to the Inland Revenue for yourself, or you can hand the job over to an accountant, or you can leave it to the Inland Revenue to do the calculations for you, as they did in the past.

For example, if you come under the new system you are required to send your first self-assessed tax return to the Inland Revenue by 30 September 1998, but only if you want the IR to make the tax calculations for you. If you decide to calculate the net tax due yourself or you hand it over to an accountant, you need only send in your tax return by 31 January 1999.

The key dates to remember are 30 September and 31 January. If you fail to send in your tax return or your tax due by these dates you can be fined £100 and later £60 for each late day, you will also be charged interest and surcharged on unpaid tax due. The self-employed will be required to make two 'payments-on account' each year, normally based on one half of their previous year's tax bill.

The key point in all of this is that, as from 5 April 1996, you must keep proper personal accounting records plus receipts for all of your income and payments that have tax implications. These receipts need to be kept for a period of five years. Since all persons who wish to manage their own finances must keep personal financial records anyway, self-assessment imposes no additional burden. Chapter 10 is devoted to a discussion of the various methods available for keeping personal financial records.

SCHEMES FOR REDUCING PERSONAL TAX

Many ingenious lawyers and other tax experts spend a good deal of their working lives thinking up schemes to reduce the burden of personal tax on their clients' income and wealth. The richer you are, the greater the scope for reducing your personal tax burden. If you live and work in several different countries during a given year, this situation provides tax experts with much scope for reducing your total tax burden.

In order to provide a flavour of what is possible, a few examples of certain tax reduction stratagems are listed below. The strategems that can be applied change year by year. As the Inland Revenue closes one loophole so another one opens.

1.   The advantages of buying rather than renting a home

There is no capital gains tax to be paid on the profits from the sale of a home that is the owner's primary residence. Interest paid on a mortgage on this primary residence up to £30 000 is allowable against tax at a 15% rate. Rent, on the other hand, is not an allowable charge against personal tax (but read Chapter 7 on renting versus buying a home).

2.   Arrange a substantial pension for yourself

The Inland Revenue are very generous in giving tax allowances to those setting up a good pension scheme for themselves. (This may relieve the

State from responsibility for looking after the pensioner in later life.) The pension contributions can be set against your income tax liability at your highest marginal rate, which may be 40%.

The income or capital gain on the assets making up your pension fund, held by an insurance company or other intermediary, are not subject to tax. If you make a lump sum payment to set up a pension scheme this payment is also allowable against tax at your highest marginal rate up to certain limits. When you retire, certain lump sum payments, up to 25% of the fund, can be paid out of the pension fund to you tax free.

3. *In writing your will, once you have ensured that your wife or husband is in a sound financial position on your death, leave the remainder of your estate, up to £200 000 (in 1996–97) to others, possibly to your children, or set up an accumulation and maintenance trust to hold the remainder of your estate on behalf of your children*

No inheritance tax will be paid on this £200 000 so long as you live for seven years after making up the trust. The £200 000 becomes what is called a 'potentially exempt transfer'.

If this is not done, the zero rate of inheritance tax imposed on an estate valued at between £0 and £200 000 on your death is wasted. It is particularly important if you and your spouse should die at the same time or shortly after one another. Certain forms of trust can, at the very least, delay the payment of tax and may be able to reduce the marginal rate of tax applied to the income from the assets transferred to the trust.

4. *Total assets of the family estate should be split roughly equally between husband and wife*

As with 3. above. On the death of either spouse the full zero-rated band of inheritance tax up to £200 000 will be used up against that part of the estate of the dead spouse that is left to the children (or other beneficiary). If this is not done the children could be landed, quite needlessly, with a heavy inheritance tax bill on the death of the second spouse. Remember that assets left in excess of £200 000 are taxed at 40% and gifts are still subject to inheritance tax for seven years after they are gifted.

5. *If you are running a business consider incorporating the business if your income from the business exceeds the basic rate band of tax (currently £3900 – £21 600 at 24%)*

You will pay tax on the profits from a small business at only the 24% rate up to £150 000 of profit. (There are other considerations here, however.)

6. *Take income in the form of goods and services rather than in cash.*

The tax on accommodation, use of car, lunch vouchers and so forth may be zero-rated or rated at a lower band than your marginal tax rate. The rules are complex here, the tax depends on the particular situation, but tax benefits are available in certain cases.

7. *Set up or take part in a profit-related pay scheme*

Half the profits from such schemes are tax free (Finance Act 1989, S 61 and Sch. 4) up to £4000 a year. This tax reduction scheme is likely to be changed on 5 April 1997 since the elimination of such schemes is included in the Chancellor's November 1996 budget proposals.

8. *Pass revenue-generating assets to your spouse if the spouse has a low income or zero income*

The spouse may not be using up all of his or her personal tax allowances. Individuals can earn up to £3900 before they have to pay any income tax. One spouse may also pay tax at a lower marginal rate than the other spouse. The key idea is to take advantage of all the tax allowances and lower tax rates available to both parties.

9. *Sell some of your assets that are standing at a profit over original cost each year to use up your maximum annual capital gains tax allowance*

A capital gain of £6300 (1996–97) can be made each year before CGT is payable. If this is passed over for a year it is lost for ever and eventually you may have to pay tax at your highest marginal rate of 40% on the accumulated capital gain. If capital gains of up to £6300 are available they should thus, if possible, be cashed yearly to absorb the full CGT allowance. The divisibility and cost of selling (and possibly buying back) the asset is also relevant. Divisible assets can be sold each year in blocks, giving a profit per block worth £6300 each (no CGT). Indivisible assets cannot be sold in blocks, so CGT is paid on value exceeding £6300. Note that both a husband and wife can claim CGT allowances in each year. 'Bed and breakfasting' shares can cost 5% of the value reinvested but this should be much less than the 40% of the profit you would pay in CGT.

10. *If you are employed and about to retire you might consider taking a tax-free 'golden handshake' of up to £30 000 rather than negotiating a part-time job for a few years as a supplement to your retirement income.*

As an employee you will have to pay tax on income of, say, £10 000 per year for three years which is being earned from your part time job. You

can, however, avoid tax on the first £30 000 of a 'golden handshake'.
Your employer may have other ideas, however.

11. *If you are an employee contributing towards a pension scheme but your
    annual contribution to the scheme is less than the maximum permissible
    then you might consider increasing your pension contributions to the
    maximum possible using an additional voluntary contribution scheme
    (either an AVC or an FSAVC), assuming the cash is available. If you are
    employed you are currently allowed to pay up to 15% of gross salary into
    such a scheme*

The pension contributions are allowable against tax at your highest
marginal rate. This might turn out to be the best investment available to
you for any surplus cash you may have. You will need to work out the
return on your net-of-tax contribution to the voluntary pension fund.

12. *Increase your life insurance cover to the maximum possible under an
    additional voluntary contribution scheme*

If you are an employee in a death-in-service scheme you can increase
your life cover by up to 2.5 times salary under an AVC scheme. The cost,
net of tax, is likely to be a good deal cheaper than any alternative form of
life cover available to you at the time since the premiums on these other
forms of cover will not be chargeable against income tax.

13. *Place some of your assets or free income into a personal equity plan (PEP)
    up to the maximum possible amount each year*

No income tax or capital gains tax is paid on income or capital gains
arising from assets held in a PEP so long as the assets are held in the PEP
for a period of five years. You can place up to £9000 into a PEP in one
year, £18 000 for a man and wife. However if the total capital profit on
assets held in any one year is less than £6300, the CGT exemption limit,
the benefits flowing from the PEP are reduced somewhat. We recall that
capital gains must exceed £6300 in any one year before CGT is payable.
Much will depend on the cost of selling and rebuying the assets, or
similar assets, outside a PEP.

14. *Save using a tax-exempt saving scheme (TESSA)*

The reason for this is the same as in point 13. above. No tax is paid on the
income from the scheme if the capital sum is left in the scheme for five
years. The benefits here are limited since the *total* amount that can be
invested in a TESSA, at £9000, is very small.

15. *Give careful consideration to the date when a financial transaction takes place*

Let us take an example. The CGT paid on the sale of an asset is based on your marginal tax rate in the year the asset is sold. If your marginal tax rate will be lower in a later year, for example after retirement, then postpone the sale until this later year. There are many other cases where the date when a transaction takes place can effect the amount of tax paid on the transaction.

16. *Set up a trust and transfer some of your assets into the trust*

A trust is a legal device that allows person A (the settlor) to transfer an asset to person B (the trustee) for the benefit of person C (the beneficiary). Many schemes for avoiding, reducing or delaying the payment of CGT and inheritance tax are built around trusts. These schemes can only be safely set up by using the services of a competent lawyer who knows about trust law since an error in even one word of the trust deed can wreck the scheme.

There are several types of trust, and the taxation of income, capital gains and inheritance differs between each type of trust. The two types of trust that are most useful in avoiding personal tax are *accumulation and maintenance trusts* and the *interest in possession trusts.*

Trusts are most useful in avoiding or reducing inheritance tax. They can be of some use in avoiding or reducing CGT but they are of very limited use in avoiding income tax. The tax benefits derived from using trusts to reduce income tax, CGT or inheritance tax are being continuously reduced by the Inland Revenue but some useful benefits remain.

In the case of an accumulation and maintenance trust the transfer of assets into the trust becomes a potentially exempt transfer. Readers are referred back to the section on inheritance tax to explain this device. If you live for seven years after placing your assets into the trust no inheritance tax is paid on these assets on your death and no tax is levied on the trust when the beneficiary receives income or capital from the trust. However the trust must pay income tax at 35% on income and *realized* capital gains. Such tax can be avoided by astute trustees.

A *discretionary trust* allows the settlor to leave assets to the children of a marriage while at the same time protecting the surviving spouse if he or she needs access to the capital or income placed in the trust. A discretionary trust provides a rather less favourable tax environment compared to the accumulation and maintenance trust. The treatment of income or capital gains is similar to the accumulation and maintenance trust but if the value of the assets placed in the trust exceeds the nil rate band (£200 000 in 1996–97) then a charge at the current inheritance tax rate (40% in 1996–97) is made on the residue. A further charge at a low rate of tax may be imposed on capital distributions from the trust.

One popular dodge is to write a life assurance policy in trust for a beneficiary and at the same time to buy an annuity that will generate sufficient income to pay the premiums on the policy. The cost of the annuity reduces the value of your estate for inheritance tax purposes and the proceeds of the life policy does not fall into your estate: it goes to the beneficiary.

Trusts can prove useful in reducing your total tax bill but they are complex devices and establishing them requires you to invest in expensive legal advice.[8]

Many other devices for reducing personal tax bills are available to the astute taxpayer. These will change from year to year as tax allowances, tax reliefs and tax laws change. The above stratagems are listed as examples of what is possible. Many books are on offer which describe in great detail the various methods of reducing your personal tax bill. Note that these books must be updated each year if they are to be of much use.[9]

SUMMARY

1. Although personal tax is an important aspect of personal financial planning, tax must never be allowed to dominate your personal financial plans. Tax rules and allowances can be changed each year in the annual budget and so tax-based plans can come to grief. Design your personal plans to achieve specific objectives and then fine-tune the plan for tax.

2. You should ensure that you are taking advantage of all tax allowances available to you. Tax avoidance is a perfectly legal activity. Only a saint or a fool pays more tax than he or she is obliged to pay. If a payment is allowable against personal tax the government is, in effect, subsidizing this activity. The rate of tax payable on income can sometimes be shifted to a lower rate band by employing various stratagems.

3. Tax evasion is illegal and can result in heavy fines. There is a grey area between tax avoidance and tax evasion called *tax avoision*. Some personal financial stratagems operate within this grey area and you need to ensure that the ingenious tax-avoidance scheme you are entering does not cross the border into tax evasion.

4. UK residents are subject to three kinds of personal tax: income tax, capital gains tax and inheritance tax.

5. Within a given tax period it is useful to know your basic rate of tax, your marginal rate and your average rate. Your marginal rate in a given situation is normally the important rate so far as tax planning is concerned.

6. Personal income from various sources are allocated to several tax schedules named Schedules A to F. Allowances and concessions are not the same under all schedules. For example you can benefit by being taxed under Schedule D rather than under Schedule E since certain expenses allowed under Schedule D are not allowed under Schedule E.

7. Any profit made on the sale of a personal asset may be subject to CGT, but there are many exceptions to this rule. For example a house which is a first home is a major example of a CGT exempt asset. A reasonable amount of capital gain can be made in any one year before CGT is payable. The rate of CGT payable depends on your marginal rate of tax for the period in question.

8. Inheritance tax is payable on assets gifted by you or on the value of your estate when you die. Many ways of avoiding inheritance tax have been devised by tax advisers; some tax experts claim that inheritance tax is, in effect, voluntary. You need to leave substantial assets before inheritance tax is payable out of your estate.

9. A wide variety of perfectly legal means of reducing your personal taxes have been devised by tax specialists. If you have a substantial income or are likely to leave a substantial estate it is almost certainly worth your while consulting with a tax expert as to how to arrange your tax affairs to minimize your tax burden.

10. Self-assessment is a new tax procedure that requires employed and retired people who have income from several sources and the self-employed to fill in a large set of self-assessment tax forms each year. They must have kept records of income and capital gains from 5 April 1996. They can calculate the tax due or leave it to the Inland Revenue. The first tax year to be assessed in this way is 6 April 1997 to 5 April 1998. This change in procedure may save the government money by reducing the number of tax inspectors. It will not benefit the taxpayer.

TEST YOUR KNOWLEDGE

1. Three types of personal tax are imposed on the income of persons resident in the UK. What are the names of these three types of personal tax and what exactly is being taxed in each case?

2. Define the difference between *tax avoidance* and *tax evasion*. Which activity is illegal? Give one example of each. What is meant by the curious term *tax avoision*?

3. Your income is assessed under various tax *schedules*. Describe the types of income assessed under Schedules D and E. Why might it be

advantageous to you for your income to be assessed under Schedule D rather than Schedule E? Dividends paid out by companies to their shareholders on ordinary shares are allocated to which tax schedule? Are these dividends paid out to you gross or net of income tax?

4. Which of the following items are subject to UK tax?

    (a) The profit on the sale of a share held in a foreign-based company.

    (b) Winnings on the Derby.

    (c) Premium bond winnings.

    (d) A gift of £10 000 from your father.

    (e) An educational grant from your local authority.

    (f) Income support provided to you because you have a low wage.

    (g) The use of a company car.

    (h) Compensation of £20 000 from your employer for loss of office.

    (i) Alimony from a divorced husband.

    (j) £70 a week rent from a lodger using a room in your home.

5. How will the new procedure of self assessment for tax work? Who will be affected?

6. What is your *marginal* rate of tax for this year? Why is your marginal rate of tax important in tax planning?

7. Assume that you take out an endowment mortgage worth £60 000. The rate of interest gross of tax on the mortgage is fixed at 8% for 5 years. Your gross earned income is £40 000 a year. You have no other income. How much interest do you pay each year, net of tax, on your mortgage? If you only earned £10 000 a year how much interest would you pay, net of tax, on your mortgage?

8. How much of a profit can you earn in one year from selling capital assets before you have to pay capital gains tax? Why is it that investing in gold coins worth £20 000 might provide a tax advantage compared to investing in a gold ornament worth exactly the same amount of money?

9. Let us assume that Mr Green owns a cottage, a second home, in Cornwall. In the tax year 1996–97 an offer comes in, out of the blue,

from an estate agent to buy Mr Green's second home for £90 000 for a client. Mr Green had bought the cottage in very good condition in 1980 for £20 000. Mr Green earns £50 000 a year and this absorbs all his tax allowances and 25% tax band for 1996–97. If the CGT inflation index has moved from 100 to 300 between 1980 and 1997, calculate how much capital gains tax Mr Green will be due to pay on the sale of the cottage in the tax year 1996–97 if he accepts the offer.

10. Suggest three assets into which you can invest your money that will not be subject to capital gains tax.

11. Mrs Amelia Black is 50 years old. Her husband Mr John Black, aged 55, dies quite suddenly from a heart attack. Mr Black owns assets with a market value of £800 000 on his death. The estate is made up of the family home worth £220 000 and equity shares worth £580 000. Assume that he leaves the family home and £250 000 of the shares to his wife, who has no other assets, and the remainder of his estate to his daughter. How much inheritance tax is payable by Mrs Black and her daughter? Suppose Mrs Black dies one year later and leaves her estate to her daughter. How much inheritance tax is payable on the estate? Assume that inheritance tax is currently at the 40% rate. Assume 1996/97 rates of tax.

12. Suppose Mr Reddy, a widower, finds out that his health is not so good and so, to avoid inheritance tax, he donates equity shares with a market value of £300 000 to his only son on 19 February 1992. Mr Reddy dies on 17 February 1997 leaving an estate worth £900 000. At the date of his death, the shares that he donated to his son are worth £400 000. How much inheritance tax must be paid on the gift by the son?

13. In the previous example the son would be due to pay some inheritance tax on the gift from his father made five years previously. This could cause him financial embarrassment if he has invested or spent the money. How could the father arrange to cover the financial risk arising out of his dying within seven years of making the gift?

14. What tax advantages accrue from setting up a personal pension fund for yourself?

15. Suggest some tax planning schemes that will assist a husband and wife to arrange their financial affairs to reduce the family tax bill to a minimum.

16. What is a *trust*? How can a trust assist in tax planning?

NOTES

1. You may have to employ an accountant in any case when tax self-assessment is introduced in the UK.

2. PEP: Personal Equity Plan. TESSA: Tax Exempt Saving Scheme. SAYE: Save As You Earn.

3. We assume that the taxpayer is resident and domiciled in the UK. If not the tax situation becomes very complicated. Let us assume that the individual taxpayer has been resident in the UK for 186 days in the given tax year.

4. If you are over 65 and your earnings are just above the £17 490 limit you might consider investing in tax-free investments such as National Saving Certificates to bring your income below the limit and so gain your age allowance.

5. If you pass an asset to your spouse the asset is valued at the original cost price on transfer. The indexation allowance is based on the original date of acquisition and the cost price.

6. If the deceased holds savings accounts in a tax haven there can be problems in accessing the asset. This is why bank accounts held in a tax haven should be joint accounts between husband and wife or between two other parties both of whom can withdraw money from the account.

7. But beware: the recipient will be liable for CGT on any profit from the sale of the asset over the value at the date of transfer.

8. The legal costs will be in the region of £300 to £500 per trust.

9. See for example the annual *Daily Mail Guide* for a simple introduction and the Allied Dunbar annual book on personal tax planning for more advanced treatment of the subject. These are listed in the 'further reading' section at the end of this book.

Keeping the score 10

WHY MUST YOU KEEP SCORE?

You cannot hope to manage your own finances successfully if you do not keep proper financial records. The recording process itself can vary from annotating your monthly bank and credit card statements in pencil to keying all your financial transactions into a computer-based personal finance package. Many of the readers of this book are likely to be busy people with little time to spare, yet it is essential to devote at least one evening a month to updating and maintaining financial records.

SELF-ASSESSMENT FOR INCOME TAX

A further reason for keeping a careful record of your finances is that the Inland Revenue, which assesses you for income tax each year, has decided to introduce a system of self-assessment based on a model used in the United States for many years. As from 5 April 1997 around nine million people in the UK will be required to fill in a self-assessment tax form at the end of each year. The financial records needed to fill in and support the data entered into this form must be retained as from 6 April 1996. An alarming number of employed persons in the UK do not seem to be aware of the duties imposed on them by this change in the method of assessing their income for income tax. If you are an employee with no other income but your salary the change will not impose much of a burden but if you are self-employed, a company director, or an employee or pensioner receiving a complex set of incomes from several different sources then it has more serious implications. You will need to maintain good financial records to fill in your annual self-assessment form.[1]

THE BASIC RECORDS THAT YOU NEED TO KEEP

The financial records you need to keep to control your financial affairs are similar to the financial records that need to be kept by a small business.[2] They are:

1.   Your monthly bank, credit and debit card statements.

2.   A personal balance sheet of your assets and liabilities.

3.   An income and expenditure account for each month and year.

4.   A lifetime cash-flow budget and a more detailed short-term cash-flow budget.

5.   A listing of all current insurance contracts.

6.   A file containing all current and past tax documentation.

7.   Details of your pension scheme or schemes including a copy of your pension scheme rule book and an estimate of your likely future pension on retirement.

8.   The title deeds or rental agreement on your home or information as to where such documents are held. A copy of any mortgage agreement.

9.   Your last will and testament including instructions to your executor.

YOUR BALANCE SHEET

Exhibit 10.1 provides an example of a personal balance sheet. At the top is a list of all the assets you own on a particular date; at the bottom is a list of all the debts owed on that same date. If you deduct your debts from the current value of your assets the difference between these two figures represents your net worth or *equity* – in other words your *current wealth*.

We suggest that you keep a note of, and proof of, the original cost of each asset you own in addition to its current value. This information can be useful for

- calculating and minimizing your liability to capital gains tax if you sell one or other of your assets and

- making insurance claims against loss or damage to your assets.

If you have not conducted this exercise before, why not work out your current wealth now? You might be surprised at the result!

Where assets of one class consist of a number of items, for example a share portfolio composed of a number of different shares, only the total value of the share portfolio should appear on the balance sheet. A breakdown of the individual list of shares should be relegated to an accompanying schedule. This keeps the balance sheet tidy.

In order to calculate your net worth you must first identify your assets and then value them. In some cases the valuing of an asset can be a tricky business, however in most cases the valuing of a financial asset is very easy. For example it is easy to value a publicly quoted share or government stock since these are quoted daily in the popular press.[3]

Financial assets	Current market value
Liquid assets	£
Cash	− 1 333
Building society deposit	25 000
Total liquid assets	23 667
Fixed interest stocks	
Government stocks	36 541
Commercial bonds	15 329
Other	5 000
Total fixed interest stocks	56 870
Equity stocks	
Equity shares	75 333
Total financial assets	155 870
Real assets	
House and land (mortgaged for £40 000)	220 000
Land: site for holiday cottage in Wales	40 000
Other real assets	21 000
Total real assets	281 000
Total value of assets	£436 870
Less: liabilities	
Endowment mortgage on house	40 000
Short-term banks loans	5 000
Hire-purchase debts	750
Total value of liabilities	45 750
Net worth (wealth) of Mr Swales	£391 120

The balance sheet separates financial assets from real assets and further differentiates the financial assets into liquid assets, fixed interest stocks and equity stocks. The breakdown of the individual assets such as equity and government stocks would be listed individually in a series of appendices that are not shown here.

EXHIBIT 10.1: Personal balance sheet of Mr Swales

In a few cases the current value of a financial asset may be more difficult to measure; for example the current value of shares that you own in a private company or the current value of an endowment insurance policy. The valuing of real assets can present you with a big problem. What, for example, is the current sale value of your home or a string of pearls or a Victorian painting by a little-known artist? An insurance valuation may be helpful in estimating the approximate value of such assets. A professional valuer will provide you with an estimated sales value but such persons can charge a hefty fee for their services, based on their valuation. Several books are published annually which provide recent selling prices at auctions of a wide range of antiques and other real assets. These values are gross of expenses and commission.

The value that you place on any asset in your current balance sheet is the current sales value of that asset, net of all selling costs. Note that the sale value of an asset, as listed in a sales catalogue supplied by a dealer, is not the relevant value to use for valuation purposes since this is the value at which the dealer will sell to you and not the value at which the dealer will buy from you. The difference between these two figures, known as the dealer's spread, can be anything up to 50% of the dealer's selling price.

The valuation of your debts presents you with much less of a problem. Debts are invariably quoted as a specific money value. The major types of debt incurred by individuals are the mortgage debt incurred in buying a house and the bank loans or hire purchase loans taken out to buy consumer goods, such as cars, on credit. A statement showing the value outstanding on your mortgage must be sent to you each year by your mortgage lender.

One major asset owned by most individuals, but often overlooked, is the paid-up value of their pension fund and the trade-in value of their life assurance policies. We do not recommend valuing these assets and including them in the personal balance sheet. The temptation to cash in such assets can be very great at certain times in life and the consequences of doing such a thing can be catastrophic for the financial future of both yourself and family. We suggest it is better to leave these assets well alone.

A debt valuation problem might arise from what are called *contingent liabilities*. An example of a contingent liability is the cost of future school fees. For example if your daughter is enrolled in a public school, fees are due to be paid in the future but there is no legal commitment on you to do so: you could withdraw your daughter from the school and send her to a State school. Until such payments actually become a legal commitment we think they are best ignored in the balance sheet, although they must be included in any future long-term cash flow budget (see below).

For most people the preparation of a personal balance sheet presents little difficulty. Most taxpayers keep a record of their financial assets in order to prepare their annual tax return and few of us own all that many real assets.

Name: John Swales

Annual income and expenditure account, 1994–96 and budget for 1997 (£)

Income	1994	1995	1996	Budget 1997
Basic salary	42 000	48 000	55 000	60 000
Commission etc.	13 500	14 100	17 740	14 000
Dividends and interest	6 700	7 400	8 100	8 530
Other income	540	720	870	900
Total income	62 740	70 220	81 710	83 430
Less: Taxation	18 822	21 066	26 147	27 532
Other deductions	5 500	5 700	6 000	6 500
Net cash inflow	38 418	43 454	49 563	49 398
Expenditure				
Mortgage (net of tax)	4 400	4 200	4 000	4 000
Household				
Rates	800	1 100	1 200	1 200
Gas	1 230	1 476	1 754	1 800
Electricity	582	603	660	700
Food, meals out	3 720	4 110	4 237	4 500
Repairs	561	1 448	754	800
House insurance	550	597	684	684
Security	600	600	600	700
Other	593	619	631	700
Total household	8 636	10 553	10 520	11 084
Transport	Mr Swales has a company car			
Fares	1 800	1 875	2 040	2 000
Mrs Swales' car	2 100	2 300	3 000	2 500
Car licence	120	120	140	140
Petrol	385	402	420	500
Insurance	230	270	330	400
Repairs	120	430	220	300
Total transport	4 755	5 397	6 150	5840
Communication				
Postage	75	85	123	120
Telephone	611	688	744	800
Computer	311	750	320	600
Risk hedging				
Insurance	430	430	430	430
Medical care plan	321	333	375	402
Children	1 800	4 000	5 000	5 000
Personal				
Clothing	2 300	2 000	2 400	2 400
Holidays	3 200	5 334	4 000	4 000
Entertainment	1 788	1 889	2 000	2 000
Subscriptions	700	750	800	900
Sundry				
Cash expenses	2 400	2 500	3 000	3 500
Total expenditure	31 727	38 909	39 862	41 076
Net saving	6 691	4 545	9 701	8 322

EXHIBIT 10.2: An income and expenditure account

YOUR INCOME AND EXPENDITURE ACCOUNT

An income and expenditure account lists all of your income and expenses at the end of each month. The monthly figures are then consolidated into an annual statement at the end of the year, such as the one presented in Exhibit 10.2, which sets out an income and expenditure account for three years plus a budget for the following year.

If you are using a computer package to prepare your accounts, such as Microsoft's 'Money' or Intuit's 'Quicken', then these figures can be analysed in many different ways without undue effort. Full accounts can be prepared each time you enter new data by simply pressing a few keys on your computer keyboard. The package can instantly sum the stored data for any period, including all of the months to date, and give you an income and expenditure account for any period you require within the time range of the stored data.

If you are an assiduous bookkeeper and have prepared a budget for your expected monthly expenditures at the beginning of the year then the computer can compare actual expenditure to budgeted expenditure for any given period, including month-by-month comparison, and highlight the major differences between budgeted and actual income and expenditures. Few of us will be tempted to go this far with our personal bookkeeping.

The precise classification of your expenditures and income will depend on your particular circumstances. As time goes by you will learn to make a finer and more useful classification of your costs. Exhibit 10.2 provides a suggested opening classification for your income and expenditures but everyone will end up with a different classification as time goes by. Personal finance computer packages also provide you with a suggested opening classification of your income and expenditures which you will modify, over time, to meet your own particular needs.

Salary data should be entered gross of all deductions and these deductions, such as tax NHI and pension contribution, should be listed separately to arrive at the net cash flow credited to your bank account at the end of each month. If you are self-employed then you are required by the tax authorities to keep a detailed record of the salary you pay yourself and any employees.

The usual sources of data on your income are the monthly payslip from your employer and the dividend and interest vouchers provided by the company or institution paying you the dividend or interest. There is a legal requirement that these vouchers provide all of the relevant data on tax and other deductions that you will need to prepare your tax return. These same data can be used to list the income in your income and expenditure account. Collecting data on your income is usually not a problem since most of your income is paid directly into one or other of your bank accounts.

The best and most accessible source of data on your expenditures will be found listed in the monthly bank statements and credit card statements that you receive each month from your bank and credit

Budget annual lifetime cash flow

Name: Margaret Gee
Occupation: retired
Age: 73 Widowed Children: 1
Assumed inflation rate: 4% per annum. Currency unit: £

Age Year	73 1996	74 1997	75 1998	76 1999	77 2000	78 2001	79 2002	80 2003	81 2004	82 2005	83 2006	84 2007	85 2008
Income													
Pension	2 500	2 600	2 704	2 812	2 925	3 042	3 163	3 290	3 421	3 558	3 701	3 849	4 003
Dividends	3 700	3 916	4 184	4 517	4 935	5 442	6 063	6 830	7 782	8 969	10 434	12 250	14 507
Other income	3 600	3 816	4 045	4 288	4 545	4 818	5 107	5 413	5 738	6 082	6 447	6 834	7 244
Total income	**9 800**	**10 332**	**10 932**	**11 617**	**12 405**	**13 301**	**14 333**	**15 532**	**16 941**	**18 610**	**20 582**	**22 932**	**25 753**
Less: tax	1 470	1 550	1 640	1 743	2 233	2 394	2 580	2 796	3 049	3 722	4 116	4 586	5 151
Total deductions	1 470	1 550	1 640	1 743	2 233	2 394	2 580	2 796	3 049	3 722	4 116	4 586	5 151
Gross cash flow	8 330	8 782	9 293	9 874	10 172	10 907	11 753	12 737	13 892	14 888	16 466	18 346	20 603
Expenditure													
Accommodation	500	525	551	579	608	638	670	704	739	776	814	855	898
Repairs	800	840	882	926	972	1 021	1 072	1 126	1 182	1 241	1 303	1 368	1 437
Utilities	600	624	649	675	702	730	759	790	821	854	888	924	961
Food	1 920	1 978	2 037	2 098	2 161	2 226	2 293	2 361	2 432	2 505	2 580	2 658	2 737
Transport	500	510	520	531	541	552	563	574	586	598	609	622	634
Clothing	500	500	500	500	500	500	500	500	500	500	500	500	500
House insurance	300	315	331	347	365	383	402	422	443	465	489	513	539
Rates	990	1 030	1 071	1 114	1 158	1 204	1 253	1 303	1 355	1 409	1 465	1 524	1 585
Recreation	900	909	918	927	937	946	955	965	975	984	994	1 004	1 014
Medical and health	300	330	363	399	439	483	531	585	643	707	778	856	942
Subs and gifts	200	200	200	200	200	200	200	200	200	200	200	200	200
Other	200	208	216	225	234	243	253	263	274	285	296	308	320
Total expenditure	**7 710**	**7 968**	**8 238**	**8 521**	**8 817**	**9 127**	**9 452**	**9 792**	**10 149**	**10 524**	**10 918**	**11 332**	**11 766**
Net surplus/deficit	620	814	1 054	1 353	1 355	1 780	2 301	2 944	3 743	4 364	5 548	7 014	8 836
Total surplus/deficit	620	1 434	2 488	3 842	5 197	6 977	9 278	12 222	15 965	20 328	25 876	32 890	41 727

Assumptions: it is assumed that the cash flow will remain constant after the age of 85

EXHIBIT 10.3: Margaret Gee – likely cash-flow scenarios assuming no serious illness or other disasters

card company. Most substantial payments nowadays are paid either by cheque, by regular bank payment or by credit card. If you receive substantial sums in cash or make substantial payments in cash then the preparation of an accurate monthly income and expenditure account presents you with more of a problem. You will need to note each item of cash income and cash expenditure as it is received or paid out. This requires a fair amount of discipline on your part which is not needed if you pay by cheque, banker's order, credit card or direct debit.

You would be wise to make all substantial payments through your bank account or by credit card. Such an approach provides you with an automatic record of all your major expenditures. This approach also offers some legal backup if, for example, you have to prove to an insurance company that you paid a particular sum for an article that has been lost or stolen.

YOUR LONG-TERM CASH-FLOW BUDGET

Your long-term cash-flow budget is the 'bottom line' so far as personal financial planning is concerned. A cash-flow budget can be prepared for a period as short one month or as long as five years beyond your life expectancy as estimated from actuarial tables.

A cash-flow budget estimates your, or your family's, inflow and outflow of cash month by month or annually over a given period of time. Exhibit 10.3 sets out an example of a 'lifetime' cash-flow budget. This budget has been prepared on behalf of a Mrs Margaret Gee, a 73-year-old widow with one son. Her life expectancy at age 73 in the year 1996 is estimated to be some 12 years. Mrs Gee's long-term cash-flow budget runs to the year 2008 when Mrs Gee, if she survives until then, will be 85 years of age. This cash-flow budget assumes an average rate of inflation of 4% per annum over the 12-year period.

A good deal of work is involved in preparing a lifetime cash-flow budget such as that set out in Exhibit 10.3. However a lifetime cash-flow budget is the most important financial statement you can construct for yourself in managing your personal finances. This statement is what accountants call the 'bottom line' of your financial planning. A lifetime cash-flow statement provides the ultimate test of the efficiency of your overall financial plan.

In order to construct a lifetime cash-flow statement you will need to estimate your future income, expenditure and net assets year by year over the given period. The statement requires you to estimate the timing and amount of the major expenditures that lie ahead such as a new house or car, the likely date of your retirement, your future pension income, your future responsibility for children until they leave the nest, and a host of other matters. The preparation of a lifetime cash-flow budget is the most demanding job you will ever undertake in managing your own finances but it is also the most rewarding one.

A long-term cash-flow budget can identify cash-flow problems that might arise in the future long before the crisis actually occurs. This allows you to take countervailing action in due time. The transition from final salary to post-retirement cash-flow estimates is a particularly important phase of long-term cash planning.

Exhibit 10.3 is based on a 'most likely' scenario. In other words it is based on the series of events that you think is most likely to happen in the future. You should also prepare several other scenarios based on less optimistic assumptions. One *worst-case scenario* which should be faced is that based on the assumption that you will fall seriously ill in the near future. Another worst-case scenario can be based on the assumption that you might die in the near future. Since death will usually trigger large life assurance payments to your dependants, serious chronic illness will usually reveal a worse long-term cash flow position than death so far as your relatives are concerned.

THE MONTHLY BUDGET

The preparation of a cash budget month by month for the year ahead is a much simpler task than preparing a lifetime cash-flow budget. If you keep good financial records the preparation of monthly cash budgets is a relatively easy job since you can use last year's accounts as a basis for estimating the coming year. Any substantial expenditures that you know will fall due in the coming year, such as a wedding or a new car or school fees, will be built into this cash-flow budget.

Once your month-by-month cash-flow budget for the coming year is complete you can check whether cash surpluses or deficits will arise in any month. This information can be used to plan how you will invest the expected surpluses and finance predicted deficits. The annual cash-flow budget allows you to plan ahead and control your monthly cash flow.

Comparing your monthly cash budget estimates with actual cash flow would be a formidable task if it were not for the new range of personal financial software that can now be bought for around £35 to £50 per package. These packages make the budgeting of personal cash flows, the entry of actual cash flows, and the identification of any differences into a relatively painless process.

YOUR PERSONAL FINANCE FILING SYSTEM: INVESTMENT, INSURANCE, HOUSING, TAX AND PENSION RECORDS

If you do not organize a comprehensive personal finance filing system early in life you will find yourself grappling with all sorts of financial problems as time goes by. Your aim should be to set up a filing system that contains all your basic financial records in one place. You should also try to set aside a specific time each month to update these records and prepare your monthly accounts. This activity should take up no more than one evening at the end of each month.

The files you need to keep in your personal finance filing system are:

- A file for your insurance policies and past insurance claims.

- All documentation referring to tax matters, particularly the annual P60 salary form from your employer and any tax assessments and repayment claims.

- Details of your pension arrangements including a copy of the company or personal pension plan that lists the latest rules and rights of the contributor.

- A copy of your last will and testament including instructions to your executor. The original copy of your will is best left with your solicitor.

- A file containing all information pertaining to your home: a copy of the title deeds or rental agreement on your house, any mortgage contract including annual repayment schedule, and details about the insurance of the home and contents and any survey report on the property.

It is advisable to keep all of those key personal finance documents in one place and to keep them separate from other personal and family documents. Placing the files in a fire resistant safe or keeping a set of photostat copies of these documents in a separate place, such as with a trusted relative or the family solicitor, is no bad idea. If all of these documents should be lost in a fire you will find that a great deal of effort is required to rebuild the files if no copy files are available. Remember to tell your spouse or executor or solicitor about the location of the files and copies.

WRITING UP YOUR FINANCIAL RECORDS

Until now we have been discussing the records you need to keep to manage your financial affairs, but how are those financial records to be set up, maintained and stored? What are the mechanics of the personal record-keeping procedure?

There can be no possible doubt that if you are computer literate then you should keep your personal financial records on a home computer. Computer-based financial records offer a level of analysis that is not feasible if your personal financial records are stored on any other medium. Unfortunately the vast majority of people, and especially older people, are not computer literate and if learning about computers is a necessary condition of managing financial affairs then few people will keep financial records and so few will be able to manage their own financial affairs. Let us first examine non-computer-based recording systems.

If you do not have the time to prepare a monthly income and expenditure statement simply annotating your monthly bank and credit card statement can provide a simple but effective alternative. The data are posted from here to an income and expenditure classification sheet:

Statement of account with National Bank PLC

Mr E Noon
17 Arcadia Avenue
Erewhon
EW17 9RH

Sheet number 174

Date 30 Feb 97

Account No. 56381

Date	Particulars	CODE	Payments	Receipts	Balance (when overdrawn marked OD)
					1489.92 Balance
1 Feb	BRITISH GAS	S/O	50.00		1439.92 Gas
	EREWHON MDC	D/D	55.20		1384.72 Rates
2 Feb	CHEQUE	263	34.92		1349.80 Books
7 Feb	DALTON PLC	BGC		1977.39	3327.19 Salary
	EREWHON	C/P 1			
	DATE OF WITHDRAWAL	5 Feb	40.00		3287.19 Cash
	CHEQUE	223	7.00		3280.19 Papers
15 Feb	BARCLAY'S BANK	C/P 1			
	DATE OF WITHDRAWAL	14 Feb	30.00		3250.19 Cash
24 Feb	RTZ Div			175.88	3426.07 Dividends
	CHEQUE	265	8.74		3417.33 Petrol
	CHEQUE	266	29.50		3387.83 Shoes
30 Feb	CHEQUE	267	3500.00		–112.17 Deposit (car) OD

The items and balance shown should be verified. Details of rates and calculations of any interest charged are available on request to this branch. The bank is not liable for loss or delay caused directly or indirectly by industrial action or by circumstances beyond its control.

EXHIBIT 10.4: A simple analysis of income and expenditure based on a monthly bank statement

PERSONAL FINANCE RECORDING SYSTEMS THAT ARE NOT COMPUTER BASED

A simple recording system, which may well be perfectly adequate for most people, is to annotate your bank and credit card statements each month and transfer the totals to a prepared income and expenditure sheet. If the bank and credit card statements are already well annotated by your bank or credit card company then all you need to do is to make notes defining each item of income and expenditure from your salary and cheque stubs on the statements themselves, total them by account, and transfer them into an income and expenditure sheet at the end of each month. Many people have found this simple procedure to be a perfectly satisfactory method of controlling their monthly income and expenditures. Exhibit 10.4 illustrates an annotated bank statement.

More formal but essentially similar systems for preparing monthly accounts are offered by several publishers. For example a company called Trakka Systems offers 'Money Trakka'. This manual system allows the user to keep records of all assets, liabilities, monthly income and expenditures, tax, insurance and pension details and so forth within a well-structured set of records.[4]

As we noted above, listing your monthly income is less of a problem. Your income should be shown gross with any deductions such as tax, national insurance and superannuation listed separately.

In summary you need to:

- learn to adopt a systematic approach to regular record keeping by listing your individual items of income and expenditure each month and then classifying them by account;

- set up a set of files to keep details of your assets, liabilities and other financial matters and to protect these files against fire.

PERSONAL FINANCE COMPUTER PACKAGES

Several times in the above discussion we have referred to a computer-based system. A computer is not an essential tool for personal financial record keeping but it certainly helps. If you know little about home computers it is unlikely that you will set out to learn about these devices simply to keep your personal accounts. However if you do have some basic knowledge of microcomputing, and particularly if you have a microcomputer at home, then one of the personal finance computer packages currently on offer in the UK will provide you with a powerful tool for keeping and analysing your personal finances. These computer packages allow you to apply a much higher level of analysis to your financial affairs than is possible if you are limited by a manual accounting system.

In recent years a wide range of personal finance computer packages have been developed which make it possible to keep your personal financial records in good shape without excessive effort. The one essential precondition to using any of these systems is that the user is computer literate. This simply means that the user should be familiar with the basic processes of using a computer. It does not mean that the user needs to be able to write a computer program.

When deciding which computer package is best suited to your needs you must first decide whether you want to use a *general* spreadsheet package designed for any kind of numerical work or a package specifically designed for handling personal finance record keeping.

SPREADSHEET PACKAGES

If you are familiar with spreadsheets then the simplest approach to maintaining financial records on a computer is to use a *spreadsheet* program. These programs, much beloved by accountants, are designed to process numerical information easily. The best known spreadsheet packages are LOTUS 1-2-3 and Microsoft's EXCEL. However these are powerful and very expensive programs that provide far more power than is needed for maintaining personal financial records. A shareware program called AS-EASY-AS is very much cheaper and is adequate for keeping personal financial records if you decide to follow the spreadsheet route.

Exhibits 10.1, 10.2 and 10.3 are examples of financial statements that can be prepared using the spreadsheet package called LOTUS 1-2-3. Statements prepared using any other spreadsheet program would look much the same. Spreadsheets will only be used to prepare personal financial records by those who use this particular type of program in some other context, possibly at work.

TAILOR-MADE PERSONAL FINANCE PACKAGES

In recent years several computer packages have been introduced onto the UK market that are specifically designed to process personal financial records. The more popular of these packages were originally designed for the US market and, between them, they have sold over 10 million copies in the USA alone.

The best known of these personal finance packages, which were originally designed for the US market but have now been redesigned for the UK market, are called 'Quicken' (sold by Intuit) and 'Money' (sold by Microsoft). There are also two packages on offer designed by British companies, called 'Moneybox' (sold by Database Direct) and 'Money Matters' (sold by GST software publishing). Since 'Quicken' and 'Money' dominate the UK personal finance market we will concentrate on these two programs.

Some packages that are sold as personal finance packages were initially designed to handle small-business bookkeeping rather than personal finance records. Thus if you are running a small business you can use one of these packages for both purposes. Several other US packages are on offer but these have not been designed for the UK market and so they are not really suitable for keeping personal financial records in the UK.

WHAT FACILITIES DO THESE PACKAGES PROVIDE?

You need to devote some time initially to setting up the system the way you want it. The package will assist you in doing this. The next step is to key all your start-up financial data into the computer. Finally you must update these initial data each month with fresh information from your bank and credit-card statements.

Once you have keyed your initial data into the computer, they, along with all the fresh data keyed in each month, give you access to an almost limitless range of financial schedules. You can change this personal database almost any way you wish. Once you know what you are doing you can produce many valuable schedules and print them out with no more than a few strokes on the keyboard.

You now have the facility to generate a current up-to-date balance sheet and net worth statement, such as those set out in Exhibits 10.1 and 10.2, any time you wish. You can produce an income and expenditure account, an investment schedule showing the cost of your securities, the current market value of each investment, your capital profit or loss on the purchase price, and the income from it, gross and net of tax.

The current market value of each investment can be regularly updated if you link your computer, via a suitable card and a modem, to a real-time share value database. You can keep a schedule of your current debts and a repayment schedule of these debts into the future if you should so wish. You can build a historical and budgeted cash-flow statement for any period within the time range of your database plus a statement of the differences between expected and actual expenditures over the given period. You can calculate the total of any specific item of income and expenditure between any two dates. A statement can be prepared reconciling your bank balance to your cheque book balance.

If you invest in an additional tax package[5] you can estimate your income tax due or reclaimable on your income for a given year and print out your tax return for that year in a format acceptable to the Inland Revenue. Some personal finance packages can be programmed to print out your cheques for the current month but this facility is of limited value if your bank cannot provide you with cheque books that are compatible with your computer and printer. Thus once you have keyed the relevant data into your personal finance computer package you have given yourself the potential for gaining rapid access to a wide range of financial analysis and financial facilities.

FINANCIAL TOOLS

In addition to keeping the score, personal finance packages also provide you with a range of financial tools to assist in making certain financial decisions. Examples of these tools, which Microsoft calls 'wizards', are given below.

The Microsoft 'Money' package provides a program to assist you in choosing between mortgage loan schemes with differing characteristics. For example you can compare loan terms offered by different lenders or different loan terms offered by the same lender.

Several computer-based personal finance packages are now offered at very reasonable prices. All of these are user friendly for those who are accustomed to running computer software, especially those familiar with the Windows environment. These packages use your monthly bank and credit card statements as the principal input medium.

Name of package	'Quicken'	'Money'	'Money Matters'	'Moneybox'
Publisher	Intuit	Microsoft	Database Direct	Sage Software
Approximate price	£50	£40	£20	£15
Suitable operating system for running program	Windows 95 and 3.1, DOS	Windows 95 and 3.1	Windows, DOS	Windows, DOS
Support provided	Unlimited	30 days unlimited	Help available	Help available
Facilities provided by most of these packages	Several different account types can be maintained such as bank, credit card, assets, loans, investment portfolio.			
	Automatically enters regular payments such as direct debits.			
	One transaction can be split and entered as several transactions.			
	Produces balance sheet, income and expenditure account, net worth statement, budget statements and investment portfolio.			
	Can reconcile bank statements with your cheque stubs.			
	Can provide reports on any item selected between two dates.			
	A single entry can update several different accounts.			
	Any specific transaction can be accessed instantly.			
	Data can be analysed into a wide range of reports.			
Other useful facilities that may be provided	A cheque printing facility.			
	A VAT calculator and summary.			
	A financial calendar.			
	Add-on packages may be offered, such as a household inventory, a package for preparing a will, tax reporting, invoicing.			
	A loan, mortgage or pension analyser can allow the user to select between the different options.			
	A saving and investment planner can analyse future scenarios.			
	A facility may be provided for converting one currency into another.			
	Password protection to prevent unauthorized entry to data.			
	A facility for producing reports in graphic form.			

EXHIBIT 10.5: Some computer-based personal finance planning packages

What would be the difference in monthly and total cost between a loan repaid over 15, 20 or 25 years? What would be the effect on monthly cost if the mortgage rate were to be increased by 2%? What would be the effect on the monthly cost of a mortgage of making an initial deposit of £20 000 rather than £10 000? This kind of procedure is called *sensitivity analysis*.

Another 'wizard' calculates the true rate of interest charged on a loan if payments are made several times a year. A 'wizard' is also provided that estimates how much you need to save per month over a given number of years to provide yourself with a given retirement income on a specific date in the future. This program allows you to vary assumptions about the rate of return on the pension fund, the rate of inflation, your initial wealth and various other factors.

An *investment analyser* is provided by some programs. This allows you to monitor the relative performance of the securities in your investment portfolio. These programs can also assist in tax planning.

One limitation of these financial tools is that few of them take UK tax allowances and rates into account when making their calculations. You need to adjust for these factors yourself or buy an add-on program designed for the UK market.

Easy access to such a wealth of personal financial information is invaluable to individuals trying to manage their own financial affairs. However, the catch is that you need to have access to quite a powerful computer, at least a 486 chip and 500 MB hard disc, plus a rudimentary knowledge of microcomputing. There is also the problem of getting the basic data into the system. A considerable volume of data must be keyed into the computer store each month from your salary slip, bank statement, credit card statement and other sources of input data. This will require you to set aside at least one evening a month to input the data into your system, process the data and print out the financial statements that you prefer to keep in hard copy. You also need to update the system from time to time by adding new accounts and attaching new 'add-on' packages.

Even if you know about the basics of microcomputing you will need to learn how to handle a fairly sophisticated computer package. Personal finance computer packages are sold on their simplicity and user friendliness. The computer buff will find them very simple. The occasional computer user might find the instruction manual, the initial installation and the running of these programs to be quite a challenge.

The writer has been told that, while many millions of personal finance computer packages have been bought, many of them are not used on a regular basis. By conventional user standards there can be no doubt that these packages are 'user friendly' but a large number of users of personal finance packages have a very limited knowledge of computing. If you find initial difficulty with your package, persevere. The rewards for successful application are considerable.

Exhibit 10.5 provides some basic information on the facilities provided by four of the more popular personal finance computer packages. All of these packages can do a good job so long as you are computer literate.

WHICH PACKAGE?

Which is the best personal finance computer package? All of the packages listed will be adequate for storing and analysing your regular income and expenditure. If you want to use the package for logging your personal finances and also keeping the books for your small business then Intuit's 'Quicken' is the best option. 'Quicken' handles VAT in a sophisticated way and provides some useful advice on managing the finances of a small business. Several 'add-on' packages, such as a home-inventory package and a tax reporting package, are offered to users of 'Quicken' which integrate smoothly with the basic 'Quicken' package. However the very fact that 'Quicken' can handle such a wide range of functions makes it a more complicated package than its rivals.

Microsoft's 'Money' package was specifically designed to assist the individual in managing their personal finances. It has the advantage of being simple and yet comprehensive at the level of personal finance. The package provides you with an income and expenditure account, a balance sheet to calculate your net worth and a sophisticated program for logging and tracking the performance of different kinds of investments. All of these reports can be printed out by striking a few keys on the computer keyboard. The well-designed 'Money wizards' allow you to apply sensitivity analysis to reviewing your options on loans, pensions and various other matters. Microsoft's 'Money' is a very comprehensive personal finance computer package.

The other packages listed are cheaper but less comprehensive. Some users may not find them quite as user friendly as 'Quicken' and 'Money'. 'Moneybox' is very good value for money. It is unique in being designed to be used by three different kinds of user: student, householder and small business. The householder section offers three levels of difficulty: beginner, expert and professional. This is an excellent idea which should be adopted by the other packages on the market. 'Moneybox' can handle VAT for the small business user.

'Money matters' provides a comprehensive package but it is rather more complex to run. A useful budgeting system is offered that identifies any expenditures that are running amok. You can run two sets of accounts, say personal and business, within a single accounting system.

All of these packages allow you to show the results in the form of graphs and charts if you find that such things help your understanding.

We conclude that Microsoft's 'Money' and Intuit's 'Quicken' are hard to fault. They both provide very comprehensive facilities at a reasonable cost. 'Money' is probably the best package for a user seeking a simple system that is solely concerned with personal finance.

Robinson (1995) provides a useful introduction to the subject of using your microcomputer to keep track of your personal finances. The book has a US orientation but provides useful information on how to optimize the use of several personal finance computer packages.

THE ADVANTAGES AND DISADVANTAGES OF PERSONAL FINANCE COMPUTER PACKAGES

A computer based personal finance recording system enjoys the following advantages over a manual recording system:

1. Entering a single financial transaction into the system can update many separate but related files at the same time. This saves you time and reduces the chance of you entering incorrect information into the system.

2. The many complex calculations are performed with extreme rapidity and accuracy. This applies especially to the several financial tools supplied as an integral part of most packages.

3. A computer-based system can be used to compile quite complex patterns of financial information. For example you can identify runs of a particular type of expense over a long period of time and the pattern can be charted. Income and expenditure trends can be identified and charted. These trends can be used to predict future patterns of expenditure.

4. The results of the various financial analyses compiled under 3. above can be printed out in a wide range of print and graphic formats.

5. The hard disc storage system in your computer provides a very compact store for all of your financial information. This data needs to be secured, but fortunately all of the data can be quickly and easily copied onto an external disc or tape for safe keeping elsewhere.

The main problems encountered when using a microcomputer to store your financial records are:

1. You need to be computer literate.

2. The financial data must be accurately keyed into the computer each month.

3. There is a need for security. You must devise and implement a regular 'backup' procedure to preserve your computer files. This procedure is essential to protect you against the possibility of your computer files, or even your computer itself, being stolen or destroyed.

4. Confidentiality. You may consider that your financial records need to be preserved from prying eyes. If this is a matter of some importance to you, select a security system that can conceal your data from external interrogation. The installation of a simple 'password' system or a basic 'encryption' system should be sufficient to protect your data against the prying eyes of all except a few computer buffs who specialize in 'hacking' into computer systems. It is difficult to protect the data contained in any computer system against the machinations of competent computer 'hackers'.

Most sophisticated finance packages and the latest operating systems on which they run provide 'password' locks on access. Simple encryption systems can be bought for a few pounds.

We conclude that a computer-based personal finance recording system is superior in almost every way to alternative recording systems. A price has to be paid for accessing these benefits and this price takes the form of having to acquire a basic knowledge of microcomputing.

If you view learning about microcomputing as a daunting prospect we suggest that you stick to a manual system like 'Money Trakka', which will provide you with a simple but quite comprehensive system for maintaining your personal financial records.

SUMMARY

1. You must keep an adequate set of financial records if you want to manage your own finances. The new system of self-assessment for income tax will force many people to keep proper financial records.

2. The basic set of financial records that you must keep up-to-date consists of a balance sheet, an income-and-expenditure account, a long-term and short-term cash-flow budget, an up-to-date file of insurance contracts, a file holding your tax documents, a file on housing, a file containing your pension documents and a file holding your will and details about your plans for inheritance.

3. You will find that it is easy to value most of your assets and liabilities. Some real assets may require you to resort to a professional valuer. The current value of your assets less your liabilities tells you your net worth – in other words your current wealth. It is best to ignore the cash-in value of your pension funds and insurance policies when calculating your net worth. 'Place not yourself in the eye of temptation.'

4. The 'bottom line' in personal financial planning is the long-term cash-flow budget. A fully developed 'lifetime' cash flow budget will require you to estimate your major cash inflows and outflows up to a

date some five years beyond your estimated average lifespan. At least two 'lifetime' cash flow scenarios should be calculated, the first based on a 'most likely' scenario and the other based on a 'worst possible' scenario. Cash-flow statements can also be prepared illustrating the financial position of your dependent relatives on the assumption of your death at various ages.

5. The simplest method for recording your income and expenditure is to annotate your monthly bank and credit card statements and transfer the month-end values to a pre-printed account. This is the least you can do. The next stage is to use a formalized manual system like 'Money Trakka'. A computer-literate reader may prefer to keep a full set of personal financial records on a microcomputer using one of the cheap but powerful personal finance computer packages currently offered on the UK market.

6. Personal finance computer packages can provide you with many unique benefits but to take advantage of these benefits you must be prepared to acquire basic computer skills and you must also be willing to devote sufficient time to keying the financial data into your system on a regular basis each month. You will also need to maintain the system and ensure the security and confidentiality of the system.

TEST YOUR KNOWLEDGE

1. You decide to set about managing your own personal financial affairs. The first thing you need to do is to prepare a set of personal finance files. What are the six basic personal finance files you need to keep to manage your financial affairs?

2. Write down what you consider to be the five most important facts about yourself that will be crucial in designing your future financial plans.

3. You want to make an estimate of your current wealth. How will you set about calculating this figure?

4. Let us suppose that you own the following assets:

(a) One thousand ordinary shares in Boots PLC.

(b) An original set of nineteenth-century cartoons.

(c) A nineteenth-century glass bowl made by Lalique.

(d) A plot of land in Tuscany.

(e) The furniture in your home.

(f) A whole-of-life annuity on your life for £2000 a year due to commence in five years' time.

(g) A 10-year-old endowment assurance policy on your life.

(h) Your home.

You wish to estimate the current value of these assets in order to prepare a balance sheet of your net worth. How would you go about valuing these particular items?

5. Assume that you inherit a stamp album from your father, a stamp collector who lived in South Africa at one time and collected nineteenth-century South African stamps. You look in a stamp catalogue from a leading dealer for each stamp and find the collection to be worth around £5000. Why is this valuation 'fools gold' so far as you are concerned? How should you value the collection?

6. In theory your current balance sheet should contain the paid-up value of your pension fund and any life assurance policies in order to arrive at a true assessment of your current wealth. However in the chapter we suggest that this might not be a wise move. Why not?

7. Use Exhibit 10.2 as a base to identify the main headings of your expenditures for the past year. Do you have any major unusual expenditures compared to Exhibit 10.2?

8. Find your last salary slip and a current dividend warrant. What information is listed on these documents? Do you understand what all of this information means?

9. 'Paying major expenditures by cash can cause future problems where score keeping is concerned.' What problems? Why is it better to make all significant expenditures using a cheque or credit card?

10. 'Your, or your family's, long-term cash flow budget is "the bottom line" so far as personal financial planning is concerned.' Why is the long-term cash-flow budget the key document in financial planning?

11. What is the current life expectancy of yourself and your spouse, if you are married? For how many years do life expectancy tables expect you to be retired if you retire at 60 or 65?

12. Suppose your long-term cash-flow budget comes up with a deficit once you retire in, say, 15 years' time. What can you do about it now?

13. Let us suppose that you are not computer literate and cannot spare the time to fill in a detailed manual personal book-keeping system. Explain the steps you would take to prepare a simple system of monthly financial records sufficient to monitor your regular monthly income and expenditures.

14. Can you name the regular tax documents and assessments you receive from your tax office each year if you are a salaried employee (that is, the documents you need to keep together in a file if you wish to keep control of your tax affairs)?

15. Keeping your personal finance records on a computer provides you with some very considerable advantages over maintaining the same records by hand. Suggest five of these key advantages.

16. If you are thinking of buying a personal finance computer package and several are available on the market, what are the key attributes of such a package that would influence your choice?

17. You have bought a personal finance computer package. You want to protect the information in your personal finance data base from prying eyes. Suggest two security devices that can assist in concealing your private financial records held on a computer from prying eyes.

NOTES

1. You can find out how self assessment effects you by phoning (0345) 1615 14. This is the number of the Inland Revenue department that deals with self-assessment. On request you will be sent explanatory material.

2. This is why all personal finance computer packages can be easily adapted to handle the financial affairs of a small business.

3. If you own a microcomputer and a modem, the value of your publicly quoted shares can be continuously updated using a package such as UPDATA from GL software which links into the stock exchange system via teletext.

4. Trakka Systems Ltd. Telephone 01276 855035. The cost is around £40.

5. See for example the tax package offered by *Which?* magazine, which can calculate your income tax liability for the given year covered by the package. You will need the Windows operating system plus a machine with 8 MB of Ram to run this useful package.

Protection against poor financial advice and fraud

11

RECENT SCANDALS IN PERSONAL FINANCE

The arena of personal finance has been wracked with scandal in recent years. The personal investor does not need to be paranoid to wonder if anyone in the personal financial industry can be trusted.

There are two problems here. The first and less serious problem arises when a personal financial adviser, who may be working for a large financial institution, gives you poor advice. The second and more serious problem arises when an adviser divests you of your assets by means of fraud. The reader is probably familiar with two of the best-publicized cases in recent years: the Barlow Clowes affair and the Dunsdale and Levitt saga. In both cases the assets of innocent investors were diverted into risky ventures rather than into the safe investment havens requested by the investors.

The failure of many 'home income plans' in 1990 and 1991 to increase the income of the investors in those schemes presents a further example of a personal finance scheme which attracted much poor publicity for the personal finance industry. Prior to 1990 many personal financial advisers had advised their elderly clients to take out a mortgage on their unmortgaged property and to invest the money so raised in securities that would, it was claimed, provide the investor with a modest additional income. Many of the investors who invested their mortgage funds into these schemes lost their money. The UK housing market crashed between 1989 and 1991 and the value of many of the homes mortgaged through these home income schemes fell below the value of the mortgage, creating a 'negative equity' situation. In addition to this calamity the income from the securities bought with the mortgage money declined and in many cases proved to be inadequate to meet the annual interest cost of the new mortgage.[1] The unfortunate mortgagees were worse off than before. Some even lost their homes.

Another scandal that surfaced in the early 1990s involved those employees who were persuaded to switch from an occupational to a personal pension plan. This switch was made with the hearty encouragement of the government of the day. Many employees who were contributing to a company occupational pension scheme were persuaded by financial advisers to leave their company scheme and switch their regular pension contributions into a personal pension plan run by a private financial institution. These switches from a company scheme into a personal pension scheme generated large commissions to the personal financial advisers who recommended the switch (and to their employers). As we note in Chapter 5 above, a company pension scheme will almost invariably provide superior benefits to a personal pension scheme and so such a switch is unlikely to benefit the employee. A subsequent analysis of a sample of such cases found that the PFAs who advised on the switch did not collect sufficient information from their clients to properly assess the advice given on the switch. In the case of this particular scam there is talk of compensation running into several hundred million pounds. It is not yet clear who will foot this huge bill. Since the government itself introduced and strongly advocated the benefits of personal pensions we would hope that the government will make a major contribution towards compensation to the victims.

Some other equally discreditable incidents occurred in other branches of the financial services industry during the 1980s. The Robert Maxwell Mirror Group pension fiasco, where some £500 million of pensioner's money went astray, and the heavy losses suffered by some 'names' guided into dubious syndicates within the Lloyd's insurance market, are well documented. In neither case has anyone so far been found guilty of sharp practice, let alone of fraud. These incidents show that the personal financial adviser has not been the only type of financial adviser to be placed in the dock during this sombre period for British finance.

These well-publicized cases are but the tip of the iceberg. By the early 1990s the dire consequences of poor advice and fraud for the finances of clients of financial advisers had become the staple diet of the personal finance columns in the British press.

As long ago as 1984 it became obvious to the British government that the public needed protection against the consequences of fraud and poor quality financial advice. A direct result of this concern was the 1986 Financial Services Act. The protection provided in the initial Bill was not satisfactory but the regulations protecting the public against poor financial advice and fraud have been gradually improved and are now reasonably comprehensive. Many loopholes in the protective framework remain to be sealed but the public is now relatively well protected against the more blatant abuses from their financial advisers. There is still much too much bad financial advice about but the protection of the public, especially against fraud, has been much improved.

THE MECHANISM OF CONTROL

One of the major risks you face when you seek financial advice is incompetence on the part of your financial adviser. How much does your financial adviser really know about the subject on which you are being advised?

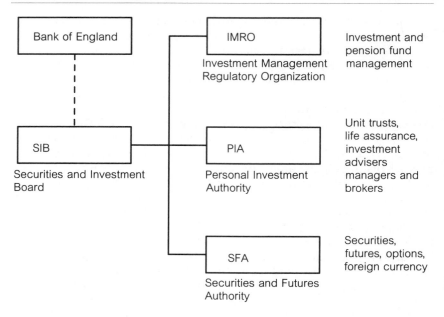

The UK financial market is, on the whole, self-regulated. The bodies that carry out the self-regulation are called the SIB, IMRO, the PIA and the SFA. Each of these organizations monitors the proper operation of a section of the market. The costs incurred by these bodies are paid for by the institutions that are being monitored.

The situation in the USA is quite different. The Securities and Exchange Commission is an arm of the US government, paid for and monitored by the government of the day in the USA.

EXHIBIT 11.1: Bodies that regulate the UK financial market

Incredible as it may seem when looked at in retrospect, prior to the Financial Services Act 1986 the qualifications required to practise as a personal financial adviser in the UK were almost non-existent. The result was that some individuals with a very limited knowledge of finance entered the industry and, by providing poor advice to their clients, lost them a great deal of money. Even worse, some criminals entered the personal finance profession with the sole objective of stealing their clients' money. Many succeeded.

The government introduced the Financial Services Act 1986 to control and monitor the efficiency and honesty of the financial services industry in the UK. The Government chose self-regulation rather than Government regulation and the main self-regulatory organizations (SROs) set up under this Act and later legislation are shown in Exhibit 11.1.

The main regulatory bodies that currently hold responsibility for regulating advisers on personal investment in the UK are the Securities and Investments Board (SIB), the Personal Investment Authority (PIA) and the Investment Managers Regulatory Organization (IMRO).

The SIB is a private limited liability company financed by members of the investment industry in the UK. The Chairman of the SIB reports annually to the Chancellor of the Exchequer who, in turn, lays a regulatory report before parliament. The SIB enjoys regulatory powers that are backed by statute. The ultimate responsibility for regulation lies with the Treasury.

The SIB and the PIA maintain a list of firms that are authorized to act as investment advisers. If you want to find out if the firm advising you is on this list you can phone (0171) 929 3652 or key into the relevant PRESTEL page (key *301# or *SIB#). The SIB is empowered to instigate criminal prosecution against any person who is found to be acting as an unauthorized investment adviser in the UK.

The Personal Investment Authority (PIA), an amalgam of two former bodies known as FIMBRA and LAUTRO, is the arm of the SIB that monitors those advisers who advise on personal investment planning and associated matters. From the date of the implementation of the Financial Services Act 1986, no adviser operating in the UK has been allowed to advise on, sell, or manage personal investments unless the adviser is authorized to do so by one or other of the regulatory bodies set up under the 1986 Act.

The current controllers who regulate personal financial advice in the UK have set themselves two objectives: to monitor entrants to the investment profession by checking that they are *competent, honest and solvent*, and to provide a set of *rules of correct conduct* that must be followed by investment advisers when dealing with their clients.

In addition to setting up the regulatory bodies mentioned above to monitor standards another Act was introduced at the same time which set up something called an *investors' compensation scheme*. This scheme will compensate you up to a fixed maximum amount, currently £48 000[2] for losses incurred by reason of bad advice from, or fraud, committed by your financial adviser.

You can claim under the scheme if you lose money by reason of negligence, incompetence or fraud by your *authorized* financial adviser. The scheme is run by an independent company called ICS Limited. The SIB supervises the scheme and compensation is paid out by the SIB, but the scheme is financed, in arrears, by a levy on members of the particular regulatory authority within which the loss occurs, such as the PIA or IMRO.

Note that 'no-advice' financial services that sell you financial products but give you no advice are not covered by the scheme. Many direct sellers fall into this category, so care should be taken when dealing with them. If you buy, but fail to take advice, there is no compensation since it is assumed that you are making your own decisions based on the literature given to you.

REGISTRATION THROUGH A RECOGNIZED PROFESSIONAL BODY (RPB)

An alternative way to register as an investment adviser is to register indirectly through a recognized professional body (RPB). Examples of RPBs include the Law Society, the Institute of Actuaries, or the Institute of Chartered Accountants in England and Wales. Note that advisers registered in this indirect fashion are excluded from the ICS scheme. These professional bodies run their own compensation scheme, which is claimed to be the equal of the SIB scheme. There have been many fewer claims against advisers registered within the various RPB schemes, probably because those registered with an RPB usually have superior qualifications and charge fees for advice given rather than accepting commission from the financial institutions selling financial products.

The scheme to regulate investment advisers came into force on 29 April 1988 but the operation of the scheme is still the subject of much criticism. There has been a great deal of buck-passing between the various parties involved in monitoring financial regulation. The concept of 'self-regulation' has come under particularly strong attack. The system 'has not worked and will not work because of the inherent conflicts of interest within it.'[3]

There is a major disagreement between the large financial institutions and the government regarding the operation of the regulatory apparatus. The kernel of the disagreement is that the large institutions believe that the small independent financial advisers should be regulated by a different organization and should operate under a different set of rules from those regulating financial advisers working for the large well-funded and well-organized financial institutions.

Major changes in the regulatory apparatus were introduced in 1995 but much dissatisfaction remains. It may be that a government organization on the lines of the Securities and Exchange Commission in the United States is needed to provide proper protection for the public. Much will depend on whether the personal finance industry continues to be driven by commission rather than by fees.

HOW DO YOU FIND A GOOD PERSONAL FINANCIAL ADVISER?

If you are seeking financial advice your most pressing problem is to find a reliable and competent financial adviser. How do you go about finding such a person?

First we should note that there is no shortage of personal financial advisers in the UK. Around 20 000 are registered with the PIA and many more work for the large financial institutions such as banks, building societies and insurance companies. There are also advisers registered with recognized professional bodies such as solicitors and qualified accountants.

The PIA is a self-regulating organization established under the Financial Services Act 1986 to ensure that those who advise on investment in the UK are fit and proper persons. The PIA regulates firms that offer independent investment advice and services to the general public.

Any person or firm that advises on investments, deals in investments, manages investments or operates collective investment schemes comes under the aegis of the PIA.

The types of investments covered are shares, debentures and bonds, government securities, unit and investment trusts and long-term insurance contracts. Warrants, options and any other rights or interests in investments are also covered.

The entity registered with the PIA can be a sole trader, a partnership or a limited company.

Before registration, the PIA must ensure that the applicant is honest, competent and solvent. The question of honesty is monitored by requiring references from reliable sources. The question of competency is addressed by requiring the applicant, at the very least, to have passed the Financial Planning Certificate of the Chartered Insurance Institute although many applicants will already hold a higher financial qualification.

With regard to solvency, a statement of personal assets and liabilities is required if the applicant is a sole trader or a member of a partnership. An opening balance sheet is required plus a forecast profit and loss account for the first year of trading. If the applicant is a company, a form must be supplied showing the issued and fully paid share capital of the company plus a statement that the shares issued are not in bearer form.

If the applicant has a criminal record of any kind, the PIA must be told.

Every applicant must have arranged professional indemnity insurance of a value acceptable to the PIA.

All members registered with the PIA must submit annual reports to the PIA. The nature of these reports depends on the category under which the member is registered. Category 1 covers all members who act as principals and handle clients' money. Category 2 covers members who handle clients' money but who do not act as principals in buying and selling shares, etc. Category 3 covers those members who neither act as principals nor handle clients' money.

Category 1 members must supply the PIA with an audited balance sheet, profit-and-loss account and statement of financial resources each year. A monthly unaudited balance sheet and profit-and-loss account and resource statement must also be supplied. Category 2 members must supply the same statements annually plus management accounts quarterly. They must also fill in a questionnaire on various aspects of their dealings annually. Category 3 members need only fill in the questionnaire and a statement of solvency once a year. Special activities such as discretionary portfolio management and transacting options and warrants require specific authorization from the PIA.

EXHIBIT 11.2: Some registration requirements of the PIA

The availability of *competent* experienced advice is another matter. Various organizations such as the Independent Financial Advisers hotline (telephone 0171 9293652) or the Institute of Financial Planning (01179 304434) will supply you, free of charge, with lists of personal financial advisers in your area. The address of these organizations are listed at the end of this book. The question of how you can find an adviser who is reliable and competent remains, however.

Your first step must be to check that the adviser is 'registered' with a regulator. This reduces the probability that the personal financial adviser is unreliable or incompetent but, alas, does not eliminate the possibility entirely. The regulator will have audited the adviser to ensure that he or she is honest, financially sound, properly qualified and insured.

Every investment adviser in the UK must be registered either directly or indirectly with one of the regulatory bodies noted above. Most personal financial advisers are registered either with the PIA or IMRO.[4]

As noted above, the PIA audits the background and competence of the applicant and if the applicant is found to be 'honest, competent and solvent' the PIA will register the adviser as a member. This registration allows the personal financial advisers to advise clients on investment and other related matters. The adviser can inform clients on a letterhead that he or she is a registered member of the PIA or some other self-regulating organization. Some of the more important conditions imposed on an applicant before he or she is accepted for registration with the PIA are set out in Exhibit 11.2.

In order to prove 'competence' to act as an investment adviser, the PFA must, as an absolute minimum educational standard, pass the three parts of the Financial Planning Certificate (FPC) of the Chartered Insurance Institute,[5] the Certificate for Financial Advisers of the Chartered Institute of Bankers (Papers 1, 2 and 3) or the Investment Advice Certificate (Papers 1, 2 and 3) of the Securities Institute. In addition, the adviser must have accumulated at least two years' practical experience in the field – three years if the adviser wishes to act as a principal. Many personal financial advisers will have already gained a more advanced financial qualification than the FPC certificate before applying for PIA membership; for example they may be qualified accountants or hold a qualification in banking, law or insurance.[6]

If your PFA is registered, has passed all three parts of a relevant certificate and has accumulated three years' experience in the job, this would suggest that the PFA possesses at least a minimum level of competence as a financial adviser.

Additional, more advanced qualifications, are now on offer. An Advanced Financial Planning Certificate is awarded by both the CII and by the CIB, these exams cover advanced topics such as tax, trusts and offshore investment. If your adviser has passed these advanced examinations he or she has demonstrated a willingness to study hard if nothing else.[7]

Checking paper qualifications is only the first step in checking out an adviser. You should also ensure that the adviser has proven experience over several years. It would also be useful to seek out a word-of-mouth recommendation from a previous client of the adviser. Not all advisers are expert in all financial products: you should check that the adviser you wish to use is an expert, or can consult an expert, if the product you are buying is a complicated product such as a pension plan.

When you have verified that the adviser is reasonably competent your next step is to check out whether the adviser is *independent* or a *tied agent* and whether he or she receives remuneration in the form of fees or commission.

INDEPENDENT OR TIED AGENT?

A personal financial adviser can choose to be *independent*. In this case the adviser can sell the financial products offered by any company. Alternatively the adviser may choose to work exclusively for a single financial institution. In this case the adviser is said to be *tied* to that institution. If the adviser is tied to a single financial institution the adviser is restricted as to the financial products that he or she can recommend to you. The adviser may only recommend the products sold by the company to which he or she is tied. These may be perfectly good products but they are selected from a restricted range.

An independent adviser can choose from among a much wider range of products. This width of choice may improve the quality of the advice given to you.

COMMISSION- OR FEE-BASED?

The final question you need to ask your financial adviser is whether his or her income is *fee based* or *commission based*. The tradition in the field of financial advice has been for most advisers to charge no fee to the client for their advice but to collect substantial commissions based on the value of the financial products that they sell to their clients. The commission is paid to the adviser by the financial institution that produces and sells the product. Since January 1995 the adviser has been required to let you know the value of the commission or other income he or she receives from selling you a financial product such as a pension plan or insurance policy. You may be surprised at the size of this commission which can run to 5% of the value of the product sold.

Where you enter into a contract to make payments for several years, as with a pension fund, the commission is often paid to the adviser in two parts: an initial substantial commission on the first year's payments plus a smaller commission on future years' payments.

Since the rate of commission paid on the financial products sold by an adviser varies a great deal between both products and institutions there is a risk that your adviser will suggest a product which pays a high commission to the adviser rather than one that is best suited to your needs. This practice is forbidden by the new regulations (see below) but regulations such as these are difficult to audit.

Fee-based financial advisers charge a fee of around £50 to £150 an hour for their services but they will deduct any commission they receive from the products sold to you from this fee. The net cost of the fee less the commission may well reduce the adviser's fee to zero or even result in you receiving a surplus on the commission. Fee-based advisers have no reason to suggest products other than those best suited to your needs.

As we mentioned above, there is nothing to stop you consulting with several advisers, some commission-based and some fee-based, and asking for an estimate of the net cost of the advice to be given to you on a particular matter. A first visit to a financial adviser is almost invariably free of charge. You can also form an opinion regarding the ability of the adviser on this first visit. Think up a few relevant but difficult questions to which you know the answer and see how the adviser performs.

THE RULE BOOKS

Every regulatory body such as the SIB and the PIA has devised a 'rule book' to control both the relations between a personal financial adviser and the client and the organization of the work of the personal financial adviser.

If a personal financial adviser who is registered with the PIA ignores these rules he or she could be subjected to criminal prosecution and any contracts entered into between the personal financial adviser and the client based on these invalid procedures would be void. It is therefore of some importance that if you are seeking advice from a personal financial adviser you should know something about these rules and regulations which have been set up to protect your interests.

At this point you may well be thinking: 'How does a regulatory body like the PIA know that the correct procedures are being implemented?' Every member registered with the PIA is visited from time to time by a representative of the PIA, a PIA auditor, who checks that the firm is complying with the rules.[8]

Some of the more important rules contained in the SIB and the PIA rule books will be described below but the only sure way to check out the rules imposed on financial advisers by the SIB, the PIA and other regulatory agencies is to read the rule book, and the associated guidelines, issued by the regulatory body concerned. These rule books can be obtained at the somewhat exorbitant charge of around £90 from the information department of the given regulator. They are also supposed to be available in the reference section of 'all good public libraries' . . . but the author could not find them in the three central public libraries that he visited.

Some of the more important rules set out in the SIB rule book are listed below.

WHO MUST REGISTER WITH A SELF-REGULATING ORGANIZATION?

If an independent personal financial adviser is dealing in, managing or advising on investing in shares, debentures, government securities, unit or investment trusts, options (but not futures), warrants or any other right or interest in investments, or is arranging long-term insurance contracts related to investment, then the personal financial adviser must be registered with an appropriate regulator.

There are one or two specific exemptions to this blanket rule. For example those who provide financial advice in newspapers or journals need not register, and those providing advice on shares in private companies are excluded, as are those providing advice on employee share schemes. Those providing casual financial advice, at a party for example, but not acting in the specific role of a financial adviser are also exempt from the rules. So you can tip that sure-fire investment at your next dinner party and not be sued by fellow diners when the share collapses in value by 50% over the following seven days.

Note that those who arrange mortgages and loans or who provide advice on investing in gold, jewellery and similar commodities are specifically excluded from supervision by the SIB.

SOME ORGANIZATIONAL RULES

An investment adviser must tell you whether he or she is an *independent financial adviser* or a *tied agent*. This is called the *polarization* rule. This declaration has important implications since a 'tied agent' can only sell you the products of the company to which he or she is tied. If a personal financial adviser is 'tied', this fact simplifies the job of the personal financial adviser somewhat since the range of possible investment choices to be considered is much reduced.

The SIB rule book states that there must be 'integrity and fair dealing' between you and your personal financial adviser. This somewhat opaque clause has caused some anguish among personal financial advisers since the precise meaning of 'integrity' and 'fair dealing' might be subject to a range of interpretations.

The independent personal financial adviser must also give *best advice* when selecting an investment plan for you. This means that the advice must be competent and impartial and place your interests before the interests of your adviser. The personal financial adviser must not bias his advice towards one organization or one product if he or she is independent. The personal financial adviser must, to the best of his ability, choose the product best suited to your needs. In other words the adviser must not choose that product that provides the highest commission available. (For example, gilts generate no commission for the personal financial adviser but might well suit the investment needs of a risk-averse investor.)

However the PIA has admitted that 'There is an element of subjective judgement in most recommendations.'[9] In other words it is not all that easy to prove whether a particular recommendation is, or is not, influenced by the level of commission offered on the product recommended.

The rules are very strict on *packaged* products provided by a group associated in some way with your personal financial adviser. In such circumstances the packaged product 'must be better at securing the client's objectives than all other products from other sources.'[10] This is a somewhat draconian requirement. It is not easy to see how such a rule can be tested.

FINDING OUT ABOUT YOU, THE CLIENT

The personal financial adviser must make a reasonable attempt to find out about your background before offering you financial advice. He or she must ask you the following questions. Are you married? Are you employed? When, if employed, do you intend to retire? What form of pension will you have on your retirement? What other investments do you hold? Do you own your own home? Is it mortgaged and if so for how much? What is your state of health? What life and other insurance do you hold? In summary, every personal financial adviser must enquire into the background of every client. Advice must not be given in a vacuum.[11]

Note that if you are asked about something important, such as your state of health, and you refuse to divulge this information to your adviser then you let your adviser off the hook. The adviser will record the fact of your refusal to answer and confirm it to you in writing. If subsequent events prove that this concealed information, poor health for example, causes you to lose money, you cannot take legal action against your adviser and hope to win your case.

If you approach an adviser and the adviser does not make proper enquiries about your background, switch to another adviser.

INVESTMENT OBJECTIVES

If you are seeking advice on investment then your personal financial adviser must agree a set of investment objectives with you. For example you must discuss the degree of risk you wish to take with your funds. The specific risks attached to any individual investment must be explained to you. The personal financial adviser must discuss with you your ability to maintain regular payments on any long-term financial contracts and the consequences of not doing so.

If the personal financial adviser is authorized to hold your money (and many are not . . . check!) the personal financial adviser must keep your money in a separate account from his own. Interest must be credited to this account at the current rate paid on commercial bank deposits and the personal financial adviser's accounts must be audited at least once a year by a qualified auditor. You should ask about these matters before you hand over your money to a personal financial adviser.

If your personal financial adviser is authorized by the PIA to manage a portfolio of your securities and you hand over your assets to be managed by your adviser then the personal financial adviser must follow certain procedures. The personal financial adviser must send you an up-to-date statement of the performance of your investments on a regular basis.

An annual report must also be sent to you providing information on such things as the sale and purchase of specific stock during the year, the income from and the costs of running the portfolio and the specific charges made by the personal financial adviser for managing your portfolio.

If your adviser sells you an investment-linked life policy then 'best advice' also applies. If your adviser makes a forecast as to the future value of the investment fund on the termination of the policy or makes a forecast as to the future profits to be earned from the policy, then both 'optimistic' and 'pessimistic' forecasts must be provided in the light of past experience. An estimate must also be provided to you regarding how much money you would receive if the life policy were to be discontinued within five years of being initiated.

ADVERTISEMENTS

The contents of any advertisement issued by a personal financial adviser registered and authorized by the PIA are strictly controlled. For example warnings on the volatility of share values and the marketability of the shares advertised must be clearly stated in the advert.

THE CUSTOMER AGREEMENT LETTER

The basis of the relationship between you and your adviser must be set out in a *customer agreement letter*. This letter will set out the services to be provided to you by the adviser, the responsibilities accepted by the adviser and the basis of the charges to be levied on you by the adviser. Read this letter carefully, it has legal import if things go wrong.

PROPER RECORDS

Proper records must be kept by your personal financial adviser on all exchanges that take place between yourself and the personal financial adviser. These records must include the facts and information relied on

The SIB requires that all financial advisers registered with them should provide all clients who buy certain defined financial products on their advice with written answers to the following questions:

1.   How much am I due to pay to enter this financial scheme?

2.   How much am I likely to get back as a return?

3.   In the case of a mortgage, is the repayment of the mortgage guaranteed under the recommended mortgage scheme?

4.   Can I move house and retain the mortgage?

5.   What deductions are made from my payments into the scheme and what are these deductions for?

6.   How much commission is deducted from my payments into the scheme?

7.   Will any bonuses be paid to me under this scheme?

EXHIBIT 11.3: Questions that must be answered by your financial adviser

by the personal financial adviser in arriving at any recommendations made to you, the client. The records must show that each recommendation was appropriate in the light of your investment objectives, your attitude to risk and any special instructions that you may have given to your adviser. These records are audited by the regulator from time to time and they will form the basis of any investigation resulting from complaints by you against your adviser.

SOME TECHNICAL RULES

In addition to the above general rules, the rule books set out some technical rules on investment advice and management. Examples of these technical rules are set out below.

- Contracts signed during a *cold call* by a personal financial adviser in the course of selling a financial product are not normally enforceable at law. There are, however, a few exceptions to this rule such as when a salesman is selling unit trusts or certain life policies.

- When a personal financial adviser is advising you on investing in certain financial products the personal financial adviser must provide written answers to the set of questions given in Exhibit 11.3. These answers are designed to inform you about the true cost of the product you are about to buy. For example the statement must set out any hidden legal or up-front costs that may not be stated in a conventional purchase contract.

- If the investment recommended to you is a *high risk investment,* for example if the personal financial adviser suggests that you invest part of your investment portfolio in such things as reverse tracker funds or warrant funds, then the adviser must inform you that such investments are *high risk, high return* investments and describe the nature of the particular risks involved *even if these risks are hedged in some way.*

- If you ask your investment adviser to manage a portfolio of your securities you must ensure that the personal financial adviser is specifically authorized by the regulator to conduct this kind of activity. Not all investment advisers are so authorized.

- The personal financial adviser managing your portfolio is specifically prohibited from 'churning' the shares in your portfolio simply to earn commission on the churning process.

- If your adviser has privileged access to a desirable stock the adviser must allocate the stock equitably between all clients and not channel all the best stock to favoured clients.

THE COMPLAINTS PROCEDURE

All registered advisers are required to set up a proper complaints procedure to deal with grievances from clients. The complaint and subsequent action on the complaint must be recorded by the personal financial adviser in the 'complaints book' and you should be meticulous in keeping a record of the correspondence between yourself and your adviser for future use.

The formal complaints procedure ensures that if your complaint is taken beyond the point of simply complaining to your adviser then a complete record of dealings between you and your adviser will be available for perusal by a third party, for example the regulator.

SOME ADDITIONAL RULES

The rules set out in the SIB rule book are supplemented by some additional rules that are set out in the PIA rule book. The SIB insists that the rules set out in the PIA rule book must be at least as strict as those set out in the SIB rule book. The PIA and its predecessors (FIMBRA and LAUTRO) have issued several 'guidance notes' that you might find helpful in clarifying and expanding the meaning of some of the PIA rules.

- Every investment adviser working for a firm that is not itself regulated must be registered with a regulatory organization such as the PIA as one who can act as an investment adviser or as a supervisor of an investment adviser.

- An independent investment adviser is required to organize a personal information system sufficient to ensure that he or she knows about all important investment products currently available on the market. Many investment databases are now stored on host computers and can be accessed directly by computer, modem and telephone. Exhibit 12.2 in Chapter 12 sets out a list of some of these databases. Many can be accessed by the Internet.

- Personal financial advisers 'are expected to consult authoritative financial journals, to be aware of the technical aspects of the various products on offer, and to be knowledgeable about the nature and past performance of the investments they may recommend.' With regard to product providers the personal financial adviser is expected to be aware of 'the solvency or financial strength of the product providers, the quality of the investment teams, specialization within the product range, contract features and terms, overall quality of service and level of charges or expenses.' These conditions impose a formidable set of research requirements on the personal financial adviser.

- Your adviser is not allowed to suggest to you that the cash or percentage returns achieved by a product or portfolio of products in the past are any indication of the returns that may be achieved in the future. When using statistical information 'members should be especially careful to compare like with like and draw the correct inferences.'[12] Personal financial advisers are instructed that they should only advise on subjects on which they are competent. If your adviser is uncertain as to his or her level of competence on a particular subject then the adviser is required to pass you on to another personal financial adviser who is competent to advise on this product or service.

- If your adviser holds any bias or interest that might influence the advice given to you this bias must be revealed to you. This does not mean that a personal financial adviser cannot recommend products in which he or she has an interest but simply that you must be informed that this is so.

- An additional requirement of *best execution* is added to the SIB requirement of 'best advice'. 'Best execution' means that the deal must be executed at the lowest price or the best terms available at that time. In particular, an investment deal must not be executed through a high-charging network that feeds a high commission to your personal financial adviser.

	Value	Approximate commission
Personal pension plan (a series of contributions)	£100 per month	£900 in first year +
Endowment policy (a series of contributions)	£150 per month	£850 in first year +
Life assurance (maximum investment plan)	£500 per year	£500 in first year +
Guaranteed income bond	£1 000 invested	£95
Unit trust	£1 000 invested	£70
Single premium bond	£1 000 invested	£65
Personal pension plan (a single premium)	£10 000 invested	£650
Investment trust saving scheme	£1 000 invested	£50
Government gilts	£1 000 invested	£0
National saving certificates	£1 000 invested	£0

The table gives some indication of the rates of commission paid to financial advisers who sell certain financial products to clients. The commission paid to financial advisers varies quite widely between product providers. The figures can only be taken as a rough guide. Note that additional commission may be paid each year to the adviser during the life of the contract.

In the case of many long-term investment contracts the rate of commission deducted and the annual management charges deducted from your investment have a greater impact on the terminal value of the fund than does the investment strategy employed by the managers of a fund. Check out the commission and annual management charges before you invest. Some funds have no initial charge and management charges of under 1% per year.

EXHIBIT 11.4: Commission paid to advisers

- The SIB rule book required that any of your funds which are held by a personal financial adviser must be audited. The PIA rule book tightens this rule by adding that the personal financial adviser's accounts must be audited at least once a year by a qualified auditor.

- Your personal financial adviser must arrange professional indemnity insurance to cover any loss arising out of his or her negligence or misconduct. Its value must be sufficient to satisfy the PIA.

- Your personal financial adviser is required to hand you a summary of the more important SIB and PIA rules that are pertinent to any transactions he or she concludes with you.

- Finally, every investment adviser registered with the PIA must be willing to submit himself or herself to interrogation and possible warning or reprimand by the PIA disciplinary panel if evidence is provided to the panel regarding his or her negligent conduct.

If a personal financial adviser should knowingly break any of the rules set out in the SIB or the PIA rule book he or she can be warned or reprimanded or fined or suspended. The ultimate sanction is that the member can be expelled from the SIB or the PIA and legal action may be taken against him or her. In effect the adviser would no longer be permitted to give advice on a wide range of personal financial matters. The adviser would have to take up another form of employment.

As from 1 January 1995 all investment advisers must declare to you any commission or fee or other reward received from a product provider on the sale of the product *whether or not you ask for this information*. Prior to this date only independent advisers were required to provide this information, and only if asked to do so by the client. A listing of commission paid to financial advisers by the sellers of financial products is provided in Exhibit 11.4. Note the high commission on pension products and endowment policies and the zero commission paid on government stock. The level of commission is not supposed to influence the advice given by a personal financial adviser but, human nature being what it is, it well might do so. Commission and management charges have a greater influence on the terminal value of many funds than does the success or failure of the investment strategy used in managing the fund.

I think the reader will agree that the above list imposes a formidable set of requirements and sanctions on personal financial advisers. If these rules are obeyed, the security aspect of personal finance should be adequately covered. The problem is that a body of evidence is building up to support the view that many personal financial advisers just do not obey or even know about these rules. This problem can be partially solved if the clients of personal financial advisers are made aware of the rules and insist on their implementation.

Since 1 January 1995 the sellers of certain financial products have been required to provide buyers with a *key features document*. An example of the information provided in this document is given in Exhibit 11.5.

AN ALTERNATIVE SCHEME FOR REGISTRATION

An alternative method of registration with a regulator is available to members of certain professional bodies such as the Institute of Chartered Accountants in England and Wales (ICAEW), the Insurance Brokers' Registration Council and the Law Society. Individuals who are members of a recognized professional body (RPB) can register with the PIA as institutional members. This does not mean that all the members of that organization can consider themselves qualified to act as independent financial advisers. They must notify the relevant RPB that they intend to provide advice to their clients on personal investment matters. Members making such an application may have to prove their competence in personal finance to their institute. They may be required to pass an additional examination and pay an additional fee to their institute for receiving the privilege of registration.

Personal financial advisers registered in this way must act as independent financial advisers and not as tied agents. However they can accept commission on products that they sell. Most advisers registered with RPBs are fee based but they need not be.

THE INVESTORS' COMPENSATION SCHEME (ICS)

We noted that if you lose money because of negligence or fraud on the part your registered adviser you can make a claim against the investors' compensation fund. The maximum amount of compensation that you can claim is currently £48 000. Your claim must be lodged with the relevant regulatory authority within six months of the loss taking place.

The ICS is run by the SIB but the costs and charges are analysed each year and passed on by the SIB to the appropriate regulatory body such as the PIA or IMRO. The PIA recovers this charge from a levy imposed annually on advisers, firms and individuals, who are registered with the PIA. The annual cost imposed on each member in any year depends on the calls on the fund in the previous year.

As noted above, all personal financial advisers are required to take out personal indemnity insurance to cover negligence claims against them. Despite this, the annual ICS charge on members of the PIA has reached a level which is considered excessive by registered members. The net effect of all of this is that honest and competent personal financial advisers have to pay for the errors of their less competent or honest colleagues.[13] The ICS is under great pressure and may not survive in its present form.

HOW CAN YOU COMPLAIN?

You cannot make a claim on the Investors' Compensation Scheme unless you can convince the SIB that you have suffered loss by reason of negligence or fraud committed by your personal financial adviser who is registered under the Financial Services Act.

WHAT ARE THE PROCEDURES YOU MUST FOLLOW TO MAKE A COMPLAINT?

You can lodge a complaint with many organizations in addition to the SIB, PIA and IMRO but in all cases you must first exhaust the complaints procedure set up by your personal financial adviser. We noted above that every firm of personal financial advisers registered under the Financial Services Act must set up a formal procedure for handling complaints received from clients. If you write to your personal financial adviser making a complaint, the personal financial adviser must reply to this complaint and log the complaint in a complaints book along with any subsequent developments with regard to the complaint.

EXHIBIT 11.5: A key features document on a 25-year endowment plan

Since 1 January 1995 the sellers of certain financial products must provide the buyers with detailed information about the product they are buying. The document below shows the key features of an endowment policy set up to cover a mortgage to be repaid in 25 years' time. All insurance companies use the same assumptions about growth rates in these key feature documents.

Basic information

NAME: Thomas Moon

ADDRESS: 16 Lunar Avenue, Skytown

DATE OF BIRTH: 16 September 1959

VALUE OF MORTGAGE: £50 000

TERM OF CONTRACT: 25 years

VALUE OF LIFE COVER: £50 000

MONTHLY PREMIUM: £150

SMOKER/NON-SMOKER: Non-smoker

What might I get back after 25 years?

Your premiums will be invested by the Amber Insurance Company. What you get back depends on how your investment grows over the years. All insurance companies use the same assumptions about the rates of growth. These assumed rates of growth are 5% per year, 7.5% per year and 10% per year. Several rates are used because no insurance company can guarantee a particular rate of growth.

If the invested funds grow at 5% per year you will get back £46 500.
If the invested funds grow at 7.5% per year you will get back £65 400.
If the invested funds grow at 10% per year you will get back £92 500.

These are not minimum or maximum figures. You could get back more or less than this.
The absolute guarantee is that you will not get back less than £32 500.

Some amounts are deducted from your annual premiums. What are the deductions for?

Amounts will be deducted from your premiums to cover commissions, expenses, charges, any surrender penalties and other adjustments.

How much will your advice cost?

The cost of the advice will depend on the size of the premium and the policy term. For arranging this policy the Amber Life Insurance Company will pay commission and provide services worth £930 initially and £27 per year thereafter.

What happens to the policy if I cash in the policy early?

The following examples will give you some idea of what you will get back under the assumption that the rate of growth in the investment will be 7.5% per year. All insurance companies use the same rate of growth, which is not guaranteed.

WARNING – THE EARLY YEARS

If you cash in during the early years you may get back less than you paid in.

Year	Total paid in to date £	Effect of deductions to date £	What you might get back £
1	1 200	1 240	0
2	2 400	1 860	729
3	3 600	2 090	1 930
4	4 800	2 360	3 220
5	6 000	2 660	4 580

THE LATER YEARS

The policy may have a terminal bonus when it matures. If so, on maturity, the amount you might get back is sharply increased. To obtain the full benefit from the policy it is important to continue paying your premiums for the whole period.

Year	Total paid in to date £	Effect of deductions to date £	What you might get back £
10	12 000	4 850	12 800
15	18 000	8 690	23 900
20	24 000	15 000	39 000
21	25 200	16 700	42 600
22	26 400	18 500	46 400
23	27 600	20 500	50 600
24	28 800	22 700	55 000
25	30 000	25 100	65 400

What difference will the deductions make to the rate of return?

The last line in the table shows that over the full 25 years the total deductions could amount to £25 100. Leaving out the cost of cover this would reduce the growth rate on the investment from 7.5% to 5.8% per year over the period.

What about inflation?

The value of money tends to fall over time. The above amounts are shown in 1997 pound values. You will be able to buy less with this amount of money in 25 years time. For example, if the rate of inflation averages 3% per year over the next 25 years then £65 400 will only be able to buy as much as £32 000 would today.

Most of the complaints made to firms giving personal financial advice are resolved by this procedure and go no further. Firms of personal financial advisers do not like complaints travelling upwards from their clients to regulators. It gives them a bad name. If, however, you are unable to settle the matter under dispute amicably within this complaints procedure, you can take your complaint to the complaints department of the regulator that monitors your personal financial adviser. This regulator is likely to be either the PIA, IMRO, the SFA or possibly the SIB itself. The regulator will review your complaint and if it thinks your complaint is justified it will take the matter up with your adviser and let you know its final decision in due course.

If the regulator considers that you have lost money because of negligence or fraud on the part of your adviser you will be permitted to make a claim against the Investors' Compensation Fund for a return of the money you have lost, up to a maximum of £48 000.

If your complaint does not concern investment but involves some other financial matter then it is possible that your financial adviser might not be registered with one of the regulators set up under the Financial Services Act of 1986. Another possibility is that the regulator might decline to support your complaint. Under these circumstances you may decide to pursue the matter using an alternative complaints procedure.

Most of the major financial institutions and professional organizations concerned with personal finance have set up their own complaints procedures. For example if you have a complaint against the actions or advice given by an employee of an insurance company and you cannot obtain satisfaction from the company itself you could approach the complaints department of the Association of British Insurers (telephone 0171 600 3333). The company, if resident in the UK, is almost certain to be a member. Alternatively you could put your complaint before the Personal Insurance Arbitration Service (telephone 0171 837 4483) if you are willing to go to arbitration. Finally, if all else fails, you can take your complaint before the insurance ombudsman (0171 928 7600). The ombudsman is unlikely to consider your case until you have exhausted all other avenues of complaint.

The banking industry and building society industry also provide ombudsmen to which you can take your complaint, but only in the last resort. Their telephone numbers are 0171 583 1395 and 0171 931 0044 respectively.

The body to which you take your complaint depends very much on the nature of your complaint. A complaint against an insurance broker can be taken up with the British Insurance and Investment Brokers Association, the broker is almost certain to be a member. If your complaint is concerned with misleading advertising or incorrect information being given to you prior to sale you could approach the Office of Fair Trading (0171 242 2858). The OFT will not pay you compensation but at least you will have the satisfaction of 'shopping' the guilty party.

If you think you have been given misleading advice about an investment but are not sure that this is so you could approach the relevant association for that type of investment. For example the Association of Investment Trust companies (0171 588 5347), the Unit Trust Association Information Unit (0171 831 0898) or the Society of Pension Consultants (0171 353 1688). These bodies have been set up to advise the public on technical and other matters concerning the particular financial product sold by their association.

Finally, you could seek a legal remedy for your complaint, but only *in extremis*. You are not likely to be granted legal aid for a financial complaint so this is an expensive solution to your problem. Finding a suitable legal adviser may also present you with a problem. You should also appreciate that your opponent could well be a very large financial institution with its own experienced and very expert legal department. The wheels of the law can grind slowly and may grind on for many years as your case progresses upward through several courts. You should only contemplate seeking a legal remedy for your financial complaint if you are seriously rich and very determined.

SOME CRITICISM OF THE CURRENT REGULATORY SYSTEM

We commented above that the current protection provided to the clients of financial advisers is fairly sound so long as the client knows about the protection provided. The efficient regulation of financial services at a reasonable cost is a major problem that is confronting all advanced industrial societies at present.[14]

The relatively meagre size of the apparatus controlling the personal finance industry in the UK means that a good number of complaints are still being levelled at the operation of the financial services industry. Let us now examine some of the complaints.

QUALIFICATIONS

Since personal financial advisers are handling and giving advice about the investment of substantial amounts of money, it has been persuasively argued that personal financial advisers should be required to pass a rather tougher set of examinations than those set at present. Even those personal financial advisers who are professionally qualified in some branch of finance other than personal finance are often not particularly well qualified to advise on personal finance. For example, qualified accountants must pass some demanding examinations to gain membership of their institute but only a small part of these examinations, the examination paper on personal taxation, is concerned with personal finance. Tough qualifying exams need to be passed to enter the Institute of Bankers or the Chartered Insurance Institute but again only a limited part of these exams is directly concerned with personal finance.

There is a need for a properly organized Institute of Personal Finance which, hopefully, could gain a Royal Charter. Entry would be by a carefully designed and *externally monitored* set of examinations. These examinations would cover the entire field of personal financial planning in some depth including investment, insurance, pensions, personal tax, raising credit and long-term housing finance. The exams would also cover the law relating to personal finance and the rules imposed by the SIB and the PIA on the work of a personal financial adviser.[15]

EARNINGS BASED ON COMMISSION

One of the most difficult problems faced by the personal finance industry in the UK stems from the fact that most personal financial advisers, or the organizations that employ them, obtain most of their income from the commission received from selling financial products. A few fee-based personal financial advisers derive their income exclusively from charging for advice, but these truly independent financial advisers are relatively few in number.[16] The term 'independent financial adviser' does not mean that the adviser receives no commission on the products that he or she sells. Some independent advisers will hand back part of this commission to their client.

If anyone is dependent on sales commission for most of his or her income, that person is primarily a salesperson, not a professional adviser. The low esteem into which the personal financial advice profession has fallen in recent years is a direct consequence of this dependence on commission attracting the wrong sort of person to the industry.

It is rumoured that, in the near future, certain insurance companies and other sellers of financial products intend to sell their products net of any commission to the financial adviser and leave the adviser to negotiate an advisory fee with his client. If this scheme is implemented it will go a long way towards solving a very serious problem for the industry.

GIVING 'BEST ADVICE'

The guidance notes provided by the PIA and its predecessors attempt to define 'best advice' but the precise definition of the words 'best advice' is still not clear to many advisers. Does 'best advice' mean that the personal financial adviser must not place his or her own financial interests before those of the client or does it have a much wider meaning? If it means the former then the meaning is clear and most right-thinking people would accept that any professional person who is not simply a salesperson should obey this rule. However if 'best advice' means that a personal financial adviser must know all the investment options available to a client in every circumstance in order to select the best possible plan available at that time the rule seems to be too demanding. Only a large organization employing many specialists could hope to meet this requirement. The sole practitioner or small-scale firm of personal financial advisers would be eliminated by this interpretation of the 'best advice' rule.

Guidance note no. 9 published by FIMBRA stated that 'there is an element of subjective judgement in most recommendations'. It would be useful if the SIB or the PIA could provide some further clarification of this comment.

WHO IS A PERSONAL FINANCIAL ADVISER?

A good deal of personal financial advice is given by professional workers who are not regulated by the SIB. For example, estate agents, auctioneers and dealers in many real assets such as gold coins give financial advice to their clients. These advisers are not covered by either the SIB or the PIA rules. If the intention of current legislation is to protect the public against poor financial advice then something should be done to monitor the advice provided by these 'indirect' investment advisers.

PERSONAL FINANCIAL ADVERTISING

The rules regarding the advertising of personal financial products need to be tightened up. The definition of personal financial advertising is not clear. What exactly is a financial advert? What exactly can be said about a product in a financial advert? What numbers should be used? For example, exactly how does the advertiser of a financial product calculate an 'optimistic' and 'pessimistic' forecast on investment returns and future investment values? How should the impact of inflation on past and future values be introduced into financial advertising? The rules regarding adjustment for inflation in particular need to be clarified and expanded.

PERSONAL FINANCIAL ADVICE FROM ABROAD

The rules of the SIB and the other regulatory bodies only apply to a personal financial adviser operating in the United Kingdom. Personal financial advisers also operate in most other countries of the world including other countries in the European Union and offshore from Britain in Jersey, Guernsey and the Isle of Man.

How can a personal financial adviser who is resident and operating abroad be regulated by the SIB or the PIA? The answer is simple: the foreign adviser cannot be regulated. These foreign-based advisers can currently sell products to you from abroad 'cold calling' by phone from Brussels or Barcelona or simply by meeting you when you are abroad. Work is currently being done to standardize the rules regarding the provision of financial services in the EU but this work is still at a very early stage and governments in continental Europe seem to be much less concerned about the exploitation of the personal investor than is the government in the UK.[17]

Many tax havens operate on the fringes of Europe. These tax havens hold several trillion of US dollars of investor funds and the value of these funds is growing exponentially year by year. Most of these 'offshore' tax havens impose much lighter legislation on fund managers than does the UK. Investor compensation is often zero or negligible.[18]

We are not suggesting that fund managers or personal financial advisers operating out of these 'off-shore' centres are dishonest, but that their conduct may well be less tightly monitored than their counterparts in the UK. This puts you, as an investor, at greater risk if you deal with foreign advisers. When moving funds into foreign tax havens you need to take care that your funds are secured against fraud.

The regulation of financial advisers in these 'offshore' centres varies a great deal in quality. Guernsey, Jersey and the Isle of Man have instituted strict controls over financial institutions operating within their borders but such strict regulation is not imposed by the authorities in all offshore centres, especially those operating far from the European theatre. The subject is currently under review by the EU and the SIB.

DIFFUSION OF KNOWLEDGE OF THE SIB AND PIA RULES

Although the rule books published by the SIB and other regulators have been around for quite some time there is an astonishing ignorance about the rules among the general public and even among personal financial advisers. It is not simply that the clients of personal financial advisers do not know their rights but it seems that many registered personal financial advisers do not know the rules under which they are supposed to operate. A research study financed by the SIB in 1993 found that 90% of the personal financial advisers approached by the researchers acted in such a way as to breach one or more of the rules as set down in the SRO rule books applying to them at that time.

A good deal more needs to be done to ensure that the rules are being implemented and that clients of personal financial advisers know about their rights. The abbreviated lists of rights that are currently required to be handed out to clients during a consultation are quite inadequate. Despite the fact that FIMBRA made compliance visits to 2826 member firms in 1993, about half their total membership at that time, compliance still appears to be inadequate in 1997.

A reduction in the cost of the PIA rule book from its current cost of £60 for members and £90 for non-members might help to disseminate the rules more widely among the community. For example the rules could be made available to enquirers on a $3\frac{1}{4}$ inch computer disc and so sold at a fraction of the present price. Even better, the rules could be placed into a database accessible through the Internet.

THE FUNDING OF THE PIA

FIMBRA suffered from a severe lack of funds from its foundation in 1988 to its termination in 1994. While most of the other regulatory bodies are funded by large and very rich organizations like banks and insurance companies, the PIA, the Cinderella of the regulatory family, is funded for the most part by around 5500 personal financial advisory firms, most of which are small firms. That regulatory body, saddled with the duty of monitoring by far the largest number of members, is thus also the one with the poorest source of funding. It is also likely that the PIA will be required to handle more complaints than the other regulatory bodies because so many of its members are less well qualified and the offices are less well run than the members of the other regulatory bodies.

Unless the government of the day is prepared to put more money into the PIA it is difficult to see how this regulator can perform its monitoring function effectively. Many advisory firms registered with the PIA are smaller than the firms registered with the other regulators, thus they need to be monitored more frequently. A substantial increase in the frequency and depth of audit of members registered with the PIA would, however, be an expensive operation that might well be beyond the current financial resources of this regulatory body.

Between 1988 and 1993 FIMBRA investigated 193 fraud cases, 93 of which were criminal in nature, and 77 members were brought to trial. Of those found guilty, 90% were sent to prison. The longest sentence handed down was the 10 years imposed on Peter Clowes.

In the UK we need a properly funded organization to monitor standards in the personal finance industry. This could be achieved by the PIA if it were adequately funded, but a better solution would be to set up a self-regulating institute on the lines of the Institute of Chartered Accountants in England and Wales to control the profession.

One condition for membership of this new institute would be that any adviser earning a living from commission would not be accepted as a member. Thus every member of the Institute of Personal Finance would be a fee based adviser as is the case with other professionals such as lawyers, accountants and architects.

SUMMARY

1. The world of personal finance has been rocked by many financial scandals in recent years. These scandals persuaded the government of the day to enact laws that forced the finance industry to clean up its act. The Financial Services Act of 1986 set up a group of self-regulating organizations within the industry and these organizations now vet all entrants to the investment profession and monitor their performance.

2. The regulator that monitors most personal investment advisers in the UK is called the Personal Investment Authority (PIA). The PIA is itself monitored by the SIB. The PIA took over responsibility for monitoring personal investment advisers from two regulators called FIMBRA and LAUTRO in July 1994. The PIA began operating on 1 January 1995.

3. All persons providing advice on, selling, or managing investments in the UK must be registered with the PIA or some other self-regulating organization. You should always check that your financial adviser is registered with one or other of the regulators. You can do this by phoning the requisite authority listed in the address lists at the end of this book or by consulting the relevant PRESTEL page.

4. If your adviser is registered with a regulator you can be confident that the adviser has studied the subject of personal finance in some detail, that the adviser has at least two to three years' experience and that the adviser has passed a test of solvency and has no criminal record.

5. Each personal financial adviser must declare himself to be either an independent adviser who can advise on and suggest the purchase of

any financial product or a 'tied agent' who sells the products of only one company. Your adviser may earn his income from commission or from fees. The advice from a fee-based adviser will not be influenced by considerations of the commission earned from products sold to you.

6. All commission and any other income earned by your adviser from products he or she has sold to you must be declared to you by the adviser whether or not you ask for this information.

7. The SIB and the PIA both publish a set of rules regulating the conduct and the qualifications required from those who advise on or manage personal investments. The rules are quite comprehensive but there is some doubt as to whether they are being universally applied by advisers.

8. The SIB rules regulate both the organization of the practice of the personal financial adviser and the method of operation of that practice. There must be 'fair dealing' between a personal financial adviser and the client and the personal financial adviser must seek to give you 'best advice' on investment matters. A personal financial adviser must find out about your personal affairs before giving you financial advice. He must agree investment objectives with you and warn you about risky investments and must not 'churn' shares to earn commission. He must allocate scarce stock equitably between clients. A letter of agreement must be signed between you and your personal financial adviser setting out the terms under which you are employing his or her services.

9. Every personal financial adviser must institute an official complaints procedure. All such complaints and your personal financial adviser's response to these complaints must be logged for possible future reference by a third party.

10. In addition to the SIB rules, there are additional rules imposed by the PIA. These state that the personal financial adviser must be knowledgeable about the financial products on which he or she is giving advice and that any bias or self interest by the personal financial adviser must be revealed to you. 'Best execution' of contracts is added to the SIB requirement of 'best advice'. Your funds must be kept separate from those of your adviser and all the funds held must be audited on a regular basis. Your personal financial adviser must take out professional indemnity insurance to cover against any losses you may incur because of the negligence or fraud of your adviser.

11. Every personal financial adviser must be willing to submit to interrogation by the PIA disciplinary panel. If found guilty of fraud

or negligence your personal financial adviser might be warned, reprimanded, fined or imprisoned.

12. An investor's compensation scheme has been set up to compensate you if you lose money through fraud or negligence on the part of your adviser. The maximum you can claim from one default is at present limited to £48 000. The ICS scheme is administered by the SIB.

13. You should beware of advice provided or products offered by advisers operating from offshore tax havens. The advice is probably as good as you would obtain elsewhere but these advisers are not so tightly controlled as those in the UK. Compensation for loss is either not available or is less generous than that available in the UK.

TEST YOUR KNOWLEDGE

1. You are seeking out a personal financial adviser to assist you in investing £100 000 left to you in your father's will. How can you find a competent personal financial adviser who will provide you with safe, impartial and competent advice?

2. You have decided to buy a house for £150 000. You need a mortgage of £100 000 to finance the purchase. Your estate agent offers to act as your adviser on raising the loan. Is the estate agent regulated by one of the regulatory agencies described in the chapter?

3. You are working in Australia and decide to invest £1000 per month in a unit trust managed by the subsidiary of a large British bank situated in Jersey. Is this investment protected by the regulatory procedures set up by the Financial Services Act 1986?

4. Several self-regulatory organizations (SROs) were set up by the Financial Services Act 1986. Which one monitors the qualifications and performance of most personal financial advisers in the UK?

5. You believe that your personal financial adviser has acted negligently and that his negligent act has lost you money. What can you do about it? What procedures should you now follow?

6. What is the Investors Compensation Scheme? How does it work? Who ultimately pays for the scheme? What is the current (1997) limit on the maximum claim under the scheme?

7. The PIA monitors entrants to the personal finance profession in the UK. What are the specific attributes of applicants for membership of the PIA that are tested by the PIA assessment committee before they

will allow an individual or firm to provide investment advice to clients? What are the minimum requirements regarding the exams they must have taken.

8. How can you find out about the rules that your financial adviser must follow when giving you advice about your investments?

9. Your personal financial adviser can be *independent* or a *tied agent*. What is the main difference between an independent and a tied agent? Does the fact that your adviser is independent affect your adviser's ability to earn commission from products sold to you?

10. 'Advice to a client must not be given in a vacuum.' What does this statement mean? Suggest five important facts which you would expect your PFA to ascertain about your background before giving you financial advice.

11. If your financial adviser manages a portfolio of your shares on your behalf, what rules apply to the information that she must supply to you on a regular basis regarding the management of your portfolio?

12. What information must a PFA supply to you regarding the risks attached to any investment he or she recommends? What is meant by a 'high risk investment'? Give two examples of high risk investments that have been given some prominence in recent years.

13. The SIB requires that there must be *integrity and fair dealing* between a personal financial adviser and her client. How would you interpret the words 'integrity and fair dealing' in the context of your personal financial adviser advising you on a choice between taking out either a repayment or an endowment mortgage to buy your first home?

14. You have visited two financial advisers and you intend to select one as your adviser. One PFA states that he will provide his advice to you 'free of charge'. The other states that she will charge you £95 an hour for financial advice. What additional questions do you need to ask before selecting which one to use, assuming that on a personal level they both appear to be competent, experienced advisers?

15. How do you personally interpret the words 'best advice' and 'best execution' in the context of the rules set down by the PIA? Can you think of examples of advice and execution that is not of the 'best' quality?

16. What is a *key features* document? What information would appear in such a document if you bought an endowment policy through an independent financial adviser and he gave you a key features document covering the deal?

17. If your authorized personal financial adviser is found guilty of negligently conducting your financial affairs what are the potential consequences for him?

18. Your personal financial adviser might become registered as a financial adviser by becoming a member of a recognized professional body (RPB). How does this difference in registration affect you?

NOTES

1. These particular schemes are now illegal and new home income schemes have been introduced that are much safer. See Chapter 6 for a fuller discussion.

2. The actual amount of compensation is 100% up to £30 000 and 90% on the next £20 000. That is £48 000 in all for a single default.

3. From a speech by Joel Joffe, former Deputy Chairman of Allied Dunbar. Quoted by Harper A. (1993) Watching their own. *CA Magazine*, May, 8.

4. IMRO is an acronym for the Investment Managers Regulatory Organization. This regulator monitors investment and pension fund management.

5. The entrants and pass rates in the three parts of the CII FPC certificate in 1995 were as follows:

Part 1
entrants: 92 000
pass rate: 73%.

Part 2
entrants: 54 000
pass rate: 68%.

Part 3
entrants 18 000
pass rate 60%.

6. The topics listed in the syllabuses of the examinations set by the various financial institutes in the UK contain very limited material on personal finance. The SIB is asking the accounting institutes to introduce more training in personal finance into the educational syllabuses of their members. Several UK universities provide undergraduate courses in financial services. These courses include some training in personal financial matters.

7. There are now a plethora of qualifications in personal finance, including: FPC, CeFA, IAC, ITC, FACT, AFPC, PIC, IMC, CFP(tm), NVQ, MSFA, AIFP, and ALIA.

8. About half the registered membership of FIMBRA (the predecessor to the PIA) were visited in 1993.

9. FIMBRA Guidance Note No. 9, Section 1.

10. FIMBRA Guidance Note No. 9, Section 5.

11. In December 1993 the SIB commissioned a pilot survey to test the amount of information that personal financial advisers collected about their clients before giving them advice on pension switching. KPMG Peat Marwick carried out the survey. The results were disappointing. Only 9% of the sample showed 'substantial compliance' with the regulation that a personal financial adviser must collect full information about the client before giving advice on switching to a personal pension. *CA Magazine,* February 1994, 12.

12. FIMBRA Guidance Note 9. Section 3.

13. The total levy attributed to FIMBRA members in 1992–93 was £15.5 million. The life assurance companies agreed to pay half of this levy. Thus the charge in 1993 was £375 per firm for category three member firms plus £290 per registered individual member. Category 1 members paid £1140 per firm and £290 per individual member.

14. In 1994/5, the budget was £21.6 million for the SIB, £5.56 million for the PIA and £3.04 million for IMRO.

15. Paper 3 of the Certificate in Financial Planning is moving in this direction but a greater depth of treatment is needed.

16. The list of addresses at the end of this book provides the name, address and telephone number of two organizations which will provide the details of five registered financial advisers who operate near you. The service is free of charge.

17. If you are interested in personal finance in Europe you can consult the *EU Financial Industry Monitor* published by Lafferty publications.

18. The Isle of Man operates an investor compensation scheme but it is less generous than that operating in the UK.

Finding out about personal finance

12

SOURCES OF PERSONAL FINANCE INFORMATION

The simplest way to finding out about personal finance is to go to a personal financial adviser. In addition there are the legal and accounting firms that run personal finance advisory services.

This chapter is concerned with advising those persons who do not seek out an adviser immediately but prefer to find out about current developments in personal finance for themselves. How should they go about it? A little knowledge of the financial products available on the market is a useful asset when discussing your personal financial problem with an adviser.

There is no shortage of advice on personal finance in the UK. Much of this advice may be found in newspapers and magazines as supplements to the considerable amount of advertising of financial products that takes place in those publications. Many books on personal finance have been published, but most of these have a short shelf life. The most recent innovation in the supply of information about personal finance comes from the ubiquitous Internet. Personal finance on the Internet is still in its infancy but the system offers great promise for the future.

BOOKS ON PERSONAL FINANCE

Books on personal finance can be divided into two categories: general introductions and books on specific topics such as pensions or tax. Many useful books on personal finance are available dealing with specific topics such as pension planning or personal investment or personal insurance.

Certain compendia of information on personal financial matters are published. These are mostly designed so that they can be consulted and updated easily by personal financial advisers and, for this reason, are rather expensive. Some of these compendia are available for reference in the reference section of central libraries. You should check to see if any of these publications are available in your own central library. Take care to check that the compendium, if looseleaf, is kept up to date by the library staff. Many are not.

Books and compendia on specialist topics such as pensions or insurance are listed at the end of this book.

FAX SERVICES

Several organizations provide detailed information on such matters as savings rates, mortgage rates, and annuity rates offered to specific categories of person. These can be accessed by faxing the requisite organization. The organization will automatically fax back between one and 10 pages of details about rates offered or premiums charged on specific financial products by various financial institutions.

The financial research organization, *Moneyfacts*, provides information on mortgage rates (8 pages), savings rates offered (8 pages), guaranteed income bonds (4), term insurance rates (6), annuity rates (7) and low-cost share dealing services (6). *Financial Adviser* provides a similar service on mortgage rates for a wide selection of different kinds of mortgages, annuity rates, instant access account rates, guaranteed income bond rates, TESSAs and National Saving rates.

NEWSPAPERS

Almost all daily and weekly newspapers carry personal finance sections. Most of this material is rather ephemeral but the advice is often of surprisingly high quality considering the speed with which it must be written. In particular, a regular check on the personal finance pages can keep you up-to-date on important current developments in personal finance. The answers in the letters columns in the personal finance sections of newspapers provide much useful information on the minutiae of personal finance. Many of these replies to readers' questions are written by advisers working for top accounting and legal firms.

Almost all daily and Sunday newspapers carry a personal finance supplement each week. The *Financial Times* runs an authoritative supplement on personal finance each Saturday.

MAGAZINES

The public in the UK is lucky to have so many high-quality journals published on personal finance. Most of these are monthly journals. Exhibit 12.1 lists most of the personal finance magazines published in the UK on a regular basis. This will prove useful to anyone seeking to find out about a specific problem in personal finance, a specific financial product, or a product provider, or simply to find out about current developments in personal finance. The quality of these articles varies but a good deal of useful information and practical advice is given. Most of these magazines provide readers with an index to articles and subjects at the end of each six-month period or year. Assembling a set of subject indices for a few years back can greatly speed your search for information on a specific topic in personal finance. You will find that many of these personal finance journals, including back copies, are stored in your central library.

Some personal finance journals are targeted at personal financial advisers, whereas others are aimed at members of the general public who are seeking advice on some aspect of personal finance. The first six titles in Exhibit 12.1(a) are magazines and journals that are targeted at personal financial advisers. The remainder are magazines and journals that are targeted at the general public. You will find that some of the most informative articles on personal finance are targeted at personal financial advisers rather than at their clients. I would advise you to consult both types of journal and not simply to limit yourself to reviewing articles aimed at the general public.

Exhibit 12.1(b) lists some of the specific information provided by two popular journals, *Planned Saving* and *Money Management*. Both of these journals are targeted at personal financial advisers. *Money Observer* provides similar data designed to be of use to the general public.

COMPUTER-BASED INFORMATION SYSTEMS

The different types of information discussed in the previous section are much better stored on a computer and accessed using hypertext. For some time now, database publishers have set up and maintained databases of information on personal finance and a myriad of other subjects in a computer store called a 'server' which allows anyone with the relevant access equipment, who is willing to pay the price, to access this information. A cheaper alternative to direct access is available on CD-ROM discs.

There are four parties involved in this type of information service. The publisher who keeps the information up-to-date, the *host* that runs the computer and maintains the technical side of the operation, the telecommunication system that links the host to the computers of the users of the system, and last, but by no means least, the user who interrogates the information system to seek answers to queries.

In theory all you need to access these databanks is a microcomputer with the relevant software installed and a modem linking you to the telephone network. In fact there are one or two quite serious obstacles in the way. First, there is the cost of access. The information providers are not charitable institutions. You must either pay a large fixed annual fee and have unrestricted access to the system or you pay a much lower annual fee but are charged a substantial cost per query raised. The second problem is the quality of your access equipment. Access to the information stored will be very slow if you are using low-powered equipment. High-powered equipment is expensive. The third problem involves finding out how to access the particular information you are

EXHIBIT 12.1(a): Journals and magazines on personal finance

Anyone interested in personal finance in the UK is fortunate in having access to a wide range of magazines on the subject. Most of these are published on a monthly basis. The first six magazines listed below are targeted at personal financial advisers. The remainder are targeted at their clients, the general public.

Money Management

Planned Savings

Financial Adviser

Mortgage Finance Gazette

Money Marketing

Money Week

Investors' Chronicle

Money Observer

Money Wise

What Investment?

What Mortgage?

What Pension?

Money Which?

Private Investor

Quarterly Review of Personal Finance

Financial Times

EXHIBIT 12.1(b) Information provided in some personal finance magazines

Personal finance magazines provide a wide range of information on financial products and financial product providers. They usually provide a selection rather than a full listing.

Planned Saving

Pension funds

> Equity, property, index-linked gilts, with-profits, currency, etc.
> Percentage gains over one and five years.
> Sector averages.

Life funds

> Most funds listed.
> Percentage gains over 1 and 5 years.
> Return on £100 with gross income reinvested over 3 months, 1 year, 3, 5 and 10 years.
> Fund size and offer to bid spread are given.

Unit trusts

> Funds in each sector are listed
> Return on £100 with gross income reinvested over 3 months, 1 year, 3, 5 and 10 years.
> The sector averages are also given.
> Fund size and offer to bid spread are given.

INVESTMENT TRUSTS

> Most funds listed.
> Return on £100 with gross income reinvested.
> Fund size given.
> The sector averages are also given.

BROKER MANAGED FUNDS

> Life and pension funds.
> Three- and 5-year performance.

Money Management

UNIT TRUSTS

> Comparative perfomance by sector.
> Exempt unit trusts.
> Unit holder index.

INVESTMENT TRUSTS

> Comparative performance by sector.

OFFSHORE FUNDS

> Currency indices.
> Sterling converted performance.
> SIB-recognized funds (and some unrecognized).
> Management groups.

ANNUITY RATES

BUILDING SOCIETY RATES

DIRECTORY OF IFAs

HEALTH PRODUCTS

> Critical illness
> Long-term care
> PHI
> PMI

INCOME BONDS

INSURANCE FUNDS

SOME INSURANCE RATES

NATIONAL SAVINGS

A SELECTION OF PEPS

PENSION FUNDS

PERSONAL PENSION PROVIDERS

SECOND-HAND ENDOWMENT POLICIES

TERM INSURANCE

seeking on such things as current insurance rates, current types of pension schemes on offer, the creditworthiness of your insurance fund, specific tax advice and so forth. All of these facts are probably available somewhere within the vast range of databases currently available, but how do you find these specific pages among the billions available?

Exhibit 12.2 lists some computer on-line databases that might be of use to those designing their own financial plans who have access to a computer, modem, telephone line and the appropriate browser software.

Most financial databases are designed to be used by specialist financial advisers such as insurance, mortgage and annuity brokers and pension advisers. The cost of access to these specialist databases is likely to be much too high for them to be used by members of the general public seeking answers to the occasional query. The public will use the Internet to seek out such information, but before we examine the uses of the Internet in more detail we must say something about the 'poor man's database', namely the CD-ROM computer disc.

CD-ROM

Directly accessing a computer-based personal finance information system may prove to be rather complicated for many persons seeking information on personal finance. A simpler alternative is to access a database stored on a CD-ROM. You will need a microcomputer and a CD-ROM reader to read off the data, but CD-ROM devices are now relatively inexpensive at £100 to £150 a unit. Accessing the information on a CD-ROM is a much simpler operation than organizing direct access to a remote database using a modem and various enquiry protocols.

At the present moment all CD-ROMs that store financial information are, so far as we are aware, targeted at companies and professional firms and are consequently rather expensive but it is only a matter of time before the publishers of CD-ROMs realize the potential market for CD-ROM discs that provide personal financial information to the general public. The information on such discs would need to be updated on a regular basis. Currently this is done with legal, tax and company information for professionals. Once a sufficient market for this type of product builds up it will become available to the general public at low cost. The key to marketing such CD-ROMs will be the simplicity with which they can be used.

PERSONAL FINANCE AND THE INTERNET

Unless you have been living in one of the remoter regions of the Kamchatka peninsula over the last few years you will have heard of the *Internet*. The Internet is a communication system that links together millions of computers, some very large, some small, into a global information network, using telephone and other lines.

The Internet serves many purposes, the best known of which is electronic mail or e-mail. Another important function of the Internet is to give users rapid access to information. This data storage aspect of the Internet can best be understood if you envisage an immense library which stores everything that has ever been published: books, reports, magazines, newspapers, the lot. All of this information is stored on individual 'pages' and if you know the requisite book and page number you can rapidly access and read anything on that particular page.

A storage system called the 'worldwide web' (WWW) is an example of such a library. If you were to write a page in WWW format, give your page an 'address' (called an URL) and then store it on the WWW, anyone on the Internet who knows the address can read the page.[1]

The Internet offers immense potential for assisting those who wish to manage their own financial affairs. Financial information that was previously only accessible to specialist financial advisers can now be downloaded from pages in the WWW and accessed by anyone with a computer, a modem, a telephone and the necessary software.

We say that the Internet offers immense *potential* because the system is still in its infancy and only a limited number of financial institutions have opened up personal finance pages on the Internet for anything other than advertising in the United Kingdom.

The Internet has the potential to provide an enquirer with rapid access to information on financial products, financial product providers, financial advisers, financial regulations and current developments in the personal finance industry.

New pages added to the Internet are coming 'on-stream' each day. However, before information about the Internet can be written down and published it is already out of date. The only way to keep up-to-date with developments is to read the current developments page on the Internet itself. This page is called 'Net News'.

HOW DO I OBTAIN INFORMATION FROM THE INTERNET?

If we return to the analogy of the WWW being a vast library with everything ever published stored in it you will immediately appreciate that such a vast data store is quite useless unless the data is classified and stored in some kind of order. The Dewey decimal system provides such a facility for public libraries.

The Internet made little progress as an information storage medium until an efficient 'search engine' was designed to index and interrogate the vast amount of data stored within it. The first enquiry engines were given exotic names like 'Trumpet', 'Mosaic' and 'Yahoo' but the real breakthrough came with the publication of the browser called 'Netscape Navigator' which allows users to access specific information held in the vast array of data bases within the Internet. Netscape navigator and other browsers include 'hypertext', a system that allows you to put your cursor on a highlighted word and jump to an explanation of that word or

EXHIBIT 12.2: Some information sources that could be useful in financial planning

Several thousand databases are now accessible to individuals who own a microcomputer and a modem linking the computer to one of the telephone networks. The number of on-line databases is expanding at such a speed that it is difficult to keep track of them. The web browser, 'ATT Interchange' can find databases that might suit your needs. Information is also stored on CD-ROMs and loose-leaf updating services. These are updated on a regular basis. Much of this information can be accessed through the Internet.

On-line databases

Name of database	Host	Publisher	Subject matter
On-line databases			
ABI/INFORM	Many	ABI	Abstracts of 800 journals in finance and economics etc
ACTUARIAL DB	Many	I.P. SHARP	National and international mortality tables and projections.
BANK OF ENGLAND	Many	DRI	800 financial indicators about the UK economy.
BANKING DB	TEXTLINE	Reuters	Information about mortgages.
BLISS	Many	GBI	Citational data base on articles on business and management.
BRAIN	Many	Brain	Information about types of mortgages, rates of interest etc.
CEEFAX FINANCE	BBC	BBC	A wide range of financial statistics from TV screen.
CNN	CNN	CNN Systems	Credit ratings for individuals and companies.
COMPANIES HOUSE	Many	Govt.	Company accounts, registration data etc.
CSO	Govt.	DRI etc.	17 500 time series on the UK economy.
DATASTREAM	Datastream	Datastream	Stock prices, dividend yields, p/e ratios etc, for 30 000 companies. Interactive system.
FIND	Pergamon	MCC	Financial institutions data base.
FINIS	Dialog	MC	Finance industry information service. Products and services available.
INFOLINK	Data-star	Infolink	Credit rating agency for individuals and companies.
INSURANCE COs DB	FIND	Tektron	Accounts of UK insurance companies plus news on same.
MEDIAT	Many	BT INS SERVICE	Life, pensions and motor insurance, price feeds, performance, On viewdata.
MICROPAL	Many	Micropal	Facts about performance of financial institutions and funds, unit trusts, investment trusts, etc.
MINTEL	Many	Mintel	
MORTGAGE 2000	Many		Loans from 150 lenders offering 2000 different mortgage schemes.
PROFILE	Many	FT	Full text of newspapers, journals, stockbroker reports, etc.
STONE & COX	Many	S & C	Comprehensive insurance and life tables.
TELESURE	Many	Telesure	Insurance rates and other data.
TEXT LINE	Reuters	Reuters	Vast array of newspapers, journal articles, etc. Full text.
Data bases on CD-ROM			
C-TEXT	CD-ROM	C-Text	Rules and regulations arising out of the Financial Services Act 1986.
FAME	CD-ROM	Jordans	Jordan's analysis of UK and other companies financial data.
MICROEXTAT	CD-ROM	Extel	Financial information on companies etc., 3500 companies, updated each week.

Update services in looseleaf binders

GEE & CO.	The compliance fact book.	SRO rules and regulations.
BLAY'S	Moneymaster.	Personal finance products from banks and bulding societies.
GEE & CO.	Financial Information Factbook	Factual information for PFAs.
IDS PENSIONS SERVICE	Pension information update	Update on all matters concerning pensions.
LAFFERTY PUB.	EU Financial Industry Monitor	Update on developments in the finance industry in the EU.
MONEY MANAGEMENT	Rate update	Weekly guide to life assurance rates etc.
STONE & COX	Life Assurance Handbook (Pub. Buckley Press)	Premium guide, policy conditions, health evidence needed, loan options, bonus declarations and much else.
STONE & COX	Individual Pensions Hand-book (Pub. Buckley Press)	Details regarding the many pension schemes offered on the financial market in the UK.

to further data on this particular topic. Currently (1997) 'Netscape Navigator' holds 80% of the market in selling Internet access providers. Microsoft's 'Internet Explorer', which is embedded in the Windows 95 operating system, is Netscape Navigator's formidable rival.

Many 'search engines' have been devised that will search through the millions of pages stored on the Web and other storage systems to find a selection of pages that *might be* relevant to your enquiry. Since many thousands of 'relevant' pages might be found these programs usually list the selected pages in order of precedence, those pages which are most likely to be of interest to you being placed at the top of the listing. A short description of the contents of each page may also be provided.

The best-known search engines are called 'Yahoo', 'Excite', 'Infoseek', 'Lycos', and 'Magellan' but there are many others. It is an interesting exercise to use more than one search engine on a query since each engine will select a different set of 'relevant' pages based on the same query.

USING THE INTERNET TO HELP MANAGE YOUR PERSONAL FINANCES

How useful is this sophisticated information retrieval system to those who want to manage their own finances in the UK? Currently the main problem with the Internet is that the data stored and selected by the search engines are heavily biased towards the US market. Any general query will pull in many pages of data which are only of interest to US citizens. However the situation is rapidly improving and the reader will find useful information on personal finance in the UK at the following Internet addresses:

http://www.iii.co.uk/about/dir/euro/index.htm

This gateway (Micropal) provides access to a vast array of information about personal financial matters in the UK. The home page allows the user to access the very extensive financial data banks maintained by Micropal. There is an extra charge for access to the full Micropal investment information system. For an individual this cost is £45 per month. The home page allows access to the following financial information: advice, news, performance, products, feedback. If the 'performance' button is pressed the user is given access to the performance over several years of a range of unit trusts, investment trusts, PEPs, and offshore funds. Another page gives access to: news and publications, investments, independent financial advisers, accountants, a financial directory, building societies, banks, insurance companies, prices of certain financial products such as shares, a selection of search engines, user groups on personal finance and miscellaneous items.

http://www.find.co.uk/

'Find' is another entry point that provides information on WEB sites concerned with personal finance.

http://www.iii.co.uk/ftmags/international/about/

This electronic magazine ('the international' investor) provides useful information on personal finance to persons living outside their home country.

http://www.offshoreinvestment.com/offshore/index.htm/

'Offshore investment magazine' is an electronic magazine providing information to foreign and expatriate investors. This is published monthly.

http://www.moneyworld.co.uk/index.htm/

'Moneyworld.uk' is an innovative site that provides a great deal of useful information for those who wish to manage their own finances in the UK. The site attempts to list all the financial service sites on the Internet in the UK. The home page provides information on the following specific topics: financial contacts, news, a daily business report, a guide to the system, a UK personal finance directory, information on mortgages, information on current savings rates, the rate of return and performance measures on various investments, a glossary and a help facility.

http://www.moneyweb.co.uk/

'Moneyweb' is another well-organized site that gives access to a wide range of information on personal finance. The index page gives access to further pages on: tax, pensions including FSAVCs, investments, whole-life assurance, term insurance, critical illness insurance, permanent health (income replacement) insurance, long-term care insurance, annuities, share information, gilts, PEPs, unit and investment trusts, viatical settlements, savings schemes and access to many interesting articles in the journals.

http://www.numa.com/index.htm

http://www.numa.com/netwatch/netwatch.htm

This site (Numa Financial Systems) gives access to much useful financial information including access to several investment calculators. The second page, called FINANCE netWATCH, keeps you up to date on financial developments on the net.
An interesting new site is

http://www.cii.co.uk

run by the Chartered Insurance Institute. It provides a large amount of information about insurance in the UK.
Deloitte Touche, the accounting firm, have set up an interesting site with information on personal tax. This may be found at

http://www.deloitte-touche.co.uk/

Auctions are conducted on the Internet. One example is AuctionWeb, which can be found at:

http://www.ebay.com/aw/

This web site auctions a wide range of collectibles but mostly in the USA. You can e-mail sellers for further information. Remember to bookmark the items you bid on.
There is even humour on the net. The site

http://rampages.onramp.net/~wnksmile

is for dealers selling costume jewellery!
You can find the latest offers from a range of financial institutions including insurance companies, banks, and building societies. Many financial institutions have created their own pages on the Internet. For example the insurance company GRE can be found on

http://www.gre.co.uk/

From these pages you can progress via your browser into other possibly more relevant pages.

FINANCIAL ADVICE ONLINE

There is currently a move towards independent financial advisers providing financial advice on the Internet. Some are providing general financial advice free of charge to enquirers and a few more enterprising firms are offering to provide a free financial health check on the financial affairs of enquirers.

The first firm of independent financial advisers to create a page on the Internet was Gaeia. Gaeia is an ethically aware investment adviser that links to 'green', environmental and social sites within the net. The address is

http://www.u-net.com/~gaeia/

Another firm called Pronoia provides general advice on investment and pensions and lists sites relevant to these activities. The address (URL) is

http://www.vossnet.co.uk/company/pronoia/

The hope is that enquirers who use these sites will also seek advice from the site provider. The site is thus a form of advertising

THE FUTURE OF PERSONAL FINANCE ON THE INTERNET

The Internet is likely to transform personal finance over the next 10 years. If we are all able to access the same data as our personal financial advisers can then the number of financial intermediaries is likely to decline sharply.

On-line banking is already with us, as is the provision of mortgage and other loans, certain types of insurance and even pensions. Closing personal finance contracts on-line will not be possible until the net is made more secure than it is at present. The financial regulators, particularly the PIA, are studying ways to make personal financial regulation more 'net friendly'.

The Internet, the worldwide web and effective browser software like Netscape navigator will, in the not-too-distant future, make managing your own finances a perfectly feasible proposition. All the information you need will be there if you are prepared to search for it.

SUMMARY

1. We are lucky to be able to access such a wealth of information on personal finance in the UK. A range of high-quality monthly journals, various compendia and sites on the Internet gives us access to most of the information we need to manage our own finances.

2. Specialist books on investment, personal pensions, personal insurance and housing finance are available. *Which?* magazine, published by the Consumers' Association, is a particularly useful source of information on financial products.

3. Some organizations continuously collect information on the cost, rate of return and relative performance of financial products, product managers and product providers. 'Moneyfacts' and 'Micropal' are examples of this genre.

4. Newspapers and monthly personal finance journals contain a wealth of information on personal finance. Some monthly journals are targeted at personal financial advisers; others are intended for their clients. The journals targeted at advisers provide the most detailed coverage of products and services. Many journals are stocked in the reference section of your central library. Indexes to articles published are usually provided every six months.

5. Computers and the Internet are transforming the personal finance industry. Much remains to be done but already a series of gateways have been provided free of charge for individuals seeking information on personal financial products, services, product providers and industry regulation. You need a powerful computer system to access this data at a reasonable speed but the potential here is enormous. 'Moneyworld UK' and 'iii Interactive' are two of the more efficiently run sites. These provide gateways to many other sites including the powerful financial database called 'Micropal'.

TEST YOUR KNOWLEDGE

1. Name three newspapers that carry extensive coverage on personal finance.

2. Name three monthly magazines on personal finance that are aimed at personal financial advisers and three that are aimed at the general public.

3. Suggest one compendium on insurance facts and one on pension facts that are available in many central libraries.

4. Name the four parties who contribute to the organization of a financial database stored on a computer, the data being accessed through a modem. What are their respective roles?

5. There are four facilities needed for accessing personal finance information stored within a remote computer system. What are these four facilities?

6. What is a CD-ROM computer disc? How could it be used to assist in designing a personal financial plan?

7. What is the Internet? How is it accessed? What are the names of the two major Internet access programs?

8. What is a *search engine* (used on the Internet)? Name four popular search engines.

9. Name three British designed personal finance sites on the Internet which collect British personal financial data.

NOTES

1. This would cost you around £100 per page to set up plus the cost of renting space on a computer host. The latter might cost you some £200 to £300 a year rental.

A simple financial planning strategy

Begin by establishing your priorities. Your insurance plan comes first. You need insurance now: after reading this book you might walk out of your front door and be hit by a meteorite. Next comes your pension plan: you do not want to spend the last quarter of your life in near poverty. The remaining plans can be taken in any order. You will need a savings and investment plan, a housing plan, a tax plan and an inheritance plan for managing your estate when you depart.

We will now suggest a series of simple plans which, for the most part, will look after themselves once they have been set up. Much more sophisticated plans can be devised but the following plans will see you through.

INSURANCE

Many forms of insurance are so cheap and provide such essential cover that it should be made a criminal offence not to take them out.

Life (or rather death) assurance

Let us start with life assurance. If you have a family and you are the breadwinner then you must take out some form of life assurance to protect your family financially if you should die. Life assurance of at least £50 000 is essential. The cheapest form of life insurance is term insurance. If you are under 40 years of age you can buy £50 000 of term insurance for 25 years ahead for a mere £4 per week! Even at the age of 60 you can obtain 10 years' cover of £50 000 for £12 per week. There is no excuse for a breadwinner not taking out term insurance.

Other forms of life assurance are more problematic. Whole life assurance is really a savings and investment scheme masquerading as an insurance scheme. Such insurance schemes, and there are many of these, must compete with other forms of investment schemes. We will discuss these schemes later under investment plans. Note that whole-life insurance pays an adviser a much higher rate of commission than term insurance. This fact might bias an adviser's advice when you are selecting a life-assurance plan.

Family income benefit is another useful and cheap form of insurance cover which will support your family for a fixed number of years ahead on your sudden death. I recommend it.

Accidental death insurance is even cheaper to buy than term insurance. Again, a breadwinner should consider covering this risk which costs very little (as little as £1 a week in some cases).

HEALTH INSURANCE

If your employer provides you with medical insurance (or PHI, or CII) then you are one of the lucky ones. If your employer does not provide this, should you pay for it yourself? The NHS is good at providing cover for acute conditions so long as you are below 60 years of age. You do not need medical insurance here. Chronic conditions are more of a problem. Unfortunately you will not get cover for pre-existing conditions. If you think you may fall prey to a chronic condition while under the age of 60 it might be wise to take out medical insurance. Study your family history for evidence of heritable conditions.

The cost of medical insurance rises sharply with age. Few of us can afford it beyond the age of 65 or thereabouts although the firms offering this service have devised some cheap schemes that provide very basic medical cover for the over-65s at a reasonably low cost.

Critical illness insurance and permanent health insurance are rather expensive once you reach 50 years of age but are not too expensive (around £25 a month) below the age of 50. These types of insurance cover you and your family against the costs of sudden unexpected illness. Critical illness insurance gives you a lump sum if you suffer from one of the stipulated serious illnesses (such as a heart attack or cancer); permanent health insurance replaces up to 75% of your income if you cannot work due to illness.

It is very reassuring to know that such cover is available if it is needed. You may think this type of illness or injury will not happen to you, but it could happen out of the blue. If you can afford it I recommend you buy either critical illness insurance or permanent health insurance.

You must insure your home if you take out a mortgage. You would be foolish not to insure your house contents, probably with the same company. Shop around for the cheapest policy.

YOUR PENSION

Most readers will already be contributing to a pension plan. If not, and you are over 30 years of age, see to it immediately. It takes 25 to 30 years to build up a decent pension for yourself on retirement.

Check out the likely value of your pension on retirement. If it is a final-salary-based plan, do the calculations now and see how much you will get after making not-too-optimistic guesses as to your final salary. If the sum provides you with less than £1500 a year net of tax on your retirement you should consider setting up an AVC or FSAVC to supplement your existing pension. These schemes are very tax efficient and beat most other saving schemes hands down.

Should you set up an AVC or a FSAVC? An AVC is administered by your company but does not provide some of the advantages attached to your company pension. It must also be transferred if you switch companies. I would advise an FSAVC. You have more control over where your FSAVC funds are invested and you can probably check out the current value and predicted future value of the fund. Both schemes are equally tax efficient.

If your company pension scheme is a money-purchase scheme, these are less efficient than final-salary-based schemes but they can still provide you with an adequate pension on retirement. If you are in a money-purchase scheme there is a much higher probability that you will need an AVC or a FSAVC to supplement your company pension.

If you are self-employed the government has set up an extremely tax-efficient regime to encourage you to set up your own pension scheme. Take advantage of it: other savings schemes will be less tax-efficient. Carry-back and carry-forward relief should be considered if your income is unstable year on year; this is a major concession by the tax authorities.

Whatever you do, do not switch from a company scheme to a personal pension. It is most unlikely that such a switch will improve your financial position unless you are thinking of leaving the country or are a grasshopper where jobs are concerned.

SAVINGS AND INVESTMENT PLANS

Your basic savings and investment plans are your pension plan and your investment in your home. Together these two plans will give you security in retirement. However we all need a nest-egg to cover financial emergencies and provide the capital for additional expenditures like a new car, freezer or that 'around the world' trip you have always promised yourself.

Most of our investment funds come from 'lump-sum' amounts arising from inheritance, the sale of an asset (such as when we move to a smaller home on retirement), the sale of a business or the lump sum from a pension fund. If you want to save additional funds you must set up a regular saving plan into which you contribute £x each month. Once such a scheme is set up you will adjust your expenditure to meet the lower income available. The saving plan should invest the money saved into a PEP fund that pays no income tax or capital gains tax.

With regard to investment you should invest in financial, not real, assets except for your home. Your investment in financial assets should be split between ordinary (equity) shares and fixed-interest stock. The proportion you invest in equity shares depends on your age. The younger you are the more you should invest in equity (say 80% equity at age 30 but only 40% at age 60). Ordinary shares have proved to be an excellent bulwark against inflation for most of this century but when inflation is low, less than 4% per annum, fixed-interest stocks have provided a higher average return than equities. If you believe that inflation will remain low for the next 20 years you might decide to increase the percentage invested in fixed-interest stocks by 20% or so.

Should you build a do-it-yourself portfolio of securities or invest in a collective investment? The answer here is simple: if you enjoy the investment game then do it yourself (but spend some time studying investment first). If you don't, and most of us don't, then invest into a collective investment like a unit trust, investment trust or tracker (index) fund and let the management of that fund take the strain.

Which type of fund should you invest in? Well all the evidence suggests that, over a long period like 20 years or so, no fund *consistently* beats any other fund, thus a tracker or index fund would seem to be the best bet. If good investment management cannot achieve a higher consistent return, why pay 1.5% to 2% each year in 'management' fees when you can get the same result from a tracker or index fund for a mere 0.5% a year. *Low management charges are crucial when measuring long-term investment return.*

Take care if you decide to invest in a 'guaranteed' fund. What is guaranteed? Income may be guaranteed but what about the eroding value of the underlying investment base? I advise extreme caution before investing in any fund which offers returns well over the odds (say over 6% a year) for many years ahead. There just must be a catch somewhere.

HOUSING FINANCE

Housing is a real asset that has stood up well to inflation but housing has proved to be a mediocre investment in terms of net return over most of this century.

What kind of mortgage should you raise to finance the purchase of your home? The reduction in tax benefits in recent years has swung the balance between the repayment and endowment mortgage in favour of the former. The repayment mortgage requires a lower monthly payment per pound of mortgage and you actually repay the mortgage over its life, although the amount repaid is low until about halfway through the mortgage period. If you will be switching homes every few years the endowment mortgage may be more suited to your needs.

With real interest rates high and inflation low you should not automatically accept the 25-year repayment period offered. Go for as short a repayment period as you can afford. Say a 15- or 20-year repayment period.

Take a fixed-rate mortgage for a longish period ahead if the fixed rate offered falls below 7% per annum. Switch mortgages by all means if a cheaper or more suitable mortgage comes on the market but calculate the break-even period first (see Exhibit 6.6).

Pension mortgages are very tax efficient but you will need advice from an expert on such mortgages in order to set one up and you will also need to have a very high income.

Mortgages denominated in foreign currencies might be a good idea with the 'Euro' on the horizon but this is a tricky area. Only experts on derivatives should apply.

YOUR TAX PLAN

Your tax strategy is very simple to frame. You want to pay as little tax as possible. Throughout this book we have pointed out a series of tax-reducing strategies and tactics. The main tax strategies concerned your pension. Investing in a pension is a very tax-efficient investment strategy since the contributions are allowed against your income tax bill and the income on the investments invested in the pension fund are free of income and capital gains tax. You cannot get better than that. Both AVCs and FSAVCs enjoy these same benefits.

Your savings can be invested in tax-free PEPs and TESSAs, and the proceeds of insurance policies, particularly critical illness insurance and permanent health insurance payments, are mostly free of tax.

No CGT is payable on capital profits from certain assets like government stock. You need pay no further tax on certain income bonds if your marginal tax rate is the basic rate. Annuities pay a very low rate of tax on income as you age beyond 70 since the monthly annuity payment is assumed to contain an element of capital repayment.

The interest on the first £30 000 of a mortgage on your first home is allowable against tax at the 15% rate in 1996–97. As we noted above, pension mortgages are particularly tax efficient.

You should ensure that you are taking full advantage of all tax allowances and tax relief available to you. Switching income and assets between a husband and wife can reduce the family tax liability quite substantially since both husband and wife are now entitled to full independent allowances. There are literally hundreds of small tax-reducing stratagems available to you. Some may only reduce your tax bill by a very small amount but in total the reduction can be very substantial. It all depends on whether you think all this tax manipulation is worth the trouble involved in setting the schemes up.

AN INHERITANCE PLAN

First you must make a will. A recent poll found that only 30% of the UK population bothers to make a will. This is a foolish economy. The lack of a will can lead to big problems for your heirs and especially to an unmarried partner.

If you die intestate your assets will go first to your spouse, second to your children, third to your parents, fourth to your brothers and sisters, fifth to your grandparents, sixth to any uncles and aunts and finally into the grateful hands of the Chancellor of the Exchequer. Why not control the ultimate destination of your assets yourself by making a will?

Some 96% of the people who die in the UK do not pay inheritance tax on their estate so if you are worrying about inheritance tax you are one of the privileged few who will leave in excess of £200 000 after making the adjustments suggested below. Make a rough calculation of how much you will leave to your heirs and if it is significantly in excess of £200 000 (in tax year 1996–97) then read on.

Gifts are exempt from inheritance tax after seven years. So if you have assets in excess of the needs of yourself and your spouse between now and your date of departure, gift them to your children or others now . . . and make sure you live on for another seven years. If you think you might not survive this long take out a decreasing term insurance policy equal to the likely tax bill which might be presented to the recipient of the gift during the next seven years if you die during this period and cede the proceeds to the person to whom you made the gift. You are allowed to make £3000 of gifts each year (£6000 over two years) which are free of tax to both you and the recipient of the gift.

One classic ploy is to buy an annuity and use the income to pay for the premiums on a life policy on your life placed in a trust for the benefit of your heir. The cost of the annuity reduces the value of your estate for the purpose of inheritance tax while the heir receives the proceeds of the life policy free of inheritance tax.

The lump sum payable out of your pension fund into your estate is not normally subject to inheritance tax. Unquoted shares in a company can be passed on to your heirs free of inheritance tax under certain conditions as can certain shares in Lloyd's insurance, woodlands and various other oddments. The moral of this is that you should check your assets to see if they qualify for any of these exemptions.

If you think you will leave substantially more than £200 000 in your estate, say several millions, see a tax-consulting lawyer. Presumably you will be able to afford the not-inconsiderable fee.

If you have covered the financial needs of your family with term insurance and family income benefit, arranged a pension to provide yourself with an adequate income on retirement, bought a house (the mortgage on which will be paid off before retirement) and minimized your inheritance tax bill . . . then you can relax. Your financial problems are solved . . . for the time being.

Solutions to 'test your knowledge' questions

CHAPTER 2

1. Maximize income and minimize risk. These two objectives conflict.

2. A financial asset is a financial contract. A real asset is a physical artefact. Examples of financial assets are ordinary shares and annuities. Examples of real assets are Victorian paintings and a Chinese water clock. Financial assets are much cheaper to protect than real assets and most provide a regular cash flow. They are cheap to buy and sell. Real assets generally do not have these characteristics.

3. The right to (a) a dividend if declared (b) the balance of value after debts paid on liquidation (c) the right to a vote at AGMs (d) liability for debts of company restricted to the par value of the share if not paid up.

4. The return consists of any dividend or interest received during a period plus the value of the rise or fall in the market value of the investment over the period.

   Zelda $12 + 25 = 37$ $37/245 = 15.1\%$

   Tarant $8 - 12 = -4$ $-4/160 = -2.5\%$

   CIK $18 + 24 = 42$ $42/375 = 11.2\%$

5. Research on share returns has shown a direct relationship between the return and the risk attached to a share. Seeking a higher return means that you must inevitably take on more risk.

6. A collective investment is a company or trust which buys a wide range of financial instruments and invites the general public to buy units or shares in the company. For example unit trusts, investment

trusts and tracker (index) funds. A company manages the portfolio for you and charges you a management fee of 0.5% to 2% of the value of the fund each year. You are buying expert management of your portfolio (you hope).

7. The managers of a 'tracker' or 'index' fund buy a set of shares to mimic a given stock exchange index such as the Financial Times 500 index. You are, in effect, buying the index. A tracker fund is very safe, specific risk is removed by diversification and the market risk is the average for all the shares in the index (one). The management charges are very low at around 0.5% per year and often there is no entry charge. You can see the value of your portfolio each day from the FT 500 or other index.

8. We leave you to work this out for yourself.

9. Equity shares of large companies. Inflation indexed government stock. If elderly, an annuity escalating at the expected rate of inflation or an inflation indexed annuity.

10. As you grow older a higher proportion of your wealth needs to be invested in fixed interest securities. You need a steady income after retirement. Annuities are a good investment for anyone over the age of 70.

11. An 'impaired' annuity might be a good investment. You need a steady worry-free income. Fixed-interest government stock will be best.

12. A tax haven charges very low or zero rates of income tax on the local income of persons living off-shore, that is not in the tax haven. Apart from low tax the tax haven may offer a compensation scheme to off-shore investors and possibly anonymity although the last is becoming less common. You can access your investment and income from virtually anywhere in the world outside communist countries.

13. Some kind of trust is the best bet, especially if the money is coming from grandparents. A split level investment trust offers some tax advantages although these have been diminished somewhat by recent legislation. See a solicitor.

14. Pick five shares each from six different industrial categories.

15. You may well be picking high risk shares that can all crash together: witness investment in Japan 1989-93 and property investment in the late 1980s and the early 1990s. You can only pick winners if you use 'insider information', which is illegal.

CHAPTER 3

1. A house can provide a regular rental.

2. Yes. Most real assets have provided excellent cover against inflation in the past.

3. Liquidity means speed of conversion into cash. Most real assets are less liquid than most financial assets. Most real assets can be sold but it can take you some time to find a buyer at a fair price. You can easily find a buyer at a poor price!

   (a) Not very except from a dealer.

   (b) Very.

   (c) Not very.

   (d) Difficult in the short term.

   (e) Very difficult in the short term at fair price.

4. The spread is the difference between the dealer's buying and selling price for the same asset. The dealer can remove most of your profit between buying and selling the asset even if the price rises. A wide spread indicates an inefficient market for a particular asset.

5. The owner must ensure adequate protection or the insurance is void. The assets must be protected in bank vaults, with drop locks, fire extinguishers and so forth. Often they cannot be moved abroad without permission.

6. Krugerrands, crates of wine, a stamp collection. Such assets can release money gradually from the asset over a period of time. This is useful if you are retired or want to use up your annual capital gains allowance.

7. Rare stamps, jewels, gold coins, *netsuke*, genetic material (highest value to weight ratio).

8. The income from certain financial assets are exempt from tax; these include PEPed investments, TESSAs. This is much less common in the case of real assets, although houses enjoy certain tax privileges.

9. (a) The authenticity of the asset. You need to obtain a certificate signed by an expert assessor if it is an antique or work of art. (b) The quality of the asset. Only real assets of the highest quality retain their value through time.

10. There are few valuable assets for which there is not an expert assessor. These are needed by sales agents and auctioneers to prove authenticity. This is a lucrative trade for the assessor so it is unlikely that the dealer cannot suggest an impartial assessor.

11. The London based antique dealers association LAPIDA will find you a dealer. You can also consult trade catalogues and antique magazines for the general public for a list of dealers in various assets. Use a search engine on the Internet to see what you can find.

12. The volume of trading is much less with real assets than with financial assets so the cost per deal is much greater. The financial markets are also exceptionally efficient. Note that you can bargain on real assets but not normally on financial assets.

13. (a) Check that the seller resides in the UK and is thus subject to UK law. (b) Check the quality of what you are buying. Is it a standard product? (c) What kind of payment system is going to be used? How will the timing of payment and despatch of the product be organized. This is a tricky business!

CHAPTER 4

1. The difference is that you do not get your capital back on the annuity. The taxation of annuity income is also different to the taxation of income from government stock.

2. Age: the older you are, the higher the income. Sex: men are offered a higher income than women at any age. Inflation: the higher the expected future inflation the higher the return offered. Health: no effect on income unless you have an 'impaired' life, in which case you can receive a much higher income. Gilts: the higher the return the higher the annuity income offered.

3. Not one penny!

4. A guaranteed annuity pays out an income on the lifetime annuity for a fixed number of years (5 or 10). So if you die soon after taking out the annuity a discounted sum equal to the present value of the future guaranteed payments is paid into your estate.

5. If you live longer than expected you winthe bet; if you live for a shorter period the insurance company wins the bet. How can you win? Keep fit!

6. The rate varies because the return on medium-term government stock varies. The insurance companies invest your money from the

annuity in such stock. Some companies pursue a more successful investment policy than others.

7. An *impaired annuity* is an annuity taken out by a very sick person. The annuitant has only a short time to live so he or she is offered a much higher return than another applicant of same age and sex who is in good health. The benefit is the higher income.

8. An *annuity certain* is an annuity that is paid out for a fixed number of years rather than for life. This type of annuity can ensure that the income is available for some known expenditure in the future, for example school fees. You cannot now spend this capital on something else!

9. A *phased annuity* is a series of annuities which come on stream on different dates, usually annually over several years. When you retire you may not want to convert all your pension fund into an annuity immediately but spread the conversion over several years, particularly if annuity rates are low on your retirement date. *Income drawdown* allows you to leave your money in your pension fund on the date of your retirement and draw out some capital to live on until you decide to convert.

10. Around 9 to 11 years. It depends upon expectations about the future inflation rate when you buy the annuity.

11. The catch is that they are very expensive per pound of annuity offered. You may be offered only 50% to 60% of the rate offered on a flat rate annuity.

12. The income from a pension fund annuity which has already benefited greatly from tax concessions is taxed like ordinary earned income. If the annuity is bought out of taxed income the rate of tax charged on the income is much lower since the income includes a partial return of capital.

13. You are expected to live for 136 months. Thus out of each £500 paid each month some £50 000 ÷ 136 = £367 is a return of capital. Thus income tax is only paid on £500 – £367 = £133. Thus you would have to pay £133 × 0.20 = £26.60 income tax each month on the purchased annuity. If this were a normal pension you would have to pay income tax of £500 x 0.23 = £115 each month. These are only rough calculations.

14. Buy (a) an inflation indexed annuity (b) a "with profits" annuity (c) an annuity escalating at 5% per year.

CHAPTER 5

1. This depends on the date of your retirement. If we assume that you retire at age 60 then you will be retired for 23 years, you will work for another 15 years and, if you started work at age 22, you will have worked for 38 years. The point of these calculations is to emphasize the relatively short period available for building up a pension.

2. The increasing proportion of the population who are aged over 60 (see Exhibit 5.2). Also the reluctance of governments to increase taxation.

3. These are listed in chapter 5.

4. You do not know (a) the value of your terminal pension fund or (b) the rate of return on annuities when you retire.

5. If you are in a final-salary-based plan you have every advantage going except if you switch companies frequently and lose money on the transfer value. 'Money purchase' schemes provide, on average, only 60% of the value of final-salary-based schemes.

6. You must find this out. Your spouse should get around 50% to 70% of your pension if you should die. A large life-assurance policy should provide a capital sum for your spouse if you die. Something should be provided for your children under 16 years of age. These benefits vary a great deal. Check them out, particularly if you are not in an occupational scheme.

7. Inflation destroys the value of a fixed-value pension. Nowadays most occupational schemes will top up a pension by up to 5% maximum to compensate for inflation in any one year. This may not apply to money purchase or personal pensions. Check this! If your pension is not inflation indexed in any way you may need to arrange a tax-efficient AVC or FSAVC to compensate for this. You can also take out an inflation-indexed annuity or an escalating annuity to compensate for inflation but these are expensive (see Chapter 4). Alternatively arrange an annuity that is based on the income from equity shares.

8. Work this out. If you are a professional worker the figure should come out at around £1500 to £2000 per month net of tax.

9. All company pensions must be portable. This is the law. The controversy arises out of the transfer value when you switch companies.

10. I calculate a figure of around £12 000.

11. An AVC is run by your existing company pension fund; an FSAVC is run by an insurance company at your request. Your employer need not know about your FSAVC unless it is large relative to your company scheme. Any employee can set up an FSAVC. (The self-employed can set up personal pensions.)

12. Some 'perks': medical insurance for yourself and your family, CII insurance, an inflation indexed pension higher than 5% per annum. If you want these perks under a personal pension you will have to pay full cost for them and they are very expensive! (See chapter 7.)

13. The fund may be listed in *Money Management* or *Planned Saving* or some other monthly journal. If so the relative performance over one, three, five and 10 years may be given. The figures may also be listed under 'iii. interactive' (MICROPAL) on the Internet.

14. From Exhibit 5.4 we see that the answer is £12 278 in 1997 pound sterling values: a 40% fall in real value. Tax may ameliorate the situation somewhat but it is still a large fall in real value. Inflation indexing is important.

15. A money purchase scheme is much cheaper to run than a final-salary-based scheme. In September 1996 the association of consulting actuaries calculated that the pensions provided by MPS schemes were only 50% of the value of FSB pensions. No obvious advantage is provided to the employee except that the employee may gain some control over the investments into which the contributions are placed.

16. Because this is where the insurance companies invest a great deal of the annuity contributions.

17. Not all annuities are inflation indexed because such annuities are very expensive. The cost can be double the cost of a flat-rate annuity at the same initial rate of return. It takes around 9 to 11 years for the inflation-indexed annuity to catch up. It depends on the rate of inflation.

18. The investment policy of the insurance company determines the annuity rate offered.

19. Mortality tables suggest that, on average, someone like Mrs Black will live for 156 months from the date of taking out the annuity. Since the capital is non-refundable 100 000 ÷ 156 = £641 of each monthly payment must be a return of capital if she lives for her 156-month predicted lifespan. Therefore the income portion of each monthly payment must be £1000 − 641 = £359. Thus Mrs Black will have to pay £359 × 23% = £82.57 each month in income tax on the

annuity income. If this were a normal pension she would have to pay £1000 × 23% = £230.

20. The pension would be worth £1000 × (100/70)= £14 300 approx. No you would not.

CHAPTER 6

1. About one third only.

2. The investment strategies employed by some insurance companies have been rather poor over the period 1980 to 1993. The return on many endowment funds has been much less than the market average. This does not apply to all endowment funds and the situation is improving rapidly in 1997.

3. A *bundled* financial product places more than one financial plan in the same financial package. A pension mortgage places a house financing plan and a pension plan within the same package. A 'bundled' product allows a seller to sell you more than one product at the same time and may provide tax advantages to the buyer. Normally separate products are more flexible than bundled products when designing an overall plan.

4. Part of your monthly endowment contribution is placed into a unit trust or trusts of your choice. You have more control over where your money is invested with a unit trust linked endowment mortgage.

5. The profit percentage of the lender on a variable rate mortgage can be kept constant no matter what happens to the market rate of interest. The lender simply increases or reduces the rate of interest you pay each month. This can also be achieved with a fixed rate mortgage but the lender must find fixed rate funds for the full term of your mortgage contract. Cheap long-term funds are hard to find even for a large financial institution so they only offer you shorter term fixed rate mortgages which can be covered forward over three to five years.

6. You can budget your cash expenses forward with a fixed-rate mortgage over the period of the mortgage.

7. Negative equity means that the value of your mortgage exceeds the market value of your house which has fallen in value. The collapse in the UK housing market between 1989 and 1995 created the above situation in many cases. It is difficult to get out from this situation until the housing market revives as it did in 1996. The number of

negative equity cases is down to 400 000 in 1997 and falling. In law you must repay your secured mortgage no matter the value you get by selling your house.

8. The variable mortgage rate depends on the market rate of interest at the time. The market rate of interest is strongly influenced by expectations about future inflation. If higher inflation is expected the mortgage rate jumps upwards very quickly. If higher inflation is expected repay your mortgage over a longer period of time and let inflation destroy the value of your mortgage to be repaid in cheaper pounds in the future.

9. Work out the 'break-even' point. Divide the cost of switching mortgages by the monthly saving on the new mortgage. Are you willing to wait for this period of time to make a profit on the switch? It is up to you to decide this.

10. (a) Interest on the first £30 000 of mortgage on first home can be offset against income tax at the 15% rate (96/97). (b) There is no CGT on the profit on sale of your first home. (c) The rent from a lodger living in single room in a house is probably exempt from income tax.

11. This is very much a personal decision. On purely economic grounds the rental option is cheaper unless there is a substantial increase in house prices over the period. The rental option costs £900 × 36 = £32 400. If you use the £100 000 as a deposit and take out a £120 000 mortgage this will cost you £800 per month alone net of tax plus the loss of income on the £100 000 investment – say, £4000 per year net of tax plus the legal and other costs. You pay the same rates in both cases. Capital appreciation of the house will have to be around 10% over the three years to cover the lower cost of rental plus the legal and other costs of buying.

12. £9000 per year is 43% of your net cash flow of £21 000. Much too high. Look for a £100 000 house. This costs only 27% of your annual net cash flow.

13. Much too risky! It looks good since you are renting half the flat, worth £100 000, for only £500 per month. But if you cannot raise the balance of the mortgage in three years time can you sell the flat then? If so, for how much? Can you take a tenant to share the cost? Will these flats be any more saleable in three years' time than they are now? No, pass this one up.

14. No. The UK has an ageing population. More houses will be sold than bought over the next 30 years. This is not a recipe for rising house prices.

15. When the value of houses in your region is standing well above the long-term trend line (1987–89), sell. Once the housing cycle brings prices well below the long term trend line (1991–93), buy.

16. The cost of land is much higher in London than in Yorkshire. This accounts for most, but not all, of the difference.

17. The £20 000 house valued in 1971 pounds is worth £20 000. The same house valued in 1989 pounds is worth 20 000 × (100 ÷ 20) = £100 000. The ratio of mortgage to house value in 1971 was 20 000 ÷ 20 000 = 100%. The ratio in 1989 was £20 000 ÷ £200 000 = 10 %. The nominal capital profit is £200 000 – 20,000 = £180 000 (ignoring other expenses). The real profit in 1971 pounds is £200 000 × (20 ÷ 100) – 20 000 = £20 000.

18. Very risky. The Swiss franc is not going into the Euro group of countries so its value may well rise against the UK currency over the next 10 years. You don't how by how much. You must repay this mortgage in Swiss francs. Do you have a Swiss franc income? You also need to calculate the break-even point on switching mortgages in midstream (see question 9. above). Is some kind of derivative protection offered by the lender? If so, at what cost?

19. Unless you believe that house prices will rise by a substantial amount in London the investment in government stock offers much less trouble than minding and maintaining a house with tenants. Note that you will pay CGT on the inflation-adjusted profit on the London house if sold.

20. An MIG policy covers the lender against loss through negative equity, not you. Such policies are very expensive if the loan value is close to the purchase value of the house.

21. The annual cost of maintaining the flat in mint condition is around £750 per annum. To earn this amount, if you pay tax at 40% on your marginal income, you will need to earn an additional £750 ÷ 0.6 = £1250. The size of a fund needed to earn £1250 per annum if it can generate 5% per annum net of tax is £1250 ÷ 0.05 = £25 000.

CHAPTER 7

1. By hedging a risk you set up a situation where an event causing the loss also causes an equivalent gain. Regarding the Glaxo shares you could sell the shares now and invest in government stock. An alternative would be to buy a 'put' option on the shares at a price close to the present price; thus if the price is lower next year you can still sell at today's price.

2.   a. No, unless you can prove an 'insurable interest'.

    b. Yes.

    c. No.

    d. No.

    e. Yes. Up to two years before divorce.

    f. Yes (slander).

    g. Yes.

    h. Yes. Via CII.

    i. Yes.

    j. No, but you can insure against not being able to pay instalments on a loan because of unemployment.

3.   If the event occurs you will suffer a loss.

4.   Yes there is. You can win money at gambling (in theory if not in practice). You cannot win money by taking out an insurance policy. You can only get back what you have already lost.

5.   a. Change the system

    b. Insure

    c. Insure. (Not in all countries!)

    d. Insure (third party injury).

    e. Change the system (go to the police).

    f. Insure (PHI).

    g. You can insure but it is very expensive.

    h. Get out of the system You may not be able to obtain insurance.

6.   I leave this to the reader. Probably serious illness, death and unemployment. You can insure against the first and second and some consequences of the third.

7.   Identify the major hazards you and your family face. Evaluate the

loss caused if such events occur. Identify which of these hazards you can insure against. Find the cost of this insurance.

8. Whole life insurance and term insurance. If you have a limited income, term insurance is cheaper per £10 000 insured. Whole-life is also a savings and investment scheme (which you may not want).

9. If you insure against ill health and never claim on the policy you are a happy man or woman. The Chinese only pay their doctors an annual fee when they are healthy!

10. A bundled financial product puts two or more financial plans in the same package. An endowment policy puts a house financing plan and a saving and investment plan in the same package. The house buyer could arrange a repayment mortgage and a PEPed saving plan instead.

11. The value of a fixed value insurance policy, such as a term policy, will be reduced by inflation. Thus if the premium rises each year by the rate of inflation so does the value of the policy. The policy retains a constant real value.

12. An *impaired* life policy assumes that the individual insured is very ill and has a shorter lifespan than a person of that age should have. The insurance company, knowing these facts, calculates a different, higher, life premium for this individual.

13. In most cases no claim will be made on a term policy. A claim will always be made on a whole-life policy if the premiums are kept up.

14. The insurance market is very inefficient but is becoming more efficient because of the Internet and direct insurance. Not all insurance companies want to operate in all insurance markets. Some insurance companies pay high commission to agents rather than cutting the cost of premiums to customers.

15. Permanent health insurance replaces your income if you fall ill with any illness which prevents you doing your job. It should be called *income replacement insurance*.

16. Permanent health insurance provides a wider degree of cover for *any* illness but you cannot work and receive PHI. Critical illness insurance pays out only on the occurrence of specific illnesses but you can still work on after receiving the insurance payment if you are able. You must choose which best suits your needs.

17. Shop around for the cheapest policy. Make full use of 'deductibles'. Buy through a group scheme if one is available.

18. If you insure with two insurance companies they may quarrel as to how damage affecting both house and contents should be shared between them.

19. (a) The jewellery must kept in a bank vault for most of the time. (b) If goods are stolen there is no liability cover from the house contents policy. (c) No cover is provided by property insurance. (d) No cover is provided for damage to your car if drunk. (e) Cover for costs is only available after two years from taking out the policy. (f) Pre-existing conditions are not covered. (g) The policy only comes into force nine months after being taken out.

20. Cross subsidy means that one group of policy holders who are at low risk pay more than justified by their claims to subsidize another group who at higher risk. Insurance companies now target groups at risk much more precisely than in the past (risk of subsidence is now assessed according to postal address). If you are at a higher-than-average risk in some way, insure now before you are targeted.

21. Those who are genetically targeted as likely to catch a serious disease far in the future may not be able to find insurance, or it may be too expensive to take up. This will make obtaining a mortgage and so forth much more difficult for such people.

22. No.

23. Make sure it is UK-based. Check in the Standard and Poors *Financial Strength* catalogue.

24. Take your case to the Insurance Arbitration Service or to the insurance ombudsman.

CHAPTER 8

1. $P \times (95 \times N + 9) \times C / 12 \times N \times (N + 1) \times (4 \times L + C)$

$12 \times (95 \times 24 + 9) \times 440 / 12 \times 24 \times (24 + 1) \times ((4 \times 1000) + 440)$

APR = 38% (approx.)

2. A discriminating lender only takes on high quality borrowers who seldom default, thus the costs of this lender are lower and so the interest charged on loans is lower.

3. The lender must give you a reason for not extending credit. If he has consulted a credit agency he must tell you which one, otherwise he is

breaking the law. You can complain to the Office of Fair Trading.

4. Write to the credit agency asking for a copy of your credit report or a form to fill in asking for this document. If it is wrong it must be changed. If you disagree with the opinion you can insert an explanation that must be sent to future enquirers.

5. With an 'open ended' source of credit the lender will not ask you what the money is to be spent on.

6. Same as (2) above. The borrowers are of higher quality; the costs to the lender are lower. Thus interest charges are lower.

7. The lower cost arises from the high quality of the security offered, namely your policy. Hire-purchase companies carry a rather higher proportion of bad debts than other lenders. They also pay commission to salespersons selling the goods.

8. The APR is the average percentage rate. In the UK (and the EC) all types of interest charged must be converted into an APR so that the rates can be compared by a discriminating borrower. You benefit by being able to select the cheapest source of credit and not being hoodwinked by an unscrupulous lender.

9. 21.93%

10. I leave this one to the reader.

11. The liquidity, that is the speed of conversion into cash, of your wealth portfolio. How easily can these assets be sold?

12. The Office of Fair Trading.

13. If you have taken it home, reviewed it, and sent it back signed to the seller. You normally have a short period of time to withdraw from a credit contract.

14. You can declare yourself bankrupt, ask for a creditors meeting, or go into administration.

15. It is difficult to get credit once you have been bankrupt. You must tell a potential future lender that you have been declared bankrupt.

16. A mortgage and a tax debt.

17. If the seller does not fulfil the contract you may be able to proceed against the credit card company for the value of the amount lost.

CHAPTER 9

1. Income tax: your personal income from all sources. Capital gains tax: profits on the sale of assets. Inheritance tax: your estate when you die plus gifts during the last seven years of your life.

2. *Tax avoidance* means using legal tax stratagems to reduce your tax bill. *Tax evasion* means concealing personal income from the UK tax authorities. Tax evasion is illegal. Examples: gifts to avoid or reduce inheritance tax. Income from part-time work paid in cash and not declared. *Tax avoision* covers tax stratagems on the border of illegality.

3. Schedule D: income from a trade or profession.

    Schedule E: income from employment.

    Schedule F: dividends.

    Some expenditures can be charged against income assessed under Schedule D which are not allowed under Schedule E. Dividends of UK based companies are paid net of tax at 20%.

4. (a), (d) partly, (g).

5. You will be sent a set of tax forms to fill in with your income and allowable expenses unless your only source of income is from your employment or pension. You can work out the tax due yourself and send a cheque to the Inland Revenue or leave the calculation to the Inland Revenue. Around nine million persons in the UK will be affected.

6. Your marginal rate of tax is 24%, the basic rate, if you use up all your allowances and exceed the minimum tax band of 20%, which is very likely (for the 1996-97 tax year). If you have a high income your marginal tax rate might be at 40%, the highest rate for income tax (unless you are over 65 and your additional income means that you lose part of the age allowance which takes your marginal rate to 36%). Your marginal rate determines the value of many, but not all, tax allowances and reliefs.

7. You will pay $60,000 \times 0.08 = £4800$ less the MIRAS tax allowance of $£30,000 \times 0.08 \times 0.15 = £360$. That is £4440. Even if you only earn £10 000 a year you get the full MIRAS allowance of £360.

8. In the 1996–97 tax year £6300. The advantage of investing in gold coins is that you can sell a few each year to use up your capital gains tax allowance but only if the price of gold coins rises in value above

the rate of UK inflation, which gold coins have not done in recent years.

9. Selling price of home £90 000

    Less: expenses of selling (say) £7000

    Net receipt £83 000

    Original cost in 1980 £20 000

    Profit before indexation £63 000

    indexation allowance

    (20 000 × 300/100) - 20 000 = £40 000

    Profit after indexation £23 000

    Less: capital gains allowance £6300

    CGT due to be paid on £16 700 at 40%

    CGT on sale of cottage £6680.

    CGT is paid at Mr Green's marginal rate of tax in that year, which is at 40%.

10. Assets held in a PEP, assets held in a pension fund, and government stock.

11. (a) If Mr Black dies leaving the home plus £250 000 to his wife, no inheritance tax is paid on this £470 000 of value. He leaves a further £330 000 of shares to his daughter. Inheritance tax must be paid on £330 000 − £200 000 = £130 000 at 40% = £52 000. If Mrs Black dies one year later leaving her entire estate to her daughter and the estate is worth, say, £400 000 net of costs then inheritance tax of £400 000 − £200 000 = £200 000 × 40% = £80 000 must be paid by the daughter.

12. The gift becomes what is called a *potentially exempt transfer*. If Mr Reddy dies within seven years of making the gift some inheritance tax is payable. Since he lived for only five years after making the gift some inheritance tax is payable. The rate after five years has fallen to 60% of the full rate of 40%, that is 60% x 40% = 24%. Since Mr Reddy left more than £200 000 of estate value in 1997 his son must pay back £300 000 (the value in 1992) times 24% to the Inland revenue. That is £72 000. Incidentally the son will have to pay CGT on these shares if

he sells them. The cost price for the purpose of CGT is £300 000 not £400 000.

13. Mr Reddy could take out a reducing term insurance policy on his life to cover the value of inheritance tax which his son must pay if he, Mr Reddy, dies within seven years. However this might be expensive if Mr Reddy is sick. It would need to be an impaired policy. It would be better to tell his son to put the money aside.

14. The contributions to the pension fund are allowed against your income tax bill at your highest marginal rate. The pension fund does not pay tax on either income or capital profits. When you retire the capital sum paid out to you on retiral (usually 25% of the fund) is not subject to tax up to the given limit.

15. Allocate ownership of the family securities (and so income) so that all tax allowances of both partners are used up in each year. If one spouse runs a business, employ the other spouse in the business. Share out the ownership of family assets so that full use is made of the capital gains allowance available to both partners when assets are sold. Place the ownership of the family home into 'tenancy in common' rather than 'joint ownership'. This opens up the possibility of minimizing the inheritance tax bill if the total family estate is substantial, well over £200 000, say one million.

16. A trust is created when one person, (A), gives assets to a legal entity called a trust (B), to hold on behalf of a third person, the beneficiary, (C). B owns the assets but has no personal interest in them. Trusts can cost around £500 to set up. A trust can be used to minimize inheritance tax by passing assets to the trust. The income of the trust can be separated from the income of A for tax purposes. The income tax avoidance potential of trusts have been somewhat exaggerated since either the trust pays tax on income at 35% or the beneficiary pays tax on the income at his or her marginal rate. Capital gains tax is paid on capital profits, usually at 35%. Trusts are very useful for deferring tax.

CHAPTER 10

1. Income and expenditure, housing, pension, insurance, tax, inheritance.

2. Needs of dependants, state of health, current wealth and income, financial objectives (long and short term), attitude to risk.

3. Identify all your assets. Value these assets. Identify all your liabilities, Value these liabilities. Deduct the value of the liabilities

from the assets. This difference is your current wealth. You might also like to evaluate future contingent liabilities like school fees and a new car and relate these values to your current wealth.

4. (a) Value in any 'good' newspaper. (b) Difficult! You need to find a professional valuer of ninteenth-century ephemera. Ask LAPIDA to find one for you. (c) Easy to value: any top class auction house will give you an estimate. (d) You will need to contact an estate agent who deals in French land. This is very tricky to value accurately. (e) It is not worth valuing this unless you own antiques, good quality carpets or suchlike. Any antique dealer will give you a sales value estimate. (f) No current value. If it can be assigned it could be discounted to a present value at, say, 5% p.a. (g) A dealer in second hand policies will give you a current sales value over the phone. (h) A local estate agent.

5. Dealers' catalogues give the price they will sell at; this bears little relation to the price they buy at. The buy/sell spread can be 30% to 50% of the dealer's sale price. This collection is worth far more as a collection than the sum of the value of the individual stamps. You need to find a broker who will find a stamp enthusiast who will buy the entire collection. You would need to find a US stamp magazine where such brokers advertise.

6. Because there are times in life when the temptation to cash in such assets is very strong. To do such a thing would gravely compromise your financial future.

7. We leave this to the reader to do for himself or herself.

8. Many deductions are made from your gross income: PAYE, superannuation, insurance, trade union dues, AVC. These deductions often take 40% of your gross salary. Many cease when you retire, which increases your post-retirement salary.

9. A cheque or credit card slip provides you with a permanent record of your expenses. This is useful for keeping score and proving the expenditure to an insurance company. Recording all cash payments calls for tight discipline on your part. There are, of course, well-known tax reasons for running a cash economy.

10. Cash is the bottom line in finance. If you have a cash surplus all your life you have no financial problems (although you may leave them to your heirs if you borrow too much). You should run a long-term cash-flow budget until five years after your predicted date of departure and ensure that it is in surplus all the way.

11. See Exhibit 4.4.

12. Take out an AVC or an FSAVC to add to your existing pension. You must save more now in a tax efficient way. The government encourages this in many ways.

13. Annotate your monthly bank and credit-card statements. Transfer the individual items to a columnar list sheet each month. Each column being an individual revenue or cost item. Add them up and list the totals. Simple but effective. I used it myself until microcomputers came into vogue.

14. Your PAYE coding number (P 2 T).

    A record of your salary, PAYE paid, NHI paid (P 60).

    Final tax assessment of total income and tax due (300 CODA).

    Record of tax due or overpaid (P 70 T).

    Your annual tax return (11 P).

15. A single entry of data, records extremely compact, fast and complex analysis of data easily done, clear printouts, data can be concealed from prying eyes using passwords or encryption.

16. This is up to the reader. Simplicity, wealth of features, whether it can do small business bookkeeping, whether it runs on your operating system, whether it is designed or redesigned for the UK market? Cost is not important since all such packages are very cheap.

17. A password system guarding entry to the personal finance files, an encryption system, a lock on the computer.

CHAPTER 11

1. Ask friends for a PFA who has been found to be competent and reliable. Contact *Money Management* to find a fee-based adviser. Contact IFA Promotions to find an independent adviser who may be commission-based. Check that the adviser is registered with an SRO. How long has he or she been advising. Check out at least two advisers and choose the one you prefer (the first interview is free). Think up a few questions to which you know the answer to test out the knowledge of your adviser before you engage him or her.

2. No.

3. No. There is a local compensation scheme in Jersey though. Check it out before you invest.

4. The PIA and IMRO.

5. Write to him. He must have set up a complaints procedure. If you do not get satisfaction write to the complaints department of his regulator, probably the PIA. If you have lost money, register your loss with the Investors' Compensation Scheme. Depending on the product you have been sold you may be able to complain to the Personal Insurance Arbitration Service or a similar body. Ultimately you could take your complaint to the PIA ombudsman but all other avenues of complaint must be exhausted first.

6. The ICS has been set up by the SIB to compensate the clients of PFAs if they lose money because of the negligence or fraud of their financial adviser. You register a complaint and proof with the ICS if you have lost money. The scheme is paid for by the personal finance industry itself not by the government. The current limit (1997) is £30 000 plus 90% of additional loss up to £20 000. That is a maximum claim of £48 000.

7. The PIA checks the competence, honesty and financial soundness of the adviser. The adviser must have passed the diploma exams set by the Chartered Institute of Insurance for personal financial advisers or their equivalent. If the adviser is a member of a recognized professional body he or she will have sat alternative examinations.

8. This is not an easy task. There are extensive rule books produced by the regulatory bodies but these are very expensive (£90). The sheet of rules attached to your contract with the adviser are inadequate. Your central library may hold a copy of the relevant rule books but don't bet on it.

9. If your adviser is *independent* he or she can sell you any financial product. If an adviser is *tied* he or she can only sell you the products sold by his or her organization. An independent adviser may well receive commission from the seller of the product. A *fee-based adviser* will pass any commission he receives to you the client.

10. Under current SIB rules an investment adviser must find out the background to the client's affairs before giving advice. For example the adviser must check up on the marital status of the client, his or her current wealth and income, pension rights, home ownership situation, health condition and much else. You need not answer these questions but the adviser must put them to you. If you decline to answer or lie to your adviser you let your adviser off the hook in any subsequent complaint regarding these particular matters.

11. The adviser must send you a statement about your portfolio at least yearly. This will show the value of the securities, the number bought

and sold, the costs of transactions, any commission charged and the adviser's fee. The strategy in handling the portfolio may also be stated: you agree to the strategy when you set up the arrangement.

12. If an investment is a 'high-risk' investment your adviser must tell you this and explain the nature of the risk *even if the risk is hedged in some way.* A high-risk investment is one where the expected income is higher than normal but so is the risk of loss. *Warrant funds* or *currency funds* are examples of risky investments.

13. An adviser must not put his or her own interest before that of the client. For example, recommending a product because it brings him or her higher commission (an endowment mortgage brings the adviser much higher commission than a repayment mortgage but a newly married couple may be very short of cash and so a repayment mortgage, the cheaper option, will suit them best, for instance).

14. Will the fee based adviser pass any commission received on to you? How much is this commission likely to be? Once you find these facts out you can compare the cost of the two advisers. Will the commission based adviser pass some of the commission on to you? Some do, but only if you ask for it.

15. 'Best advice' means putting the client's interests first and knowing about all relevant financial products. 'Best execution' means buying or selling the client's product at the lowest cost or highest return available at that time. Question 13 above gives an example of advice that is not the 'best'. Selling a product on a market with a wide buy-sell spread when a market with a narrower buy-sell spread is available is an example of execution that is not the 'best'.

16. All relevant information to assist you in understanding the financial consequences of your contract is given. See Exhibit 11.5.

17. He can be reprimanded, fined, debarred from further practising as an investment adviser or sent to jail.

18. It does not affect you as a client. You must take your complaint to the relevant professional body with which your adviser is registered.

CHAPTER 12

1. *The Daily Telegraph,* the *Daily Mail,* the *Financial Times.*

2. Advisers: *Money Management; Planned Savings; Money Marketing.*

   General Public: *Money Observer; MoneyWise; What Investment.*

3. *Stone and Cox Life Assurance Handbook* (Buckley Press).

    Stone and Cox Individual Pensions Handbook (Buckley Press)

4. The publisher (who puts the facts into the base and keeps them up-to-date), the host (the computer that stores the data), the telephone system (that connects the main computer to the user, the software designer (who designs a search engine that allows the user to find what he or she wants to know from the data base) . . . and the user (who interrogates the service).

5. A computer, a modem and telephone, an internet access package, say, Netscape Navigator, and a search engine (a software package like 'Excite' or 'Yahoo').

6. In theory data on personal finance could be stored on a CD-ROM computer disc and updated regularly, say each month. This would make access to data easier to achieve than on the Internet. For example, a personal finance CD-ROM information system could be maintained by central public libraries.

7. The Internet is a worldwide information system. Computers in many countries are linked via telephone cable. Data is stored on 'pages', for example within the worldwide web system. Each page has an access address. The system needs an efficient search tool to be useful. The two most popular internet access systems are the Netscape Navigator and Microsoft's Internet Explorer.

8. A search engine is a software tool that allows an enquirer to find relevant pages within an Internet storage system like the worldwide web. Many search engines are offered on the market. The most popular currently are Yahoo, Excite, Lycos and Infoseek. You type in the keyword or words and the search engine hunts through the millions of pages for you. The results are listed in order of probable relevance to your query.

9. *Moneyworld, iii interactive* and *Money Web*. (Type in one or other of these names and you will go straight to the site.)

Changes to personal taxation, 1997–98

The following changes in personal taxation were put forward by the Chancellor of the Exchequer in his November 1996 budget. If passed by Parliament these changes will apply from 6 April 1997.

	1996–7 (£)	1997–8 (£)
Basic tax rate	24p	23p
Personal allowance	3 765	4045
Married couples allowance	1 790	1830
Tax bands at 20%	3 900	4100
at 24%	25 500	26 100 (at 23%)
Capital gains exemption	6 300	6 500
Inheritance tax threshold	200 000	215 000
Pensions earnings cap	82 200	84 000
Insurance premium tax	2.5%	4%
Room rental tax exemption limit	3 250	4 250

PEP and MIRAS limits remained unchanged.

Venture capital trusts can raise additional capital above the 10% limit.

Some useful addresses and telephone numbers

Regulatory organizations

PIA
Personal Investment Authority
1 Canada Square
Canary Wharf
London
E14 5AZ   Tel. 0171 538 8860

PIA Pensions Unit   Tel. 0171 417 7001
(contact re. mis-selling of pensions)

PIA Ombudsman
Third floor
Centre Point
103 New Oxford Street
London WC1A 1QH   Tel. 0171 240 3838

Securities and Investments Board
Gavrelle House
2–14 Bunhill Row
London   Tel. 0171 638 1240
EC1Y 8RA   Tel. 0171 929 3652
(to check if an adviser is authorized)

IMRO
Investment Managers Regulatory Organization
9 Broadwalk House
5 Appold Street
London
EC2A 2LL   Tel. 0171 628 6022

Securities and Futures Authority (SFA)
Cottons Centre
Cottons Lane
London
SE1 2QB   Tel. 0171 378 9000

Office of Fair Trading
Field House
15–25 Bream's Building
London
EC4A 1PR   Tel. 0171 242 2858

Compensation for loss because of negligence or fraud

Investors Compensation Scheme (ICS)
Gavrelle House
2–14 Bunhill Row
London
EC1Y 8RA   Tel. 0171 628 8820

(Maximum claim: first £30 000 plus 90% of the next £20 000 to £48 000.)

Insurance

Association of British Insurers
51 Gresham Street
London
EC2V 7HQ   Tel. 0171 600 3333

The Insurance Ombudsman
City Gate One
135 Park Street
London
SE1 9EA   Tel. 071 928 7600

(exhaust all other complaint routes before making your claim.)

Personal Insurance Arbitration Service
Chartered Institute of Arbitrators
24 Angel Gate
London
EC1V 2RS   Tel. 0171 837 4483

Insurance Brokers Registration Council
15 St Helen's Place
London
EC3A 6DS   Tel. 0171 588 4387

Investment

Association of Investment Trust Companies
Park House
16 Finsbury Circus
London
EC2M 7JJ   Tel. 0171 588 5347

Unit Trust Association Information Unit
65 Kingsway
London
WC2B 6TD   Tel. 0171 831 0898

Premium Bonds
National Savings Department
Lytham St Annes
FY0 1YN   Tel. 0645 645 000

Annuity direct
27 Paul Street
London
EC2A 4JU   Tel. 0171 588 9393

The Annuity Bureau   Tel. 0171 495 1495

Safe Home Income Plans (SHIP).   Tel: 0181 390 8166
                                           (number of Hinton & Wild
                                           (Home Plans) Ltd)

S & P UK Life Financial Strength Digest
Garden House
18 Finsbury Circus
London
EC2M 7BP   Tel. 0171 826 3581

(to measure strength of life funds)

Incorporated Society of Valuers and Auctioneers
3 Cadogan Gate
London
SW1X 0AS   Tel. 0171 235 2282

Investment Ombudsman
6 Frederick's Place
London
EC2R 8BT   Tel. 0171 796 3065

Pensions

Society of Pension Consultants   Tel. 0171 353 1688

The Institute of Actuaries
Staple Inn Hall
High Holborn
London
WC1V 7JQ   Tel. 0171 242 0106

Occupational Pensions Advisory Service
11 Belgrave Road
London
SW1V 1RB   Tel. 0171 233 8080

(they will supply you with a list of experts on various aspects of
pensions)

Pensions Registry Service
PO Box 1NN
Newcastle-upon-Tyne   Tel. 0191 225 6393

Pensions Ombudsman
11 Belgrave Road
London
SW1V 1RB   Tel. 0171 834 9144

Banking

Banking Ombudsman
70 Gray's Inn Road
London
WC1X 8NB   Tel. 0171 404 9944

Building societies

Building Societies Commission
15 Great Marlborough Street
London
W1V 2LL   Tel. 0171 437 9992

Building Society Ombudsman
Millbank Tower
London
SW1P 4QP   Tel. 0171 931 0044

To find a personal financial adviser

The Money Management Register of Fee-Based Advisers
Matrix Data Ltd
FREEPOST 22 (SW 1565)
London
W1E 7EZ   Tel. 01272 769444

Independent Financial Advice Promotion
28 Grenville Street
London   Tel. 0171 831 4027
EC1N 8SU   Tel. 0117 971 1177 (hotline)

(will provide a listing of IFAs who live near you)

Institute of Financial Planning   Tel. 0117 930 4434

(provides list of certified financial planners near you)

APCIMS   Tel. 0171 247 7080
112 Middlesex Street
London
E1 7HY

(if you want to find a stockbroker)

Information about rates, premiums, prices, annuity rates, etc

Financial Adviser (fax information service: each product allocated a
different fax number. For example 0897 439411 is the number to fax to
find the top five fixed rate mortgages)

Moneyfacts
Laundry Loke
North Walsham   Tel. 01692 500765
Norfolk   Fax 0336 400236 (an example:
NR28 0BD   this is the fax no. for annuity rates)

(fax information service: each product is allocated a separate fax
number)

Micropal   Tel. 0181 741 4100

(Computer data base of financial information. Very extensive information base but expensive to access using the Internet.)

Which?
Freepost
PO Box 44
Hertford X
SG14 1SH   Tel. 0800 252100 (freephone service)

(the magazine provides much useful information and advice on personal financial matters)

School fees investment advice

Independent Schools Information Service
56 Buckingham Gate
London
SW1E 6AG   Tel. 0171 630 8793

Some useful further reading

INVESTING IN FINANCIAL ASSETS

BZW (1992) *Gilt Equity Study*, Barclays De Zoete Wedd, London.

A careful study of the relative returns from safe fixed-interest securities and ordinary shares from 1918 to 1990. Equities win the race by a length.

Chase de Vere (1996) *PEP Guide*, Chase de Vere, London

Analyses performance of the many hundreds of PEPs on offer.

Gray, B. (1993) *Beginners Guide to Investment*, Investor's Chronicle/ Century Business Books, London.

A guide to investing your wealth in a sensible way. Written with great clarity and avoids jargon. Explains the pros and cons of the different kinds of investment available to an investor in the UK.

Chamberlain, G. (1990) *Trading in Options*, Woodhead-Faulkner, London.

Explains how to do it, if you feel like losing your shirt.

Frost, A. and Hager, D. (1990) *Debt Securities*, Heinemann, London.

A careful study of the nature of the various debt securities that are available for investment.

McHattie, A. (1992) *The Investor's Guide to Warrants*, FT/Pitman, London.

See comment on Chamberlain above.

Littlefair, H. (1996) *Allied Dunbar Investment and Savings Guide*, Longman, London.

Another useful book from this reliable stable.

386 Some useful further reading

INVESTING IN REAL ASSETS

Travers, S.A. (1990) *The Investor's Guide to Coin Trading*, Wiley, New York.

A comprehensive guide to the market in trading valuable coins. Useful advice on buying, selling and getting coins properly certified as genuine.

Mitchell, S. and Reeds, B. (Eds) (1996) *Coins of England and the UK*, Seaby, London.

ANNUITIES

Williamson, G.K. (1993) *All About Annuities*, Wiley, New York.

A guide to the different kinds of annuities offered by insurance companies. Strong US bias.

MANAGING YOUR PENSION

Bean, B. and others (1996) *Retirement Planning Guide*, Allied Dunbar/ Longman, London.

A useful collection of facts about pension provision in the UK.

Financial Times, *FT Pensions Book (1996)* FT Financial Publishing, London.

This includes three sections on (a) personal pensions (b) 'top-up' pensions and (c) executive and directors' pensions.

Harrison, D. (1995) *Pension Power*, John Wiley, Chichester

A most detailed introduction to the pension scene in the UK. Highly recommended.

Oldfield, M. (1992) *Understanding Pension Schemes*, Format Publishing, London.

Oldfield, M. (1994) *Understanding Occupational Pension Schemes*, Tolley, London.

A detailed study of the structure and operation of occupational pension schemes.

Stone & Cox (Quarterly) *Individual Pensions Handbook*, Buckley Press, London.

These regularly updated tables provide a wealth of information on current pension schemes offered by insurance and other companies.

HOUSING FINANCE

Barr, A. and Barr, R. (1994) *Which Way to Buy, Sell and Move House?* Which? Consumers' Guide, London.

Some helpful advice on buying and selling your home.

Nationwide Anglia Building Society (Quarterly) *Quarterly Bulletin on House Prices.*

Quarterly bulletins on house prices and other housing matters in the various regions of the UK.

INSURANCE

Dickson, G. and Steele, J. (1995) *Introduction to Insurance*, Pitman, London.

An introduction to the insurance market and the insurance industry.

Raine, P. (1996) *Planning your Personal Insurance*, Foulsham, London.

A useful guide to planning your insurance cover.

Stone & Cox (Quarterly) *Life Assurance Handbook*, Buckley Press, London.

The bible of the insurance salesman. Regularly updated tables give much information about current insurance policies, premiums, policy conditions, medical requirements, loan options on policies etc.

CONSUMER CREDIT

Burgess R. (1991) *The Law of Borrowing*, Sweet & Maxwell, London.

Information on the legal side of credit management

Edwards, B. (Ed.) (1990) *Credit Management Handbook*, Gower, London.

How the professionals do it.

Jones, S. (1989) *The Law Relating to Credit Cards*, Blackwell, London.

All you will ever want to know about this subject.

Spears, J. (1993) *Money Costs Money*, Spears, London.

A useful collection of facts about personal credit and the raising of loans.

Which? (1995) How Does Your Bank Rate? *Which?* October, Consumers Association, London.

A critical listing of the services provided by banks including the provision of credit.

PERSONAL TAXES

Barlow, J.S. (1996) *Wills, Administration and Taxation*, Sweet & Maxwell, London.

Ernst & Young (1996) *Tax Savers' Companion*, John Wiley/Ernst & Young, London.

Covers the most recent budget and provides an extensive guide to tax strategies for the individual and for small companies. Some overall financial advice is given in the context of designing a tax strategy.

Marshall, C. (1996) *Life Assurance and Pensions Handbook*, Taxbriefs.

Mellows, D. (1992) *Taxation for Executors and Trustees*, Butterworth, London.

A useful reference book on a very tricky subject.

Sharp, I. N. (1994) *Self-Assessment: Dealing with the New Income Tax Regime*, ICAEW, London.

A simple guide to the new system of self-assessment for income tax which will effect 9 million tax-payers.

Sinclair, W. I. (1996) *Allied Dunbar Tax Guide*, Allied Dunbar/Longman, London.

A readable but still comprehensive guide to UK personal and company taxation. Lots of tips about reducing your personal tax bill.

Sinclair, W.I. and Silke, P.D. (1996) *Capital Taxes and Estate Planning Guide*, Allied Dunbar/Longman, London.

Slevin, K. (1993) *Capital Gains Tax*, CCH, London.

The standard work for the layman on the subject.

Tingley, K. R. (1996) *Daily Mail Income Tax Guide*, Chapmans Publishers, London.

A hardy annual. It explains how to calculate your personal tax liability. Introduces you to the vagaries of income tax, capital gains tax and inheritance tax. Some advice is given on reducing your tax burden.

RECORDING YOUR FINANCIAL TRANSACTIONS

Begg, P. (1994) In the money: personal finance software, *Personal Computer World*, August, pp 422-9.

Hahn, H. (1996) *The Internet: Complete Reference*, Osborne McGraw Hill, New York.

Comprehensive reference work on accessing the internet.

Krol, E. (1994) *The Whole Internet: User's Guide and Catalogue*, O'Reilly, New York.

A very detailed guide to accessing the internet.

Robinson, P. (1995) *Personal Finance on your Computer*, MIS Publishers, New York.

Useful technically but strong US bias.

Schofield, S. (1994) *The PC Plus Modem and Communications Guidebook*, Future Business Books, London.

This book explains how to access the Internet and associated matters. UK based unlike most of the other books from across the Atlantic.

REGULATION OF FINANCIAL SERVICES

DTI (1985) *Financial Dervices in the UK*, DTI Report CMD 9632

A detailed impartial report on the state of the industry in 1985. The basis for much of the later legislation.

Elkington W. (1987) *Abbey Financial Rights Handbook*, Roster Limited , London.

A useful introduction to the rights of the individual with regard to dealing with financial institutions, personal financial advisers and investment managers.

Gower, L. (1984) *Review of Investor Protection in the UK*, CMD 9125, HMSO, London.

The key report which persuaded the government to act to protect investors in the UK. Still very relevant despite it's vintage.

THE RULE BOOKS OF THE REGULATORY ORGANISATIONS

The SIB rule book from the SIB
The PIA Rule Book from the PIA
The IMRO rule book from IMRO

The guidelines published by these regulators to clarify certain rules are also essential reading if you want to check that your financial adviser is playing by the rules. All of these books are available from the appropriate authority.

OTHER USEFUL BOOKS ON PERSONAL FINANCE

Cartledge, P.C. (1991) *Financial Arithmetic*, Euromoney Books, London.

This provides some basic introduction on how to do discounting, compounding and how to calculate rates of return on various financial products.

Johnson Fry (1996) *The Personal Finance Pocket Book,* Johnson Fry PLC/ NTC Publications, London.

A miniature treasure trove of statistics on personal finance. Small but perfectly formed reference work.

Shim, J. and Siegal, S. (1991) *Personal Finance*, Schaum's Outline Series, New York.

An American textbook. The book supplies the reader with hundreds of simple calculations to test the users ability to make calculations in investment, insurance, housing, pensions and many other areas of personal finance.

Vaitilingam, R. (1993) *The Financial Times Guide to Using the Financial Pages*, Pitman, London.

A useful guide to the jargon of the financial world plus explanations as to how to read the voluminous statistical tables in the *Financial Times*.

GENERAL INTRODUCTIONS TO PERSONAL FINANCE

Lofthouse, S. (1996) *How to Fix your Finances,* John Wiley, London.

Covers a remarkably wide range of topics and pays great attention to specific details. A good reference book.

Lowe, J. (1996) *Be your Own Financial Adviser,* Which? consumer guide, Consumers' Association, London.

A book from a reliable stable. Admirably practical guide to selecting financial products. This really is written for the layman with many flow charts designed to assist in understanding complex selection processes.

Mitchell, A. (1995) *Guide to Personal Finance,* Viking/Penguin Books, London.

An excellent introduction to the basics of personal finance, packed with useful information for the DIY enthusiast in financial planning. Strong on the legal side.

Philip, S. (1994) *Kelly's Financial Planning for the Individual,* Gee/Binder Hamlyn, London.

A general guide but particularly strong on details regarding individual investments, trusts and taxation of investments.

Robson Rhodes (1996), *Personal Financial Planning Manual,* Butterworth, London.

An informative listing of what one should do on a regular basis to arrange one's personal financial affairs.

Stillerman, B. (1996) *Stoy Hayward Guide to Personal Financial Planning,* Century Business, London.

Another listing of actions to be taken by DIY enthusiasts in the personal finance field. Strong on taxation.

Glossary

Adjuster	A representative who helps to settle insurance claims.
Annuity (lifetime)	A contract that guarantees a lifetime income of a certain amount, often fixed in value.
Annuity certain	An annuity (see above) that lasts for a fixed period.
APR	The true rate of interest on a loan.
AVC	Additional voluntary contributions to a pension fund operated by your employer.
Bearer bonds	Bonds that are assumed to be owned by the person possessing them.
Bearish	Pessimistic about the future.
Bed and breakfast	Selling some shares and then buying them back immediately.
Best advice	A financial adviser must choose the best product, not the one that offers the highest commission.
Beta	Measure of change in the return on a share compared to the change in the return on the market.
Bond	A financial product that offers a fixed return. Used incorrectly to describe many insurance products.
Bond rating	Measure of the relative safety of a bond.
Broker	Someone who buys and sells something for someone else, for example shares or currency.
Bullish	Optimistic about the future.
Capital bonds	Bonds offering the possibility of a large capital gain but little or no income for, say, five years.
CGT	Capital gains tax

Certificate of deposit	Funds placed on deposit with a bank at a fixed rate of interest. May be negotiable.
Codicil	An addition to an existing will.
Collateral	A specific asset provided as security for a loan.
Contracting out	Coming out of the SERPS pension scheme and into a private pension scheme.
Counter-cyclical share	A share that moves against the market trend.
Credit line	A form of automatic loan from a bank.
Credit scoring	Method of assessing creditworthiness.
Deductible	You must pay this minimum amount before the insurance company pays anything.
Dividend yield	The percentage of dividend paid on a share to the value of the share.
Double indemnity	Doubling the insurance payment due because of death by accident.
Drawdown	Drawing down income from a pension fund instead of taking the pension via an annuity.
Effective rate of interest	The true rate as against the nominal rate which may be incorrect.
Endowment insurance	The insured receives a sum of money on death or at the end of a stipulated period.
Equity	The proportion of the value of an asset which is available to the owner of the asset.
Equity share	Another name for an ordinary share.
Escalating annuity	An annuity the income from which rises by x% per year.
Estate planning	Planning an estate to minimize inheritance tax.
Executor	The person chosen to manage the instructions in a will.
Exit charge	Charge on owner for selling a financial product, imposed by the managers of the fund.
FIMBRA	Body that used to supervise investment advisers. Now the PIA.
Financial assets	Assets that are represented by documents that give a right to a future cash flow.
Financial instrument	Any financial product that can be bought or sold. Share, bond, option etc.

Floating rate bonds	Bonds that pay a variable rate of interest depending on the current market rate.
FSAVC	Free standing additional voluntary contribution to a pension fund.
Fund switching	Investor can switch funds from one fund to another at zero cost.
Funded pension plan	The contributions are invested in an independent fund that pays the pension.
Gearing ratio	Ratio between the value of an asset and the loan secured on that asset.
Gilts	Government stocks.
Grace period	Once insurance premium is due you may be given a few days to pay before insurance is terminated.
Growth stock	A share expected to rise in value over a long period.
Guaranteed renewal	An insurance policy that can be renewed without conditions (e.g. medical examinations)
Guaranteed income or growth bond	Lump sum investment linked to an insurance policy which provides a guaranteed return.
Hedging	A technique to eliminate risk by taking opposite position to exposed position.
Home income scheme	A scheme that allows an elderly home owner to receive income from the value of the home.
IAFP	International Association of Financial Planners, head office in Atlanta Georgia, USA.
Index-linked gilts	Government stock, the return from which is guaranteed against inflation.
IFA	Independent financial adviser.
Insurance bond	The value of both capital and income is guaranteed but not inflation indexed.
Inter vivos trust	A trust created during grantor's lifetime.
Investment trust	A portfolio of shares quoted on the Stock Exchange which can be partly financed by debt.
Irrevocable trust	Assets placed in such a trust are no longer available to the creator of the trust.
LAUTRO	Body that, in the past, supervised certain market insurance products and unit trusts.
Level term life insurance	Policy that pays out the same amount no matter when you die.

Liquidity	The ability to easily change an asset into cash.
Low load charge	A unit trust that charges less than normal for running the fund.
Lump sum from pension fund	The amount you receive (when you retire) from your pension fund.
Marginal tax rate	The highest rate of tax paid by a taxpayer (40%) in the United Kingdom.
Market risk	The loss on a share caused by market movements.
Maximum investment plan	An investment scheme masquerading as an insurance scheme.
MIRAS	Mortgage interest relief at source. Tax benefit to houseowners who have a mortgage.
Money purchase	Pension contributions are paid into a pension fund which is converted into an annuity on retirement.
Mortgage endowment plan	Only interest is paid until the end of the loan period when capital is paid out of the endowment policy.
Mortgage indemnity insurance	Covers the lender against the risk of a fall in house prices uncovering loan value.
Mutual fund	US term for unit trust.
Net worth	Total assets less liabilities.
No-load fund	No front-end fee charged by the managers of the fund. Only an annual management fee.
Nominal value	Value in current money terms.
Non-contributing pension	All contributions made by employer.
OEIC	Open-ended investment company. Investment innovation introduced from Europe
Offshore fund	Any fund managed outside the UK. Usually refers to a fund managed in a tax haven.
Open-market option	If you have an OMO you can choose an annuity from any company on retirement.
Option	The right, but not the obligation, to buy or sell an asset under fixed terms.
Overdraft	Variable bank loan.
PEP	Personal equity plan. The income and any capital gained from it is tax free.
PFA	Personal financial adviser.

Permanent health insurance (PHI)	An insurance policy that will replace up to 75% of your income if you fall seriously ill.
PIA	Personal Investment Authority.
PIBS	Permanent interest-bearing shares.
Portable pension	Pension that can be moved from one firm to another without difficulty.
Potentially exempt transfer	If you make a gift during your lifetime, the recipient may have to pay inheritance tax.
Pound cost averaging	Buying shares on a regular basis. You need not worry about the stock market cycle.
Preferred shares	Shares paying a fixed dividend, usually redeemable.
Present value	Discounted present value of future amount.
Private medical insurance (PMI)	Covers medical bills in private hospital if you fall ill.
P/E ratio	Price to 'earnings per share' ratio.
Qualifying insurance policy	Only such a policy benefits from various tax reliefs on payout from policy.
Real asset	A physical asset. For example a house, jewellery, gold, an antique clock, etc.
Replacement value	Insurance term for current cost of replacing asset lost or damaged.
Second mortgage	A second mortgage on an existing property.
Self-assessment for tax	New tax system introduced on 6 April 1997. You can work out your own tax bill.
Selling short	Selling shares you do not own.
SERPS	UK government pension scheme. An addition to the basic State pension scheme.
SIB	Securities and Investment Board. It supervises some financial markets.
Simple interest	Interest paid on original capital, not past interest.
Single premium annuity	Annuity financed with a single lump payment.
Split capital investment trust	Income and capital gain on the shares in the trust is separated but held by different owners.
SRO	Self-regulatory organization (e.g. SIB, PIA).
Surrender value of policy	What you get if you surrender an insurance policy early.

Tax haven	A foreign country that charges very low or no tax on income of offshore investors.
Term insurance	Life insurance for a fixed period of time. No capital value at end of period.
TESSA	Fixed interest investment on which no tax is paid if held for five years. Maximum investment £9000.
Testament trust	A trust that only comes into operation after death
Tied agent	An agent who only sells the products of a specific company.
Transfer value of pension	Value of pension rights transferred from one company to another
Trust	A legal device whereby person A transfers property to person B for the benefit of C.
Unfunded pension	Pension paid out of current contributions.
Unit trust	A collective investment managed by professional investors and held by trustees.
Viatical settlement	Payment out of life policy to a terminally ill person before death.
Variable life assurance	Premium and value varies with inflation.
Waiting period	An insurance device to reduce premiums. No payment until some fixed period has elapsed.
Warrant	The right to buy a share at or after a given date in the future at a given price.
Whole life assurance	Terminal value payable normally on death.
Withholding tax	Tax deducted at source by payer of revenue.
Yield	The net of tax return on an investment.
Zero coupon bond	A bond that is bought below face value but pays no interest before repayment.
Zero dividend preference shares	The portion of a split-level investment trust that receives no dividends, only capital.

Index